ASTROLOGICAL INSIGHTS INTO PERSONALITY

Also by ACS Publications, Inc.

ASTROLOGICAL INSIGHTS INTO PERSONALITY

Betty Lundsted

Published by
ACS Publications, Inc.
P.O. Box 16430
San Diego, California 92116-0430

International Standard Book Number 0-917086-22-8

Printed in the United States of America

Published by ACS Publications, Inc.
P.O. Box 34487
San Diego, CA 92103-0802

First Printing, July, 1980
Second Printing, February, 1981
Third Printing, December, 1982
Fourth Printing, March, 1984
Fifth Printing, February, 1986
Sixth Printing, December, 1987
Seventh Printing, July, 1989

This book is dedicated to those people who believed it should exist. And special thanks to Neil Michelsen, Patricia Morimando and Marsha Kaplan for their encouragement.

CONTENTS

ASTROLOGICAL INSIGHTS INTO PERSONALITY

THIS BOOK WAS WRITTEN BECAUSE I HAVE PERSONALLY experienced the possibilities for growth and awareness that can occur when astrological symbols are used as a tool for understanding the processes taking place within the individual. Because I was so enthusiastic about what I learned in regard to my own development as a result of exploring this symbolism, I started teaching what I knew. I watched my students and clients develop exciting personal insights into their needs, drives and motivations. Because of the positive feedback from students, I wanted to share this kind of information with a readership that might never come to New York City to study with me personally—or who might never take a course in astrology that covers insights into the motivation behind personality development. The material presented here can be used by the beginner or the advanced student as well as the professional. It relates the symbolism of astrology with the diagnosis and interpretation of the early childhood environment, and discusses the possible links between the childhood experiences and adult behavior.

I came into astrology with a background in other fields, so that my conclusions are based on a correlation of Eastern philosophy, metaphysics, awareness of Religious Science and a long and interesting pursuit of Jungian psychology from a layman's level. The ancient myths related by Joseph Campbell in his series *The Masks of God*; humanity's search for a spiritual identity described in much of Jung's work; and certain concepts regarding the masculine and feminine principles discussed by M. Esther Harding in her work *Women's Mysteries*, opened up a whole new world for me.

It was easy to combine these spiritual philosophies with astrology, for the symbolism is universal. For instance, the astrological houses symbolize the struggle for consciousness discussed in various religious philosophies. The planets and aspects not only indicate how we search for that consciousness, but also describe the preconceived notions that we absorb from the family environment. I was amazed to discover that minutes after people are born, the major emotional and spiritual confrontations of life could be known. Although each of us has free will and we choose how we wish to use our energy, the natal chart shows our natural perimeters. For example, an Aries cannot become a Gemini type, but that Aries can choose to be a happy or an unhappy Aries. His Aries qualities can be understood from the birth chart even though his response to environmental conditions or his natural potential cannot.

Many people are born on the same day, and many people have charts that are very similar. This further indicates that we each have choices. We are free to use or misuse our energy any way we wish. We are tested at various times during our life, and as a result of our reaction to these testing periods, our entire life can change. We choose very individual kinds of life experience for we react to the symbolism within us, and each person elects to use his energy differently. The natal chart could be termed a symbol of our opportunity in life.

> Listen! A sower went out to sow. And it happened that as he sowed, some seed fell along the footpath; and the birds came and ate it up. Some seed fell on rocky ground, where it had little soil, and it sprouted quickly because it had no depth of earth; but when the sun rose the young corn was scorched, and as it had no root it withered away. Some seed fell among thistles; and the thistles shot up and choked the corn, and it yielded no crop. And some of the seed fell into good soil, where it came up and grew, and bore fruit; and the yield was thirtyfold, sixtyfold, even a hundredfold. (St. Mark, Chapter 4, lines 3-8.)

> He said also, "How shall we picture the kingdom of God, or by what parable shall we describe it? It is like the mustard seed, which is smaller than any seed in the ground at its sowing. But once sown, it springs up and grows taller than any other plant, and forms branches so large that the birds can settle in its shade." (St. Mark, Chapter 4, lines 30-32.)

The above material relates to two basic astrological patterns indicating personal potential. Many people can be born with the same or similar personal planets and houses—that is, you're born the same day, month, and year, in the same time period and in the same geographical location as someone else. Because the houses and the aspects are almost the same, the childhood environment can be the factor that encourages or discourages the individual's development. An awareness of the potential within can help an individual reprogram himself so that his life "seed" falls on fertile ground.

In the same generation a pattern is also observable because the more slow moving planets form aspects that are called generation aspects. They indicate pressures that an entire generation will confront on the journey through life. This concept of choice—how we each choose to use our energy, how we each choose to grapple with our problems—was an exciting one for me because it encouraged me to believe that life has a purpose. Each philosophical and religious group has its own theory as to why the soul wishes to continue. But astrology gave me a symbolism that explained the idea of reincarnation. A mass of people (or souls) are involved in the evolution process—so that someday the Aquarian age will be able to take place. In the meantime, we are learning how to love, how to share and how to care for one another in the midst of all the emotional and physical poverty caused by not understanding how to use our energy. The world soul is maturing. It's exciting!

In mythological and mystical literature the magic circle is said to protect us; it saves us from the "fates." In medieval times, astrologers began to use the circle as a vehicle to present astrological symbols that indicate a person's life path. It could be said that each birth chart is our individual "magic circle." Within it are the symbols that explain our growth pattern and the kinds of life experiences that may occur in the process of self-discovery. This circle may contain the key to the riddle of life if we learn how to read it. Once we understand the riddle, or find the key to "know thyself," we are protected by our own energy, our own circle.

The term "becoming" has been used to indicate the state of consciousness at any given moment. The capacity for becoming can be enhanced or quickened by using the knowledge hidden within the astrological symbols. We know that our capacity for becoming is influenced by family experience as well as by the environment, for psychological research has been done in this area. Recent research has even shown that the mind is more than ninety percent unconscious. This means that we may now need to evaluate how much of our personality is ego-centered consciousness and how much our lives are motivated by some subconscious drive. Subconscious drives may be better understood after exploring the natal horoscope because it may show how the effect of early childhood programming relates to the drives within. It is not uncommon to hear people say, "I don't know why I did that, I don't know why I reacted that way." Astrology can be used as a tool to understand "why."

There is always a relationship between the seed and the crop. If we understand the seed, we can better cultivate the crop. Granted, when we plant spinach seeds, we'll get a spinach crop, but it can be healthy or unhealthy spinach depending on the environment and how we consciously choose to nurture the seed. If an adult has a Mars–Moon square, it may be said that he was exposed to that energy in his early environment. If that is so, in order to free himself of the Mars–Moon square outlook on life, he must first determine where it may have come from in his childhood. This book is written to help those interested in exploring the possibilities of the early childhood environmental factors as they relate to astrological symbolism. Some facets of chart interpretation are covered and others are ignored, for this book isn't intended to replace the textbooks already in existence.

Serious students of astrology have been working for years to establish the science in the academic community. The academicians of recent times are unfamiliar with this ancient wisdom and have mistakenly branded astrology as a fortune-telling device. Astrologers have been apprehensive about writing explicitly serious material, for they too have been influenced by the opinions of the scientific community. Much of the astrological symbolism became esoteric because of this. It became difficult for new students to obtain serious interpretations of certain planetary configurations and the possibilities of human behavior they symbolized. Students have had to learn from a teacher or from personal experience. Teachers haven't published because many have feared that their words might be misunderstood or misinterpreted, or that the information will be misused by people who think astrology is only a parlor game.

Laymen interested in what is commonly called self-awareness have read psychological research papers intended for professionals in the field, such as the case histories of famous researchers like Carl Jung, Sigmund Freud and others. Often the student has read of a case of schizophrenia and felt that all the symptoms applied to him! If the psychological researcher was limited by the possibility of offending a reader who may be unable to assimilate the information in some reasonable manner or perspective, the psychological research available today would be much inhibited. The reader of this book, therefore, must assume responsibility for any condition that he creates within himself by misunderstanding or misusing the information presented here. If the reader is unfamiliar with basic psychology, metaphysics, or philosophical approaches, it is suggested that those subjects be pursued so that the astrological symbolism might be better understood. A bibliography has been included for those who may be interested in pursuing the subjects that led to many of the conclusions presented here.

The serious researcher or student is encouraged to respond to the ideas and formulas contained herein. Inquiries or comments should be directed to me in care of the publisher.

I: THE BASICS

I-1: MOMMY, DADDY & THE KID

THIS CHAPTER IS INTENDED TO EXPOSE THE READER TO A
general overview of parent-child relationships, and how these relationships
can be seen in the natal chart. The roles of parent-child, the need for a
parent image and the blocks that confuse parent-child issues are explored.
In Section II (Planets and Aspects) the influence of the parents' relationship
on the child's development is discussed. If we are to comprehend natal
aspects in perspective, it's important to understand the "typical" resentments and confusions of parent and child during the normal maturation
process.

When we consider mother-father-child relationships, we often approach
the subject with a great deal of prejudice. We tend to view parents and
children through distorted eyes—we are blinded by our love or hate, our
disappointment, our overattachment, etc. In order to understand the relationships, or the problems connected with the various roles in family life,
it helps to be aware of the fact that we are often caught in both roles, since
we are usually both children and parents!

In a recent lecture about planetary aspects, the speaker was describing
the effect of a particular aspect on a child. A mother in the audience had a
child with that aspect. She responded to the speaker's description by saying, "But I was always there, I responded to every cry, to every need!"
The fact is there is no way a parent can or should respond to a child's every
need. The child elects to come into the universe, and presumably the
parents elect to handle the responsibility for that child. We can try to do
everything humanly possible for our children, but we may not always
satisfy them. I wonder if we are supposed to. Children misunderstand
parents at some point or other, and parents misunderstand children. The
only thing we can do is become aware that these misunderstandings are
unavoidable.

For example, a Fire sign child, born with a Fire sign Moon as well, was raised by two Earth sign people who did not have Fire signs strong in their horoscopes. There was no way that the parents could understand the child's idealism! The parents were not deliberately trying to hurt the child; the child was unable to understand the parents' needs as well. They knew each other, they cared for each other, but they couldn't really relate to each other.

When we look at the birth chart, we are essentially looking at the formation of a personality. If we consider the horoscope of the child as a reflection of the early childhood environment, then we may logically consider the horoscope as a road map of the emotional life based on the child's reaction to the parents' relationship.

If we can read the aspects in an adult's chart accurately, we may assume that there had to be some childhood experience to cause that aspect to manifest later in life. Mom is the first woman we see and Dad is the first man we see; and because we have no other life experience to compare them with, we assume that Mom and Dad are "normal," i.e., they behave in a "normal" way to each other—they are "normal" human beings. The value system prevalent in the marriage at the time of the birth of the child is the value system that is instilled within the personality of the child.

Most psychologists say the problems they counsel in their adult patients have been formed in the personality by the age of five. I would offer that they are formed more probably by the age of three. We pop into the universe with lots of intuition. This means that we are able to sense and feel the environment, much like we can if we go to a foreign country without knowledge of the language but find ourselves capable of discerning whether people are angry or happy, fighting or loving. A child senses the relationship between the parents in much the same way. Baby often sleeps in the parents' bedroom, a silent witness to their sexual and emotional relationship, which influences the child's reaction to sexuality in later life (on a subconscious level). And Baby is around when Mom is complaining about Dad to her girl friends, or when Dad is throwing a temper tantrum at Mom when dinner isn't ready. Baby feels how the parents handle crises, emotional warmth and everyday activities in the home.

None of the early childhood experience is readily accessible to the conscious mind as we mature. The picture and feeling memories have been stored in the subconscious mind—they haven't been discussed with anybody. To make self-diagnosis more difficult, around the age of three the child begins to broaden his range of experience by reaching out into the backyard or the nursery school. We are told that a personality is developed as we grow. Sociologists infer that a school or social environment can influence or change a child. What does this mean in reference to the aspects in the natal chart? And if a child is responding to the environment, is it responding via the aspects in the chart?

When we study astrology, we learn that a chart can be read five minutes after a child is born, so astrologers are priviledged to see a child's emotional experience or expectancy of experience before it has happened. We may have to decide for ourselves which came first, the chart or the environment.

If you compare the horoscopes of the child and the parents you will see that there is a relationship between them in planetary terms. For example, *you* are the transits to your parents' charts because your natal planets are their transits on the day you are born! If a child is born when Mom is going through her Saturn return, and if the kid's Saturn also conjuncts the father's Sun, the child will subconsciously evoke memories of that period in the parents, even as the child grows. (Mom's Saturn return may have been productive or unhappy; Dad's Sun–Saturn transit may have been a very unhappy period for him. Subconsciously they remember that when "Junior" was born life was awful or life was wonderful!) If two children have the same father and one child's Saturn conjuncts the father's Sun while the other child's Jupiter conjuncts the father's Sun, you will witness two different relationships between father and child. You can also see some basic relating problems by looking into the Cardinal, Fixed and Mutable squares between the charts of parent and child. The squares have difficulty in getting along together.

We think that we must love our parents and that parents must love children, but the chart comparison between parent and child may not be an easy or an amicable one. Psychologists say that parents respond differently to each of their children because one child is the eldest, one is the middle, one is the youngest, etc. These factors are certainly something to consider, but astrologers have other diagnostic tools at their disposal: the chart pattern, the signs, the planets, the houses and the aspects.

If the personality can be read from the horoscope—and a person with Mars square Venus (for example) has a certain personality—the child must have learned this from the parents' relationship and, most important, from his or her *reaction* to the parents' relationship. If Mom is the first woman that the child sees and Dad is the first man, then the interrelationship that goes on between Mom and Dad has to be influential in developing the child's concepts. Most parents feel that children have no awareness—but if that is true, how can the psychologist say that adult problems are formulated by the age of five? Granted, in the first few years of life children don't hold great intellectual conversations with their parents—but they can feel.

Often when parents are arguing, the six-month-old baby will begin to cry because it is sensitive to what is going on. Recent investigations in hypnosis have been quite revealing. People in hypnotic trance seem able to recall past experiences all the way back to the birth trauma.

We play roles and we also cast people into them. A child is a child and not often seen as a "person." Parents feel that they can influence their children, mold them, make them into the "spitting" image of themselves by exposing their children to circumstances, environment and experience.

Parents are amazed when their children disappoint them and don't behave in the way they intended, or don't follow in their footsteps as far as career is concerned. Parents are hurt when their children don't understand or appreciate the things done to promote their welfare.

Children are just as guilty of casting their parents into roles. They identify with "mommy" and "daddy" and seldom see Mom as a woman and Dad as a man. Young children are extremely demanding of Mom and Dad (and necessarily so, for they need lots of food and care). As they grow, they demand as much as parents are able or willing to give—and more. During various time periods in the growth cycle, children demand different things of parents, and often will align themselves with the parent who will give permission or understanding. So it's "me and Dad" against Mom, or vice versa. And there are times when children see life in terms of "me against Mom *and* Dad." This is all part of the natural maturing process.

In some circumstances, children want parental role models, even though the models are negative. A case in point is an eleven-year-old I worked with, who was very upset about his parents' divorce. He tried for two years to reunite them. He wanted them together even though he was aware of the following circumstances: The father was unreliable; he spent many years at home, claiming that he could not get a job, so the family was supported by the wife. He felt guilty about not pulling his own weight financially, so he abused his wife and child. The child had been so severely abused by the age of six that no other adult could discipline him in any normal fashion. When the marriage ended, the husband was forced to find a job but he refused to support the child. When he had weekly custody of his son, he performed sexually with other women in front of the child.

In the face of all these harsh and painful physical and emotional experiences as well as seeing his mother hospitalized from beatings, the child still wanted his parents to get back together.

Other situations of this type helped me to understand a child's need for a *parent image* regardless of what that image is. If violence is a part of the experience, then these children must feel that violence is "normal."

Counseling people about the origins of personality (or even looking into your own origins) can be a very delicate experience. We are exposing a sensitive area. Most people who come for readings feel as though they are victims in some way. It's Mom's fault or Dad's fault that life is not kind. They may be right—they probably got very little training in terms of how to handle the stark realities of life. But we must keep in mind that most parents do not consciously try to destroy a child. I know some very neurotic parents, people who are going through periods of personal crisis, who are disoriented, and who would not pass too many "responsibility" tests! But they are not *trying* to destroy their children.

Parents may not know what they are supposed to teach a child. Humans (especially in the Western culture, or the Christian/Judaic ethic) do not really raise their children to prepare themselves for adulthood. We say that we do, but we seldom do what we say. Parents often feel that they are doing the best for their children by covering the "realities" of life and exposing the children to a rose-colored universe. For example, many parents are unable to teach their children about sexuality. Most young people I've counseled receive no sensible information about sex from their parents. (How can these young people avoid being emotionally hurt if they begin their sex lives with taboos and fears and guilts? And won't these emotional hurts breed an unexpressed resentment toward the parents?) So when it comes time for young adults to venture out into the universe on their own, they are forced to fight two battles at once. One battle is the fear of approaching the unknown universe, and the other is the fight to get rid of the influence of Mom/Dad.

Parents often do not understand that there may be a certain amount of competition between parent and child. Granted, the child may be competitive, but what about the parental jealousy that can manifest on a man-to-man or woman-to-woman basis? The mother or father can be competitive with the youngster but we have difficulty recognizing it sometimes. To understand this, observe the teen-age girl whose mother dresses "younger" than her daughter...who infers that the kid will never be as feminine as she is...who may resent her daughter's dating...who may make innuendoes about what her daughter is "doing" on those dates...and who may even be too "friendly" with her daughter's dates.

Have you ever noticed the father who criticizes every move his teen-age son makes? Dad questions the kid's selection of college, summer jobs and girls. Or the father who won't support the sensible ideas that his son has. There may be constant references to the boy as being a "dummy" and an "idiot" or other derogatory remarks rather than words that are supportive and helpful.

I've watched the parents who constantly nag their children, where all conversations with children turn into parent-child harassment. I wonder if these parents subconsciously feel threatened or resentful of the child's ensuing independence. Consider also the idea of "trust" between parent and child. Parents lay a groundwork of morality and then don't trust their children to live that morality. Many teen-agers are completely crushed by this lack of trust.

Teen-agers rebel against their parents to get free so that they can join the adult universe. Literature is fraught with this "quest for freedom." The mythology of various cultures shows the Hero (the young man) fighting his father for independence by passing tests. Hercules is mythologically important for many students of astrology since the twelve labors have often been interpreted as a quest for the self in terms of the zodiac. There also is the myth of the "father killing." This myth does not mean that one goes out and physically maims the father, but in order to *be* a father, you must first free yourself from the authority of your own father. The young woman in mythology must also fight to develop from ingenue to woman, but usually she must confront her husband's mother!

When we look at the animal kingdom we see some interesting phenomena regarding parent and child. A female kitten, for example, grows into cathood and gives birth to a litter of kittens. We do not see her paying obeisance to her mother, who may reside on the same farm. In fact, we will see two mother cats together, on an equal basis, sharing the responsibilities of motherhood. In the human species, seldom do we find mother and daughter greeting life as two women, or a father and son greeting life as two men.

In "Two Women," a movie made in the late 50s, a mother and daughter are women together, forced into the role because of war. They are forced to deal with sexuality in its more unattractive aspects. In the movie, mother and daughter are both raped. Sophia Loren does a magnificent job of portraying the grief of a mother forced to watch her daughter experiencing sex for the first time under terrifying conditions. The arena of war forces her to experience life with her daughter as two women; but later in the movie she reverts to the mother-daughter role when her daughter begins a relationship with a young man. She never talks with her child about their rape experience, and she slaps her when she thinks that the girl is seeing a man. Most women don't teach their daughters how to cope with sex or rape.

We often see the father-son tradition played out in epics like the movie "All My Sons." Edward G. Robinson plays a patriarchal role, demeaning his sons so much that they can never leave home. He refuses to pay them proper wages when they work for him; the sons are forced to bring their wives home to daddy because they can't afford a home of their own. This movie illustrates a father who systematically robs his sons of their manhood; but as the drama unfolds, it becomes apparent that he is not consciously aware of what he is doing.

Misuse of parental authority can cause great hostility and misery. Why? Because as children we are afraid to go against the parent figure; but in order to become adults, we must—while everything in our religion and culture says that we must not. The parent, too, is easily caught in the parent-child game because children are very dependent when they are young. The parent becomes so accustomed to doing everything for the child that two basic problems usually arise. One, the child becomes the center of the family unit and constantly interrupts family life because the parents don't teach the child that it must share. Two, the parent won't let the child "leave the nest" when the time comes. Of course, the problem of leaving the nest does not occur until the teen years, while the spoiled child syndrome usually manifests between the ages of three and ten.

Let's look at the jealous parent for a moment. Jealousy shows up when an overprotective parent tries to keep a child from developing, or living out the normal life pattern of an adult. For example, the mother who does not want her son to marry—to have, in fact, a woman of his own. She raises her son around such ideas as "women are bad" (all women except her, that is!) and talks of young girls being cheap, instilling in the boy certain guilts about his own sexuality. The guilts are shown in the chart, but how they will manifest in adult behavior is unknown. So this son must fight his way clear of the possessive mother influence.

A daughter may have a jealous or competitive father—a man who doesn't want his "little girl" to grow up and have an adult life of her own. The parent often overprotects his child and feels that all boys are out to "get" her, to misuse her. The girl will be better off if she is taught about the effect of sexual experimentation on her emotional and physical self. Sometimes these fathers had a double standard in their own youth. They fear that all young men will misuse women in general, like they may have. Unconscious, unadmitted incestuous desires could be questioned as well.

Once the age of 18 is reached, any dwelling on parental failures is really a waste of time. This is far easier to say than to do! But in order to get on a positive mental track, we may have to let go of the past. If Aristotle Onassis had spent his adult life blaming his mom and dad for his meager beginnings, he wouldn't have had the time to achieve all that he did in the material world. If we choose to develop along more spiritual or more creative levels than Onassis chose, we still must let go of the past. Understanding the natal chart can help us to let go, to work through difficult personality patterns, to bring out positive energies and maturity.

One of the biggest problems we have to solve is the parental love-hate dichotomy. We are embarrassed about being seriously involved in hating our parents, but I've heard it so much that I don't think it's abnormal. People who really dislike Mom and Dad can seldom talk about it, and when it comes out it is with a great deal of passion and/or venom. When the "love connection" between parent and child is looked for, no direct answers are found, not even in religion. The words used are *respect* and *honor*, not *love*. A parent provides life, shelter and food until we are old enough to care for ourselves. We owe them honor and respect for that. But lovingness is not necessary in order to perform the responsibilities of raising a child. We think that "nice" people love each other—but reality shows us something different.

In order to resolve the love-hate conflict, the resentments must be faced and accepted without guilt. The aspects in the chart (which can explain the source of the conflict) can be understood. We go to a doctor to cure our physical illnesses; and we can use astrology to diagnose what our emotional problems might be in order to cure them too! When we first work with our natal chart, we often feel like a "victim." As we work through our chart, we may see that our "victimization" is the *center* of our growth potential.

When people come to hear about their natal chart, they usually are in a conflict period which needs resolving. If the problem needing resolution can be understood, then the planets and the aspects that they make begin to represent strengths and energies which can be used constructively by the individual. It is the astrologer's job to make the client aware of this.

We unconsciously pattern ourselves after the stronger parent—but diagnosing who the stronger parent is can be a problem! We try to judge the stonger parent *now*, but we form our bond with the stronger parent *then*. Parents change—a marriage is a series of cycles, because all human relationships exist in terms of cycles. When talking to clients about stronger parent influence, you may find that they have difficulty remembering who the stronger parent was. Not only have their parents changed, but the clients' views about their parents have changed as well as their views about what a parent should be. When an attempt is made to understand who the stronger or more influential parent is, the blind spots must first be considered. To reiterate briefly, these blind spots are the roles that we force on each other, the animosity caused by parent-child competition, the confusion and anger we may feel when we start to go our own way in life. These blind spots are inevitable.

The horoscope is a key to the determination of the mother-father influence. We've forgotten what we picked up and stored in our subconscious mind. So the chart can be the tool that solves the mystery. We tend to get our basic life values from our "dominant" parent. That's the parent who is stronger when we are age 0-3. The stronger parent can be determined by checking the Sun sign polarity. The positive sign people (Fire and Air signs) are strongly influenced by the father; the negative sign people (Earth and Water signs) are strongly influenced by the mother. Obviously every child is influenced by the mother. But the child also seems able to sense whether or not the mother respects or fears the father. (For more details, see Chapter 3, Polarities.)

The dominant parent is not necessarily the parent we love best or relate to best, but the one who influences our goals in life in our later years. For example, Leo children are born into a family with a very strong father image from age 0-3. Father issues rules and regulations about life from an impersonal point of view. He seldom explains why the rules and regulations exist. So Leo kids grow up with a lot of self-imposed rules and regulations. It is not uncommon to hear them say "I can't do that, one does not do that, one does not carry oneself that way." They really don't know *why* they have these values, nor can they readily *explain* their code of ethics except that "one just does." They can only change the value system when they explore the relationship with the father. This does not mean that they are little carbon copies of Dad, but they do tend to get stuck in ruts and life positions that seem very limited to the other eleven signs of the zodiac!

Taurus children, on the other hand, are mother-dominated. Their value system will be based on their reaction to Mother's value system. They may

not like her, but they will base their philosophy of life on Mother's opinions and on their reactions to her opinions. For example, if your parent is
a chain-smoker, you may grow up to be one too. Or you may have strong
feelings about not smoking because you lived with a heavy smoker. The
dominant parent may well be an unfavored parent; dominance does not
imply love. The child with trines and sextiles to the Sun may have a much
better relationship with the dominant parent than will the child who has
afflictions to the Sun.

The Sun position also symbolizes the physical father (and how he
behaves) in the child's early home environment. The negative or feminine
sign Sun implies that the father is not the strongest member of the family
when the child is born. It shows that the father's influence is passive, or
what is traditionally expressed as feminine-receptive. This does not mean
that the father is feminine, but that he is passive about running the
household, the marriage and the family at the time the child is born. The
aspects to the Sun indicate just how the father influences the child at a time
in life when it is important to the child's development.

The Moon represents the child's physical mother. It indicates how she
presents herself physically and how she influences the emotional side of the
child's personality. The placement of the Moon by sign, house and aspects
indicates the type of feminine influence the child receives in terms of
mothering, nurturing and loving, and how the child responds to emotional situations. An afflicted Moon in the natal chart means that Mom has
some difficulty in adjusting to certain aspects of relating emotionally; the
child will sense it and perhaps copy it later in life.

The Saturn and Venus placements are also important in evaluating the
influence of the parents. These placements seem to indicate the *psychological*
impact of the parents. Saturn represents authority and the effect of father
on the child's development. In a traditional sense, the first authority figure
that greets the child is the father. He is gone during the day and comes
home in the evening and lays down the law. In legal and civil matters, no
matter how strong the mother is, the father has control. So when Saturn is
afflicted, there are some problems with the *concept* of authority. Afflictions
to Saturn can also mean that the father's psychological influence may keep
the child from maturing easily, or it may influence the child's emotional or
sexual development in some way.

Venus represents the psychological influence of the mother. If Venus
also represents the ability to appreciate love and to accept love, or to
develop a concept of loving, then what the mother thinks about this during the child's early life can be most influential. It seems that when Venus
is afflicted, Mom has some conceptual problems about love and what
femininity is all about. She transfers a poor image of the feminine to the
child. If the child is female, the girl may have psychological blocks
concerning her feminine values, which may include self-value. If the child
is a boy, he may have trouble expressing love to a woman or may not value
his emotional needs, or both.

When Saturn and Venus afflict each other (the conjunction, square or opposition), this can indicate that the relationship between the parents is psychologically damaging to the child. These children go into adult relationships with little confidence or joy. They don't expect to share, they seem to expect to lose. They look for flaws in a relationship, and when they look, they usually find them! They don't want to discuss problems; when one is brought up, they assume that the relationship is over and they withdraw. These people tend to look for enormous guarantees and reassurances from the partner without offering any in return. I wonder if the interaction between the parents was so negative that these individuals become frightened of ever committing themselves to sharing. To work free of this influence, they must examine their memories of their parents' relationship.

When the chart is looked at from the viewpoint of being a picture of the parents' marriage at a certain period in time, it should be remembered that the child reacts to the parents in terms of the child's needs. For example, adopted children land in families where the adopted parents dole out the same aspects as would their real parents. It's uncanny. Just as transits, progressions or directions work in synchronicity, so do the circumstances present in our universe when we arrive here!

This leads me to say one small word about reincarnation. I can't prove it, but the following theory makes some sense to me. If we have different aspects to work out, perhaps they are the clues to why we were reincarnated this time around. After all, if we understood the "game" of life and understood all the rules, then the learning about it, the playing of the game, might not be any fun!

THE HOROSCOPE WHEEL CAN BE CONSIDERED FROM A symbolic point. The ancients worked with symbols that we can understand when we examine the planets and the houses as they are said to rule the twelve signs. The houses in the natural zodiac represent the twelve basic functions in life. (See Figure 1.) Each house describes the qualities and concepts represented by the ruling signs and planets.

In an ancient religious manuscript, the author discusses the concept that the entire zodiac represents a person. The macrocosm and the microcosm reflect each other. "As above, so below." In order to realize the full potential of personality and creativity in a lifetime, all the signs should be integrated within the individual. This integration process will make us "whole." For example, Aquarius rules the natural eleventh house. When Aquarius happens to rule the third house in a timed birth chart, the qualities and concepts of Aquarius have to be incorporated into the Gemini (third house) part of the person. This applies to all the houses throughout the chart. The integration of the qualities of the sign ruling a house indicates a person's own special kind of individuality. This information can be used for better self-understanding on a personal level, a mundane level, a creative level and a spiritual level.

Many representations of the masculine and feminine principles use black to symbolize matter, or the feminine principle, and white to symbolize "idea," or the masculine principle. (See Figure 2.) In the color spectrum, white indicates the absence of color or the ability to reflect all the rays in the spectrum; black is the combination or total absorption of all existing colors. Hindu symbolism includes the "Shiva/Shava" dichotomy represented by black and white...the absence of life (or the life force) in the spiritual conception, and the necessity of flesh (the color black) to realize and manifest the spiritual self into a living reality. The esoteric philosophies always get around to expressing the need for physical

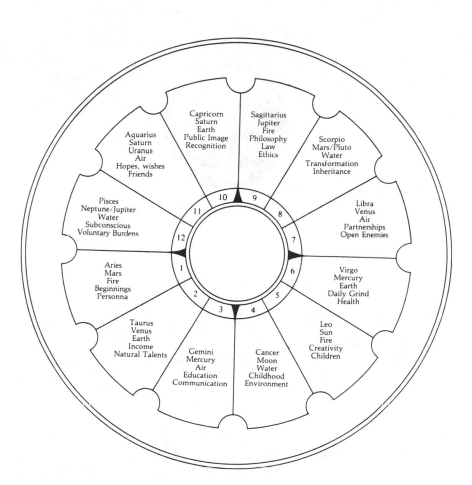

Figure 1.

manifestation in order for the soul to evolve, to raise its consciousness. And consciousness is raised by the melding of the masculine and feminine principles.

All the signs of the zodiac are represented in each birth chart, and every person is a special combination of the masculine and feminine principles. We each have the potential to become androgynous.

By reflecting on this ancient symbolism, the normal conflicts in life can be better understood. Some people assume life must be easy, that if we

Figure 2. The symbol for the Tao in Chinese philosopy. Black represents the feminine principle, and when reprinted correctly the black portion is at the bottom. It means that feminine relates to night, to Moon, to the material universe. The feminine principle follows the masculine. Manifestation always follows idea. The top half is the daylight half. It represents the masculine principle, the Logos, the ability to "see" as Plato discusses it. The two colors are intertwined, forever together, forever necessary, a "whole."

don't have an easy time of it someone must have done us a disservice. However, there are natural squares and oppositions in the zodiac, and as we examine them we begin to discover that change and growth can come out of discomfort, discord and conflict.

In Figure 3 we see the masculine and feminine houses forming a natural square to each other. In the natural zodiac, Aries rules the first house, Libra the seventh; Cancer rules the fourth house, Capricorn the tenth. Aries and Libra are masculine; Cancer and Capricorn are feminine.

The Cardinal houses, or the angular houses as they are sometimes called, are the focal points in our life. These signs form what is sometimes known as our personal "cross," our personal areas of stress. In various religious philosophies, the cross has particular significance. The Christian cross is more generally known, but the cross has been used in all recorded civilizations. The ankh came from Egypt, the swastika was originally an Egyptian and Hindu symbol. (The Nazis changed the meaning of this symbol drastically.) The cross has often been used to symbolize the pain caused when the spirit is trying to express itself in the material universe. The

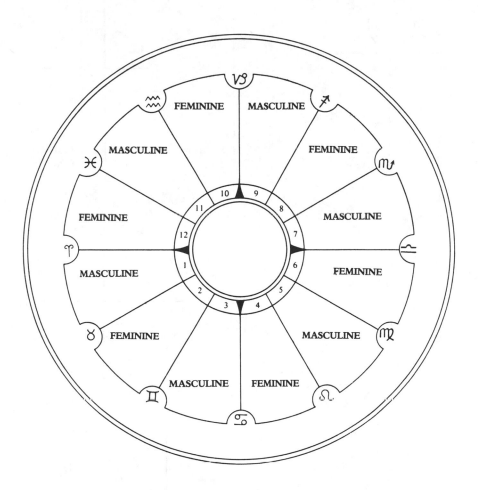

Figure 3. The position of masculine and feminine signs in the wheel shows "idea" followed by "manifestation" in the life pattern. Masculine houses have to do with action, idea, communication. Feminine houses indicate material possessions, position in life and spiritual development.

spirit or soul must be encased in matter (a physical body) in order to express itself. Idea must take form. The creative energy must manifest physically in order to become conscious.

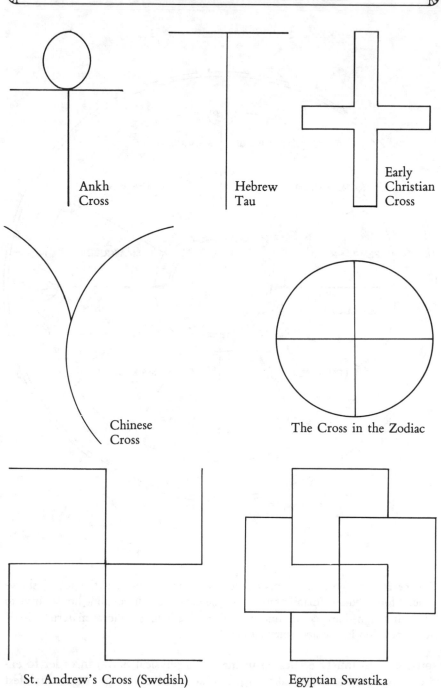

Ankh Cross

Hebrew Tau

Early Christian Cross

Chinese Cross

The Cross in the Zodiac

St. Andrew's Cross (Swedish)

Egyptian Swastika

Figure 4. Some ancient symbols of the cross. All these crosses symbolize life, and they appear in all religious motifs.

THE CARDINAL HOUSES

The angles of the cross formed by the first, fourth, seventh and tenth houses represent each individual's philosophical or creative concept of the spirit, or the Logos, encased in matter. In a personal sense, the various phases of life need to be experienced in order for consciousness to evolve to a higher plane. These struggles or experiences are symbolized by the Cardinal conflicts. Generally, the angles are either in a square or in opposition to each other. (There is an exception to this in the case of intercepted houses. If you're lucky enough to miss the squares in your angles, bless you!)

The first house rules our physical body, the way we present ourselves to others and the way we begin things. The seventh house indicates how we see and accept our business and marital partners and how the public reacts to us. Since these houses naturally oppose each other, it can be concluded that some compromises are generally required regarding self-expression and a close relationship with another person. Compromises are also made between self-expression and the general public. Because this opposition includes the natural seventh house of Libra, it may be assumed that this compromise teaches a kind of balance. It requires us to take notice of our actions every now and then! It seems the marriage relationship is naturally one of compromise—and perhaps a happy compromise can be worked out if we understand the nature and the symbolism of those two houses.

The fourth house rules the influence of the early childhood environment, the influence of heredity and the atmosphere created by the parents in the early childhood. The tenth house indicates what we are striving for in the world, the public image and honors that we reach for. We often reach for world position based on a pattern instilled by our childhood experience. Sometimes the fourth house blocks us, sometimes it encourages us.

In regard to the fourth and tenth houses, there seems to be a lot of confusion about which house represents which parent. Perhaps an examination of the symbolism of the natural rulerships will be of help. The fourth house in the natural zodiac is ruled by the sign Cancer. Cancer rules the stomach and breasts; it is described by the word *nurturing*; it indicates mothering. On the other hand, Capricorn indicates the position we look to hold in the world, the honors that we strive for. Capricorn is symbolized by the mountain goat climbing to the top of the mountain. People born under the sign Capricorn are often looking to get to the top of the corporate structure. Saturn rules Capricorn and the natural tenth house, and it usually symbolizes the authoritarian influence in the material world.

The twelve houses are also used to symbolize the time of day. The first house indicates the morning, the tenth house represents noon, the seventh house indicates six o'clock in the evening, and the fourth house indicates midnight. The lower half of the wheel represents night, the upper half of the wheel indicates day. From a philosophical point, day is associated with light, and light indicates the masculine principle—the idea, the ability to "see," to know. Night represents the feminine principle. The Sun rules the day. The Moon is the Sun's wife in ancient mythology, and she rules the night. Taking these symbols into consideration, it seems that the ancients intended the natural house of the Moon to symbolize the maternal influence.

The opposition between the fourth and tenth houses is not unlike the opposition between the first and the seventh. Since the fourth and tenth represent the parents, these houses show their relationship compromise. The actions of our parents influence the type of compromise we will make with our own partners.

The arms of the cross are symbolic of our basic life conflicts. They show that it's natural for these functions to have difficulty expressing in the personality. Perhaps the interaction caused by the squares from the first to the fourth, from the fourth to the seventh, from the seventh to the tenth, and from the tenth to the first indicates tension is necessary for growth and maturation to take place. The first house (how we begin things, our physical body) squares the fourth (our early childhood environment). Everything we start, from career interest to physical expression in life, is influenced by our early childhood environment. When we have planets arguing between the first and fourth houses, there is even more energy and more conflict to work with in terms of self-expression. These conflicts can make us productive human beings. We start things based on our reaction to the early childhood experience. If we received encouragement early in life, we have less trouble beginning new things. If we are thwarted or hindered early in life, we have to learn to give ourselves encouragement.

The fourth house (the early childhood environment) squares the seventh (the house of marriage and partnerships). How many parents approve of the person their son or daughter marries? And if the parent approves of the marriage, does the person have a chart that happens to have the fourth house in harmony with the seventh? Usually there is some conflict between the marriage partner and in-laws. Sometimes the conflict is expressed as a difficulty in leaving Mom and going on to the marriage partner. Sometimes family loyalty gets in the way of partner fidelity. Women and men want to return home to inherited family responsibilities and to the familiar experience. Or, the marriage partner may make us change. For example, a husband may restrict his wife in some way; he may put her in an uncomfortable environment. Sometimes the wife doesn't want to move away from her family. And we are all familiar with mother-in-law jokes!

The seventh house squares the tenth. Marriage partners often have conflicting values. One partner may not be encouraging or supportive of the career development of the other. A husband sometimes won't let his wife pursue her goals because they don't complement his. Sometimes a wife wants children at the same time that her husband wants to make a career change, and he can't afford to make it if he has to support a family. The partner's needs can often force a husband or wife to bend the career goals. On a less personal level, the tenth house is the recognition we look for in the world, and the seventh represents the general public's reaction to us. Sometimes the public won't give us what we want. Some compromises must be made.

The tenth house represents our idea of public recognition and the honors that we strive for, and it squares the first house which shows the way we present ourselves and the way we begin things. This conflict between the houses can indicate the kinds of problems we make for ourselves in terms of career. It indicates what we want versus what we project. The first house can indicate what we may be good at in terms of career. But the work we do well might not agree with what we want from the world, or with what the world is ready to give us. In order to get what we want from the world (tenth) an adjustment or a compromise is sometimes necessary in the way we present ourselves (first). In other words, if we really want what we say we want, we have to dress the part!

Apparently, the main issues in life conflict with each other! The arms of the cross need to be brought together in some way in order for the healthy energies inherent within to develop. It may be concluded that tension causes growth. The process of individuation involves chaos as well as harmony. In his book *The Courage to Create*, Rollo May says that out of chaos comes creativity. The various religions and mythologies indicate that the universe was created out of chaos. Chaos can be a friend, a teacher and the source of creative potential. Perhaps we can learn to relax with it if we understand it as such.

THE FIXED HOUSES

The Fixed signs in the natural zodiac (Taurus, Leo, Scorpio and Aquarius) also square each other. The second house indicates natural talents. It argues with the fifth house ability to create. The friction between the second and fifth houses can express on many levels: income goes out on children; earning a living may take time and energy from the development of our creative self; income or the need for income conflicts with the fun we want to have since the fifth house represents any interests we may have in gambling, risk-taking and entertaining. People who live on loans or charge cards may have a second-fifth house conflict!

The fifth house squares the eighth. Our creative ability may be stifled because of our partner's financial problems, or money may be paid out for legal fees, taxes, etc. The eighth house indicates how we respect other people's property and ideas; the fifth indicates our own creative ideas. The dichotomy between doing what we want to do and respecting someone else's right to do their own thing will be met. The fifth-eighth house square also signifies some of the conflicts between flirtation/romance versus what you really believe about sexuality and reproduction. Leo represents ideal love; Scorpio symbolizes reproduction. Sexual problems can be indicated by the eighth house.

The eighth house is ruled by Scorpio. It represents our concern with regeneration, transformation, our feelings and attitudes about other people's ideas and property. It indicates our concepts about death, inheritance, taxes, the partner's money, etc. The eleventh house shows our friends, advisors, our hopes and wishes and ideas of humanitarianism. The square between these two houses indicates the conflict between accepting other people's ideas, respecting the fact that their ideas are different than our own (eighth) and how that difference can affect friendship (eleventh). If we won't respect or listen to another's ideas, how can they help us?

Last, but not least, the eleventh house squares the second—the conflict between friends and their needs versus our income. Perhaps our friend doesn't recognize our natural talents; perhaps our social involvements blind us to the fact that our path in life may be different from the one our friends travel. This can keep us from developing our own special talents.

The Fixed house oppositions cause a compromise to take place as the tension builds between the various ideas involved in the opposition. The second house represents natural talents, how we earn our income; the eighth house indicates what we think of other people's ideas and creativity, as well as how we spend our money, and how we respond to the inherited responsibilities of our environment. The second-eighth house opposition causes us to compromise. In the process of individuation the natural talents and the natural urges of the second house will have to be compromised with the values of others, for we cannot inspire others to grow (or even ourselves) if we do not consider the world around us. Transformation is a personal experience that can only be shared through personal love and understanding. When the compromise is not understood, we tend to force our new ideas on others.

The opposition between the fifth house and the eleventh house causes a need for compromise between our concept of creativity and its effect on our friends, or our creativity and its application to our hopes and wishes. The fifth house rules children; the eleventh rules friends. A parent must compromise between the needs of the family versus an interest in developing friendships. The personal cycle of becoming conscious, or undergoing a personal transformation, will always involve the Fixed house oppositions. The second house is our natural talents and the eighth stresses inherited responsibilities. The eighth can be interpreted in terms of what we inherit due to the genetic process—inherited karma, inherited disease, etc.; the fifth may be seen as our personal creativity being hampered by our advisors or by the general qualities of Aquarius symbolized by humanitarianism. Our ideas of protection toward our children or our protectiveness about creative ideas may not be accepted by the Aquarian humanitarian ethic. For example: a mother may love her child even though he's the neighborhood "junkie." The authorities arrest him because he sells drugs to other teen-agers. The social structure benefits but the mother is upset. She doesn't approve of junkies, but she wants to protect her child. This is a very real emotional dilemma that confronts many parents—that of love versus the law, or love versus what is good for society.

THE MUTABLE HOUSES

The Mutable, or changeable, houses are the third, sixth, ninth and twelfth. They are ruled by Gemini, Virgo, Sagittarius and Pisces, respectively. These houses represent the areas of change in life. They indicate our natural ability to communicate on various levels.

The third house is the Gemini part of us. It indicates how we react to public school, and reflects the environment surrounding brothers, sisters and kids our own age. It indicates how we communicate on an everyday level, and has influence over writing and talking in general. It indicates how we will work with groups and with the educative process.

It squares the sixth house of duties, obligations and service to others. The desire to associate with our peers sometimes interferes with our daily grind. Because the sixth house indicates how we handle daily responsibilities, it also has bearing on our health. Constant conflicts between the third and sixth houses, the routines of daily living, are the pressures that often build disease. Since the third house indicates siblings and relatives and the sixth house involves the daily routine, we can see these conflicts at work. They are the family arguments, the arguments at work—all the daily hassles.

The sixth house squares the ninth. The old astrology books call the ninth the house of religion and philosophy. In the old days we were identified by our religion, for it was our philosophy. Today it may be defined as the philosophy we practice in life. What happens when our life philosophy can't be put into practice? The ninth squares the sixth and opposes the third. If we can't practice our philosophy of life through the way we communicate (third) and our job (sixth), we create tensions. Physical tension is the body saying it can't handle any more of the internal pressure. Metaphysicians report that illness is the result of the body rebelling against what we have done to it either emotionally or physically.

The ninth house squares the twelfth—philosophy of life versus personal burdens. The twelfth house has been called the house of self-undoing. The twelfth seems to be the karmic house, the one that indicates what we have come here to work out. People interested in reincarnation say that it indicates natural abilities we have brought with us from a previous life. These abilities need developing and conscious use in this life. If the qualities of the twelfth aren't used consciously, they may become a part of our own "undoing." It may be that understanding and compassion come from this house, and those qualities may need to become integrated with ninth house concepts.

The twelfth house has been called unconscious or hidden. Planets (or parts of personality) in this house are brought into consciousness with difficulty. The square between the ninth and the twelfth houses shows the philosophical problems engendered when we are not totally conscious of our motivations, reactions or fears. The old dictum of "know thyself" is important here, for when the ninth house and the twelfth don't agree, ignorance of universal law does not keep us from suffering the penalties.

The oppositions between the Mutable houses show the compromise between the various phases in communication. Our ability to communicate ranges from personal expression to our ability to communicate with the god-consciousness in the universe. In order for us to grow, the Mutable houses indicate that we must function well in several areas. Consider the compromise between the third house (daily communication) and the ninth house (personal philosophy). Idiomatically, it means "put your money where your mouth is!"

The opposition between the sixth and the twelfth houses causes a compromise to happen between our daily responsibilities and the burdens we voluntarily assume; perhaps also a compromise between our health and the subconscious patterns that need to be integrated into consciousness. As we compromise in these areas, we are forced to meld our consciousness with that of the universe, and also to become aware of the concept that each of us is a part of one never ending whole.

Perhaps the ancient philosophers were not so naive after all. As modern science deals with such things as quantum theory and black holes, we come around again to the consciousness that has been written about in the esoteric philosophies. Only our language is new.

THE ANCIENT SEVEN

The ancient houses were ruled by seven planets. Each house had a natural ruler and the rulers repeat themselves. (See Figure 5.)

The numerical order of the planets is: Mars (1), Venus (2), Mercury (3), a break in the pattern with the Moon (4) and the Sun (5). The pattern then repeats in reverse: Mercury (6), Venus (7) and Mars (8). Jupiter is added at the ninth house, Saturn rules both the tenth and eleventh, and Jupiter repeats at the twelfth house. A basic pattern can be noted: Mars, Venus, Mercury followed by Mercury, Venus, Mars. Jupiter and Saturn are introduced, then Saturn and Jupiter, and the pattern is completed.

Each planet rules two signs (except for the Sun and Moon) and has both masculine and feminine value. (See table 1.) From a symbolic point, each planet is androgynous.

The numerical value of the houses ruled by Mars, Venus and Mercury adds up to nine. When the Sun and Moon are combined, the fourth and fifth houses, the number is again nine. The Jupiter and Saturn combination adds up to twenty-one, which breaks down to three. The other

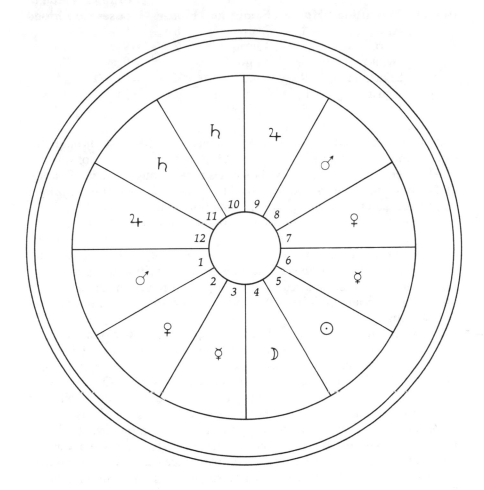

Figure 5. The planets in the ancient wheel. Uranus, Neptune and Pluto were not yet discovered.

obvious three is the twelve that stands for the twelve houses. The number twelve appears in religion as the twelve apostles, the twelve tribes of Israel, and in the twelve months of the calendar year, etc. In the ancient philosophies numbers were very important. There are many more numbers in the zodiac, but here the symbology seems obviously planned.

Venus, Mars and Mercury have the same combined numerical value as the Sun and Moon combined, and have been called the personal planets.

Table I

Planet	Masculine	House	Feminine	House	Number Value of Houses Combined
♂	Aries	1	Scorpio	8	= 9
♀	Libra	7	Taurus	2	= 9
☿	Gemini	3	Virgo	6	= 9
♃	Sagittarius	9	Pisces	12	= 21 = 3
♄	Aquarius	11	Capricorn	10	= 21 = 3
☉ ☽	Leo	5	Cancer	4	= 9

The houses involved in personal development are the first through the eighth, and they are ruled by the personal planets. The houses of spiritual development are symbolized by the houses nine through twelve. It seems that in order to transcend the personal life we must incorporate the Jupiter and Saturn parts of ourselves and become universal.

We get to spiritual consciousness through the transformation coming out of the eighth house, which is ruled by Scorpio. We regenerate at that point. The feminine side of the planet Mars rules Scorpio. It's the receptive (or feminine) side of ourselves that leads us into spiritual transformation. (See Chapter 3.) Unchanneled Mars energy often represents anger. When this energy is channeled it becomes productive, creative and, through Scorpio, spiritual.

Following the symbolism of this ancient wheel, one may wonder whether or not the creativity of the Sun ever gets to manifest itself. It seems that according to the houses, the presentation of the physical self is ruled by Mars. Yet the creative self is expressed by the Sun. On the road to consciousness, can it be that some people's Suns lie dormant, breathing life but never understanding the fantastic message of house symbolism?

Mars rules the first house and is opposed by Venus in the seventh. In the area of relationships, the first house (Mars) indicates how we act at the beginning. The first house signifies how others see us, how we begin new endeavors—it's our best foot forward, so to speak! The seventh house (Venus) represents how the general public responds to us. More importantly it represents the Venusian qualities we want our partner to have; it often indicates the kind of partner we draw.

The opposition takes place between Mars and Venus again, but this time it's between Venus in the second and Mars in the eighth house. This opposition indicates a compromise between what we want in life (second) and how we handle other people's ideas and finances (eighth). (Some astrologers consider the eighth house the money house of the marriage partner.) The opposition indicates what we draw to us financially, and how we will be treated karmically as well as legally. The eighth house represents the feminine side of Mars, and it also indicates what we draw to us in regard to inheritance and perhaps our inherited responsibilities toward others. Referring to Jung's definition of the feminine in nature or the *anima*, the feminine side of both Mars and Venus (symbolized by the second and eighth houses) has to do with the materialistic side of life and how we are led through it into a possibility of higher consciousness. The lesser side of the second and eighth houses is economical, materialistic—money and partner's money. The more evolved side of this opposition manifests as the tension and compromise caused when we investigate the concept of our own soul or our own personal talent (second) and our ideas about the transformation of others (eighth). This particular tension is that very real soul-searching experience we face every time we discover something about the universe: knowledge is beautiful and it makes us feel wonderful, but what do we turn into when we "force" our personal knowledge on someone else?

Mercury rules the third house and opposes Jupiter in the ninth house. The daily expression of our life philosophy—how we talk to our peers, what we communicate to neighbors—compromises our philosophical attitudes in some way. The compromise lies between what we say as we communicate on an everyday level (third) and what we believe (ninth). We may believe one thing (ninth) but say or espouse something else (third). The opposition in the natural zodiac suggests that we have to *learn* to live our philosophy or beliefs by putting them into practice in our everyday life. A "good Christian" goes to church every Sunday, but what does he do during the rest of the week? The opposition involves the conflict between "Do as I say, not as I do," and has to be handled by each individual who wants to attain a higher consciousness.

In the personal sense, in order to recognize the polarity between Jupiter and Mercury we must be able to relate to the universe around us in a positive sense. This involves solving any conflict between what we learned early in life and what is learned later as we mature. The third house opposing the ninth compromises "lower education" and "higher education." The lower consciousness (third) should be integrated into the higher conscious mind (ninth). Once this conflict is overcome, we go on to solving the cross that is caused by considering the opposition between the sixth and the twelfth houses as well.

Mercury ruling the sixth house indicates a different form of communication—the communication connected with service to others. In the old days it indicated how one dealt with servants, but today it indicates how one handles the daily grind and the fellow employee. The twelfth house indicates how we've elevated our consciousness—what our spiritual values are. Our daily work relates to our spirituality just as our communication with peers and family relates to our personal philosophy. The twelfth house has been known as the house of self-undoing—and may be another cause of why we become ill since it opposes the sixth. Perhaps the self-undoing (or illness) takes place when we are not conscious of our mission in this life. We bring talents into this life from a past life, according to those involved in reincarnation. We may suppress parts of our personality by letting them remain unconscious in the twelfth. We are karmically or spiritually responsible for ourselves on both a conscious and an unconscious level. In order for the soul to evolve, all the aspects of Jupiter and Mercury must be understood. If not, the polarity remains either masculine or feminine instead of becoming an androgynous symbol.

To look at this polarity another way, Mercury *requires* us to communicate, for it rules both the third and the sixth houses, forming a natural square. Family (third) versus employee (sixth)—can we express ourselves in a constructive way in both areas? The two sides of Jupiter represent philosophy and law (ninth) as well as compassion and understanding (twelfth). The Mutable squares and oppositions require that we change, for Mutable implies a changeability, and with the change comes the responsibility for our actions. All the houses and signs are necessary to accomplish the transformation.

We come now to the Sun, Moon and Saturn. Saturn opposes both the Sun and the Moon in the natural zodiac.

The Moon rules the fourth (the house of early childhood environment) and is opposed by Saturn in the tenth. The tenth house represents how we are judged in the world as well as the public status we are seeking. The way in which we go about making a mark in the world is determined by how we respond to our childhood environment—how we are nurtured. For example, when a child is learning to walk and after three steps it falls, the child is becoming aware of Saturn (in this case gravity). When the child goes to school for the first time, it sees Saturn as the authority figure who stands in its way, or the universal structure that stands in its way. We learn through the fourth-tenth house polarity that we must understand what we are doing in order to accomplish our stated purpose. When children are nurtured and encouraged in childhood, it is easier for them to confront the world. However, when children have had unhappy childhood experiences, they can be motivated to change their lot by accomplishing great things.

Saturn opposing the Moon indicates a balance must be achieved when we are too emotional. If the Moon also represents our feelings, our physical body, our subconscious self, then we must direct our emotion in order to realize our potential in the universe. Our friends and family may tolerate our immaturity but Saturn won't. When we refuse to grow or mature, Saturn comes along and pulls the rug out, forcing us to take the necessary steps for growth. Saturn can be called the "Cosmic Cop."

The balance between mothering and fathering is shown between the fourth and the tenth. Cancer symbolizes the nurturing, feeding and encouragement that comes from the feminine principle. The mothering principle determines the development of our emotional responses. The nurturing ability is symbolized by the Moon.

Fathering ties in with authority, discipline, action taken to direct the child into adult society. The fathering principle is supposed to show us how to deal with authority figures, how to make our way in the world when we leave the nest. This differs from the mothering principle, which shelters us and gives us solace when the world hurts us. Obviously this is all symbolic, for our parents may not be perfect models of the mother/father principle.

Note that both the fourth and the tenth houses are feminine. The child symbolizes the manifestation of the soul in matter. Both parents are part of the material universe, for they are physical beings. Both parents are a part of the feminine principle, which brings spirit into manifestation—the child.

The masculine representation of Saturn in the positive sign of Aquarius opposes the positive sign of Leo (the Sun) in the fifth house. This Sun symbolizes our spiritual self. The expression of the spiritual self will be compromised by Saturn because our ideas must be channeled or crystallized. The fifth house is the creative self; Saturn in the eleventh stands as advisor, guide, the Wise Old Man who leads us to the realization of our hopes and wishes. This Sun–Saturn opposition is the one that develops us spiritually. It makes us evolve our consciousness in the true spirit of Aquarius. We develop as a humanitarian through the blending of this opposition.

Saturn on a symbolic level is both Mother Nature and the Wise Old Man, an androgynous figure. Saturn has always represented universal law in terms of both the masculine and feminine principles. In order for the Sun–Moon energy to develop in the personality, it must be disciplined, or channeled into maturity. As we confront life and meet with these two characters, Mother Nature and the Wise Old Man, we grow, mature and evolve. We live through many cycles in life. Many Americans get caught in the youth culture, and because of that they do not value wisdom and maturity on a psychic or internal level. This limits the growth process, for if we do not value the Wise Old Man we can never become wise. The last cycle in life gives us time for spiritual development. When we become restricted by the war between masculine and feminine, we don't become a happy, healthy combination of the two, and we miss out on the most creative cycle in life. The universe was not our enemy in the ancient philosophies. To "know thyself" was not a task without joy. The alchemists called it the *opus magnus*—the great work.

The growth of an individual, the exploration of all the possibilities of personality in the process of individuation, requires that the polarities become balanced. Each of the planets has both a masculine and feminine side. The masculine side of Mars (Aries) opposes the masculine side of Venus (Libra): "I act" versus "I share;" my self-expression versus my partner's self-expression; my physical activity versus someone else's. Here Mars is physical action, the male principle. The masculine side of Venus represents our *ideas* of balance and love. The masculine or intellectual concept of love comes from Libra.

The feminine side of Venus (Taurus) opposes the feminine side of Mars

(Scorpio): the desire for material acquisition balanced by the desire for transformation. The feminine Venus represents physical sensuality, or the appreciation of physical pleasures, which comes from her rulership of Taurus. The feminine side of Mars describes reproduction, or bringing something into physical being. This may be children as well as a personal transformation of the life force that brings us into a different consciousness. This side of Mars–Venus, the feminine side, regenerates physically or spiritually or both.

The masculine-feminine sides of Mercury and Jupiter pattern themselves after the natural houses as well. Mercury in Gemini is masculine—pure thought, idea, the "word." Jupiter is masculine in Sagittarius, where we formulate our religious philosophy, our ethics of behavior. In order that our ethics can manifest in the physical plane, Mercury becomes feminine, or materializes, in Virgo. Jupiter becomes feminine in Pisces. The "word" becomes deed.

The feminine side of Mercury–Jupiter develops our ability to live out our ideas, to develop our spiritual awareness. The unevolved side of Virgo manifests in criticism, and such people criticize everything from the weather to the one they love. But the higher side of Virgo is service: can we put our ethics into action that shows in our daily routine? We all know people who "mouth" spiritual verses but don't follow through when their emotions (or their finances) become involved. Pisces manifest the Sagittarian ethics of Jupiter—can we really be evolved, or are we only giving lip service to spiritual awareness? If we only think about our code of ethics and never act it out, we won't be able to manifest the feminine side of the Jupiter–Mercury configuration. The Virgo–Pisces axis lifts us to spiritual heights.

The masculine-feminine interplay is different in regard to Moon–Saturn and Sun–Saturn. Saturn represents structure. Emotional strength, centering the emotional and physical self, developing confidence in emotional situations, developing intuition and feeling come out in the interaction between feminine Saturn and the Moon. We should be strong enough to handle emotional feelings or reactions without becoming bitter or unsatisfied. The symbol of the Moon opposing Saturn from the fourth to the tenth houses gives us a perspective regarding life that resolves itself in the interplay between the two planets. This interplay has been illustrated in literature on many occasions—especially when the child (the third party) is taught to compromise. The symbols are played out because of the different roles the mother and father play.

In Steinbeck's *The Red Pony*,* the mother offers love, compassion and understanding; the father offers harshness. He gives his son "man's" answers. The child is hurt by his father's reactions to most of the events

---

**John Steinbeck, *The Red Pony*, Penguin Books, New York, 1976, p. 175.

described in the story. The boy is even afraid of his father (and don't we all fear the reality of "nature?"). The reader is drawn to take sides with the boy because of the emotional play. But at the end of the story, the boy begins to understand his father's ways. He begins to accept his Saturn. "That's the way life is," says Saturn. "Make your peace with it." The pain of a child growing up is similar to the pain felt by an adult growing up. The boy felt real emotional pain when his pony died, and as adults we feel real emotional pain when something we love dies—whether it be a pony, a loved one, or the death of an idea.

The Saturn–Moon opposition says that we must go on, and as we go on our perspective must change. Steinbeck expresses these ideas in a wonderfully philosophical manner. When the pony died, the boy stopped trusting the man who tried to save the animal. He thought this man (Billy) was invincible, and he learned that no one is. At the end of the book the boy is going out to kill some mice on the farm, and he mentions to Billy, "I'll bet they don't know what's going to happen to them today." And the pony trainer answers, "No, nor you either, nor me, nor anyone."

On the masculine side, the spiritual self becomes centered or self-confident when the conflict between Saturn and the Sun is resolved. In order to evolve consciousness, we must learn to center our energy on more than one level. If we pursue the world of idea through expanded consciousness, these ideas need to be incorporated into the life style; for it is the life style that essentially tests any idea we have. When we are thrown by mental or emotional experiences, we have not properly tested our Saturn. For example, some children are protected by their parents so that they never see "reality." When they go into the adult world, they may be shocked at what is considered "normal procedure." When Saturn in its masculine sense (Aquarius) is incorporated into the family experience, children have more opportunities to test themselves. That testing, or that awareness, becomes a friend.

When the masculine-feminine polarity is unbalanced, it becomes easier for the *anima* or the *animus** part of the personality to be in control. Erratic love-hate polarities can momentarily take over the conscious personality, and we suddenly realize we have not made any progress. Conscious awareness, when properly developed, does not fail us in times of crisis. A crisis can be considered as a lack of the maturity needed to handle the "age" we are living through.

The symbols of the natural house oppositions indicate the compromises needed in life and how a personality will evolve in order to develop the potential of its life. The houses represent natural or universal law. They symbolize departments in life that can be worked out through the channeling of energy. When there are planets in these houses that also oppose each other, the aspects can be used as a guide to understanding the nature of the compromise.

---

*Feminine and masculine components, respectively. See Chapter 3 for further definition.

The chart gets very complicated when the time and place of birth are added because the houses become different than the natural houses. Instead of having Aries on the first house, Gemini may be there. This indicates that new beginnings are approached in a Gemini manner, and Mercury (ruler of Gemini) combines with Mars (the natural ruler of the first house). The first house combines with the third, so instead of using physical action to begin things (like an Aries Ascendant would) the mind will be used—mental action will be taken.

If Virgo is rising instead of Aries, this will tend to self-criticism because Virgo is the "mental discriminator." Action is taken only after analyzing all the details. People with this Ascendant may work in a highly organized manner and tend to complete whatever is begun. But the first house has combined with the sixth house if Virgo is rising. Those who don't understand the Virgo energy may be very confused, for the details of new beginnings confuse them. They may be sensitive to criticism from other people because too much criticism was received in the early environment.

With Cancer on the Ascendant, the Mars first house activity has an emphasis added from the Moon. Any new beginning will be both an emotional and a physical endeavor. The natural first house has combined with the fourth. These people may overreact when beginning something new because it is an emotional experience as well as a physical one. On the constructive side, Cancer rising can be nurturing and can make an excellent teacher; it usually functions well in the helping professions. When a person doesn't recognize the combination of action and emotion, there may be a lot of body tension. Every new beginning is regarded with caution and emotional apprehension.

The chart is an architectural plan of the life-riddle for each individual. If the plan is understood as it is illustrated in the ancient horoscope wheel, it becomes easier to cooperate with the universal energies in order for us to realize our potential. If the various stages of growth which are available to us are recognized, life and the process of maturing become very exciting! Each new day is a new growth process, each decade brings new awareness, and each phase of life is a welcome transformation.

I-3: POLARITIES

ASTROLOGY, AS IT STANDS TODAY, WAS PASSED DOWN TO us primarily through Ptolemy and those who interpreted his work. In the interpretation process, Ptolemy's original definitions may have been distorted because of changing social and philosophical attitudes. Ancient astrology seems to have a philosophical and symbolic basis.

Ptolemy said, "Again, among the twelve signs, six are called masculine and diurnal, and six feminine and nocturnal. They are arranged in alternate order, one after the other, as the day is followed by the night, and as the male is coupled with the female.

"The commencement, it has been already said, belongs to Aries; since the moisture of the spring forms an introduction for the other seasons. And, as the male sex governs, and the active principle takes precedence of the passive, the signs of Aries and Libra are consequently considered to be masculine and diurnal. These signs describe the equinoctial circle, and from them proceed the principal variation, and most powerful agitation, of all things. The signs immediately following them are feminine and nocturnal; and the rest are consecutively arranged as masculine and feminine, by alternate order.*"

Early religious philosophies used the words "masculine" and "feminine" to differentiate between the world of idea, the Logos—knowledge that comes from the mind—and the manifestation of these ideas in the material universe. The Logos (symbolized by male) formulates the idea, and the feminine principle (symbolized by female) manifests the "child," or the complete entity, into the material universe.

The masculine and feminine principles seem to be misunderstood today in astrology, as well as in other areas of our society. In primitive religions or philosophies, the female principle was dominant because the female gave

---

*Ptolemy's Tetrabiblos, translated by J.M. Ashmand, W. Foulsham & Co., Ltd., London, 1917, pp. 35 f.

birth. The birth process was highly respected because it was easily visible and awesome. The Logos (or idea) was not visible or measurable. One could not see that it was the masculine principle (or the idea) that fertilized the egg that produced the visible. As the human species developed, a philosophical war also seemed to develop over which was better—the masculine principle or the feminine principle. The war probably developed because most people did not understand the basis of the symbolism. The symbols were applied to the biological male and the biological female, and people forgot that these principles are permanently intertwined in each other.

Because the masculine and feminine principles can be symbolized in human form, it is easy to misinterpret the philosophical concept and endow physical man with the power of the "male principle" and physical woman with the power of the "female principle." This misunderstanding separates the symbols used to define the life force and we end up with two halves. There is a third symbol that represents the complete or "whole" person—an androgynous symbol that is *both* male and female. It appears in all major religions as the male with one breast (or one half of the body is female, the other half is male). Religious symbolism was esoteric or "occult" in the old days. The meaning of the symbols was taught to a chosen few.

Carl Jung restated the problem and brought out into the open the idea that human beings are composed of a *combination* of the masculine and feminine. (For more details see his work "Answer to Job.") Jung says that the masculine principle represents the principle of perfection, and that the feminine principle represents the principle of completeness. In order to grow as human beings, in order to get a concept of self, we need to recognize the *combination* of these principles within ourselves and others.

Using the zodiac as a symbol, the philosophical concept can be seen at work in astrology. Fire and Air signs are positive, or symbolically masculine. We can see certain kinds of mental activity coming from the signs of Aries, Gemini, Leo, Libra, Sagittarius and Aquarius. For example, people who enter the zodiac in the sign Aries are highly idealistic; they have one thing in common as a group—they are aggressively involved in pursuing ideals and causes. They can be ardent intellectual promoters of a cause or idea that interests them. Those who enter the zodiac through the sign Gemini are interested in ideas, all forms of education, all forms of communication, the media, film, the spoken and written word. Leo is again oriented toward the ideal—how things ought to be. Leos have strong feelings about the ideal life situation—ideal behavior, ideal authority figures, ideal religions, etc. When Leos are not living up to the ideal, it's usually because they've been hurt. Librans are the great democrats. They are interested in pursuing the intellectual—how ideas, education and art can benefit the community. Sagittarians are the most theoretical of the idealists—they are the philosophers, often becoming involved in the political ideal in order to bring law to the masses; hence the lawyer and the politician. Aquarians are the great humanitarians, not in the personal sense especially, but in the sense of groups. They think in terms of humanity, the ideals that the species can grow toward. They are known as the bringers of the ''Aquarian Age,'' the lifting of consciousness onto a plane of awareness that surpasses or bypasses sexuality.

The negative signs are symbolic of the feminine or the completeness principle. They are the Earth and Water signs Taurus, Cancer, Virgo, Scorpio, Capricorn and Pisces. They are capable of manifesting the ideas brought here by the positive signs. Taureans are highly practical, scientific and realistic. They sort out the Aries ideas and bring the good ones into physical reality. Cancer has an uncanny sense of what the common people need and is able to provide it, putting Gemini ideas into practice. The Virgo sorts through the Leo ideas and manifests the perfectionism sent into the universe by Leo. Scorpio tries to manifest a transformation in all that it sees. It follows Libra, so Scorpios are interested in the physical or spiritual welfare of the group. Capricorn follows Sagittarius and brings the concept of law into manifestation from a physical point of view. Sagittarius is interested in the law, the idea, the philosophy; Capricorn wants to see these a reality. When this manifests on the physical plane, we have the corporate structure, the presidency, the religious minister. Pisces follows Aquarius and brings about the physical manifestation of the Aquarian humanitarian idea, touched with the aspect of individual human kindness and sympathy.

These ideas may not manifest in the physical, individual personality; they are symbolic. We strive to learn how to use our energy; few of us are born with the ability to live out our natural talents from birth—we have to learn how to use them! Christ said (St. Mark, Chapter 4) that we sow many mustard seeds hoping that some will grow. Some land on rock, some on fertile ground. When we observe all the people born on the same day with similar astrological patterns, we can begin to see that those charts are like mustard seeds. Perhaps one will grow to accomplish something in the universe, to help the species to raise its consciousness. When we look at our charts from this perspective, we see a beautiful order and purpose in the universe.

The masculine and feminine principles exist in the symbolism of the zodiac, and they exist as well in the individual. In the personal sense, the positive Sun signs (Fire and Air) indicate the presence of a strong father image (or stress the masculine principle). When people born in these signs are 0-3 years old, they see Daddy as the dominant parent. They find the father to be more influential in the parents' relationship, and so they copy the father's mannerisms.

The ideals a father passes on to a son work quite well in our social structure. We have an affirmative cultural reaction to outgoing, strong male types. The positive sign male empathizes with his mother, but he knows women are not as important as men. He basically respects authority figures and will work in a traditional authoritarian situation, such as the corporate structure. He feels comfortable working around men and not so comfortable working with women, especially if these women are in executive positions.

The female born in a positive sign, however, is a different matter. She is father-dominated, more interested in a career and ideas than in domestic issues, so traditionally she has had more trouble fitting into the social structure. She can seem too "bossy," too intellectual, too independent, too involved in profession, too involved in masculine ideas. This can cause men to be uncomfortable with her, or can cause her to be uncomfortable with her status as a woman. She may not like her femininity; she may be too sensitive to being designated a "mere" woman. If she doesn't understand where she gets her value system from, she may spend years in agony because she can't figure out her unhappiness, or her rejection of self. She may try to put herself in positions that are basically uncomfortable for her—e.g., the woman who has five kids to prove to herself that she's really a woman. These women seem to need outside interests or a career as well as kids.

The positive sign female, when she's in her late teens and early twenties, may listen too readily to men and place too much importance on the words they offer. Daddy was important, therefore men are important, what men say is more important than what women say. These women often make friends with men rather than with women because they undervalue the feminine self.

When women seem to be having trouble recognizing the woman-worth in themselves, I recommend a book by M. Esther Harding called *Women's Mysteries*. It can provide them with an historical concept of the role of women as expressed through the goddess. Literature is readily available about male symbolism, but not so readily available about the female. As women understand more about the masculine/feminine philosophical principle, they will garner a sense of self-worth and build much better relationships.

The negative, or feminine, signs are the Water and Earth signs—Taurus, Cancer, Virgo, Scorpio, Capricorn and Pisces. These people are born into a strongly mother-dominated atmosphere. They get a big dose of the feminine principle as children! The father is more passive or physical in nature, and less of an authority figure. The job of authority is handled by the mother. In some cases the father is missing (which seems to happen more often in the Cancer or Scorpio type).

The female born in a negative, or feminine, polarity is comfortable about the duties and powers of being a woman because she picks up the character traits and concepts of strength from her mother. Sometimes the feminine principle is overdeveloped and the woman is not conscious of her strength or power. When this occurs, she can be overwhelming, which can cause her to have difficulty in her relationships.

On the other hand, the male born in a feminine polarity is less sure of himself in the male-dominated world because he has been raised in a mother-dominated situation. It seems to him (on a subconscious level) that he is not as strong as women are. He is more "feminine," or intuitive, than the positive sign man. Some identity problems can arise regarding the value concepts of men because he comes out of an environment that does not have an important male figure. A side effect, then, for men in negative signs, is a basic lack of respect for authority figures since most authority figures are male. Negative sign men are capable of strongly innovative careers because they have little respect for the contemporary regime and want to change it. Or they may become antisocial to the extent of breaking the law. These men need counseling that encourages them to *use* their intuition, which they usually bury under a cover of male chauvinism. Male chauvinism in the negative sign man is usually an indication of basic insecurity about self-worth. They listen too much to the female, take women too seriously, and have difficulty expressing themselves around women (much like their positive sign female counterparts). They often feel that a problem must be mentally solved before it can be discussed with women. This comes from the mother-dominated atmosphere—where women have all the answers—and it can all be changed when these men understand what causes the lack of communication!

Some people have difficulty in relating to the concept of their Sun sign polarity. They don't consciously remember the 0-3 year period in their lives, and sometimes the circumstances don't seem to add up. When this situation occurs it is recommended that they try to recall as much of the childhood as they can, and give the polarity idea some thought before rejecting it. The examples of circumstances brought up in Chapter 1, Mommy, Daddy and "the Kid," can be investigated. Also, consider that astrological patterns may bring up the possibility of letting some family skeletons out of the closet!

For example, I had an interesting experience with a young client whose real-life father did not seem to match the description of the father according to her chart. I mentioned that the father image in the chart was confused and I wondered if her real father was the man she knew as "Daddy." As a typical nineteen-year-old, she rushed home to tell her mother what I had said. An irate phone call came in from the mother, indicating that I was ruining her marriage. When I asked the mother if the child was illegitimate she told me that she had been married to another man, divorced him when the child was two-and-one-half-years old and remarried. The child was led to believe the second husband was her real father. However, she remembered her real father, and when she questioned her mother about the man, she was told that this was some kind of fantasy, not fact. The child began to doubt her sanity; she began taking hard drugs when she was thirteen. (This is why she had come in for a counseling session.) I felt that until the child was able to verify and accept her early memories, she would not be free of the drug problem. The mother finally admitted to the paternity of the child, but by this time the real father was dead. The girl was only able to learn about her father by discussing him with relatives. She was deprived of ever knowing her real father, and because she was a father-dominated person, he was important to her. (P.S. She did kick the drugs, and her mother decided to go into astrological therapy in order to begin to uncover some of the reasons for her attempt at the deception in the first place.)

Literature gives many instances of mental instability (or spiritual illness) caused by either parental distortion of information or a child's inability to accept an unpleasant life event happening to a parent. The children's classic *Heidi* illustrates conscious grief; *Cinderella* illustrates the conscious loss of love experienced by a child who lives with her stepmother and therefore has to discover her true potential and feeling-identity through her eventual contact with a "prince." Another childhood favorite of mine is *The Secret Garden*, by Frances H. Burnett. It is about a boy whose mother dies in childbirth. The boy is unable to get to know his father because the father blames him for his mother's death. The child is raised by maids while the father travels. The key to the boy's mother and her history, as well as the eventual meeting with his father, takes place after he discovers how to get into the "secret garden" that had been his mother's.

Many suspense stories have been written about difficult mental conditions created by a child's reaction to a parent's behavior. One of these stories was made into a suspense movie, and although I can no longer remember the title, the plot serves as an illustration of the dilemma. A young girl is being treated for a mental dysfunction. We learn that she witnessed a fire when she was about five, and her mental condition has been unstable ever since. She spent several years in an institution during her adolescence. The audience learns that her mother had been killed in the fire. The young girl had gone into her mother's bedroom during a party in order to try on her Mom's prized necklace. While there, the parents came into the room and the child hid to avoid discovery. She witnessed a bitter fight and the father killed her mother and set the house on fire. In the panic caused by the fire, she escaped unnoticed but she later had no memory of the fire or her mother's death. Her "mental condition" is cured when the fire incident is handled consciously and she is removed from her father's custody.

This story vividly illustrates the mental anguish that can be caused when a child knows something about a parent and can't accept the knowledge. When a child witnesses a traumatic event, more often than not the memory is suppressed. When an astrologer gets too close to a "painful" memory, a client may not wish to pursue the subject any longer. This is where the therapist comes in, for a therapeutic setting can help any individual work through to the discovery of painful memories, which can lead to a new perspective.

A child may either misinterpret or remember a painful event, while the parent may not give the "whole truth" of the incident when discussing it with the child. Parents often think it is better for children not to know the truth, but in some cases it isn't better at all. Years ago, we were a society of people struggling for mere survival. Now survival is pretty well taken care of, and Americans especially are much more involved in developing a sense of consciousness. We can afford to ask "WHY." If we were only survival oriented, we wouldn't be spending so much money on therapy, we wouldn't be looking for spiritual answers. We can now afford to look within, and perhaps it's becoming a necessity.

In examining the parent domination in the chart, as well as other factors that influence personal principles or patterns developed by the child's interaction with the parent, the examination must be made with an open mind. For example, consider a positive sign kid who is father-dominated but whose mom swears there was no man around. I would question this tactfully and gently, for astrology says there was a man around. But how do we get to that information? A friend of mine gave birth to a Leo child shortly after she and her husband divorced. This child will grow up to say there was no man around in his early years because Mom and Dad were divorced and Mom did not remarry. I happen to *know* there is a man around, and he's helped this woman as much as any man can without being married to her. He doesn't live with her, but he spends most of his free time with her. Eventually they will marry, but the child will probably be three or four years old by the time it happens. Of course she will tell the child he had no masculine image around when he was born, because if she tells him the truth she will be admitting to having an "affair." Many parents avoid telling their children the intimate details of what they consider to be "grown-up" business.

After determining the basic Sun sign polarity, the "trinity" in the chart—the combination of Sun, Moon and Ascendant—can be used as another key to understand how the positive and negative polarities (or the masculine-feminine principle) manifest within us. The Sun represents the spirit, or the true self; the Moon represents how we feel, how we respond to life; the Ascendant represents how we start things, how we present ourselves.

Jung said a man is basically 60% male and 40% female. The female, or recessive, part of the male he called *anima*. A woman is 60% female and 40% male, and her recessive male part is called the *animus*. Much has been written by Jung and others about the definition of the anima and the animus and how each can be observed in a personality. This concept can be defined in astrological terms as polarity. To help with the process of diagnosing the trinity in the chart, a part of the Jungian definition of anima and animus should be taken into consideration:

> The anima is a personification of all feminine psychological tendencies in a
> man's psyche, such as vague feelings and moods, prophetic hunches, recep-

tiveness to the irrational, capacity for personal life, feeling for nature, and, last but not least—his relation to the unconscious...the character of a man's anima is as a rule shaped by his mother. If he feels that his mother had a negative influence on him, his anima will often express itself in irritable, depressed moods, uncertainty, insecurity, and touchiness.

"There are just as many important positive aspects. The anima is, for instance, responsible for the fact that a man is able to find the right marriage partner. Another function is at least equally important: Whenever a man's logical mind is incapable of discerning facts that are hidden in his unconscious, the anima helps him dig them out. Even more vital is the role that the anima plays in putting a man's mind in tune with the right inner values and thereby opening the way into more profound inner depths...

All these aspects of the anima...can be projected so that they appear to the man to be the qualities of some particular woman. It is the presence of the anima that causes a man to suddenly fall in love when he sees a woman for the first time and knows at once that this is 'she.' "*

The masculine and feminine Sun sign polarities can indicate the balance of power in a personality—which parent the value system comes from. The trinity gives an added insight into personality formation and how the masculine-feminine principle is likely to be projected by an individual.

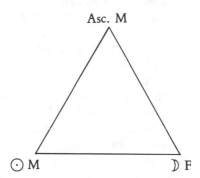

Figure 6. A trinity with two masculine and one feminine planet.

A male born with two masculine planets and one feminine planet in his trinity (Figure 6) is reasonably well balanced. That is, he fulfills Jung's definition of 60% male 40% female; the percentage of masculine and feminine is balanced in favor of his sex. He has an easier time working through some of his personal problems because he doesn't have the additional problems attached to the overpowering anima figure to handle at the same time. He feels comfortable in his culture.

---

*From "The Process of Individuation" by Marie-Louise von Franz in *Man and His Symbols* by Carl G. Jung et al; © 1964, Aldus Books, London. Quote from the Dell edition, 1964, pp. 186 ff.

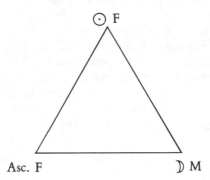

Figure 7. A trinity with two feminine and one masculine planet.

The male who has two feminine planets and one masculine planet in his trinity (Figure 7) is not so well grounded. The 60-40 percentage is beginning to get off balance. The influence of the feminine, or the influence from his mother, is heavier. He may be more easily "anima controlled," or irrational. He is more intuitive, more emotional, more feeling and more sensitive then men are "supposed" to be, and this may make him uncomfortable in his social environment. If he doesn't recognize the feeling part of himself, he may wind up being overly irritable, even "bitchy." He will be more inclined to project his anima image onto a woman and blame her for his ills.

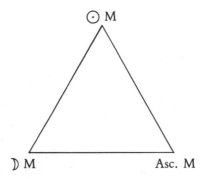

Figure 8. A trinity with three masculine planets.

The male with three masculine planets in his trinity (Figure 8) is lacking an inner feminine image. When the trinity is all positive signs, the person functions completely from mind or "spirit." This type of man is essentially all male—all ideas and ideals. He lives in his mind. He thinks about everything he does—he may even think his feelings. He has trouble communicating with women because he rarely listens to what they say. He is more likely to project his feminine or feeling values onto a physical woman, who probably won't live up to his expectations! He may expect her to be a fairytale image. He may have difficulty accepting a woman as a human being, one who is prone to human error! This may indicate that he wanders from woman to woman looking for the perfect lady in gossamer and lace. At the other end of this pendulum is the man who becomes physically violent when the woman he loves doesn't behave as his anima *should*. The chances are that he has difficulty communicating what kind of behavior he expects from his female companions, for he may not even be conscious of what he is projecting. He is a very mental and idealistic person though, and capable of intellectual and even spiritual relationships with those he loves. However, a woman in love with a man who has this setup may feel that she has to work very hard to be truly understood.

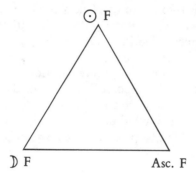

Figure 9. A trinity with three feminine planets.

The male with three feminine planets in his trinity (Figure 9) has problems of a different nature. Feminine planets endow intuition and emotional response-ability, which are traditionally designated to women. He may not be the "John Wayne" type because he feels things too acutely. He may lack confidence in his "manhood," meaning that he is a bit apprehensive about his social behavior (on an unconscious level). This particular combination gives a man the ability to feel and to develop his intuition, his creative self. He can have warm, emotional relationships with members of the opposite sex because they can relate to him easily, if he's open. Often, the owner of this combination tries to act "tough"—acts the role of the male chauvinist—in order to protect his sensitive emotional self. In the social structure that we live in a man "ain't supposed" to cry, to feel, to relate on a warm emotional level. A man with this setup can play the role of Don Juan, trying to prove to himself and everyone else that he is really masculine by having many sexual encounters. But sex doesn't really develop personal security, for every time he meets a new woman he has to re-establish himself, and the beat goes on! This man is a wonderful and warm person once he feels comfortable with his natural energy.

The Jungian definition of the animus is:

The male personification of the unconscious in woman—the animus—exhibits both good and bad aspects, as does the anima in man. But the animus does not so often appear in the form of an erotic fantasy or mood; it is more apt to take the form of a hidden "sacred" conviction. When such a conviction is preached with a loud, insistent, masculine voice or imposed on others by means of brutal emotional scenes, the underlying masculinity in a woman is easily recognized. However, even in a woman who is outwardly very feminine the animus can be an equally hard, inexorable power. One may suddenly find oneself up against something in a woman that is obstinate, cold and completely inaccessible....

One of the favorite themes that the animus repeats endlessly in the ruminations of this kind of woman goes like this: "The only thing in the world that I want is love—and he doesn't love me;" or "In this situation there are only two possibilities—and both are equally bad." (The animus never believes in exceptions.) One can rarely contradict an animus opinion because it is usually right in a general way; yet it seldom seems to fit the individual situation. It is apt to be an opinion that seems reasonable but beside the point....

Just as the character of a man's anima is shaped by his mother, so the animus is basically influenced by a woman's father. The father endows his daughter's animus with the special coloring of unarguable, incontestably "true" convictions—convictions that never include the personal reality of the woman herself as she actually is....

...the animus [can represent a particular figure] that lures women away from all human relationships and especially all contacts with real men....

Like the anima, the animus does not merely consist of negative qualities such as brutality, recklessness, empty talk, and silent, obstinate, evil ideas. He too has a very positive and valuable side; he too can build a bridge to the Self through his creative activity....

...her animus can turn into an invaluable inner companion who endows her with the masculine qualities of initiative, courage, objectivity, and spiritual wisdom....

...On this highest level he becomes a mediator of the religious experience whereby life acquires new meaning....sometimes connects the woman's mind with the spiritual evolution of her age, and can thereby make her even more receptive than a man to new creative ideas....*

*From "The Process of Individuation" by Marie-Louise von Franz in *Man and His Symbols* by Carl G. Jung et al., © 1964, Aldus Books, London. Quote from the Dell edition, 1964, pp. 198ff.

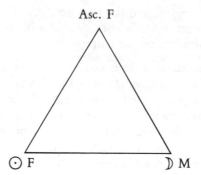

Figure 10. A trinity with two feminine and one masculine planet.

A woman's trinity indicates the manifestation of personality and the balance of feminine traits versus the animus. The woman who has two feminine planets and one masculine planet (Figure 10) in her trinity is fairly well balanced. According to Jung's 60/40 definition of the feminine-masculine energy present in the biological type, she's comfortable. She can work through personality problems easier than some of the other combinations. She will handle her life crises better for she is not burdened with an overpowering animus.

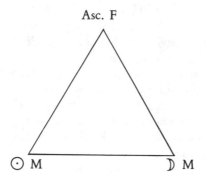

Figure 11. A trinity with two masculine and one feminine planet

The woman who has two masculine planets and one feminine planet in her trinity (Figure 11) is beginning to go out of balance. She can be animus controlled more easily; she can manifest her personality in such a masculine way that she is not well received. She can seem too aggressive. She may not value her feminine self, and she may not truly value the biological role in which she was cast. She may be overly aggressive with men; she may value an intellectual companion more than an emotional one; she may value professional standing more than a personal relationship. This type of woman should not avoid developing her masculine traits (the intellect), but the feminine side of her personality should also be acknowledged and respected. As the masculine traits are developed and used in perspective, she can use the healthy energies and discard the less useful ones. However, feelings are felt, not thought.

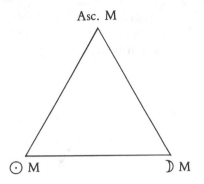

Figure 12. A trinity with three masculine planets.

A woman with three masculine planets in her trinity (Figure 12) is a super intellectual type. She thinks about everything she does; she communicates emotions on an intellectual basis rather than on a feeling level. She doesn't really feel sure of her femininity (subconsciously), so there may be a lot of compensation. Overcompensation takes place when she appears too feminine or too sexy. In order to gain attention as a woman, she may overexpose her body and then get angry when someone notices! This woman may be sexually mistreated, even raped, because she sets herself up for it. On the one hand she wants a relationship that is highly intellectual, and on the other she wants to be reassured that she's a woman.

For example, Marilyn Monroe had three masculine planets in her trinity. She was considered one of the most beautiful women in the world, and people couldn't understand why this beautiful woman was so troubled. When her chart is looked at from a psychological point of view, her dilemma can be seen. She was feminine (on the outside) and beautiful, but she didn't really believe it. She needed constant reassurance that she was good at her job and that she was an attractive woman.

In counseling young women who have positive trinities, I've learned that many of them have been raped more than once. Yet, they continue to dress in a very provocative fashion. Men don't often know how to handle women who have this kind of energy. These women look so female on the outside that the average man assumes that the "dish" knows what she's doing! Men also have trouble comprehending that they really want to *talk*—to have an intellectual relationship. This type of woman presents herself as intellectualy as any man can; she comes not from a feeling point or from an intuitive point, but from an intellectual point. So the man sees the lovely lady but hears the masculine conversation (and ideas) and doesn't know what to do.

Some women solve the problem by having five kids in order to prove to themselves that they're women. But a woman with this kind of energy also needs to have some kind of career, even if it's only running the local PTA, for the "idea" energy needs to be used. When she becomes aware of her energy balance, she can begin to solve the problem. As she develops a personal sense of worth and self-understanding, she will change her outer appearance.

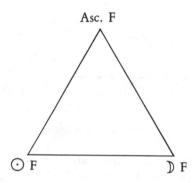

Figure 13. A trinity with three feminine planets.

When a woman is born with three feminine planets in her trinity (Figure 13), she's a very feminine, female type lady. She is very powerful because her mother was super strong. This lady will become aware of her strength as a woman in this lifetime. She lacks the masculine image in her psyche, so she will tend to project her animus on any man that comes in sight. It's very hard for men to live up to her idea of what a man is. Her image is probably full of "knights in shining armor" and standards from King Arthur and the Knights of the Round Table. And when the man doesn't live up to this image, it's off with one man and on with the next. Once she becomes aware that she does this, it's easy to balance the energy.

When the animus image is projected onto someone we expect that person to do all the things that we should be doing for ourselves. For example, "I can't be what I could be, for he won't help me." That's the job the animus does for us according to Jung's definition.

The masculine and feminine principles symbolize the interrelationship between thinking and feeling. In the discussion of the polarities as they manifest in the trinity of personality, the terms anima and animus are mentioned. Neither of these discussions has anything to do with homosexuality. Sometimes clients and students think that a female with an overdeveloped animus or a man with an overdeveloped anima is homosexual. Actually, the balance of masculine and feminine planets in the natal chart is a better indicator of how comfortable or uncomfortable we feel in our biological roles. Our choices about sexuality seem to come from something else. A woman with eight masculine planets in her chart can be as good a mother and woman as can a woman with eight feminine planets. And a man with lots of feminine planets can be as happy being heterosexual as can a man with many masculine planets.

Last but not least, the planets in the chart are counted in order to see what that balance is. When there are seven or eight Fire and Air planets in a chart, there is a lot of masculine energy. These people are thinkers—they intellectualize everything they do. A man born with eight masculine planets will be a very mental, spiritual, thinking person. He may have trouble expressing his feelings; he may intellectualize sex; he may have trouble combining sex and love. (He may actually separate sex and love!)

A woman with seven or eight masculine planets in her chart will have an interesting life experience because she will have to balance the idea of masculine and feminine in her life style. She is similar to her masculine trinity sister and will have to come to terms with her feminine self. If she does not, she may resent her femininity in some way. She may resent the biological role and/or responsibilities of being a woman. When she gets into her 40s, she may have more medical problems than other women; for example, hysterectomies are not uncommon for such women. Because she functions in such an intellectual manner, she may be the kind of client who comes to an astrologer and speaks about various kinds of social-sexual problems. This woman may not feel secure in regard to her femininity and may project an overfeminine image. When men respond to this image, she may be uncomfortable, and may also be subjected to unwelcome sexual advances. She may even be subjected to rape—and often women are raped by people they know. (For obvious reasons, these rapes are unreported.) A woman in this dilemma needs understanding and counseling. We each draw life situations to us because we need to learn something. Until we understand what it is we do to compensate for our inner feelings of "lack," our opportunities for growth remain limited. This type of woman may grow to resent men; she may get involved with women's liberation from the wrong point of view—namely that of disliking men. She would be better off involved in raising her own consciousness to include the values of being a woman.

If these women have unconsciously rejected the biological role of woman, they may not have children. Sometimes these are the women who keep trying to have children but can't get pregnant.

When there are seven or eight Earth or Water planets in the chart, there is a lot of feminine energy. Since the feminine principle symbolizes manifestation, these people can be highly productive. They may tend to use more strategy or guile to get what they want than their positive chart counterparts. The female with eight negative planets is very feminine, much like her negative trinity sister. She will have to learn about her tremendous power and strength in this lifetime. The problems that manifest from this energy may concern an overemphasis on materialism—too much concentration on the material in life and not enough concentration on spiritual or inner development. These problems manifest in relationships where one partner is extremely materialistic and the other is not. The female with a strong emphasis of feminine planets often comes on like the overwhelming mother figures in ancient religions and philosophies, such as Kali, the Hindu goddess who gives birth and eats her young. These women can unintentionally overwhelm their men and their male children unless they learn to become conscious of their energy.

The man with seven or eight feminine planets in his chart is also a materialist. He may feel out of step with the idea of "man" in his culture. He will be very intuitive, sensitive and emotional. He'll struggle with the idea of Don Juanism in his lifetime. He sees life in emotional terms. He may even unconsciously regard himself as feminine. This implies an insecurity about masculinity—what it is, how to be a "man." The outward behavior of this kind of person can be called chauvinistic. He may project a heavy male image to compensate for his sensitivity. Inside he's a very emotional and intuitive, warm and sensitive human being. If he learns to listen to his intuitive self, he'll be able to produce creatively in whichever direction he wishes. If he is uncomfortable with this feeling self, he *may* be homosexual, or will at least worry about it.

The masculine and feminine principles basically indicate the balance of idea and manifestation within us. Both are necessary for a balanced life. There have always been four forces present in philosophy and religion. They have been the qualities associated with Fire, Air, Earth and Water. Fire and Air have represented the manifestation of the seed—Earth to plant it in and Water to grow it with. So Fire and Air represent the mind and the soul, Earth and Water represent the body and the continuation of the species.

When we examine how these universal forces are present within us, we get an idea of what parts of us need to be developed so that we can achieve a well-rounded concept of the universe. The twelve signs are symbolically present in every individual because we each have twelve houses in our chart and twelve signs represented in our personal circle in the zodiac. As the balance of masculine and feminine energy in our chart is understood, we can begin to know what we need in order to become more fulfilled and happy men and women.

WE ARE ALL REACHING FOR SOMETHING: SOME OF US strive for power, some for spirituality; others seek wealth or material security while others look for emotional experiences or pleasure on a sensual level. We all live and die, we all laugh and cry—but what moves one person may not move another. The Cardinal-Fixed-Mutable and the Fire-Earth-Air-Water breakdown in the personal horoscope can give an insight into individual drives and needs. These modes and elements indicate on a very basic level what the individual's natural energy flow is and what that person is seeking in this life.

MODES

The modes of emanation (or the quadruplicities, as they are sometimes called) are determined by counting the number of planets in the Cardinal, Fixed and Mutable signs. There are eight planets plus the Sun and the Moon in the traditional horoscope. If the different numerical combinations are understood, the energy flow of different individuals can be determined. The ideal average between the Cardinal, Fixed and Mutable signs is a 3-3-4 ratio. However, there are charts with more exotic accumulations of energy. For example: 1 Cardinal, 2 Fixed, 7 Mutable. People with an equal energy balance (the 3-3-4) can handle life crises better than those who must train the 1-2-7 breakdown to function to their advantage.

The Cardinal signs are Aries, Cancer, Libra and Capricorn. Cardinal signs are basically accomplishment oriented. They are each aggressive in their own way. Cardinal energy symbolizes the angles in life, as discussed in Chapter 2. Aries symbolizes the energy of personal accomplishment. This accomplishment is sometimes seen by others as aggression, but Aries carries with it the energy of Mars—the starting energy in the zodiac. Thus Aries is considered a pioneer—the sign of new beginnings. Cancer symbolizes the energy of emotion—the power of emotional involvement that can range from the intense mother-nurturing possessive love to the love of power and material possessions. Libra symbolizes another kind of energy—that of diplomatic aggression. It's the power of the mind or the intellect that can be used for accomplishment. Capricorn symbolizes the aggression necessary for management and leadership. Therefore, the Cardinal planets show the individual's aggression level—or the energy level. These energies are dynamic. In order to follow through on any project, the basic energy must be there.

People with zero to one planets in Cardinal signs don't seem to have a great deal of physical energy. They want to take on responsibilities which they may not have the physical energy to fulfill. When planning activities, it may be helpful if these people will take into consideration the needs of their Sun sign in relation to the responsibilities they wish to assume.

For example, Aries people with only one Cardinal planet will want to get involved in all kinds of activities because Aries enjoys getting involved with many new ideas. But the Cardinal energy is a clue that they may not be able to handle the responsibility of many activities because the energy won't hold up. Taurus people with one Cardinal planet will move more slowly than Aries; they tend to conserve their energy, they don't burst into activities like Aries do and therefore don't burn themselves out as quickly. Taureans with one Cardinal planet may feel sluggish, lacking in physical energy.

Some Sun signs are always late because they can't get out of the house to keep appointments or get to a job on time. Overscheduling is often a problem that needs to be solved. A lack of Cardinal planets means the Fixed and Mutable signs are well represented. The accent group will give insight into the natural energy flow of the personality.

When there are five or more planets in Cardinal signs, there is dynamic energy. These people often jump into situations without forethought. They're dynamos, but the energy needs channeling. These are the children that go! go! go! and wear out parents. This energy can, however, be highly productive in adults. When most of the energy is Cardinal, they tend to act before thinking through the situation. They can be impatient and thoughtless to the point where half their energies are spent in getting out of unnecessary scrapes. If for some reason they can't act out their inclinations, this energy may be turned inward, producing tremendous inner tension. When this happens, tension-based illnesses may occur because the circumstances in the person's life won't tolerate the living out of the energy within.

The Fixed signs are Taurus, Leo, Scorpio and Aquarius. Fixed signs indicate how stable the individual is by nature and how much the inner self is believed in. The degree of stubbornness, rigidity and fixed opinions is indicated by this balance. Fixed signs indicate how much the person wants to build, since the Fixed signs are the builders of the zodiac. They also indicate ideas about soul, spirituality, transformation, ethics and humanitarianism.

Zero to one planets in Fixed signs indicates a lack of natural built in feelings of stability, or self-assurance. However, a paucity of Fixed signs maybe offset by having a lot of Earth planets, which will be discussed later in this chapter. People who lack Fixed planets can be easily swayed by others because they are not strongly opinionated personalities. They feel the various life crises acutely because they don't have a strongly rooted sense of self. They want to build stability and security around them, for they are compensating for a lack of it within. When this legitimate personal need is understood, they will be able to provide themselves with whatever it takes to keep them comfortable. These people will develop a trust in themselves as they go through the life experience.

Five or more planets in Fixed signs show a natural surety of conviction, and possibly downright stubbornness! It's hard to change people with lots of Fixed signs; it may be difficult for them to adapt to new ideas or to change jobs, and it's easier for them to get caught in ruts. The personality is firmly entrenched—it stands against the storm. These are sturdy people. A majority of Fixed planets is both a blessing and a curse. On the one hand they make for stability, endurance and survival. On the other they indicate an unwillingness to change, to alter beliefs, to learn new things or listen to others' opinions. Consciousness of the Fixed sign dilemma facilitates the working out of some of the negative traits and the development of the constructive side.

The Mutable signs are Gemini, Virgo, Sagittarius and Pisces. Planets in these signs indicate how much energy we are able to put into the concept of change. They indicate how easily we bend to outside influence, how susceptible we are, how open we are.

Zero to one planets in Mutable signs indicates a bundle in Cardinal and/or Fixed, which gives a clue to the energy type. A low count in Mutables indicates people who are not normally interested in change or in thinking new thoughts or in being swayed by outside opinions—they are not fad conscious. An absence of Mutables will show when these individuals participate in relationships; in a partnership they may not be interested in coping with the needs or the interests of the other. These people are not naturally group oriented; they tend to work better alone rather than as team players.

Those with five or more planets in Mutable signs tend to listen to everybody! They can be swayed by anyone who has a ''rap'' together. They may have difficulty listening to their inner needs because everybody else makes so much sense. These people are known as Mutable types, which means that it's easy for them to change, to adapt to new conditions; but they may be so adaptable that they never make a decision. These people can bring new ideas and concepts into the social structure. They explore new philosophies, new attitudes and new trends. It's important for them to learn to assess their personal needs, for too much of their life may be lived for others.

ELEMENTS

The ancient philosophies subscribe to four basic states of matter. In astrology they are called the triplicities or elements. It is important to understand the qualities of Fire, Earth, Air, and Water as they manifest in the world, and in the human psyche. The elements can be used to understand how we direct ourselves. The human being is always motivated toward something. Karmic astrologers say we draw the life experience that helps us to develop our consciousness. As we seek psychological wholeness, we seek experience from outside ourselves which we do not innately possess. *The elements we lack seem to symbolize the qualities we try to develop.* An easy way to understand what we need versus what we have is through the element balance, or imbalance. When we have plenty of one quality, we don't need more. When we lack a quality, we reach out to absorb what seems to be missing in our life experience.

The elements can be used to determine what the individual has in terms of inner qualities, and what the individual feels is lacking and, therefore, will search out in life. A scale of 1-10 is used, counting the eight planets plus the Sun and the Moon. The elements indicate the departments in life that are of most interest to each individual. We seem to play down the elements that are well represented and go about the business of seeking those we lack. When we establish relationships, we often draw people to us who have an energy balance that compensates or completes ours. We are interested in developing the empty categories and seem to be somewhat self-conscious about using the categories that are well represented.

The Fire signs are Aries, Leo and Sagittarius. Zero to one planets in Fire signs suggests a *need* for fire, or the quality of fire in the life. People with no Fire planets need lots of love and attention. They may expect too much attention from parents or loved ones. They may be asking for so much adoration that it's humanly impossible to satisfy that need. When the lack of Fire is handled in an immature fashion, there is usually a demand to be the center of attention. These people interrupt conversations or change them; they get angry when the world doesn't hang on their every word. People who lack Fire need to be known for what they do in a career sense. By using this energy in their careers, they may have a better chance at productive relationships. They need lots of reinforcement about love—they need to be told they are loved forty times a day! It is essential for them to learn to share, to understand that their needs for attention may be too demanding, that they may not be allowing their partners a space of their own.

People with five or more Fire planets are usually quite shy. The old textbooks say these people should be very fiery and attention seeking—but lots of Fire seems to express in the opposite way. Those with lots of Fire are open and joyous and idealistic *with people they know well*, but they are rather shy in unfamiliar circumstances and around strangers or people they don't know. Lots of Fire can cause problems in relationships; the heavy Fire people don't communicate their needs easily. They seem to have difficulty in asking for what they want in a relationship—they resent people who are unable to read their minds! They think that if you love them you must "know" what they want without their having to ask for it. Since they can tune into their partner's needs, they expect it in return. For example: The five Fire person has a birthday coming up. The lover forgets. Five Fire won't remind his lover that his birthday is due, or even that he likes to celebrate the event, and he resents being forgotten. Lots of Fire also symbolizes high ideals. These individuals may look for idealistic love affairs and can be hurt by the 'human-ness'' of their partners. Romantic ideals may include a combination of Jane Eyre, Mary Poppins and King Arthur and the Knights of the Round Table. Looking for knights in shining armor or maids in gossamer and lace increases the chances for disappointments in honest relationships.

Sexually, too many Fire planets can be limiting. The Fire signs are idealistic; they want their minds read. When sexual needs are present, Fire people won't communicate their needs to a partner. They feel romantic and want to make love, but won't let the partner know. Because the partner doesn't pick up on their needs, the owners of Fire planets get angry, hurt, etc. This can cause the beginning of a separation between the lovers, because Fire people may withdraw and build resentments. The predominance of Fire planets in a chart can indicate an innate difficulty in working through relating problems because feelings get easily hurt and ideals get smashed. When these people learn to regard themselves with a sense of humor, they are then able to put themselves into perspective and will pick ideals that can be lived.

The Earth signs are Taurus, Virgo and Capricorn. Our sense of security comes from the Earth signs in our chart. They indicate how much material security we have, how determined we are, and, like the Fixed signs, the Earth signs tell us something about how we weather the storms in life.

People with zero to one Earth signs are not naturally self-assured. This seems to be the mark of the money-maker, for this group finds both financial and emotional security important. They can be go-getters in the material sense. They want a nice home in a good section of town, money in the bank and lots of love. They don't function well living from week to week—they need more security than that. People with no Earth planets are more likely to suffer in their personal relationships. Love is important, emotional security is necessary; therefore, they often cling to unproductive relationships rather than face the possibility of standing alone. These are the people who stay in a bad marriage because of the house or the life style or the income.

Consider what can happen when a female with an Aries Sun has no Earth planets. She is idealistic; and in her early twenties, often she is looking for a knight in shining armor—a good person with lots of potential who may be financially unestablished. *And she has no Earth planets.* She needs to know there is money coming in, but she may be in love with a penniless painter who lives from day to day. In order to have a relationship with him, she must sacrifice a part of herself—her own need for security. Part of her wants to pursue the ideal, and part of her wants to establish a financial fund. Perhaps she decides to accept him the way he is, and then she'll try to establish some security on the side—a bank account that might secure them for a rainy day. But he may learn about her "stash" and convince her to spend it all on paints and canvas for him to work with. The frustration that takes place in situations like this is difficult to compromise. She has both ideals and financial needs. In order to satisfy both parts of her personality, she needs to find someone who complements her.

People with five or more planets in Earth signs tend to be a bit rigid and stubborn in outlook. Financial security is not important, so these people don't always react diplomatically toward their boss, or to instructions from other people, especially when those instructions include admonitions about behavior! In money matters, they can enjoy the fruits of financial success but won't stay in situations they don't approve of in order to maintain financial security. As much as they can enjoy and appreciate love, they won't sell their souls for it; they can take love or leave it. These people are self-sufficient and that can be both good and bad. In relationships, it will be wise for them to consider the possibility that they may be too dogmatic. Lots of Earth can make them too stubborn, too rigid, sometimes too angry. They want what they want when they want it, without considering the other fellow's needs or desires. It's their way or no way. (If you happen to love someone with lots of Earth, keep in mind that they won't be pushed too far.)

The Air signs are Gemini, Libra and Aquarius. Air signs generally indicate an interest in communication. When we lack Air signs, we tend to overemphasize intellectual development; if we have lots of Air, we learn best through communication with others.

When there are zero to one planets in Air signs, it means that the quality of Air is missing. Intellect is missing and therefore Air, or intellectual development, is sought. These people are generally curious; they read a lot or study subjects that interest them. Those who can't afford college will study on their own. A lot of Fire planets and no Air planets tends to produce a bookworm! People with no Air tend to enjoy learning about theory and systems. Their minds are always open to learning something new. They make interesting and diverse companions.

If there are five or more planets in Air signs, it may be that this life trip does not involve the intellect any more than intellectual development is necessary to further career goals. If the career requires some college education or a Master's degree, these people will get it; but this may also be a person who prefers communicating with other people rather than reading. People with five or more Air signs usually need to work around constantly changing surroundings; they like to know and communicate with a wide variety of people. They are interested in learning by talking and listening. They are often happy in the media-related occupations or in a teaching profession because they enjoy sharing what they learn. These are the writers and reporters, the people who work well with constant change. They are involved in contemporary groups—women's liberation, civil and equal rights movements and political causes.

The Water signs are Cancer, Scorpio and Pisces. The number of planets in Water signs in the chart indicates the individual's natural feeling, intuitive and psychic abilities. A lack of Water sends us on a life trip that includes searching for love, feeling and the development of our intuitive abilities. When we have a majority of planets in Water signs, we may be afraid to give of our emotions and we may be afraid to express our natural intuitive abilities.

People who have zero to one Water planets tend to milk each emotional experience for all it's worth. It seems that when a natural dose of emotion is lacking, it is sought. So these people throw themselves into emotional situations and feel them all as much as possible. Every little nuance of an emotional situation is lived through, and whether the experience is good or bad, these individuals *feel*. People with an average amount of Water planets may feel that their Water-less friends are overreacting to life. But the no-Water people are *seeking* these intense experiences. As the no-Water people mature they realize that they suffer more than their friends with more Water do, and they begin to withdraw from the unnecessary emotional experience in favor of what makes a more serious impact. For those readers who are familiar with the Mary Hartman character, Mary was a good example of the no-Water reaction.

On the other hand, people with five or more Water planets are so sensitive and emotional that they tend to lock up their feelings and have a fear of intense emotional involvements. These people can appear to be hard or cold because there is a wall of protection around them. There may be a fear of emotional involvements because they question whether or not they can survive the ordeal if their relationships don't work out. They may be methodical in their everyday activities because they don't want the Water to flow all over the place! On an inner level, they are tremendously sensitive, often very psychic and interested in some form of spiritual development or the occult.

One of the complaints one hears about lots of Water in a chart is the hardness associated with emotional responses. It seems that these people go through the motions of being in love, but their feelings are often so bottled up that the partner never feels loved. People with lots of Water need to learn to take a chance, to trust themselves in emotional situations. They can teach themselves to give to others without fearing that they will lose everything. Water is one of the most powerful substances in the universe. If fire burns it, it turns to steam and comes back as water; if earth eats it, it eventually turns into a stream or a spring; if air evaporates it, it comes back to the universe as rain. Water does not need to fear the environment since it constantly returns to its own place.

It seems we seek what we lack in our horoscope. If we have many planets in one particular mode of emanation, we tend to draw people who operate out of a different mode. Their energy will balance ours, but we may resent the balance. A person with five Cardinal planets may relate to someone who has five Fixed planets. Obviously their opinions and reactions to life will be different. The Cardinal person wants to be on the go all the time, and the Fixed sign wants to stay put. As they relate, one will begin to affect the other. They may choose to help each other or they may resent each other.

We also draw to us the elements that we are missing in our natal chart. This often shows up in relationships. A person with lots of Fire and Earth will draw someone who has lots of Air and Water. They promptly have difficulty understanding each other! If we think of a relationship in terms of a circle, the person who compensates for our ''lacks'' can help us to become a better rounded individual. For example, when a person with no Earth enters a relationship with someone who has a lot of Earth, they can balance each other. The no-Earth person may be oriented toward financial security at the expense of other aspects of life; the person with a lot of Earth may be so independent and stubborn that he cannot accomplish what he wants to in terms of career. As these two people get to know each other, a sense of balance can be attained.

The problems caused by the element differences between people are sometimes very easy to solve. For example, one of my clients came in for a chart comparison. She didn't understand her husband and wondered if the marriage was worth it. She had no Fire and no Earth. One of the things she really wanted in life was a home in the country. Her husband had lots of Fire and lots of Earth, and he eventually bought the house for her but he wouldn't take care of it. We discussed the basic difference in energy, and she began to understand that she was creating the problem (and other problems as well) because of the basic differences in interests. She began to regard the situation with a sense of humor. As she shared this information with her husband he began to understand his reactions to her as well, and they started relating to each other again. The element balance is an important thing to understand when considering what we need versus what our partners need.

The breakdown of elements and modes in a chart can show a great deal about a person. For example, Marilyn Monroe had 2 Fire, 0 Earth, 4 Water, 4 Air. Basically, we can tell that the two Fire gave her a healthy need for attention and love. She may have been a bit too demanding as far as her need for attention was concerned. Three planets in Fire would have given her a "normal" break, but when two Fire and zero Earth are together, there is a basic insecurity in the individual. That insecurity required her to seek attention and security from outside herself. The zero Earth indicates that she had no strong sense of inner security, so she wanted to be loved; she also wanted to accumulate financial security. The four Air planets indicate that she was not as interested in reading books about life as she was in communicating with people, being in the public eye, and having new faces to look at. But she was not really sure about what she wanted from people. The four Water would have influenced her reactions—she reached out for love (two Fire) but she was afraid to give (four Water). The lack of Earth indicates a need for emotional security. But the high Water count would have kept her from ever really giving herself to anyone, from sharing herself completely, because she would have been afraid of losing. This kind of internal battle is simple to diagnose astrologically, but it's a difficult one to overcome for the person who owns it. Marilyn could have reduced the internal panic if she had known what her needs were. She needed love; but in order to get love it must be given—especially if one wants to keep it. Once we understand our security needs, we can begin to build strong relationships that encourage us to grow—and we begin to leave the relationships that only enhance our insecurities.

Marilyn had 2 Cardinal, 4 Fixed and 4 Mutable planets. The two Cardinals indicate a lack of physical stamina. She had a lot of endurance (from the four Fixed), but she probably questioned herself a lot. The four Mutable planets cause the questions: she would have replayed her decisions, questioned whether her decisions were right or wrong, and probably ended up hanging onto the decision because she had trouble letting go. She had a personality that vacilated between fixity of purpose and questioning of goals and attitudes. She probably was open one day and stubborn the next.

Considering the mode dilemma along with the fact that she had no Earth and only one Fire, we can begin to understand the questions she constantly asked herself. Four Mutable planets ask a lot of questions and start many new projects but rarely finish what they start. With two Cardinal planets, she didn't have much physical stamina. Being a Gemini, she was interested in Gemini activities, including lots of change. The one Fire planet needed attention all the time...and no Earth planets indicate that when she didn't get enough attention she would feel extremely insecure.

This balance of energy makes for an interesting personality and gives the option for an interesting life. This dilemma does not have to end in suicide. These people can produce a great deal when they become aware of their energy level, the kinds of questions they will have, their security needs and their relationship needs.

Elvis Presley had a different setup: 1 Fire, 4 Earth, 2 Air, 3 Water. This indicates a different type of person. The one Fire planet drove him out into the world looking for attention (much like Marilyn), but he balanced his need for attention with the four Earth planets. He wanted attention, but he wouldn't give up his ethics for it. He wanted to do things his way; he was not the kind of person who would stay in a relationship when things weren't going the way he wanted them to. The two Air planets suggest that he had a curious mind and that he pursued his interests. The three Water planets indicate that he was senstive and emotional but not abnormally so. He does not appear to be as afraid of relationships as Marilyn, for he has less Water planets than she. The difficulty for this setup is the dilemma between the one Fire planet and the four Earth—the need for attention and the inability to give when it is necessary. It seems that lots of Earth planets want what they want when they want it, and the partner's needs don't matter; they often don't consider what their partner's needs might be. It is not inconceivable that Elvis was a difficult man to deal with in personal relationships: he had the element breakdown of a demanding lover. Marilyn, with her zero Earth, would stay in a bad relationship a lot longer than Elvis would, because she needed emotional security and he didn't.

Looking at Elvis in terms of mode, there are 6 Cardinals, 2 Fixed, 2 Mutable signs. This indicates a person with a phenomenal amount of energy. Elvis could really work and might have been able to hold to fantastic schedules in a tireless fashion. Six Cardinal planets have a tendency to plunge into the future without looking ahead or even considering the consequences. The two Fixed planets indicate that he was moderately sure of himself. The two Mutables show that he was somewhat unwilling to change. He probably never even thought about it.

Elvis gave the world a certain kind of sound and a certain kind of music in a particular era, and he did not change with the pop market. He dropped out of the music world and the "top forty," unlike other singers whose styles have changed with the times. He was resurrected when we returned to the "oldies." It may be that his two Mutable planets didn't adapt to new programming easily. The two Mutables coupled with the four Earth planets suggest that he probably didn't want to change with the times. He wanted to do his thing...and probably didn't care whether anyone liked it or not.

As another example, a person with 5 Fire, 5 Earth, 0 Water and 0 Air will have a unique personality. The keyword here is anger. The zero Water indicates he is seeking emotional experience. The lack of Air provides a curious mind and interest in developing the intellect. But the emphasis on Fire indicates extreme idealism, perhaps an overdeveloped sense of ethics. The five Earth planets indicate a certain rigidity, stubbornness and a kind of selfishness. Lots of Earth planets want what they want at the moment they want it. The high Fire count indicates difficulty expressing needs and wishes to the loved one. In a relationship, this person is apt to hold in resentments that cannot be expressed because the Fire sign ethics won't allow the expression of such anger. The energy gets bottled up within the individual, and a great deal of tension manifests. In order to cure the tension, the individual will have to learn to express his needs and understand the needs of others, and to put ideals into perspective according to his needs. Often, people with many Fire planets have a tremendous code of ethics, and the basis for these ethics are not examined. One hears words like "there ought to be a law" or "that's not fair," or other statements that don't acknowledge universal law. Such narrow principles seldom enhance a relationship.

When 0 Fire is combined with 7 Air, and 1 Earth and 2 Water planets are added, the personality expresses this way: the individual seeks a great deal of personal attention (no Fire) and constantly looks for an audience. The preponderance of Air planets encourages the social life, so these individuals may seem to be those "empty" gadabouts who run from party to party having a grand time. The learning experience often comes from socializing with people from different walks of life; they enjoy meeting new people. They may not be up on current events except as they hear about them from their friends. The lack of Earth enhances feelings of insecurity; they are not sure where they stand. When people learn from socializing, and they have no Fire planets, they can be excessively demanding. The no-Earth planets want to be loved, but the no Fire wants attention. This combination often produces a flirt. When these people feel insecure in their personal relationships, the solution to the insecurity is flirtation. The person they love may get tired of living with a flirt and leave. The insecurity deepens. The personal insecurity may be offset by financial security, so they find ways to earn money. As they become more mistrustful, it becomes easier to get into more and more shallow relationships, unless the pattern is broken.

Three Fire planets, 0 Earth, 0 Air and 7 Water planets express differently. Idealism comes from the Fire and practicality comes from the Water balance. The Water keeps these individuals from trusting in a relationship and the three Fire gives just enough Fire for a tendency toward shyness. When their emotional needs are not met, they will become insecure (no Earth), and they need to be told how much they are loved. But they seem "cold" to others, so no one tells them. The Fire and Water combination causes "steam," or tension, which is difficult to live with. They will seek to develop financial security because of the no Earth, and often relate to the world through ideas gleaned from books, which they read in order to avoid getting emotionally involved. Once they begin to trust people, they can form interesting relationships. But the emotional part of relating will be difficult because they don't want to put all their eggs in one basket. This type will change as the Sun sign changes. In this example, there could only be a Fire or a Water sign Sun. The Fire sign Sun will be very noble and constrained... the sense of idealism will be highly developed and may perhaps be a factor that causes rigidity. If the Sun is a Water sign, this will be a moody and impenetrable type who may be very difficult to get to know.

Experimenting with the different combinations of mode and element teaches us to synthesize the various combinations of energy so that we can better understand the drives of individuals very different from ourselves.

I-5: THE ASTROLOGICAL SIGNS

IF A CHART IS TO BE ANALYZED GIVING SPECIAL attention to the *foundation* of personality, then the qualities of the signs through which the Sun enters the zodiac must be carefully considered. These points of entry into the universe will give a special emphasis to certain characteristics and needs. The Sun sign also indicates the power parent at the time the child's personality is forming (ages 0-3).

A planet will pick up some of the characteristics of the sign it's in. However, the dominant parent factor cannot be applied to any planet but the Sun. For instance, Mars in Cancer will pick up the qualities of Cancer—the sensitivity, the possessiveness, the tendency to act like a little girl or boy, or the tendency to act like a parent figure (a big momma or daddy). But it doesn't say which parent is dominant.

Usually, the signs are presented one by one in the natural order of the zodiac, but here they are presented according to their elements. The secret of how the chart works can be discovered if the meanings of the elements are thoroughly understood.

FIRE SIGNS

When the Sun is in one of the Fire signs of Aries, Leo or Sagittarius, the individual is known for being enthusiastic and idealistic. The child born in a Fire sign tends to be extremely sensitive and is often misunderstood by the parents. Some conflict between parent and child concerning personal values will cause the Fire sign person to develop sensitive reactions regarding ideals.

The element indicates which parent is more important to the child. "Importance" should not be confused with "love"—for either a love or a hate polarity can be at work between the parent and the child. The important thing to remember is that the child is more strongly influenced by one parent. Fire sign children are influenced by the father more than the mother. The child tends to pick up the philosophical attitudes that are expressed by the power parent—and the power parent is determined between ages 0-3. This power parent is based on the child's subjective idea of power.

In the Fire signs, the child is always emotionally close to the mother, but as the child matures, one often finds that this affection really borders on compassion. Mother is a "poor dear," and Fire sign girls decide that they will never be caught in the same life style as Mom; Fire sign sons feel concern and compassion for their mother, and worry that they may be too emotionally close to her.

The father may not know how strongly he influences his child. But he does; Fire sign children think that Daddy's are more important than anybody. Aries, Leo and Sagittarian children will try to imitate the father's value system, and will try to assert themselves in the world in a "fatherly" way. (See Chapter 3.)

Fire signs are more intellectually aggressive than physically aggressive. They tend to chase ideals—and when they suffer, they suffer because of their ideal. Fire signs are often referred to as proud people. They are extremely idealistic and perhaps too perfectionistic, each sign behaving so for its own reasons. A strong sense of ethics is found among the constructive manifestations of Fire signs. When they are unethical, it's usually because they have judged themselves as failures and are looking to suffer even more than they already have. They seem to be paying dues to some cosmic collector!

ARIES. The Aries type is the most personal of the Fire signs, and it is often seen as selfish. Aries people are not selfish on purpose, but they tend to be thoughtless. They pursue their own interests with enthusiasm and seldom realize that what they are doing might overwhelm or hurt another individual. If this is pointed out to Aries, they will be hurt and usually defensive. After giving some thought to the situation, they'll probably apologize. When Aries discover they have hurt or disregarded someone, they are often filled with remorse. It's a combination of idealism and enthusiasm. As Aries people mature, they begin out of necessity to cultivate patience in order to lessen the hurt feelings around them.

Aries usually say "no" to anything suggested to them at the time the suggestion is made. But the saving grace of the Aries breed is that they do go away and think about what you've said, and eventually you'll see that they adopt your suggestions, if those suggestions are good. Aries are always in a hurry, rushing into the future looking to accomplish something—and they don't always know what that mysterious "something" is. They are trained at an early age to react to accomplishment because Daddy thinks it's important. The father may not accomplish anything in the world's definition of the word, but it must be kept in mind that a child's perception of adult behavior may be very different from an adult's.

The Aries child may have a parent who either talks about accomplishment or who feels guilty when enough isn't being done around the home; Aries may also have a parent who actually is an accomplishment-oriented individual. These children tend to be born to parents who "worry" about accomplishment. The father of the Aries child is a man who seems to be respected or idealized for his work. He may only be a laborer, but he is good at his job. He may also be unhappy; if he is a laborer and he wants to be a businessman, for example, he may retreat into the power plays that frustrated people choose in order to express their discomfort. When the Aries child is small, Daddy comes home either as a "big deal" or as a tyrant; and depending on the particular father type, the child will develop his own behavior pattern accordingly.

The mother is seen as a service figure—it isn't that the Aries child hates the mother, but the mother figure is someone who provides a service. In the case of the father-tyrant, the Aries sees the mother as a "poor, frightened creature" who stays in a difficult marriage because she doesn't know how to change her circumstances. The Aries child may be defensive of the mother, may take Mom's side in quarrels between Mom and Dad, and will try to help the mother as soon as Aries is old enough to provide emotional or financial support. However, the mother gets more pity and compassion than love from this child—and Aries will in some way, as an adult, emulate the father's position.

This is the way it works: The Aries male is often uncomfortable about his love for his mother—he may care for Mom more than the Aries female does. He may think that he's too close to Mom emotionally, perhaps too much like her as far as his emotional reactions are concerned. If this is the case, he may avoid her as he becomes an adult. He wants to be as much like his father as possible. Emotional closeness to his mother usually doesn't enhance his self-image. The Fire sign person has some natural confusion about sexuality—for them, sex includes ideals as well as action and feeling. The idealistic types feel a bit embarrassed about sexuality, so the Aries male tends to treat women like little girls or daughters—and he plays the father. It may be that when his personality was forming, he saw his father treat his mother like a little girl. It is not uncommon for the mother of an Aries child to call her husband "Father" during the child's formative years!

The Aries male has an image of Woman that combines Lolita with the maids in King Arthur's court. He wants a genteel woman who doesn't swear, who presents herself like a little lady, who doesn't confront him; and he's generally a male chauvinist as a young man. The youthful innocent he is pursuing must also fit his anima image—a long-tressed damsel in distress. He gets easily disappointed in love situations because he tends to pick the Cancer type female for a partner. She often turns out to be much stronger than she looks; he then finds he has trouble running the relationship. He is not really sure of himself in romantic situations—or in relationship situations in general. His Fire sign idealism trys to maintain a courtship throughout a love relationship because that's what he thinks love is. As soon as he sees hair curlers or has to work through a problem that requires some kind of compromise, the "romance" is not as wonderful as it once was.

The Aries female has compassion for her mother—but she vows never to put herself into the same situation that her mother is in. She doesn't want her mother's career, or her mother's kind of marriage. She may be so father dominated (either through love or hate) that she actually ends up being a "better man" than most men. In other words, it's important to the Aries woman that she act like a "man" and not like a "woman"—that she be "rational" rather than "emotional." When she marries, she often marries a childish man so that she is, in essence, the head of the household. . .like Daddy.

She tries to prove herself by doing everything well; she therefore has difficulty letting her partner do anything. It's easy to fall into the trap, for the Aries female can't stand to watch a man do a chore the hard way—so she does it for him. Sooner or later she notices that he isn't doing anything—since she has done everything so well, why should he? Ultimately, some event occurs that is so stressful to her that she falls apart and has no one to help her out of her dilemma because her man doesn't realize that she really needs help. She can be so overpowering in her identification with "fatherdom" that she runs away from all the mature folks and winds up loving people who need to be saved.

This is exemplified in the positive sign female who has an overdose of the masculine principle within her system and within her environment. When this principle is not understood, both the personal life and the career can be affected by this misunderstanding. The misunderstood masculine principle causes one to imitate culturally defined "masculine" behavior. It is possible for an Aries female to develop a career, to develop her mind, and find enjoyable and creative outlets for expression when she understands what kind of energy she is blessed with. Jung's definition of the "animus" may give a better understanding of the problem. (See Chapter 3.) The positive sign female unconsciously lends more credence to the animus, and thereby loses a part of her sense of feminine values. When a woman has no real sense of the feminine within herself—that is, she doesn't think women are worth much—she often tries to be what she considers "manly." This has nothing to do with homosexuality; it merely indicates the kind of hardness that can be involved in developing the personality.

Aries women can be extremely competitive with their fathers later in life; they can unconsciously illustrate the strength of the mythic Father image. For example, when an Aries female is involved with family situations, she often tries to outdo her father. She may even try to take away her father's position in his marriage. A case in point is an Aries female who rushed into the middle of her parents' marriage at a time when the mother was critically ill. The father wanted to do one thing, the daughter wanted to do another. The daughter didn't ask her mother what *she* wanted in terms of therapy. Instead, Aries took over the solution of the problem. The moral of the story is that she was trying to be "a better man" to her mother than her father was. Of course, this attitude alienated everyone in the family and poor Aries couldn't understand why.

When Aries don't understand their energy, when they don't understand what motivates them to action, their wonderful Aries ideas can be wasted because they may not be presented in an acceptable manner. The Aries female, in her quest for being helpful to others, may push ideas on people when they aren't ready to accept those ideas, or when those ideas haven't been asked for.

The influence of the father on the Aries female turns her into the Scarlet O'Hara type—one who runs from strong men, who tends to approach males like another male because that's what Daddy would have done. When Aries examine their reactions to life, they'll find that they resemble the father in an uncomfortable fashion. Idealism has to be tempered, for too much idealism means that we are living in an unreal world. It means that we make unrealistic demands on our partners and then become wounded when these demands are unanswered. Aries people tend to ask for things that are selfish—in other words, they don't consider the needs of their partner. They often don't know how to voice their ideals, and when their feelings are hurt, they get buried inside and are not shared. When Aries people decide to abandon idealism, they tend to put themselves into strange types of relationships which can hurt them even more. For example, the Aries male (who is basically loyal and idealistic) may get into sexual relationships that have no meaning, therefore debasing his emotional and sexual needs. Or the Aries female may draw to her the type of men who have some unhealthy sexual habits. In order to participate with these men, she must turn off a part of her personality, for she is a romantic idealist.

When there is a planet other than the Sun in Aries, some of the Aries characteristics rub off on the energy of the planet. For example, Venus in Aries indicates a person who has an extremely idealistic concept of love. Love relationships "should" be ideal, intellectual and at the same time aggressive. This makes for a person with a "lusty" mind! When Mars is in Aries, the action of the individual takes on an aggressive note—but it is an aggressive intellectual action more than a physically aggressive type, unless the Mars is carrying afflictions. Since Aries is always in a hurry, Mars in Aries is too—and you can figure out what that means when it comes to sex! Saturn in Aries operates a little differently. The Aries intellect is influenced by Saturn, so these people take the intellect seriously. As young people they may fear their intellectual capacity. This fear manifests as a basic fear of not being "smart" enough, so there is a tendency toward shyness when it comes to intellectual matters. Or due to this fear, the pendulum swings the other way and university degrees are pursued with zeal!

LEO. Leo is also a Fire sign, but the Leo energy expresses differently from the Aries. Aries are personally and emotionally idealistic whereas the Leo type is far more intellectual about it. Leos are not as selfish as Aries. Like Aries, Leos are born into a father-dominated atmosphere, but the effect of the father shows in a different way. For example, Leos live in a more intellectual fantasy world than do Aries.

Religion and ethics are important to Leos because they usually get overdosed with both when they are children. They get a wonderful but unrealistic code of ethics from the father. Because they are immersed in ethics, in rigid codes of behavior, Leos impose difficult life situations on themselves. The difficulties tie into a subconscious message these children pick up from the father. Ethics can be a subtle cover for the disease called perfectionism. Perfectionism doesn't leave any margin for error, and when one must be perfect, one becomes either horriby judgmental of the behavior of others, or one becomes frightened of doing anything new. Heaven forbid a mistake should be made while trying something new! This subconscious need is a difficult position for Leos to work out of; they restrict themselves and say things like "I wouldn't be caught dead doing that."

Approval is another quality Leos pick up from the father...all Leos want to be approved of. Many people think Leos are pompous, but that doesn't seem to be the case—they are really in need of approval. They are afraid that they may not get it. So they withdraw, waiting for some sign of appreciation. It's important for Leos to learn *self*-approval, for that is the key to the proper use of their energy. When approval comes from within, one doesn't need to look outside oneself for recognition. This frees up the natural energy for constructive purposes.

Idealism is very much a part of Leos—they can radiate enthusiasm for new causes and new ideas which they have a basic respect for. They are not afraid to accept responsibility. Once their word is given, they try to stick to it. This puts Leo types into managerial positions, for they take responsibility seriously.

The entire life is affected by the influence of the father because the ethics learned from him are applied to every possible life situation. There are standards for work, for social life, for love. In exploring the parental experience with Leos, they don't find their ethics really coming from the mother. Clients who have either been abandoned by the father or who have been born into a family where the father is very old, seem to have the most difficulty getting in touch with themselves. For Leos who have no visible father influence it's most difficult. They don't know where they get their standards from, they don't know where the influence comes from, and they can end up feeling like outcasts. Leos born into unusual situations, such as not easily fitting into the environment because of a racial or an ethnic or a religious split between the parents, may live lives of self-condemnation.

The other side of Leo manifests when the child decides that the universe just will not approve of him, or will not respect him; he therefore has no self-respect. A Leo woman will throw herself into the most demeaning of situations involving her love life, and a Leo man may take on a sexual relationship that causes him tremendous inner pain. For example, I was consulted by a Leo man living in an "open marriage;" who said it was wonderful. It took several meetings before he admitted that he had agreed to this kind of experience because of his wife. She decided he was not sexually interesting enough for her. He couldn't force himself to consider losing her and his status in the community. When an idealistic person succumbs to a situation he doesn't think is ethical, the inner pain is heartbreaking. Fire signs can die of a broken heart; when they become wounded and hurt, they may begin causing pain to themselves. One may conclude that the Fire sign person is more susceptible to masochism than some of the other signs.

The Leo female is influenced by the attitudes of her father. She therefore tends to look for a place in the world that either puts her into a profession or in a place of trust in a business situation. She needs approval on her job, and she needs to be treated with "proper respect" at all times or she gets very hurt and outwardly quite negative. As far as her father's influence on her romantic life is concerned, she, too, like her Aries sister, is looking for a knight in shining armor to come and save her from her plight. But he must let her be the boss after he gets her! These needs cause confusion in relationships. A Leo woman will often align herself with inferior types of men, for she, too, is being the "masculine" head of the household. Since she wants approval, she finds it difficult to let her mate get close to her. She can't let anyone see her imperfections. Her married life is often based on what she thinks she must do in order to maintain approval from the community. She will stay in bad situations because, as the old adage goes, she made her bed and now must lie in it. Often she lies in that bed because her husband gave her approval and respect before the marriage—and she was so flattered by it that she never looked to see what kind of person he really was.

Some Leo women have been so adversely affected by the father image that they don't function well sexually. They want the absolutely perfect partner and, therefore, tend to judge each new candidate so harshly that they can reach sixty years of age and wind up never marrying. Rigid codes of behavior regarding sexual activity may be strictly enforced, so much so that the Leo female never gets a chance to experience life without guilt. Usually this happens when the Leo child is raised with a strong religious upbringing. One of my Leo clients "saved herself" until she was forty-two years old and married a man who wanted her to be a virgin. When the knot was tied, she found that he was impotent. At forty-four she had been married for two years and still was a virgin. Obviously not all Leos are so adversely influenced by the father, but the natal chart will give a good idea about the effect of idealistic ethical training regarding sex.

The Leo male is one who normally has a double standard. He wants to be strong like his father, he wants to be perfect like he thinks his father is, and he spends his life trying to live up to his father's standards. He can pursue a career in a responsible way and assume positions of authority. Leos often choose a profession or a career in high management. If the early environment does not encourage education, the adult Leo will look for work where he is known and respected for his integrity and ability. Leos are trustworthy and devoted employees if they are given a responsible position, and often they will assume responsiblity that they are not being paid for. They give their all for the position they hold, and expect respect and approval for what they have done. Leo men can be terribly wounded if they are shoved in a corner after having given twenty years to a company.

Again, there is a need for counseling regarding self-approval rather than looking to others for it. When we are centered within ourselves we can withdraw from the emotions of the situation at hand and begin to see how the situation is really going.

When Leos give their trust to someone, they seldom re-evaluate it. For example, friendships formed early in the life are held in the same regard years later even though those friends may have changed considerably. Leos have a tremendous loyalty toward established friendships. If the friend has had a change of values or ethics, Leo doesn't want to see where the friend has gone. He will defend his friend to the end!

The idealism of Leos often draws them toward working in the political arena, but poor Leo doesn't do too well there. They bring idealism into the ball game, and find it difficult to handle the political situations—the deals, the graft, the political compromises that are sometimes made within the various political party structures. They may trust their fellow politicians too much, not realizing that each new election brings about a change in attitude for "the party." They may not recognize the wheeler-dealers until it's too late, and their reputations can suffer. The inner suffering that Leos feel is not always visible, but the pain is intense.

The Leo male brings idealism into his relationships as well. He wants to be king in his castle, which is fine. But when things are not going his way he tends to withdraw into silence and loneliness. It's difficult for him to talk about his sensitivities and hurts in a relationship (and no matter how much we love each other, we will sometimes unknowingly hurt each other). The Leo is so sensitive that one sees him withdraw when another person inadvertantly uses words he doesn't understand—or if he feels his position isn't respected enough. Many Leo men don't want their wives to work because they feel their position in the community will be jeopardized.

Their standards are noble. Because of this, they may even have sexual difficulties, for "one doesn't have sex with a woman one loves." Leos can put the people they love on such a high pedestal that they don't want to touch the loved one. If the Leo man marries a comfortably sensual sexual woman, she may begin to resent the fact that she doesn't get the loving she needs—or that she has what is called the "dull" lover who just goes through the motions with no feeling. Often, Leo men who come from a background where sex was forbidden don't have a strong sexual relationship with their wives. They may function better with a woman they don't love, for then they can relate to her sexually. The idealism of the Fire signs is not always easy to live with. Idealism has to be re-evaluated on a conscious level if there is to be a happy and fulfilling emotional life. Leos tend to live lives of quiet desperation because they don't question the basis of their ethical decisions. Their reasons are often "one simply does."

We've heard that Leos can be judgmental—and they can be. They usually apply the ethics learned from the father on the universe around them, without considering the fact that each person is different. Each of us has a path to walk, and each of us must find our answers for ourselves. Leos try to tell us how to live without considering what our needs are. And there is more to judgment—for it often makes the judge "better" than the person judged. Perfection is Leo and the rest of the world is not as good. This quality sounds distasteful—but it is merely an offshoot of the need for approval. "I want approval," says Leo, "so I will disapprove of you."

The creative energy will manifest in Leo types when they re-evaluate their personal ethics, examine the foundation of any ethical decisions, and consider developing a code of ethics that allows them to grow.

When there are planets in Leo other than the Sun the parental influence is not picked up, but some of the traits of Leo are. For example, Venus in Leo indicates that our concept of love is idealistic, and that we want to be approved of and respected by our loved ones. This makes us sensitive to the person we love, for we want their approval. One of the problems coming out of Leo planets is confusion in regard to the words "respect" and "love": they do not mean the same thing, and Venus in Leo often confuses the issue. It *is* possible to love people who don't carry themselves in a respectable way all the time. When Mars is in Leo, those qualities are added to our actions. We can act pompously, or proudly; we can act in a socially acceptable way, or we can demand approval for our actions. Saturn in Leo never feels it has enough respect or approval, and this can make for a "touchy" person. Saturn in Leo produces individuals with a sense of ethics; and because they take themselves seriously and like to be treated with respect, they often have a sense of respect for others.

SAGITTARIUS. Sagittarius is the last and most impersonal of the Fire signs. The idealism of Sagittarius is less personal than either Aries or

Leo. Sagittarians are more involved in causes, politics, in formulating the law, and they have ideas about religion and/or philosophy. They too come from a home that is strongly influenced by the father. But often, Sagittarians are angry at the father. It seems he is quite fond of them when they are little but later forsakes them for some other interest as they grow older. The Sagittarian types are looking for approval and respect from the father, while at the same time they want to be independent of him. For some reason known only to Sagittarians, they think Daddy is a successful person, and like all the Fire signs, they feel that it is impossible to measure up to his greatness.

Most Sagittarians grow up in an atmosphere of enough food and shelter, but they seem to feel left out in the emotional department. They seem to radiate self-confidence and enthusiasm, but inside they often question their personal values. Again, here is the Fire sign dilemma—ideals can be so lofty that the Fire sign person can't possibly live up to them.

Sagittarians pursue ideals and ideas in an independent way. They are interested in all aspects of the concept of freedom. The political quest for freedom often involves the concept of revolution. However, when it comes down to the actual fighting, Sagittarians don't want to be involved—it's cold and uncomfortable on the battlefield, and suddenly philosophy seems to be the direction in which to travel! This type can be the great fireside revolutionary. Sagittarians who become interested in politics often have the same problems Leos have. As they become more involved in the political arena, they find that it's not as idealistic as it seemed at first. They don't care for the political compromises that take place—or graft, or dealings that are less than idealistic.

No idealist likes to be in situations that are not "fair." "The world isn't fair; there ought to be a law," say the Fire signs. After a number of hurts over the years—hurts caused by the unfairness of life—one begins to notice that Mother Nature is not fair either! She does not support "fairness" in the life structure of the universe. It's the Fire sign people who work to develop a sense of fairness and justice, for the universe does not make moral judgments. Westerners regard certain Eastern practices with abhorrence because they seem so unfair, so inhuman. But our ideals will not allow us to see that life is a constant stream of transformation and change. Life is a force much like that of symbolic water, for it keeps on "a-keepin on." Perhaps some insight can be gained as to why Fire signs don't understand Water signs and vice versa if the difference in the symbols of the two is taken into consideration.

In the area of the Sagittarian's relationships, the father has a great deal of influence. He is a person who loves companionship and camaraderie. He likes typically male things—sports events, the hunt, the "man-and-his-dog" stuff in life. The child is influenced by this, and the effect manifests differently in the male and the female as they each mature. And because Sagittarians are so involved with ethics and justice and the theory of what is going on in the universe, they often find personal relationships difficult.

The Sagittarian female comes into the universe with a strong dose of father influence. The influence of the masculine principle interferes with the development of her concept of her feminine self. Her mother's influence is very weak; and like her Aries and Leo sisters, the Sagittarian feels sympathy for her Mom.

She wants to be known for her mind, for her ability to be rational, to comprehend information in the same logical manner that a man is purported to. She is, however, a female; and lurking behind her sports events, her politics, and her career responsibilities, is that nagging fear that she may not be as feminine as she could be—or that men don't appreciate her femaleness. Her conscious mind doesn't think that she's worried, but her unconscious mind knows that she is biologically female. So an interesting battle takes place within her. She presents herself as an intellectual, with the body language of a sexpot. The men she talks with don't really understand what is expected of them, and she sometimes causes unpleasant and unwanted advances to be made upon her. She doesn't want to be known as a sexual type; she really wants a relationship built on intellectual sharing. She wants companionship like Daddy had, and like she once had with her Dad. As long as she rejects her femaleness—the biological energy present in her life structure—she is the victim of animus projection. (See Chapter 3.) In relationships she will always be a bit disappointed because no man can live up to her projection of the knight in shining armor. Because of her sexual projection, and the reaction of men to it, she can develop a dislike for men because she thinks that all they want from a woman is sex. But the situation can be cured when she understands her own needs. The masculine principle is strong in her and can be used profitably for career development. The feminine body can easily be incorporated with the masculine principle, for we all are a combination of both. Investigations into what a "woman" is, or what a woman can be can be very helpful to her. We all are a combination of energies, and when this is understood we can then proceed through life without resentment of our biological gender, and interact with people with interest rather than defensiveness.

The Sagittarian male has a slightly different influence coming from the father image. He wants to be as successful as his father, but doesn't believe that he can ever be the man Daddy is, or the companion Daddy is. He has lofty ideals that he brings into his career—but Daddy was a casual man who didn't hurry or rush or take responsibility too seriously. Life just seemed to "happen" to his father.

The Sagittarian child doesn't know how to follow through on activities, and doesn't think that one should work too hard since Daddy didn't. What he doesn't understand is that his father may have worked very hard to establish himself, but the Sagittarian kid didn't witness that period. So he doesn't work as hard as he can, and his lofty ideals and revolutionary ideas may never see fruition. He may wind up being supported by his wife, for life circumstances bring him into situations that cause those results.

As far as his concept of his maleness is concerned, he's learned the companionship attitudes that his father had, and he's coupled them with idealism. Fire sign men have such lofty ideals about love that it sometimes becomes difficult for them to have a love relationship on the physical plane since so much guilt is attached to the earthy aspects of sex. The Sagittarian male may be a bit shamefaced about his sexual needs and may, therefore, approach women with such tactlessness that he unconsciously makes sure he never "scores." He may love one woman and have sex with another. He may trade in a good emotional sexual relationship for good basic companionship. He may choose to relate to the fellows in the locker room, following all the sports events faithfully, rather than building a strong relationship with a female.

He comes from a father-dominated atmosphere—and this means Dads are important and Moms are not. So he may limit his relationships with women, feeling that they are cooks and domestics and not companions. If most of his relationships are with men and he feels love in these friendships, he may wonder if he is really a "man" because he knows that he's uncomfortable with the opposite sex.

Both Sagittarians will learn about honesty in their lifetime. They pride themselves on being idealists and on being honest like Daddy is. But often they are not honest with themselves. The female wants to be a masculine companion and can avoid her feminine self. The male wants to be a companion to his mate but wonders about his masculine self. Both need to allow themselves to be emotional as well as intellectual. Learning how to give love is an important step for them.

Honesty expresses itself in other ways as well: Sagittarians pride themselves on being honest in situations where honesty becomes rather tactless. In the process of being brutally honest, they may shatter someone else's self-image, or cast aspersions on another individual. Then they wonder why people withdraw. It has been said that Sagittarians have foot-in-mouth disease because they say things that hurt or shock other people. You ask "How does my hair look?" and Sag says "Gee, it looks nice *today*," implying that you haven't been looking well lately! This tactlessness doesn't go over big in business either. Sagittarians learn as they grow older that some questions in life don't need to be answered—they learn how to listen. Learning to listen is one of the qualities of a judge—justice and truth and fairness are qualities that can be used in a positive Jupiterian way. And in order to judge fairly, one must listen to the whole story.

When there are planets in Sagittarius, the qualities of freedom and independence are added to the definition of the planet. Venus in Sagittarius indicates a person who wants an idealistic love relationship, and freedom as well. This can make for a wholesome, straightforward relationship, or it can indicate someone who confuses falling in love with a loss of freedom. Mars in Sagittarius indicates an independent person—one who acts freely, idealistically, independently—and perhaps one who doesn't want to work in a situation where he can't move around. Saturn in Sagittarius indicates a person who takes independence very seriously, who perhaps feels not enough freedom, and one who may resent any ties that bind and limit a sense of freedom and independence. Saturn here also indicates a person involved with the law—universal as well as governmental—and one who is interested in justice.

EARTH SIGNS

The Earth signs are Taurus, Virgo and Capricorn. They are generally practical by nature, and they want a life that makes some kind of sense. The Earth signs seek to stabilize. They tend to be good at following through on projects, and are often the dedicated workers of the zodiac and therefore trusted with responsibilities in terms of career. Because they are mother dominated, they look for materialistic answers to their questions. An Earth sign follows every fire sign. Earth takes the Fire sign ideals and incorporates reality and practical application into the Fire sign dream.

TAURUS. The Taurus child is born into a mother-dominated household, since the sign is a negative, or feminine, polarity. The father is probably present but passive. When the father figure is passive, the mother has to take on the family responsibilities. The child begins to pattern its decisions and values according to the mother's life philosophy.

The Taurus person is Venus ruled. Many people undervalue the Taurus types because they look to be easygoing and perhaps a little weak. This is not the case. The childhood does not encourage children born in this sign to respond spontaneously. Therefore, Taureans rarely feel comfortable displaying reactions either in a career situation or in a relationship. The mother is an overpowering figure who manipulates the child with so much "mother" love that Taureans hesitate to express themselves honestly or easily. It has been said that Taurus is stubborn, angry and sometimes rigid. All Fixed signs are, and Taureans try to build environments that they can depend on since not much in the childhood was dependable.

Material acquisitions help create a feeling of a stable universe. Taureans are often drawn to the money professions for security reasons. The Taurus banker is not avoiding relationships with people and is not really pursuing money for money's sake, but is attempting to work in a stable environment. The world of finance is dependable—a dollar is a dollar (more or less!) every day of the week. The Taurus person is afraid to establish relationships with people because those people may change their attitudes toward their relationships from one day to the next.

Taureans are quite sensual and need some emotional commitment in order to be fulfilled. When relationships frighten them, they may avoid the emotional sensuality of sex and enjoy the sensuality of food, ending up with weight problems. They may also retreat into religious and philosophical orders which can protect them from living out their emotional needs. The irony here is that the validity of philosophical beliefs cannot be tested if they are not experienced through emotional involvements.

The Taurus female is raised in a strongly mother-dominated atmosphere. Here the animus concept is different from that of the Fire sign woman. The animus figure for the Taurus female is colored by the fact that, as a child, she doesn't see her father make many meaningful decisions. Because her father is passive, she will unconsciously assume all men are passive. However, she sides with her father emotionally; for the two of them, Daddy and the child, can side with each other against this strong maternal force that is sometimes overwhelming.

The Taurus woman wants a relationship with a man, but after she gets him she begins to treat him much like her mother treated her father—as an object to be controlled and manipulated. The young Taurus female does not consciously try to manage men; she may not even be aware that the men around her feel "managed;" but she may find later in life that her relationship with her husband is very similar to the one her mother had with the father.

She is a strong and opinionated type. As she develops she'll learn how to make solidarity, materialism, a search for the spiritually creative side of life, warmth and enthusiasm positive working forces within her. The fear comes into her relationships when she succumbs to dishonesty. It's difficult for Taureans to offend someone they love, and often they are dishonest with a lover. They become quite angry when they don't get what they want or when they are misunderstood. The anger is buried inside and begins to manifest when the throat becomes restricted, because tension settles in the Taurean throat.

The Taurus female has difficulty accepting rejection. She also gets angry when her man doesn't feel happy with her, for she has given up so much of herself in order to secure that happiness. She eventually learns that if she expresses and shares herself honestly, she will draw a person to her that really likes her.

The problems with her femininity often come from the fact that her mother is overwhelming and jealously competitive with her as Taurus develops, especially during her teen years. Often, the mother of a Taurus girl competes with her daughter so heavily that the girl has no sense of her own feminine worth. The irony is that Taurus is one of the most sensual and feminine of the signs. The female is sensual and sexual; she brings men into her life because of her feminine approach to them—an approach highly seasoned with an animal sexuality that is hard to pass up. For example, look at the combination of energies present in Barbra Streisand: managerial ability, talent and sensuality. Although Barbra may not be considered one of the world's great beauties, she is dynamic and she is magnetic.

The Taurus male has a different set of problems. He is a male born into a mother-dominated household with a passive father. His values are determined by his reaction to his mother's values. He also must cope with the fact that he's a male who has to prove how "good" he is to his mother. The mother is super strong and seems to have all the answers as far as this child is concerned. Under these circumstances, the child becomes very careful about what he says to mother, for she may shoot him down. This subconscious feeling is carried over into later relationships with women, causing a dichotomy within the Taurus male. He's interested in women, enjoys communicating with them, yet feels apprehensive about sharing his not fully formed ideas for fear of being rejected.

It seems that when the Taurus male is a child, his mother is so strong that she overwhelms his father; his father either remains passive (which disappoints the child) or causes the child to dislike and basically reject his father because he isn't a "man" to his wife. The Taurus boy seems to be in the middle of his parents' relationship. He is a child who is allowed to sleep with Mommy and Daddy. Sometimes the father leaves, and the Taurus child then becomes an even closer companion to his mother. Because he loves his mother, he feels guilty about becoming involved with other women. This can lead to problems in his own marriage. He sometimes has difficulty determining where his priorities are: his mother's needs or his wife's needs. He thinks that it's important to show his mother how responsible he's become, so he may take on obligations he doesn't want.

Sometimes the mother's influence is so strong that the Taurus male develops a big unspoken fear in his psyche called "Am I really gay?" When a mother is too close emotionally to her child, the influence affects the images in his psyche. Affection becomes confused with sexuality; affection can be confused with loyalty. Something also happens to the ability to express the creative self, for when the mother's influence is too strong, she can overwhelm his ability to use his creative processes. Taurus is creative but is often afraid to use the creative energy for anything other than building fortresses emotionally.

This child tends to hold in tension because the early environment doesn't encourage spontaneous response to difficulties or to normal childhood fears. Taureans form habits that include the holding of tension. If the tension is not released or faced, it builds and builds until the body falls apart and Taurus winds up with some medical problem. These medical problems are signals that the inner tensions are not being released and that new habits must be formed—habits which include the proper use of the building talents that Taurus has at its disposal.

When there are planets in Taurus, the characteristics of the sign become incorporated into the planetary symbols. For example, Saturn in Taurus fears the practical, fears that it is not practical enough, and takes sensuality seriously. This can mean that the person becomes seriously involved in sensual relationships, or fears them. When Mars is in Taurus, the person acts like a Taurus, tries to act in a practical manner, carries himself in a rational way, and wants and enjoys a sensuous sexual relationship. Venus in Taurus indicates a person who has a concept of love that is more on the practical side; sensuality is enjoyed, but the material side of life is also important. This individual may include material possessions as a part of the criteria for a love relationship.

VIRGO. The Virgo child enters a mother-dominated environment. The Sun is again in a feminine polarity, which indicates that the father is a passive figure. There is a different expression of the earth element in the Virgo since the childhood environment stresses education and mental development.

For centuries Virgos have been told that they are too critical, too intellectual, too rational, too involved with education, too involved with finding fault in others, and that they emphasize petty details rather than concentrating on main issues. It seems to be true—these qualities are often a part of a Virgo's character. But how are these character traits developed?

Virgo is born into a family where Mom is quite put out with Dad. In many instances, Virgo is born when the mother decides to have a much-wanted child. She then goes through the crisis of having to stay home from work to take care of the kid. The work environment offered office relationships that were enjoyable; the office offered a chance to exchange information with others that is usually lost when a woman stays at home to take care of a child's needs. This mother begins to resent her husband, for after the child is born she can't afford baby sitters since the family has just lost her income.

Or, the Virgo child is born into a family where one more child is another financial responsibility that is added to an already heavy burden. The mother resents her position and begins to question her husband's ability to support his family. She not only criticizes her husband, but doubtless criticizes her own mother, her in-laws and the whole neighborhood. It isn't too long before she gets around to criticizing the little Virgo as well. Because the mother is such a dominant force, the criticism that she offers is taken quite seriously by the child.

In general, Virgos have a serious need to be appreciated and needed as they reach adulthood. They choose occupations which are necessary, which provide service for different groups; or they tend to become involved in occupations where they are overworked and underpaid. They are an employer's delight because they often give more time to a job than they are being paid for. Their problems begin when they start to find fault with everything and everybody around them. The motive is simple: "If I can find fault with you before you find fault with me, then everything is ok." Children raised by highly critical parents are going to grow up to be critical adults. We pick up our basic patterns of behavior from our parents. The attitudes we encounter as children are deposited in our subconscious very early in life. As we get older and look inside ourselves, we sometimes notice with amazement that we have become a carbon copy of one of our parents!

The mother may instill values in her child that will also discourage Virgo from feeling comfortable in certain adult aspects of relationships. Often, the mother of a Virgo goes through an antisexual period during the kid's infancy. She worries a lot about hygiene, and the normal functions of the body are often regarded with distaste. Mothers of Virgo infants have been observed to have extremely negative reactions to the job of changing dirty diapers. All children wear diapers, and all humans eliminate body waste. However, when a child's diaper is changed with disgust, and the child is only two or three months old, it begins to feel that the disgust relates to some unsatisfactory behavior on its part. If one shows disgust or disdain to a dog while it's in the training process, it can be trained not to eat! A child exposed to this response will develop guilts about natural functions, including sexuality. Most Virgos feel guilty about their sex life and handle sex with embarrassment, or not at all. However, Virgo is an earth sign—its symbol is the Virgin holding a sheaf of wheat or grain. Grain has long been a symbol of the crop that sustains life. We often use the word "earthy" to indicate someone who is practical and sensual and a part of the earth. Virgo children have trouble compromising between their sexual desires and their sexual attitudes.

The Virgo female grows up in an environment in which she is close to her mother, but this closeness may be either of the love or hate polarity. She feels criticized and unsure of herself. She doesn't have a lot of confidence in her ability to handle life experience, since her childhood was full of admonitions and criticisms. As she progresses into her teens, her body starts making demands and inquiries into her sexuality. Many young Virgo girls have early sexual experiences because they are looking for "a port in the storm." They also want to understand how it feels to be a woman. Some Virgos marry for the first time in order to get away from home and mother. But as time goes by, the Virgo begins to feel guilty about her sexuality because the power of the subconscious pulls on her rational mind. She may even grow to resent her sexual needs.

She often goes back to college after marriage to get her degree so that she can go back to work in a professional capacity. At that time she begins to treat her husband much like her mother treated her father, and disappointments begin to happen in the relationship—they begin to grow apart.

The Virgo male has a more difficult time of it. He is a mother-dominated child in an atmosphere where his father is criticized and rejected. As he grows up, he's quite angry that his father is so incompetent. He feels that if his father were a better provider, his mother (the center of his universe) wouldn't be so unhappy. Consequently, the Virgo often works too hard on a job in order to prove he isn't the "no-good" that Daddy was, and he gets very angry when his work is not appreciated.

He gets the same dose of bacteria phobia and disgust that his sister did from his mother, and he enters adulthood with a bit of a sexual double standard. He wants to be sexually involved, yet he thinks sex is a little vulgar. The Virgo male can carry a great deal of resentment towards his mother. If she is really overpowering, and if she is intensely critical of him and his dad, the boy may not want to have any involvement with women at all; for every time he sees a woman he sees the characteristics of his mother.

Men born into feminine signs, as was discussed in Chapter 3, have more trouble dealing with women than do their masculine sign counterparts. Because Mother ran the household, because Mother seemed to be the ruler of the universe, it is more difficult for these men to converse freely with women; subconsciously, they think that women have "the power." When they learn "the power" is really related to the concept of the feminine principle, and that this power is in them and can be used in a material sense for building something in the material universe—whether the building is intellectual or physical—then they are free to see men and women as human beings. Until they reach an understanding of the masculine and feminine principles operating in the universe, they will over-listen to women. It's difficult for them to have a disagreement with a woman; they can't easily handle opinions from a woman and overreact to what she says. A woman may have no idea that the Virgo male is reacting to her in this way. She just notices that he's too detailed, too involved in statistics, too involved in proving his points by quoting passages from all the books he's read, and she can't get a straightforward conversation out of him. If it happens to be a positive sign woman (who wants to be respected in her own right by men in general) encountering a Virgo male, these two can engage in a most interesting argument, all based on the sub-conscious drives within them!

If Virgos want to form real relationships, they need to sincerely dedicate themselves to the art of relating. It's something they need to learn because when they were children they didn't see relating between their parents. Their parents essentially play "Mr. and Mrs." roles; the man-woman factor in the relationship was impersonal. Virgos have to figure out for themselves what a relationship is, how to do it, and whether or not they feel they can take a chance with it.

Perhaps the most difficult thing to understand about Virgos is that it's normal for them to criticize people they are fond of—they criticize when they care enough to criticize at their very best! However, they don't accept criticism very well because they're already a self-critical group; so they don't want to hear any suggestions from a partner. When they realize that they need to share their mind and their emotions with someone they care for, when they begin to care enough to care about how their partner feels, when they can give up being self-defensive every time a serious discussion takes place, then they are on the road to having a good relationship.

Planets in the sign of Virgo pick up some of these qualities. A person with Venus in Virgo is basically analytical about love, criticizes the loved one and anything that is liked. This energy can be used as a "critic" on a professional level. Mars in Virgo becomes very technical, which is wonderful to apply to a career. But what happens with sex? Sex handled in a technical and detached manner is not particularly emotional. Saturn in Virgo takes being criticized very seriously, and doubts its own intellectual capacity. This doubt will show up more in a young child, and in an adult as an overdeveloped intellectual or analytical capacity.

CAPRICORN. Children born into the mother-dominated sign of Capricorn obtain the values of traditional business and the corporate power structure and the ability to go about attaining power, from the influence of the mother. Father again is a passive figure. However, most Capricorns have a father who is a respected member of the family, but one who is untouchable and uninvolved in the family structure. So the immediate decisions about running the family are left in the hands of the mother, and in the child's eyes she runs the universe. When Daddy comes home, he just upsets the applecart, for the little Capricorn is the second-in-command during Daddy's absence. Capricorns usually feel apprehensive about confronting the father, unlike the other Earth signs.

Capricorn's mother is very traditional in her attitudes. She runs a Saturnian household where children are to be seen and not heard. Capricorn children are usually quite well behaved, and they tend to frown on too much frivolity in life. They take responsibilities seriously. Even their sense of humor is serious—it's often cynical or satirical; funny stories are told with a straight face.

Mother wants to go places in life, and Capricorn children pick up this vibration from her. She instills in them a sense of management, a sense of power, and a need for power and control, for she is a powerful and controlling figure. She uses every piece of information at hand so that she can keep her family in line. Capricorns learn how to do this from her.

Capricorns go out into the world looking for a place to climb, and want to be the head of something at all costs. What they often don't understand is that they are born leaders. One enters the zodiac in this sign because one is ready to learn about the responsibility of power. If they are in a hurry to get ahead in life, Capricorns will use any means available, including using people to get what they want. This sign is sometimes considered the mercenary of the zodiac. If they will learn to wait, to earn their position, they will be better off. The natural vibration of Capricorn (and Saturn) will put them into positions of authority if they train themselves properly.

When the Capricorn female grows up she wants to leave home to get away from the strong mother influence. She doesn't immediately realize that she has the same strengths and ability to manipulate others that her mother has. It would be wise of her to select a mate carefully; she needs to unite with a man who has strong power drives and ambitions to match her own. If he doesn't, she'll get angry and will try to destroy him emotionally. She doesn't understand her own strength in her youth. As a teen-ager, Capricorn often looks like the Ugly Duckling; for this reason, she may not have a great deal of faith in her femininity. However, after she reaches thirty there's a transformation and she keeps on looking attractive even into her seventies. She can be a terrific partner for any man who wants to develop a business or political career, because she will work tirelessly with a man who wants to go somewhere.

She needs to learn how to relate emotionally because she feels uncomfortable with this aspect of herself. Emotional responses imply that one is out of control, and she wants to know what is going on in her universe at all times. She represents that part of the feminine principle that has to do with building and collecting and overseeing the universe. She wants to create boundaries, but emotional expression has to do with letting down boundaries. In order to feel emotionally fulfilled, she will need to learn to let go of some of the control and work with the concept of universal flow. It will never let her down.

The Capricorn male uses his energy a little differently. He has a great deal of respect for his mother, and particularly notices how she handles her husband. He wants to be Daddy when he grows up, but he has to use his mother's habit patterns to get where his father got. She is the strength his Dad relies upon, and he will pattern himself after her. She handles men in a certain way, and he will imitate her particular and individual pattern. He, too, can be so involved with getting to the top that he doesn't notice the means which he uses in order to get there. Materialists seldom do, for the end often justifies the means. However, the Capricorn power trip is a long and powerful one, and he can get to the top of the corporate structure the right way or the wrong way. Again, Capricorn has been given power in the zodiac, and the task he has in this life is to learn the responsibility of power. He must learn how to delegate responsibility to the proper people, and he must learn how to see who these proper people are; he must learn how to leave emotions and loyalties out of his decisions. He must also learn how to trust people he cares for.

Capricorns tend to want to have absolute control in their relationships. Sometimes they marry for the wrong reasons and feel insecure because of it. The Capricorn male can enhance his life position by marrying the boss's daughter, or the "right woman" who fits in with the moves he wants to make as he climbs up the social ladder. However, the love and trust part of the relationship may be missing. When this occurs, he has to control her. In a sense he has to be protective of his status and his control, so he wants to be entirely aware of everything going on with his wife. He will resent any friendships she makes, and he can distort the truth so that it looks to be in his favor. When one controls a relationship, this only serves to build more inner feelings of insecurity and, eventually, symptoms of paranoia.

When a person is too controlling, he can't think of everything, and sooner or later the situation blows up.

It has been said that Capricorn falls from high places. The symbol for Capricorn is the Mountain Goat, climbing to the top of the mountain. The trick is for Capricorn to develop its sure-footedness in order to climb the mountain without falling. Some people think Capricorns should give up the climb; but the importance here is that of developing the qualities of an experienced mountain climber so that he can reach the top and do some good. The universe needs leadership, guidance into new traditions, and help to establish order and purpose in the social structure. Capricorn is an Earth sign; it follows the Fire sign of Sagittarius. Sagittarians bring about theories of law and order and the spiritual or philosophical growth of the individual. Capricorn is here to carry these theories into being, into existence. There is good reason for Capricorn types to develop sure-footedness; they have the responsibility for building strong traditions and institutions in a symbolic sense. Those of us who use our power in a thoughtless or selfish way will eventually have that power taken from us, for it seems to be the way of the universe.

Capricorn is the most theoretical of the Earth signs. All the Earth signs have something to do with the manifestation of an idea into reality in the universe. The pattern of Earth and Fire around the horoscope wheel shows the union of the masculine and feminine principles. As humanity cooperates with energies present in the universe, each new generation forms its own tao symbol in consciousness. The problem with the material, or feminine, polarity signs stems from a desire to keep everything static in the material universe.

When there are planets in the sign of Capricorn, they will pick up qualities of the sign to some degree. Venus in Capricorn indicates a person who wants to be a Capricorn, who wants to be stable and traditional about love matters. Mars in Capricorn indicates action motivated by control. This is a person who acts in a traditional manner, whose actions are colored by power and control, who wants to always act in control and may not be spontaneous. Saturn in Capricorn manifests as "I take tradition seriously," or "I fear tradition," or "I feel restricted by tradition or authority."

AIR SIGNS

People born with the Sun in one of the Air signs are born communicators. The Air signs symbolize the various kinds of communication that exist in our universe. These are the people interested in exploring the world of the mind. They live in their heads or minds, they are mental people, they react to life from a mental point. They enjoy exploring the world of words, education, the various levels of philosophy and spirituality or a combination of the above. These children usually wind up in families where no one communicates in a way that a child can understand; such circumstances can send the Air signs on a search for the meaning of words, the meaning of the mind and all the related fields of communication.

GEMINI. Gemini people are born into the most personal of the Air signs. They wonder where they fit in the scheme of things. They have lots of "me," "I," and "my" in their consciousness, and their life experience requires the incorporation of self into a larger universe. Geminis are raised in a father-dominated atmosphere. Communication between the parents is difficult for these children to understand, because disagreements between the parents are solved with words and not with deeds. Since young children don't understand what words mean, they are uncertain as to what the fuss is all about. But, they do know something important is going on because the parents are upset by these strange words. Gemini children learn to use words well, for they are good imitators; but often they don't know what the words mean. The comedian Irwin Cory has played on the Gemini dilemma by doing a comedy routine in which the words are *almost* right but not quite. Because Geminis find communication intriguing, they pursue either the world of conversation or the world of books. The media becomes important to them, and therefore they make great contributions in that area.

Geminis are explorers of the intellect and are naturally very curious people. Their curiosity is manifested in several ways, depending on the childhood environment. If little or no education is available, or if there are too many Air signs in the chart, they want to talk: they learn by talking, they entertain by talking, and they like a lively and entertaining social life. Each person they meet is a new source of information or entertainment. As they seek each new experience they forget the old sources. This can cause conflict in their love relationships because their partner may resent all the new people. If the background was more intellectual, or placed more stress on education, Geminis will explore the world of the intellect and pursue the study of language and/or education. In addition, they are enthusiastic about sharing information and social activities with all kinds of new and interesting people. However, the more educated Geminis have the same problem as those who aren't: they have trouble maintaining interest in an on-going relationship.

The parents of Gemini children have some interesting reactions to each other in terms of body language. The impact of the words they react to fascinate Geminis, who feel left out. Geminis often try to recreate these situations in adult life and in their relationships. They need verbal interchanges with their mates. This interchange can start with harmless banter and work its way into bickering. If the mate of a Gemini doesn't understand the Gemini need to see a *reaction* (body language) to words, and if the mate doesn't respond appropriately to the situation, terrible verbal fights can ensue, leaving lots of hurt feelings and misunderstandings. After the fight, Gemini feels wonderful but the mate is ready to pack; and after a long series of these interchanges, the Gemini may find he's lost a partner.

One of the relationship difficulties for Geminis stems from a fear or a disinterest in working through problems to some compatible compromise or solution. Since they are social at heart, it's easier for them to run off and explore the new and different rather than to work through a serious situation with an "old" partner. This type of Gemini needs to learn to work through disagreements without becoming resentful.

The Gemini female child admires her father, who is very often a respectable professional. Or, if Daddy is not a professional of some sort, he usually is known for something he accomplished that was special. She wants to be special like he is, but there is a resentment directed toward him along with the admiration. At some time in her childhood when it was important that she have his attention, he ignored her. And so, she brings her resentment for her father into her adult life.

Because Gemini is a mental sign, it isn't always easy for the female to incorporate her emotional needs into her professional life. She sometimes looks at her body and physical needs as alien to her. She tends to select a mate based on his ability to mentally stimulate her, and she wants companionship with a partner almost as much as the Sagittarian female does. She loves the company of men because she feels she can share her ideas with them; being born in a masculine polarity, she wants to feed her intellect. Because of this polarity, she may reject her feminine self. The less evolved Gemini type avoids the company of women because she basically doesn't respect the position of woman. As she becomes more conscious, she begins to cherish her relationships with women who are interested in mental development like she is. She may even find conversations with women more stimulating than the ones she has with men for there are no sexual overtones.

The Gemini male is known as a gadabout. He's difficult to own because he's always off exploring the universe. He rarely opens up with men and seems to enjoy the company of women more. He likes to flirt. Because he doesn't really trust other men, he will develop few male friendships. This mistrust seems to come from his relationship with his father.

During childhood, he wants to be with Daddy, but like his Gemini sister, is in some way rejected by Dad at a time when he trusts him and needs him—hence Gemini's suspicion of men. When he picks a partner, he chooses a companion or a woman with whom he is friendly, for he seldom bases his serious relationships on sex alone. He is emotionally attached to his mother; he used her as an extra support when he was young, so he often picks a super strong woman he can "hide behind" or depend upon. An exceptionally handsome Gemini male seldom chooses to be with a "pretty" woman; he tends to pick a reliable type.

It seems that the parents handle situations in the early childhood of Gemini children with an overemphasis on the intellectual. The child is rewarded for doing "things," and doesn't really understand *why* he is being rewarded. Adult life situations are not clearly understood, for hearty emotional responses were handled with words by the parents. The child matures only to learn that other people cope with emotional situations differently. Geminis may not understand what others want from them. Feelings of resentment may accompany responsibilities, for they don't know what is expected, or they may feel that their intellectual freedom is being restricted. The Gemini group worships "freedom of the mind."

In personal relationships, Geminis feel misunderstood for the emotion called love is conveyed to another in an intellectual manner. Words are more important than gestures, but the other eleven signs don't respond to this kind of a demonstration of love very easily. When a Gemini says he loves you, he may love you with all his heart, but he has difficulty demonstrating that love. First of all, his intense feelings may be completely different in the morning! Second, he may feel threatened when you tell him that he is not acting as though he loves you. Neither the male nor the female want to be put on the spot where love is concerned. Love is a lofty ideal that can be thought about, fantasied about, dreamed about. For the Gemini, the words "I love you" might be a sufficient demonstration of affection, and might not engender another period of affection for six months. As Gemini matures, he will learn that he has to give more than mere words. And here comes the test, for Geminis often feel that the needs of the loved one involve testing, and they resent it.

As far as career responsibilities are concerned, Geminis tend to get into the water over their heads. A basic difficulty affecting both sexes concerns direct and honest communication. It is easier to assume what the Gemini thinks the other party wants to hear than to handle delicate situations directly. The Gemini has a reputation for being two-faced, but the double personality has a basis in the early childhood environment. In order to be well received, Gemini assumes that others won't accept what he has to say. So he changes it.

For example, a client came to me with a difficult problem to solve—she had undertaken to rewrite a book for a professor at a local university and had been unable to accomplish her goal in the time period given her. Rather than tell the professor that she hadn't even started the project, she told him it was almost done. She thought that he wanted to hear that. Since she also worked for him in another capacity, she feared that she would lose her job when he discovered the book had not been rewritten. She was right! Her question to me was, "What can I tell him that will allow me to get away with this faux pas?"

Another Gemini was invited to a party he didn't wish to attend. Rather than call his host and decline the invitation, he called and told the host that he had an interview in Philadelphia and therefore couldn't attend the party. The irony of the story is that the party was being held at nine o'clock on a Saturday evening, and everyone knew that Gemini wasn't going for a job interview at that time. Unnecessary feelings were hurt, and the Gemini added to an already untrustworthy reputation. When this kind of behavior is applied in career situations, the Gemini may get fired.

It seems that Gemini people don't understand where they fit in. They keep looking for a secure place in the universe, and this need for security is often the cause of the double talk that takes place. A dilemma is caused when the need to belong conflicts with apprehension about being restricted, for Geminis don't want to be "beholden." The conflict is intensified because they may not understand directions or instructions that go along with handling job responsibilities. Rather than asking how a particular job should be handled, they tend to make corporate decisions on their own. They often feel that asking questions will indicate to fellow employees that they don't have the qualifications for the job.

Sometimes Geminis even color their resumes. One client of mine applied for a job with a phoney degree. Another obtained a prospectus from a large company, learned the names of several important men on the Board of Directors and then went to the personnel department with a "verbal" recommendation from them. The people in the department didn't confirm the recommendation because it came from a VIP. Gemini worked for the company for two years before his action was discovered!

Geminis minimize or maximize any life situation based on the interests of the moment. The most common manifestation of this ability is the "Gemini time system." They tend to be late or early. If they enjoy what they are doing, time flies. If not, it drags. If they are on time, they're probably bored with what they were doing before they came. It is not uncommon for Geminis to be totally surprised that they are two hours late for dinner.

When there are planets in the sign of Gemini, a controversial or contradictory flavor is added to the personality as well as an interest in the pursuit of the intellectual. Venus in Gemini indicates a person who wants to be like a Gemini, one who wishes to develop the traits and interests of a Gemini and appreciates controversial ideas or behavior patterns. Mars in Gemini indicates one who acts in a controversial manner, and one whose actions will be based on thoughts. This indicates a person who is apt to take mental action. It can indicate that there are lots of ideas about sexuality, which could make for an interesting or an unusual lover. Saturn in Gemini feels restricted by the controversial, takes new ideas and education seriously, and may even become a teacher of some sort. People with Saturn here are concerned with education, either because they are afraid of their intellect or because they want to pursue the intellectual in a serious manner.

LIBRA. Libra is the second of the Air signs and is more intellectual and less personal than Gemini. The family situation for Libra is one of dissention between the mother and father. Often, Libran children are born at a critical time in the marriage relationship: the parents may be staying together "for the sake of the children." When children hear parents discussing these reasons for the marriage staying together, they feel excessively beholden to the parents; this can cause deep-rooted resentments. Because of the tense family situation, Librans develop a sense of diplomacy; they try to soothe the troubled waters and to smooth over rough situations between the parents. The habit gets so ingrained that it becomes difficult for Libran children to voice their real feelings or real angers or real disagreements with those around them. Because their feelings and ideas are not easily expressed, this holding in turns into rage that is directed inward upon the body. Often, the "idea" that they support is more important than their "personal feelings." Their diplomatic actions seldom soothe their own troubled personalities. Words don't make the emotional Libran feel any better, and often they have strange and mysterious diseases that need medical attention. Hypochondria results when there is no other outlet for emotional needs.

Because their parents stayed together for appearance sake, Librans find it important to create a good social image. The danger is that they may only create a social image and never get a real and honest life style going for themselves. Their relationships may be more socially acceptable than meaningful, and they may stay in emotionally damaging relationships because they need the image. They either have marriages that give them social support, or they may be so afraid of marriage that they never enter into it. Many unmarried Librans are reacting to their early childhood environment: they saw so much dissention and disharmony between their parents that they feel all marriages are like that.

We all bring into our relationships what we saw happening in our early childhood environment unless we make a conscious effort to change. Unconscious Librans recreate their childhood circumstances and enter into a relationship with wonderful expectations but turn it into the inevitable cold war of their youth. They seldom say what they mean; and when their feelings are hurt, they will wait for some appropriate time to intellectually attack the partner. This is done with well-chosen words designed to cut the other person to the quick. The partner either stays and suffers, or leaves.

The Air sign curiosity manifests differently in Librans than in Geminis, for they are interested in social acceptance rather than the controversial positions in the world. Librans pursue education, and enjoy being known as mediators in the universe. The rest of us love to have them solve our problems for they have the ability to bring diverse people together in a spirit of cooperation. They often go into the learned professions: doctor, lawyer, psychologist, or corporate management. When they are not interested in pursuing a diplomatic or political career, they enjoy pursuing anything that brings beauty into the life. Because their childhood circumstances were not pleasant, they are drawn to any occupation that brings pleasure, beauty, or harmony into the life of another. Librans pursue interior decoration, antiques, the fashion or cosmetic industry. The tension in the childhood brings Librans into the pursuit of the classical forms of entertainment. Classical music is soothing to the troubled brow; the dance is a work of art. This group of people can be involved in creating new art forms for the general public.

Since Librans seldom like to look too far below the surface, their personal problems are very difficult to solve. As soon as they begin therapy or any related type of treatment, they become upset. They don't want to look at the years of suppressed anger. First of all, most people do not want to seriously admit that they are angry with their parents, and they don't want to admit that hostility lingers within due to having had so much difficulty in expressing real emotions. People who have close contact with Librans are sometimes surprised at the anger and hostility beneath the surface of the personality. We are taught that the Venus ruled signs of Taurus and Libra are warm, loving, easygoing and placid people. They are not. They are merely fantastic actors and diplomats!

In considering the concept of beauty and our ability to appreciate beauty and love, we encounter the various forms of maya projection. Maya is the Hindu goddess who represents the world of illusion and beauty. This symbol is meant to teach that beauty is an illusion. We must look beneath the surface to find the truth. When we look at the beauty of Libran people, we don't often see the pain inside, but it is there. And it needs to be understood so that they can let it go.

Air signs are meant to bring new ideas into formation or new ideas into acceptance by the present-day consciousness. Libra follows the symbol of Virgo. The analytical Virgo sorts through all the chaff and sifts out the valuable grain. The Libran takes the grain, the ideas that Virgo has left, and lifts them one step higher in consciousness. Libra asks, "How can we take these ideas and make them work? Where do we go from here?" And after Virgo has stripped each idea of its protective covering and harvested the crop, Libra tries to make it all lovely and beautiful. As Libra works on these new ideas they are picked up by Scorpio and transformed. Every Air sign increases awareness.

The Libran woman has more difficulties making it in the universe than the Libran man since she's a female born into a masculine polarity. Because the masculine principle is strong within her, she wants to be known as a professional, as a woman with meaningful ideas and as a rational human being. She looks very feminine and is usually very attractive, but she doesn't really believe in being feminine for she wants the status and rank that is often given to males. She enters into marital relationships with hostility because she doesn't want to be known as a "housewife." She wants an intellectual relationship, but often she is so pretty that she is seen merely as a lovely object. When she's continually treated like a lovely plaything she becomes angry and will attack her partner. Because she wants to enhance her social position, Libra will often get into relationships that can be defined as masochistic. She will allow herself to be emotionally abused while her need for a social image is being satisfied. Because her parents argued so much during her childhood, and because there was so much tension between them, it doesn't seem abnormal to her to live in the same environment when she reaches adulthood.

The Libran male, on the other hand, can be more in control of his circumstances because males are generally bigger and stronger. He, too, gets into a tense marriage in which he feels that he has to soothe the relationship rather than express his feelings. This results in open hostility later on. He becomes angry and hostile due to the fact that it is difficult for him to express his feelings or his needs. He may spend more money than he makes, or feel that he has to keep up with the "Joneses" in order to keep his image in the community. If he is immature and abuses his credit cards in order to keep up his image, this can create lots of tension when he has to face all his creditors. The Libran male is also quite physically attractive, and his partner often doesn't understand his internal tensions because he looks so good on the outside. She may misinterpret his moods and feel that when he is depressed he is really unhappy with her, when in reality it's himself he's unhappy with. He rarely gets the understanding and affection he needs. Until he learns to ask for what he needs directly, and until he learns to express how he feels honestly instead of placating others, he will be lonely.

When a planet is in the sign of Libra, the qualities of Libra are added to the symbolism of the planet. Venus in Libra indicates a person who wants to be a Libran type, one who sees love in terms of a smooth, lovely, beautiful experience. Since this is what is wanted, the person will settle for relationships that look good on the outside rather than building firm relationships. Mars in Libra usually indicates a person who acts like a diplomat, is aggressive with words, and one whose actions may come out of suppressed anger or one who takes action to soothe those around him. Saturn in Libra picks up the restrictions based on Libran qualities. The person takes social acceptability seriously; he feels that he may lack social acceptance and that he has to earn it all the time. He takes the social graces seriously, and wants to surround himself with gracious situations rather than cope with probable truths. Saturn in Libra can take social acceptance so seriously that the individual may even become bigoted in some way, depending on environmental conditions.

AQUARIUS. Aquarian children come into a very impersonal household. The father runs the show and instills in his child the philosophical basis for life. The father is interested in the unusual and the unorthodox, and may have what the neighbors think are strange or odd involvements politically or philosophically. He lives in his mind and is often quite distant from his child. Aquarian children want approval and acceptance from their father, so they grow up to pursue the world of "the idea" even more thoroughly than the rest of the Air signs. For some reason, Aquarians don't fit into the expectations of the family or the environment, and they grow up feeling there is some mysterious plastic wall between them and the rest of the neighborhood. This instills a feeling of loneliness, causing them to spend a great deal of time as adults looking for groups they can join in order to achieve a sense of belonging somewhere. However, because so many years pass without the "belonging" experience, Aquarians tend to question everything—every tradition, every group moral—and seldom stay involved very long with any one idea. This separation from other children (Aquarians can be alone in a crowd) serves to give them impetus to develop their minds more than other children, so the Aquarian types can be infinitely creative. Because the child doesn't fit in, the adult doesn't fit in either. Aquarians end up being the square peg in the round hole as far as society is concerned. The "misfit" complex has benefits however: innovations and inventions are created by those who hear the beat of a different drummer.

Aquarians bring new concepts to everything they touch. They make innovations in social work, spirituality, humanitarian areas and the scientific world. They take the traditional ideas that Capricorn presents and bring them into new perspectives. This creative ability doesn't always make them popular, and can even compound the Aquarians' difficulty in fitting in with the group. Natural talents or abilities are seldom recognized when attention is focused on what is lacking: the Aquarian focus is on belonging somewhere when it should be on the creative process.

Aquarians are raised in an impersonal atmosphere—one of ideas, intellect and words. Life situations are handled by their parents with rationality. Aquarian children don't see anyone reacting in an intense and personal way. It is difficult for them to develop the personal side of relationships because they have so little experience from the childhood environment to guide them. When personal problems arise, they tend to be solved with theories and ideas, which is more appropriate for dealing with concepts than with people. Although Aquarians can be social innovators in theory, it becomes hard to put theory into practice in personal relationships; they feel more comfortable in groups than in one-to-one situations.

The Aquarian woman is interested in following in her father's footsteps. Like her other positive sign sisters, she wants to be known as a career woman. She's unsure of herself sexually for her mother doesn't present a sexually feminine image. Since her father is known for his unconventional stands, she wants to be known for hers—therefore, she will pursue anything that seems different or unusual. She remains unsure of herself as a woman, for when concentration is on mental abilities, the physical side remains unfamiliar. She may want to reassure herself that she is a woman, but she gets nervous when too much attention is paid to her body. The dilemma concerns which direction to follow, the intellect or the emotions, and she vacillates back and forth. When she's feeling emotionally insecure she can become what is commonly called promiscuous. But she isn't promiscuous at heart—she's only searching for her identity. As she gains a sense of identity, or if she gets hurt enough, she'll stop. She has to learn that self-assurance comes from within and can't be gained through approval from others.

The Aquarian male has trouble settling into a relationship because he, as well as the Aquarian female, has a strong need for social interaction and intellectually stimulating relationships. Since he also questions his sexuality, he may experiment with sex for a while until he figures out which direction he wants to move in. Most of his problems in relationships stem from the fact that he is too impersonal. He doesn't know how to give personal reassurances or the emotional responses necessary to his partner. He needs to learn how to operate in a personal relationship. He doesn't know what is expected of him.

When he was a child, his mother often protected him against the violence (either mental or physical) of his father. Consequently, the Aquarian male is chary of accepting help from a woman. His mother asks that he never forget her and that she helped him, and he's afraid all women will require the same commitment. He can be an interesting and diverse partner if his need for freedom is understood.

When there are planets in Aquarius, they pick up the qualities of unconventionality, the unorthodox, or new-age ideas. Venus in Aquarius wants to be an Aquarian; the appreciation of love is unusual, unorthodox, and mental in nature. The needs of love relationships will stem from the unconventional, so this is the person who falls in love with the handsome stranger, or the person who loves someone who has an unusual career or life path. When Mars is in Aquarius, the person acts in an unconventional manner or may act in a new-age way, and may be interested in unusual sexuality (which can manifest either as unorthodox sexual behavior, or a lot of mental thought is added to the concept of sex). Saturn in Aquarius places restrictions on the unconventional and will manifest either as a person who is afraid of anything new and different, or one who takes unusual new-age ideas very seriously.

WATER SIGNS

Water symbolizes the changing nature of the universe. It is a physical manifestation of change for it is permanent on the one hand and ever changing on the other. The course of the river gradually changes, the ocean keeps making new shores, and springs keep spilling forth nourishing the earth. The Water signs bring feeling and intuitive understanding to the ideas and concepts of the Air signs. Water planets are necessary for the truly creative process, for the water lends feeling to the most lofty idea.

CANCER. Cancer is the most personal of the Water signs. Because Cancerian children respond to their environment so intensely, they are among the most sensitive in the universe. The ruling planet of this sign is the Moon, and the Moon rules the tides and symbolizes the "great mood changer." This sign is not an easy one to live out, for the emotional tensions and sensitivities create great inner turmoil in these individuals. It is for this reason that many people don't recognize the power of the Cancerian types. This is a Cardinal sign, full of energy and possessing a great ambition to do something in the world. Yet, this driving ambition is difficult to see because of the emotional tensions.

It has been said that Cancerians are the orphans of the zodiac, that more Cancerian children than any other sign have lost a mother or father. (This also happens when the Moon is in Cancer or when Cancer is the Ascendant.) It has also been said that when Cancerians are lucky enough to have kept both parents, they nevertheless feel emotionally orphaned or emotionally deprived.

Cancer arrives in a mother-dominated world. The mother rules the marriage at the time of the child's birth. Sometimes it seems to Cancer that mother rules the universe because the father is missing. The father can be absent for many good reasons: he may be in the military, he may be traveling, etc. The child doesn't know why he's absent, or even that he exists—Cancer only knows that mothers do everything. And the mother seems to be a particular type of person: she's highly manipulative; she controls the people around her by never showing her personality as *woman*; she handles people by *acting the role* of mother surrogate or by acting the role of helpless little girl. The child sees this kind of behavior and grows up to act just like Mom. The Cancerian girl plays Big Momma or Helpless Little Girl; the Cancerian boy plays Big Daddy or Helpless (and cute) Little Boy. Everyone plays roles at one time or another, but Cancerian types have little experience in how to play the role of adult men or women. They control their relationships by being a parent or child, and sometimes this behavior causes difficulties in the career and relationships.

The Cancerian female presents herself as a helpless little thing who needs protection. She marries a man who will save her from her environment. But, she develops into a very strong woman, for she is mother dominated. And since she is a female, it's easy for her to imitate her mother. She usually has no idea of her strength until she reaches thirty. She felt left out when she was an infant; her mother's love was not apparant. Consequently, she wants security as an adult. So, when she feels uncomfortable in a relationship, she'll use her wiles to regain control: either by playing helpless so that her partner will have to take care of her, or by being insecure, which usually manifests in wonderful jealousies. When there is insecurity there is a tendency to over compensate, so she may be jealous of her husband's friends or even of his business. She may be the type who calls him at his office twenty times a day; or she may pull scenes if he arrives home late from the office because he stopped to talk with someone after work. She may become a parasite, looking for constant reassurance of his love and affection. The irony here is that although she needs love and affection, she may have difficulty giving it in return because she never saw her mother give it. She learned through observing her mom that one must control men, manipulate them gently, in order to get what one wants. She learns what her mom teaches so well that she tends to have a lot of "gimme" in her personality until she matures out of it. If she wants a role-playing relationship, these traits are fine. But if she's looking for a meaningful adult relationship with another person, these traits will stand in the way of its development.

Because her mother was so competent, the Cancerian female becomes quite aggressive in the career area. She wants to make money so she can spend it. She wants to have a nice home to return to when she gets tired of the world. The Cancerian type is not the homebody we hear about; she prefers to have a nice home available to her, but she has to be out in the world exploring and feeling with the masses of people. (The Moon rules the general public.) She does well in her career once she settles into something that interests her. Many Cancerian women have jobs that include travel. She looks for executive power, for that is one way to use the Great Mother energy in a constructive sense.

The Cancerian male has more trouble getting free of his early childhood environment. He's raised in a mother-dominated atmosphere. He realizes that women are strong and powerful, and adopts his mother's mannerisms and attitudes. He may either be too emotionally close to his mother—a momma's boy—or he may really dislike her and later make the women in his life pay the dues for his mother hatred. In any event, he usually prefers the company of women; they are easier for him to talk with, they are more familiar. He enters relationships playing the role of Big Daddy or Little Boy. Whichever role he begins with, once the relationship is established, it is not surprising to see the Cancerian male playing Little Boy, for he thinks this will get him what he wants. He, too, is looking for emotional fulfillment and affection, but usually something akin to "mother love" is more important than a sexual relationship. Sometimes he establishes sexual relationships outside his marriage; he doesn't want one with his wife since she's playing the role of mother for him.

He needs lots of attention, and when he can't get it, he tries to make his wife angry. This is usually the time the Cancerian male starts playing around. But, he plays around to get caught. Getting caught arouses his wife's ire and this signifies to him that she still cares. However, this is a dangerous way to secure his wife's attention. It may be the beginning of the end of the relationship! He is looking for a love that he is seldom able to return. His mother was not a giver, he didn't learn how to give as a child, so giving becomes something that is learned in his adult life. The

Cancerian type holds on to what he has and keeps asking for more, all the while giving little in return.

The Cancerian man may not be quite as interested in a career as the Cancerian woman. He may have ambition or not—usually the motivation for accomplishment comes from impetus elsewhere in the chart. He can do well in a job situation if he so desires, for he can play father surrogate and be Big Daddy to all the people in his office, or he can play Little Boy and sell products better than anyone else in the zodiac. A Cancerian salesman makes lots of sales because he adopts the Little Boy role which doesn't threaten the authority of his customers. Cancer walks home with nice commissions over the years! If he has problems holding a job, it's usually because he's too much of a rebel. Mother-dominated signs (with Cancer at the top of the list) have little respect for male authority figures. They are emotional and moody, and don't often care about father-approval, so they can be controversial and rebellious in the traditional business setting. They need freedom on the job, and they need to be interested in what they are doing or they won't fit into the business atmosphere.

Cancer is the sign that indicates nurturing and growth. Both the males and females have the capability to teach and train, to encourage and help others. This is a good indication that they will do well in the helping professions, that they make good teachers and that they can be helpful to people in general. They can also use this nurturing ability to develop a business that plays on the "fad" consciousness of the public. There's no better horse trader in the zodiac.

Cancerians are moody and intuitive. They function much better when they listen to their intuition rather than their intellect. Because no one paid attention to what Cancerian children said at home, it sometimes becomes very important for them to get a college education, for the "grades" prove to the world that they really are as smart as everyone else. They are often put down as children since they have *emotional* reactions to what goes on around them as opposed to "rational" reactions. However, the emotional reaction is the start of the intuitive process, and the rest of the signs have to take courses to reopen the channels of the intuitive process! Cancerians respond better to feelings than to words. If you want them to respond to you or to a situation, ask them how they *feel* about it rather than what they *think*. When Cancerians reject their intuitive energy, they become very stiff and overrational. It's usually a cover for a wonderful intuitive self they haven't learned to value. It needs to come out.

Planets in Cancer indicate that some of the qualities of Cancer will manifest in the personality: possessiveness, jealousy, sensitivity, intuition and a need for affection are involved. Venus in Cancer indicates a desire to be a Cancer; to be sensitive and possessive and emotional; to respond to love with sensitivity, apprehension, a great deal of feeling. Mars in Cancer acts like a Cancer; the person acts on emotional responses, acts emotionally, acts sensitively, acts possessively. Saturn in Cancer takes possessiveness seriously, is concerned about security, fears emotional involvements, or feels a lack of sensitivity or intuition in its being.

SCORPIO. Scorpio children are also born in a mother-dominated atmosphere. They, too, do not come into an environment that is warm and loving, and a parent may be missing. There is often a death in the family a few days before a Scorpio is born. This effects the emotional set of the parents, for the person who dies is someone they love. This circumstance brings an attitude of grief into the small child's life. Often Scorpios are unwanted children, and sometimes they are the eleven-pound babies born into a seven-month marriage. Or, they are just one more child in a family that can't afford another mouth to feed at this point in time.

Scorpios born in this type of atmosphere pick up all the unpleasant vibrations. Like any infant, Scorpio needs lots of attention and love, but the father ignores the child and the mother often gives only minimum care: food, shelter, diaper changes, etc. There is little affection, warmth and holding. Later, the parents feel guilty about not giving this child love and try to make it up by spoiling him, or by providing many opportunities in life. But, the little Scorpio isn't buying it. The child needs affection early in life, and the allowance and extra privileges he gets later on don't mean anything; and the parents end up thinking the child is ungrateful.

Because of the early experience, Scorpios are on a life-long search for love and affection. They search for the mother love that was missed in childhood. Scorpios have a reputation as the "super sexed" sign of the zodiac, but they aren't as sexy as they would have us think. The young Scorpio male and female confuse sex with love. If you have sex with someone they will love you, thinks Scorpio. So they learn how to be good at sex; but people who have a relationship with Scorpios often find that after the relationship has been established, the sexual part of it is not nearly as important as it was. Affection becomes more important to Scorpios. When young Scorpios feel insecure, they try to create sexual situations; it makes them feel secure when they think someone "loves" them. (If you love an immature Scorpio, and you are perceptive, you may feel that sex for them is not merely sensual pleasure but is used to control you.)

Scorpios are born to go through great personal transformations. The life is such that either they spend a lifetime trying to create a family experience for themselves, or they go into the business of self-transformation. The problem here is one of direction. Often Scorpios try both—they want to manage a tight household *and* transform the world at the same time. Because they felt unaccepted in their early childhood, acceptance becomes important to them. In the attempt to become accepted, confusion arises when they try to lay down the law to others and try to control the behavior of others. As they judge and control and push others, they become quite unpopular and don't really understand why. The Scorpio search for identity is a real one; and one of the things they learn is that the search is a personal one—it isn't one of transforming the world first and yourself later! In the process of discovering the meaning of their existence they uncover lots of information on the way. The sign is known for its investigative abilities.

As far as career is concerned, Scorpio types can go in many directions. They often choose to become involved in the corporate structure, which is like a family for them. The new-found family can approve of them, promote them, and they belong. Usually the corporate type of Scorpio is indicating a need for father approval, which may mean that the father was either harsh or quite distant from Scorpio. We often seek in our adult life what we lacked in our childhood.

Scorpios are also drawn to all kinds of scientific and social research, for their investigative minds can be put to good use in this area. Detective or police work, analysis of any kind is good for this sign. There is an interest in the various aspects of the medical profession; this field brings out the research abilities as well as the transformational or healing quality of Scorpio.

The Scorpio female grows up to be strong and secretive like her mother, and she often copies her mother's mannerisms. This gives her magnetism and an air of secrecy. She carries within her, however, a feeling of personal insecurity, a sense of worthlessness that can only be assuaged by getting into love relationships. She can use her sexuality for power. She gives herself sexually until she has what she wants under control, and then she stops. The person she relates to feels confounded when this happens, for he got involved with this ''sexy'' lady who is no longer warm. He becomes suspicious and begins to wonder if she is seeing someone else. Sometimes the young Scorpio female marries a man who treats her badly because she thinks she doesn't deserve more than that. As she matures, she finds she wants more from a relationship than second-rate treatment, so she leaves. In her search for a strong man, she manipulates, she's magnetic, and like the female spider in her web, she catches her guy. But if he turns out to be too powerful, if she can't control him, she may get so uncomfortable that she leaves him.

The undeveloped Scorpio female stays close to her mother. If there's too much maternal influence in her adult life, it's difficult for her to form a good relationship with her husband. He feels he has two women—his wife and his mother-in-law. He may get fed up and leave. The more evolved Scorpio female looks for a relationship that will teach her something because she's a searcher. She needs someone to share her growth with, to share her learning experiences. These are fascinating women.

The Scorpio male has a harder time of it than the Scorpio female. He carries a fantastic sexual reputation from all the dime-store astrology books, and he doesn't feel sexy inside. He wants a love relationship that includes plenty of mother love and affection, the kind of affection he missed out on when he was younger. He often chooses older women to relate to, sometimes heavy-set women with big bosoms—all symbolic of the search for Mother. He is inscrutible, hard to get to know and moody. All of this serves to make him extremely magnetic to some women. However, he confuses sex with love, and finds it difficult to return the love that may be given to him since he saw little of it given when he was a child. He feels uncomfortable admitting that he loves someone: he thinks this leaves him open for attack.

Seldom is the Scorpio male child not criticized and put down by someone in his family. The secrecy that Scorpio projects is a cover for the fear of rejection. The Scorpio child is extremely intuitive and "knowing," and he is laughed at or rejected when he tries to share his thoughts. Rather than face more rejection, he learns to keep his thoughts to himself—and grows into the tall, dark "fascinating" stranger.

Both the male and the female of this sign have tension related illnesses. The Scorpio personality is so moody, so emotional, so sensitive, so intuitive, and so afraid to share emotion for fear of rejection, that all these feelings are pushed down inside and they churn around and around in the digestive and intestinal tracts. As Scorpios hit their forties, the tension begins to tell, and they are more prone to high-tension disorders or intestinal and digestive stress diseases.

They need to learn to share. As Scorpios learn to share their ideas and dreams and hopes they begin to find out if anyone really likes them. It's so important to Scorpios to have meaningful and intense relationships that it's more profitable to be open in the long run. They draw people who are impressed with their "mysterious" act, but their true selves are never really known. It is far more rewarding to be open and be either rejected or accepted. If we are rejected, we didn't have anything to begin with; if we are accepted, we have the start of what may become a wonderful, intense experience with another person.

Planets in Scorpio pick up some of the intensity and magnetism of the sign type. Venus in Scorpio is not an easy one however. The Scorpio child feels unwanted; therefore, Venus in Scorpio *wants* to feel unwanted. It is a setup for the masochist—the person who suffers in love affairs. Mars in Scorpio acts like a Scorpio would—in a searching manner as an investigator, or unwanted. Saturn in Scorpio takes rejection seriously, takes research seriously. These are the people who like to build families. When rejection is taken seriously, one may assume one is unwanted in most situations and become extremely defensive—or one may approach new situations with great caution.

PISCES. This is the most theoretical, or the least personal, of the Water signs. It seems that Pisces people arrive in this universe through a difficult birth: the mother may have a long or difficult labor, or the child is born with some "strange" disease, like eczema. Often Pisces children get a fever or the flu early in life, and several days are spent worrying whether they'll make it through the experience without brain damage. They pick up this worry from their parents because Pisceans are so intuitive. They begin to worry a lot about their health and welfare at an early age.

The mother of a Pisces is a lady who worries a lot and who is afraid of everything: she worries about getting robbed, mugged and killed. She worries about life—and in the middle of all her worry she plays the martyr role. She will accept her fate, she sighs, and the little Pisces soaks up these vibrations. These children are so intuitive and all-knowing that they often make their parents uncomfortable. One mother of a Pisces confided in me that her brother came for a brief visit when her child was six months old. When the child was about four, the brother reappeared and the Pisces asked uncle where his beard was, since he'd had one the last time the child saw him. The mother couldn't believe what she heard. She had no photographs of her brother and had not discussed his beard with the child. The memory these children have is terrific. Karmic astrologers feel that Pisces types bring a lot of past-life fears, apprehensions and knowledge with them into this life. Perhaps this is why Pisceans are so creative and intuitive. However, the early childhood environment usually creates a fear of developing their intuition—and as spiritual as this sign is, they often fear exploring the occult, the religious or the more spiritual sides of life. It may be that their fear of spirituality or their fear of developing their intuition comes from the fact that they knew too much as children; that every time they came up with some interesting information they were either turned off, disciplined or made fun of by one of their parents. So Pisceans bury the spiritual self deep inside. The more intuitive they are, the more antireligion they may be; the more psychic they are, the more they're against the occult in any form.

The more Pisceans reject their natural creativity and reject their natural intuitive abilities and try to become hard, rational adults like some of the other sign types, the more miserable they become. It isn't unusual for them to immerse themselves in alcohol or drugs. They seldom become skid-row alcoholics since they enjoy the easy life too much. They are the ''miraculous'' alcoholics who drink at night but manage to show up for work every morning. They can be the ''week-end'' alcoholics or drug abusers. Sometimes they go for alcohol because they can't cope with their intuitive or psychic experiences. If these experiences don't manifest during the day, they sometimes manifest at night during dreaming. The dream experience can be so overwhelming for Pisceans that they start drinking, since alcohol dulls the dream process. Prophetic dreams can be hard for anyone to take when one doesn't know why one is having them or doesn't know how to work with the energy in a more positive sense.

The Pisces female enters her adult life with many of her mother's expectations and habits. She often resents the power of her mother, and she also resents her father because he didn't stand up for himself in the marital relationship. Pisces picks men that are as weak as her father was, and then resents them for being that way. She tends to choose someone she feels sorry for when she picks her first marriage partner. After she becomes conscious of what she has done, she begins to feel sorry for herself—and a little bit of the martyr begins to come out. She confuses sympathy with love and doesn't understand that a love relationship can't be shared with someone she feels pity for. Pisces should use her strong altruistic tendencies for work rather than marriage. She suffers a great deal, either with an incompetetent lover or husband, or with someone who mistreats her. When she learns to pick better material, when she decides that although her mother suffered it isn't necessary for her to, she will get involved with healthy relationships.

The Pisces male makes the same mistake as the Pisces female. When he is younger, he also marries a person he feels sorry for. Or, the first ''big'' love affair is with someone who needs to be saved from themselves or from something else. He soon finds that he has to take care of this woman all the time and that he really doesn't have anyone to share his life with, and so he tries to get out of the relationship. However, if he fails to work his way out of the martyr syndrome that his mother taught him is normal behavior, he will continue to make a martyr of himself in any relationship he forms. He will continue to expect to be a martyr, to be mistreated, to be misused. He needs to learn to talk out his problems. When there are difficulties that need to be worked through in the process of a maturing relationship, he tends to withdraw and suffer. This is a habit he learned from Mom, and he doesn't know any other way to behave. He can, if he wants to, learn how to make a relationship work by giving as much as he expects to get. However, the Water signs have trouble giving in a personal sense. They're more concerned with getting; they worry about how much they'll get from a partnership. They don't get much guidance in their childhood environment that teaches them the give-and-take necessary in a relationship.

Since Pisces is a theoretical sign, these people are interested in the theory behind the idea, and much like the Aquarian, they are an impersonal group of people. They talk about feeling, they talk about spiritual evolvement, they talk about how spiritually evolved and conscious they are. But when the time comes for being understanding or open in their own personal relationships, they tend to be more verbal than actual. They are mother imitators, and whatever the mother gave the father is often what Pisceans give their partner, friends and business associates. Often the mother was a user, and Pisceans can use people too. Sometimes one hears from them only when they need something. They may never ask you how you are, or if you feel ok, but they'll tell you how miserable they feel and how much they need. When one observes Pisceans over a long period of time, one begins to notice that they don't really need that much, that they aren't doing badly and that they complain more than is necessary. One may even begin to suspect that they enjoy complaining. They are here to learn spiritual awareness. It seems that they bring a lot of knowledge from the "other side," but they are here to learn how to put this knowledge into practice.

As far as profession is concerned, Pisceans usually do quite well, they tend to get the breaks in life and often wind up in positions they don't really have the background or experience for. They're usually drawn to the classical theater, literature and art, or the humanitarian fields. They are also drawn to the pleasant social-service positions like a maitre d' or manager of a great resort hotel, and positions that make a comfortable living. The creative Pisceans sometimes sell out, electing to take the easy money rather than using their creative energies. When this occurs, they suffer because that energy remains untapped. Some Pisceans may like money so much that the female can be drawn to the oldest profession in the world; she thinks she won't have to work too hard. Again, the spiritual urges in Pisceans hurt when such types of decisions are made, and they suffer later in life.

Pisces children need lots of encouragement in early childhood. They should be exposed to music and dance and creative endeavors in general. They often live in a fantasy world full of imaginary playmates, creating a universe of their own when the family structure is too harsh for them to cope with. This ability to create fantasy can be channeled in such a way that the child becomes an extremely creative adult, offering wonderful things to the rest of the world. Einstein was a Pisces who used his retreat into the "windows of the mind" to bring a new perspective to the scientific community. All Pisceans have a piece of this gift, and it's there to be used. However, in order that Pisceans may use their creative energies, they must give up the martyr role, unless, of course, they're going on the stage to act the part of Joan of Arc.

When there are planets in the sign of Pisces, one becomes sensitive, intuitive and also martyred! Venus in Pisces indicates a personality that is influenced by a mother who felt martyred. This is a person who feels that to be in love one must suffer and go into great realms of tragic experience. When Mars is in Pisces, the individual acts like a martyr, acts as though he suffers a great deal. This is a person who can be martyred in emotional situations or in business deals. There is also sensitivity and intuitiveness. Saturn in Pisces takes martyrdom seriously—and this usually means that the person worries a lot. It means that if there is nothing to worry about, he often makes up something. He fears the psychic or intuitive side of himself and may view the occult with great suspicion.

EPILOGUE

It seems that the Fire signs are full of ideals and avoid dealing with physical situations that will crumble their rose-colored concepts of the universe. Then come the Earth signs, bringing practicality and common sense into the world in addition to bringing the ideals of the Fire signs into physical manifestation. Air signs follow Earth and react to it, for they take the physical manifestation and add the theory of spirituality, or the beginnings of mental development. The mental attitudes take over the physical needs, and the person tends to live in the mind more than in the body. The Water signs come along and add feelings to ideals, combining ideals and spiritual development.

Completeness takes place when Fire, Earth, Air and Water are incorporated into the personality. The internal dilemma can be diagnosed from considering the elements.

II: PLANETS AND ASPECTS

INTRODUCTION

THE PLANETS AND THE MAJOR ASPECTS ARE HANDLED IN this section. The Sun and Moon are defined first, and the rest of the planets follow in their natural order. The aspects color the function of each planet in a chart. The various changes and stresses that may be felt when aspects are present are explored. Planets and aspects are also affected by their house placement. For example, a square taking place between the second and fifth houses may function a little differently from that same square involving the first and fourth houses. These differences become so complicated that they are not being covered in this book. Chapter 2 in Section I may suffice as a basis for understanding these complications.

In order to more easily understand the basics, the aspects are presented in a "cookbook" manner, although it is impossible to use a "cookbook' method when actually reading a chart. Any aspect will be colored by house placement; the Sun sign colors the personality and alters how an aspect may be used by different individuals. Each astrologer must master the art of synthesis because each chart is different. The existence of free will further indicates that each person chooses how he responds to his inner energy level. All aspect manifestations will be influenced by age, maturity, the concept of self-responsibility and exposure to alternatives in life. Aspects can signify internal pain and tension. Even those who have transformed their lives will relate to what they previously lived through or rechanneled.

The table on page 105 includes the major mathematical divisions of the circle that are considered when creating an aspect. Some aspects are considered hard (square, opposition) and others soft (sextile, trine). Astrologers define the various aspects differently; the old astrology books refer to the soft aspects as benefic, the hard aspects as malefic, for example. Each student will determine how he or she chooses to define them. It should be remembered that if people have only benefic or soft aspects, they may not develop character and strength. Because some of the most difficult aspects are found in the charts of highly accomplished people, perhaps these difficult aspects are not totally malefic.

Table 2

Aspect	Degrees Apart	Energy Keyword
Conjunction	0°	More of/a blending
Sextile	60°	Facilitative
Square	90°	Frustrating
Trine	120°	Easy/cooperative
Opposition	180°	Compromising/tension
Quincunx	150°	Straining

Briefly, I see the aspects functioning as follows:

CONJUNCTION. The influence of a conjunction seems to vary depending on the planets involved. The aspect can be read as "more of," and each planet's function is colored by the other. The affect of Saturn, for example, in conjunction to the Sun may be restrictive, while Mars conjunct the Sun adds the quality of activity or action.

SEXTILE. This seems to be an easy aspect, but it can indicate so much ease that it may never really be put to use. It has been suggested that it indicates undeveloped talent. The sextile can be of help in the process of finding constructive outlets or when trying to alleviate tension caused by more difficult aspects in the chart.

SQUARE. I think the square is one of the most difficult aspects for it indicates frustration. It causes excessive energy to be directed against one or both of the planets involved in the square. The blocks symbolized by the aspect may remain as stumbling blocks or be rechanneled into stepping stones. The square signifies where personal energy needs to be channeled differently. Each person chooses to use the square energy, for it can be used constructively or destructively. Squares signify internal tension; two parts of the personality are at war with each other within the individual.

TRINE. This aspect has been considered the easiest of aspects. Some feel it indicates good luck; others feel that it signifies an easy expression of talents or facets of life that are symbolized by the planets involved in the trine. The energy is so "easy" that it can be indicative of other kinds of problems. The trine may place an element emphasis in the personality as well. Fire signs may become overly idealistic and therefore more easily hurt, etc. Perspectives may become distorted because of the cooperation between the planets.

OPPOSITION. Many astrologers see this as one of the most difficult aspects. Because the opposition includes the idea of polarity (Aries always opposes Libra, for example), I feel that it is more easily compromised and worked out than is the square. When two planets are in opposition, there is a need to compromise, to alleviate tension, to develop temperance. This aspect does create great internal dissatisfaction, but once it is understood, the aspect carries enough energy so that it can be converted into more constructive expression.

QUINCUNX. This aspect indicates strain and has been considered the classic health aspect. Two ideas or two life activities are straining against each other, but not in as difficult an angle as that of the square or opposition. Because the tension is not clearly visible, two facets of personality may conflict while the owner does nothing to bring them together. Time and energy may be wasted, and eventually the body rebels. The energy can be released as it is understood and allowed to function in some kind of perspective.

ORBS. Each aspect has an orb of influence. For example, the conjunction aspect indicates two planets 0 degrees apart, or in the same degree. An orb is allowed to affect this relationship so that a planet at 15 degrees of Aries is said to be conjunct another planet at 17 degrees of Aries.

Orbs are a hotly debated issue between astrologers. Some use very small orbs while others use large ones. I've noticed that astrologers using small orbs also use the minor aspects (such as the semi-square, the semi-sextile, etc.). Astrologers using larger orbs often use only the major aspects. I tend to use large orbs. The conjunction, trine, square and opposition get ten degrees, while the sextile gets six and the quincunx five. When the Sun or Moon are involved in an aspect, I might even stretch the orb to fifteen degrees since clients have physically felt them working as they are described under the various sections. However, I don't stretch the Sun and Moon orbs for a sextile or a quincunx. Each astrologer will work with an orb of influence that feels comfortable.

THE PROCESS OF INDIVIDUATION STARTS TAKING PLACE when we begin to integrate the Sun consciousness with that of the planets and the various aspects in the chart. When we start to become conscious we are in fact beginning the trip that Jung describes—the search for the spiritual or conscious self. We become like Gautama Buddha or Jason in his search for the Golden Fleece or Hesse's Narcissus and Goldmund. We start on our own Hero's journey, the private journey of a soul seeking to find itself. How can anyone want to avoid that?

The Sun is the spiritual force that gives us life. The energy of the Sun seems to enter us when we are born and leave us when we die. It seems to be the force or energy of spirit, perhaps the indicator of what our spiritual values are, what our life drives will be and what we will eventually understand if we are to fulfill our destiny. The Sun supplies the life energy to our solar system and it supplies the life energy to the astrological symbolism of our body. We incarnate into certain segments of the zodiac so that we can learn about those degrees of experience. In each lifetime we learn about values, philosophies and feelings in direct relation to the values ascribed to the zodiac. We incarnate into certain family types because we must have a certain type of life or family experience in order to get started on our life path this time around.

The Sun can be used to indicate how our physical father manifests himself when our personality is forming: how we feel about him and what kind of value system we get from him. The aspects to the Sun indicate how our Dad reacts to life when we are born. Since we can't readily remember the circumstances of our early environment, the Sun position (and the aspects to the Sun) help us to understand the kind of atmosphere we were exposed to. When the Sun is afflicted, it means that Dad is going through changes at the time of our birth. Because he does not feel good about himself during this period, he affects our sense of self. When the sense of self is afflicted, we may become spiritually ill as discussed by Jung in much of his work. Much of the work done with psychotherapy helps us free ourselves from the effect of our parents. By looking at the astrological chart, we can also see what brings about the unhappiness in the parent-child relationship.

SUN–MOON ASPECTS

The strongest aspect the Sun can make is with the Moon. The Moon is indicative of the mother influence in the chart. The Moon also indicates how we feel and indicates how our mother feels about herself when we are born. The physical and emotional problems she is living through that affect us are expressed through the aspects to our Moon. When Mom and Dad aren't getting along too well, we have afflictions from the Sun to the Moon. As far as a child is concerned, it doesn't really matter whether or not Mom and Dad get along together except when considering the subject of self-worth. When a child is born with a square or opposition between the Sun and Moon, some kind of hostility is indicated between the mother and father. Hostility or grief may be evident because the relationship isn't what the parents expected it to be. Whatever the cause, the child picks up the unrest, and it seems to the child that Fathers and Mothers have conflict. Because emotional responsibility develops in each of us as a result of the parental influence, the person with afflictions between Sun and Moon often has more self-doubt regarding relationships than other people. This makes it difficult for the individual to find a comfortable place in the universe. The nurturing qualities of the Moon are in conflict with the creative self. The person is at odds over what to be and what to feel. When this is examined in terms of modes, the conflict may be understood.

SUN–MOON AFFLICTIONS IN CARDINAL SIGNS. Consider a Cardinal Sun square Moon. We know that Cardinal signs are action signs in the zodiac. But each of them takes action differently. For example, Aries is outgoing, idealistic, aggressive on an intellectual level, and full of the "masculine principle." The square to Cancer makes for conflict that is readily understandable, for Cancer takes emotional action. It gives the qualities of sensitivity, nurturing, feeling, possessiveness, and the "feminine principle." Simply stated the conflict between these two is *idea* versus *manifestation*; idea versus feeling; the Aries idealism versus the Cancer practicality; the Aries need for an intellectual approach to life and the Cancer need to *feel* the life experience; the argument between the ideal versus material acquisition. When the self responds to life one way and the emotional nature responds to life another, the tug of war between the two often forces a lessening of self-expression as well as an apprehension about expressing feelings. Because we can't ignore either part of the personality, we tend to suppress one side until it bursts forth in some kind of explosion. We then compensate by "behaving well" until the energy releases again. If we understand that both energies are valid, we can learn a way to express both, and the personality is then at peace with itself.

The planetary square between Aries and Cancer symbolizes a "rational" father and an "emotional" mother—an idea-based father versus a possessive, overpowering mother. The parents don't pool their energies well, they seem to be pulling against each other. The child sees dissension as a normal part of the living experience, but the dissension within the personality slows down the growing process. It can eventually lead to the development of well-earned consciousness that is formed because of the inner tension. However, the developmental process isn't easy. (See Section I, Chapter 5).

SUN–MOON AFFLICTIONS IN FIXED SIGNS . Consider an Aquarius Sun opposed by a Leo Moon. Here there are Fixed planets in the personality rather than Cardinal, and where a Cardinal person tends to plunge into action, the Fixed signs cope. They are more rigid, more strongly rooted people who tend to hang onto personality problems. The Aquarian Sun seeks acceptance by its peers. Aquarians are father-dominated, and they are eccentric. They want attention and acceptance at the same time that they enjoy being different. The Aquarian type likes the innovative, the unorthodox. Combine this with a Leo Moon: someone who responds to the world "proudly," and who wants approval and respect from others. The Sun–Moon opposition reflects a struggle between the parents that encompasses eccentricity and approval. The child needs both influences from both parents; yet, in the life struggle, the influence of the father will win. This puts the young adult into the interesting position of wanting to be different and wanting approval for it. The spiritual self is at odds with the emotions and makes for an interesting but painful dichotomy within the individual. The vacillation in personality varies from the qualities of Aquarius to those of Leo. If both qualities are understood and incorporated into different phases of the personality on a conscious level, the person will eventually gain inner peace.

The opposition between Aquarius and Leo tells of a split in the parental relationship which occurred at some point before the child was three years old. It may be that the father was into something that the mother didn't approve of, or that her sense of community respect and approval was affected by her husband's behavior. If the parents stayed together, they evidently worked out the discrepancy in the relationship. If they separated, they didn't work it out—which causes another set of problems for the child. It seems to be easier to pull the qualities of the opposition together when the parents stay together, for the child then sees the overall solidarity of the parents. If a separation occured it is more difficult for the person to resolve the differences between self and emotions.

SUN–MOON AFFLICTIONS IN MUTABLE SIGNS. Consider a female with Virgo Sun square a Sagittarius Moon. Here is a female child born into a mother-dominated home, and a child who feels emotionally close to her father (see Section I, Chapter 5, Sagittarius). Mother rules the universe, but Dad is a loser, and so is the girl child. She will be apt to build companionship bonds with Dad—''her and Dad'' against Mom. She will often prefer her father in her childhood memories, not because she really respected him or because he ran the marriage, but because she and Dad were in cahoots against Mom.

The Virgo child hears a lot of criticism about her father from her mother, and Mom wants the Virgo kid on her side. (See Section I, Chapter 5, Virgo.) The guilt of loving Dad and not getting Mom's permission to do so causes tension in the child. The parents battle as well, for the square represents dissension between them. The father may choose independence rather than the castration battle, so he may leave the marriage. If he stays, he may become extremely aloof. (It's interesting to check the polarity of the children born later in the marriage, for it can give a clue as to how the parents grew—who was winning in the marriage.)

The child will grow up to feel unsure about how to express the father/mother values—or how to express the mental and emotional self. The Virgo female wants to be as strong as her mother, but when she becomes emotionally involved in a love relationship the unconscious will send up images of the Sun–Moon square from her early childhood. She may cut relationships short because she fears a loss of independence.

This aspect can also indicate an extremely independent mother and an overly passive father. However, the father may be passive because he loses the battle with his wife and stays in the marriage because he loves his children. If this is the case the child may grow up to fear inadequate, passive men; and until she clears up the childhood impact on her psyche, she will probably draw that type to her as an adult.

Astrologers do not need to guess the early childhood environment for a client. Since each family is different, and each child is influenced by their particular mother and father, all an astrologer need do is to point the client in the direction of parental influence and leave the client to discover the details. The point is to discover the key to unlocking the blocks—and each client must do it for himself. The astrologer is merely a guide on the road.

The conflict between the Sun and Moon indicates a life-long search for identity. Many people who have the square are unhappy. They look for answers by getting into therapy, by looking into religion or philosophy, or use some other means that may help them to understand why they are here in this universe. Although the aspect doesn't bestow happiness, it can lead to a very interesting and spiritually developed life.

SUN–MOON CONJUNCTION. This indicates that one parent is both mother and father to the child, one parent is very strong and out-influences the other. This may mean that one parent is missing so that the other is forced to take both roles. Sometimes it means that one parent is ill and the other must pick up all the parental responsibilities for the child. Most of the time, the stronger parent can be discovered by observing the polarity of the Sun and Moon, for it indicates that either the mother or the father was super strong.

In trying to discover the early childhood environment, the parents may not be truthful about what was going on at that time. One of my clients (positive Sun conjunct Moon) said that her mother was her sole influence and that her father was not around, that her mother did everything for her as a small child. I disagreed and asked that she check again with her mother. She later affirmed that when she explained to her mother that her astrologer told her the father was influential, the mother agreed. Mom had been very sick and the man who was my client's father (although not her legal father) had taken care of the child for more than a year until her mother recovered sufficiently to handle the responsibility. Unfortunately, not all parents are so open, and it makes things difficult for us when we are trying to trace our patterns or our roots.

SUN–MOON TRINE OR SEXTILE. These aspects indicate that Mom and Dad like the relationship they have when the child is born. The child may not like the relationship or the parents, but the parents have what they want! Children have difficulty understanding that their concept of parents' marriage is not the only one. If parents argue, the child may feel that arguments indicate a "bad" marriage. However, the parents may enjoy the arguments. The qualities of the parents' relationship are often brought into the child's adult relationship because they are familiar to the child.

People born with Sun–Moon sextile or trine have the energy to manifest the self in a productive way. The father had a beneficial influence on the child and was seen as a productive, strong person whose authority is accepted. When these children reach adulthood, they are able to work cooperatively with authority figures, and will be received well by those in authority.

Here the emotional self is in accord with the spiritual self. This quality can be both good and bad, for it influences the quality of self-perspective. For example, a Fire sign trine will be super idealistic, a Water sign trine can be super emotional and the personality may be one-sided because of that. As these people become self-aware, they can use this energy in a constructive manner to develop easy interpersonal relationships. The results of the development are healthy in that people with Sun trine Jupiter, for example, can accomplish what they want to. The problem comes when the trine or sextile puts the personality in such accord with itself that it justifies itself rather than examining the modus operandi that may cause pain in the life. The Fire sign trine makes one so idealistic that the feelings may be hurt in relationships; the Water sign trine overemphasizes protecting the feelings and emotions; the Air sign trine tries to think through situations that may require feeling; the Earth sign trine may overjustify the quality of practicality or accumulation. The trines and sextiles between the Sun and Moon can be further looked into by reviewing Chapter 3 in Section I, the positive-negative trinities.

SUN–MERCURY ASPECTS

Mercury cannot make many aspects to the Sun. This planet travels in such close association with the Sun that it can be best used to indicate how versatile a Sun sign is. Mercury is either in the same sign as the Sun or one sign behind or ahead of it. For example, if the Sun is in Cancer, Mercury has to be either in Cancer, Gemini or Leo. When both Mercury and the Sun are in Cancer, the person not only is a Cancer but also *talks* and communicates like a Cancer. Since Mercury represents the five senses as well as the mind, Mercury in Cancer people hear, speak and relate via the five senses in a Cancerian way—an emotional way. These people will more obviously reflect the qualities of the Cancerian type. If, on the other hand, there is a Cancer Sun with Mercury in Gemini, the qualities of Cancer will be present, but they will be expressed through Mercury in Gemini. This makes for an interesting type, for when Mercury follows the Sun it tends to observe and report the things in life that interest them. Cancerians with Mercury in Gemini are controversial Cancerians. This sometimes makes for difficulties. Since Mercury indicates the way we communicate, the communication in Gemini will be controversial, sometimes contrary. These types may not express their Cancerian needs. Cancer is possessive, emotional and sensitive. Mercury in Gemini is controversial, intellectual, curious. Mercury in Gemini wants to discuss subjects for the sheer fun of it.

The Mercury placement in Gemini may spur these Cancerians to express a greater curiosity than they can comfortably handle emotionally. For example, consider a Cancer female who is possessive of her lover or husband, who's very sensitive and whose feelings are easily hurt, but she communicates "liberation" to her man because of the Mercury placement. He listens to her words and, therefore, may not understand that when he flirts outrageously at parties she's dying inside. In order to compensate for the great jealousy that she's engendered in herself by telling him that he can talk with anyone he wants to, she is reduced to a basic Cancerian reaction and has to overflirt. Her Mercury in Gemini says that he can talk with anyone, yet her Cancer security needs may not be recognized or discussed with her partner. When these types talk with a Gemini attitude and cover their Cancerian needs, those they want to relate to may have difficulty understanding what they want!

When Mercury is in Leo with the Sun in Cancer, the combination becomes very sensitive. The behavior pattern and value system comes from Cancer: sensitive, mothering, nurturing, posessive. When Mercury is in Leo, one communicates "proudly." There is a strong need for respect. These people might use "proud words" or "proud reactions" to cover their sensitivity, and this tends to close them off. On the constructive side, this setup indicates far-reaching futuristic types of Cancerians, those who can combine the Cancer and Leo characteristics. The mind is interested in things of the future, the theory of life, the theory of feeling. They may elect a career oriented toward the development of a modern outlook in a traditional field.

Because Mercury travels close to the Sun, there are no squares, oppositions, trines or sextiles between them. Mercury is the messenger. It merely helps us express the qualities of our sign type, and this expression, whether it agrees with the Sun or not, helps prepare us for growth. It is often thought to be easier to have Mercury in the same sign as the Sun, for this gives the ability to express more of what is truly felt. The Mercury placement tells how a person will talk about himself; that is, what kind of Aries or Taurus or Gemini he is. This placement can give insight to an astrologer when reading charts, for it helps to understand what a client will respond to. The aspects to Mercury can cloud the personal issues that may need to be handled. If the astrologer knows that the Mercury aspects hide the Sun, or speak for the sun, then she or he can develop a perspective regarding what people say versus what they need versus what they do.

SUN–VENUS ASPECTS

Venus is similar to Mercury in that it is never far from the Sun. Venus is usually in the same sign as the Sun or one behind or ahead of it. Venus doesn't quite make a sextile to the Sun; it travels just a few degrees out of orb. Venus represents what we want in life: the finer pleasures, the things we want around us, the person we want to be, the way we appreciate art, the way we appreciate love. It helps to define how we *receive* loving as well as our intellectual concept of what we think love is. The Venus position in relation to the Sun sign gives a clue to what people are (Sun) and how this relates to what they *want to be* (Venus). When people talk about what they want to be, it is usually Venus talking.

People with Venus in the same sign as the Sun usually are quite satisfied to be themselves, whatever that is. They have the potential to like themselves if the conjunction is not afflicted by another planet. It can make them very smug and self-satisfied, for they like being the person they are. For example, a Virgo with Venus conjunct the Sun may really enjoy being overly critical. When we try to work out our ties to our parents, or when we try to understand our life, Venus conjunct the Sun can be difficult; for, we tend to stay in our rut rather than try to get out of it. Venus in the same sign as the Sun may indicate that a conscious decision has to be made before we can look at the motivation for what we do in some serious manner.

When Venus conjuncts the Sun, the father either overaffects the child or the child subconsciously plays the role of the mother in order to gain Daddy's approval (Venus indicates a tie to the mother, Sun indicates the physical father. For more details, see Chapter 4 in this section). This closeness to the father may be difficult to understand or to become conscious of, and the only time it becomes important is when the person is in the process of self-examination regarding relationships. A woman with Venus conjunct her Sun is tied to her father from a subconscious psychological point. She may marry her "father" or a man who has the same attributes as her father. If she has Venus conjunct the Sun and no other emotional blocks (by aspect) in her chart, this problem is relatively easy to work with if she wants to be free of the influence. But if her Moon, Venus and the Sun are afflicted, her chart becomes more obscure to work through, the struggle for consciousness becomes more complex. If she is interested in developing relationships that do not include the father image, she must find a way to understand the conflict.

A man with Venus conjunct his Sun is emotionally close to his father, and the aspects to the Sun–Venus conjunction will indicate how this closeness will take place. A Cancer male with Venus conjunct his Sun has an affinity with Dad, but Dad is a "loser" because, for Cancer, Mother rules the universe. By the age of three, this child will have picked up a combination of feelings because of his response to his parents. His behavior will be much like his mother's and his value system will be derived from her; yet, there is a closeness to Dad that can make him turn on Mom and want to align himself with his father or with people who resemble his father. When he reaches adulthood, he may be a very dedicated worker who wants to accomplish in the business world, and a person who avoids relationships because he is suspicious of the complexities involved. He may be a person who clings to relationships with males whom he considers important, who are fatherly types to him. He may feel that in order to survive he must present himself as a child, as a little boy. If he aligns himself with his father, he may feel it necessary to protect himself from women. His relationships with women may be coated with an attitude of male chauvinism. If this Cancer also has Gemini, Virgo or Libra planets, he may experience a crisis of sexuality; he may feel unsure as to which sexual role he wants to play—whether to be hetero-or homosexual. The final decision is not really important to anyone but himself, for his reaction to his life experience and his emotional experience will only please or hurt *him*. When Venus conjuncts the Sun, the psychological influence of the mother (Venus) is very close to the father image on a physical level (Sun). The child sees the parents' roles jumbled together and this can confuse him. A boy child may use his mother's "role" games to get close to his Dad.

This is not an uncommon image, for many of us are born with this aspect. It depicts a relationship that is not uncommon among parents. The power parent is determined by the Sun sign; yet, when Venus conjuncts the Sun, the mother has a close rapport with the father, which may not be confirmed by the rest of the chart, by the power parent, or by what she says about her husband. In other words, no matter what she says about her husband to the contrary, she really likes the way he is. This confuses the child. In adult relationships it causes the following problems: a mother-dominated male may use his mother's tactics to get on with men as an adult; a father-dominated male feels that there should be some mystical-bond between his lady and himself, and is disappointed when he doesn't feel it; a mother-dominated female will feel a closeness to her dad that she can't understand, so it's a combination of love and resentment; the father-dominated female may marry a man in her father's image.

The only time it is necessary to understand these types of aspects is when "something" keeps interfering with the development of meaningful, lasting emotional relationships. When we think our problems happen to us because we only meet "awful people," we need to look inside ourselves to understand what has been programmed into our subconscious selves—for this program is the one we draw to us. It cures itself when we become conscious of it.

When Venus is in the sign before or after the Sun, it tends to alter the sign type. The Sun is the indicator of what we are here to understand and experience. When Venus is in another sign, we prefer the qualities of that sign rather than expressing the needs of our Sun sign. For example, I have a female client with Sun in Capricorn and Venus in Aquarius. Capricorn women are strong; they have a built-in power source that needs proper channeling. Contemporary Capricorn women tend to fear their innate power, for the word is unpopular today. But their trip this lifetime includes learning to use power in perspective. My client avoided the traditional role of woman, and wanted nothing to do with "power" or with men who were powerful. She had been raised in an intellectual atmosphere. Her Venus in Aquarius wanted to be different—and she insisted on being known as an unconventional type. She began living with an unknown artist whose main claim to "art" was his hippie clothing and his ability to smoke pot. When she came to me, she was not well physically because her spirit was ill—she was not using her energy well. Capricorn women make good working partners with a man they trust and believe in—but the man she chose was uninterested in her helping him. We talked about her needs, and it is hoped that she will find someone she can build a nest with. (When we first learn that we can do more for ourselves if we understand what we need from life, we have to *work* through our feelings and our emotional ties. They are not and should not be broken immediately. A process is set in motion. When the time is right, the old and unproductive relationships dissolve and new growth bursts forth, much like the budding of a new leaf. It doesn't need to be forced.)

A Capricorn with Venus in Sagittarius will function differently. There is the Capricorn base, a person who functions well in an executive capacity or in big business, one who has the same power source within, but a Capricorn who is more outspoken than usual. These people go out on a limb, they are not quite so careful as they would be with Venus in Capricorn, and they have strong urges to be free. It's important for them to have time for themselves. The internal battle develops when they become adults: they accept responsibilities, yet there is a strong urge to have freedom. The keywords for Capricorn and Sagittarius, responsibility and freedom, may be at odds with each other from time to time. When they establish themselves in a marriage and in business, they may be somewhat dissatisfied in both areas. Because the sense of responsibility is strong within the Capricorn soul, the Sagittarian planets may be reduced to "druthers" and dreams, only to burst forth in the cycle that hits about the age of forty (transiting Uranus opposing natal Uranus), when caution is thrown to the winds. Or, the Capricorn may start to contemplate some kind of separation.

When Venus appears in a different sign than the Sun, it can bring the quality of open-mindedness to the individual, for it helps the Sun develop alternative perspectives. However, it tends to develop a "missing the boat" complex, which occurs when a person doesn't have a sense of self. These are often the people who study the occult, or who study psychology, or who go into various analytical programs, and still manage to avoid dealing with themselves. They may chase the wrong goals, for the "I am" part of the self gets lost in the fervor of the "I want" pursuit.

SUN–MARS ASPECTS

The Sun represents the spiritual self, the "I am" part of the self. The Sun sign and the aspects to the Sun indicate something about the behavior of the physical father when the child was 0-3 years old. Mars represents action; it's the "I act" principle and describes the kind of action a person will take. When the Sun and Mars are combined by aspect, it can be determined whether or not the self can be acted out in a constructive way. When we act against the Sun, we place limitations on our potential. Hard aspects indicate an early childhood environment that is not conducive to easy self-realization, for the father does not provide an image that will make it easy for the child to mature into a constructive-action person. Constructive action will have to be learned. When the hard aspects are understood intellectually, the energy can be channeled into consciousness, becoming even stronger and more productive than the easy aspects.

Mars also indicates our special kind of sexuality. Something of a person's sexual response to self and to other people can be determined by examining the aspects between Mars and the Sun.

SUN–MARS CONJUNCTION. This aspect should be read only after considering the other aspects that involve the Sun–Mars conjunction. Mars heats up anything that it touches, so it tends to give energy and spontaneity. When Mars conjuncts the Sun, the personality is acted out, it can be volatile, it can be quick to act and react. When reading this aspect it's important to remember in what sign the conjunction takes place in order to evaluate how the energy will express.

For example, Sun–Mars in Aries presents fiery, idealistic, spontaneous types if the Sun is not afflicted. These are people who are highly idealistic and oriented toward intellectual accomplishment. Their ideals or ethics are very close to the surface, so these individuals can go off on a tangent for good or bad, depending on the development of the reasoning powers. They can overprotect a friend, or they can explode in anger over any violation of their ideals. The father of this type is spontaneous and quick to act, and the Aries Sun–Mars child imitates him. This aspect gives fantastic vitality and quick healing power. The temperature tends to run high, and the energy can be disciplined into highly constructive areas.

However, the Sun–Mars conjunction in Pisces will pick up the qualities of Pisces and will tend to be more sensitive, more apprehensive, more frightened than the average Piscean. Pisces is apprehensive, fearful of the future, as well as psychic and intuitive. Mars here will enhance all these qualities, the good as well as the others. The fears will be picked up from the father, and by understanding the father's hangups (while the child was developing) insight can be gained into what will cause the person to over-react. Mars adds intensity to the Sun so there is a stonger vitality than without the presence of Mars.

Look to see how Mars is aspected, to see whether or not it is an easy conjunction or not. Easy conjunctions give added energy, but when other planets are involved, how those aspects affect the Sun must be considered.

SUN–MARS SEXTILE. This child is born into an atmosphere that provides a good influence. The energy around the father is constructive. Whether or not the child can appreciate the father remains to be diagnosed via the Sun sign. For example, an Aries child with Mars in Gemini sextile the Sun comes from a strongly father-dominated background; the father is an intellectual type and uses his energy constructively. The child probably admires his father. A Scorpio child, born into a mother-dominated atmosphere, with Mars in Virgo sextile the Sun, will function from a different background. The Scorpio child doesn't value the father much, for he is a passive figure, and the mother runs the universe. Mars in Virgo (in sextile to the Sun) indicates that the father is not such a bad guy; he's a bit critical of the kid, but he's using his energy as creatively as he can. The child may not value the father as much as the mother however, so a counselor might want to explore ideas symbolized by the sextile, to ascertain if the father is able to get through to the child to show him how to use the energy. As the child matures, this energy will become more apparent and can be trained to function in constructive directions. The sextile needs to be trained. Most astrologers recognize that sextiles bring talent, but the talent has to be consciously nurtured for it to be of any lasting value.

SUN–MARS SQUARE. If the Sun symbolizes who we are or what we are to become, and Mars symbolizes how we act, and the square indicates a conflict or a frustration or an "acting against" something, then we may conclude that the Sun square Mars indicates a tendency to act against oneself. In psychological terminology, this is an indication of a self-destructive type. How the self-destruction will manifest will depend on the sign type and how the Mars is aspected elsewhere in the chart.

For example, the Sun symbolizes the father in his physical representation to the child. With Mars square the Sun, it looks as if Dad is not functioning on a constructive level when the child is born. Not that he is unkind, but more that he is being unkind to himself. Consider the possibility of a child born to a man going through his Saturn return, who has many career decisions to make, who is torn between selling out for the salary or taking a lower salary and causing some financial hardship on the family while he pursues a new career. If his decision is to stay where he is because the money is good, the child may be born with Mars square the Sun. The father is doing something that is not good for him.

The aspect can also indicate a difficult social environment, for these aspects happen when we are racially or ethnically discriminated against within the community. Mars square the Sun may indicate a black person born in a white community rather than in a black section of town; or a Jew born in a Protestant community; or a Protestant born in a Catholic community; or an Irishman born in an Italian community, etc. This baby tends to "sop up" the vibes in the neighborhood. Children who have absorbed the negative energy that occurs when Mom and Dad are not liked or approved of by the neighbors, tend to have little fear when they grow older. Children and adults with Mars square the Sun may have no real sense of danger. They sometimes live or walk in bad neighborhoods without being protective of themselves; they get themselves into questionable situations which others (who don't have the aspect) wouldn't dream of.

When Mars squares the Sun, there is an interesting energy at play. It's called "I act against my self, my spiritual self, sometimes my own needs." This can be tempered with understanding and a development of consciousness, or by learning to assume responsibility for the situations we create in our life. For example, Sun in Taurus square Mars in Leo. The dilemma is caused by qualities symbolized by Taurus and Leo that don't mix well. Taurean people cover anger, they are emotional, possessive, and they don't share their feelings or emotional reactions easily. They tend to blow up when the energy has built up enough to create an explosion. Mars in Leo people want to act and react proudly, want to act and react to others based on the respect they are given. They want to be approved of for their actions, and they are acting out the ethics of idealism. How can one be idealistic *and* possessive? Or socially approved *and* extremely sensual? The actions (and even the sex drive, for that is represented by Mars) can be harmful or unsatisfying in relation to expressing the needs of the self. Because Leo is more involved with social approval, the rage and emotional turmoil that Taurus normally has to work out will be even more closely held in. This kind of energy causes inner pain to happen in people. Some of the pain can be alleviated when the energy is understood.

The person with Cancer Mars square Sun in Aries has a different kind of energy flow. The Aries is idealistic, interested in intellectual accomplishment, wants to approach new life situations from an intellectual point. The Aries person is always in a hurry. Mars in Cancer says, "I act emotionally." Aries is intellectual. So the dilemma is caused by the Aries person who responds to life emotionally instead of intellectually or rationally; the Aries person is in a hurry mentally, but the Cancer Mars wants to feel things out and then, crablike, sidle up to this new thing. The Aries considers fairness an aspect of his concept of love, but Mars in Cancer reacts emotionally and even possessively in love situations, a character trait that is not particularly idealistic! When pursuing love situations, the sex drive (Mars) may pull the person toward a relationship full of emotional polarities but where no intellectual relating can be shared. So the emotional and sexual needs of the individual may unwittingly involve him in relationships that hinder his intellectual or spiritual development.

Self-destruction can take place many ways—it can manifest as a dead brain, or in relationships that don't include trust, or in emotional relationships that cause so much internal misery that we don't want to face it; and so we then satisfy our needs or drown our needs in alcohol or junk food. We can fall in love with hopeless alcoholics, or junkies, or people who cannot treat us lovingly in return—these are all part of the self-destruct syndrome. It ties in with the concept of self-worth. We don't think we can have it all.

In order to work with this energy in a constructive way, we must figure out a way to use the qualities of both signs in a harmonious manner. We can teach ourselves to be constructive in our approach to career. With Mars square the Sun, we may not handle ourselves well in career situations. We may not consider our career goals and needs before we take physical action. If we teach ourselves to stop and think before we do something, we can change this energy into productive energy for ourselves. As far as our emotional life is concerned, we can often change how we handle our relationships by discussing our needs with the person with whom we are trying to relate.

People with Mars square the Sun (Mars also symbolizing sexuality, and the Sun being the self) often pick lovers who don't encourage their self-development. When an Aries female with Mars in Cancer picks a lover who doesn't want her to have a career (and Aries women want to be professionals on some level), she has a dilemma. The Mars in Cancer says that she must be nurturing to her sexual partner; she wants to be mothering, emotional, and wants to act out all the Cancer qualities—but she wants to work as well. Most Aries women like to be mothers and work too. When the Aries female is stuck with cooking and domesticity for years on end, her soul suffers and she can become rather neurotic. Both energies need to be fed. The square tends to feed one side at the expense of the other. When this takes place, divorce is more apt to occur, or she becomes a "bitter woman" staying in a marriage and not giving much to its development.

The man who has a Mars square the Sun is often hurting himself in his business endeavors. He has to carefully train himself to see business opportunities. The man who has Mars in Virgo square Sun in Sagittarius wants freedom and wants an open-minded partner. Yet he himself acts critically; he can be so critical of himself that he doesn't get anything done. He may have a critical sex partner or he may be critical of her. He wants someone who responds to him on an intellectual level, but he may choose to marry a woman who is so nit-picky that the Sagittarian part of himself just dies.

When these types can't admit to failure, or assume all the blame for everything, they can work their way into diseases that are rare and incurable because that gets them out of the relationship. They no longer have to be responsible. Obviously this pattern won't present itself until mature adulthood. This is a hard pattern for a 20-to 25-year-old to understand. Yet, when these individuals reach the age of forty, they may be able to look back and see the difficult life they made for themselves in the same way the father did.

The Mars aspect will always be influenced by the stronger parent; the pattern comes from the stronger parent. In order to diagnose the pattern, the astrologer must be able to evaluate the parents' mental and emotional attitudes when the child was very young.

SUN–MARS TRINE. These people have the ability to work well and are capable of accomplishment in the world; the choice that they will make has to do with what they consider accomplishment to be. The decision will be formed from the energies attached to the Sun sign regarding ethics, values and philosophical outlook. Mars represents "I act," and the Sun represents "I am." When these two energies work together, these people have an opportunity to make a mark in the universe. Whether or not the energy is used this way is a personal decision.

The father brings a healthy image to the child when it is born; the family atmosphere shows the child how to accomplish what it sets out to do. Because the family helps and encourages the child, and because the father is under a favorable influence when the child is born, the child may expect that all his endeavors will be encouraged and appreciated by those around him. He may find that Mom and Dad give more support than his peers. If this happens, the child may give up too easily when things don't go his way. His individual persistence level may be determined by considering the Sun sign, what the fallibilities are, and how Saturn is aspected in his natal chart. All in all, people born with this aspect have ample opportunity to get "mission impossible" accomplished.

SUN–MARS OPPOSITION. The opposition and the square work in a similar manner. The Sun is the essential spirit, the possibility of creativity within the individual. It represents the self as well as authority figures, men in general, and the power of the traditional authority figure. Mars represents "I act" and how the person manifests ideas into physical action. It represents how a person will consider sexuality, especially as sexuality relates to the general well-being of the soul, or the growth potential within the individual.

When Mars opposes the Sun, the child is born into a family that is not particularly welcome in the community. The child has little sense of danger, no sense of impending doom or impending action that may be harmful to some aspect of the self. The internal dilemma is that of self struggling for survival in the face of action taken that may hurt the self. These setups are not always physically dangerous, so don't look at Mars–Sun afflictions as only physically destructive! This energy can express itself in many other ways.

The Mars–Sun affliction can indicate a person who takes physical chances. This may be a racecar driver or a person who chooses to fight impossible odds. It may be an individual who gets into one scrape after another. Or it can indicate a person whose sexual needs cause a compromise of self. An example would be the woman who falls in love with a man who is not productive, or a man who is unable to support her. A man with Mars opposing his Sun may have one good job after another and lose them because of some petty problem in the work area. The aspect generally indicates that the "I act" part of the self doesn't easily cooperate with the "I am" part of the self, and the energy has to be consciously raised to a productive level. Any hard aspect (the squares and oppositions) can be more productive than the trines if the owner of the aspect becomes conscious of the energy play and works to take responsibility for it.

The childhood family environment of the Sun–Mars opposition includes strife. The father does things to himself that are not constructive when this child is born. The child will pick up the unconstructive energy pattern. More important, the child thinks that failing or a lack of accomplishment is a "normal" trait. The influence can be subtle. For example in one family the four children have remained close to the parents even though they are all in their thirties. They insist that their family ties are loving and wonderful, yet none of them have married and started families of their own. One daughter (a father-dominated child with Mars opposing the Sun) has found it difficult to establish herself in any profession that complements her talent. She has wandered from one career to another, one idea of profession to another, and has had difficulty staying in anything long enough to follow through. Daddy was a failure as a man when this girl was born, and she seems determined to follow in his footsteps and fail too. When pursuing the idea of family turmoil with her, she finally admitted, as did the rest of her family, that Mom and Dad were violent and unpredictable when the kids were young. The violence and unpredictability were so intense that these people find it difficult to commit themselves to an emotional love relationship as adults.

This type of childhood environment can manifest a subconscious fear of establishing a family, for the psyche may think that babies will create the same childhood tensions again. We seldom understand this consciously (without therapy) for it is often easier to say that one has not found a suitable or responsible partner, and therefore "I can't have the children that I'd love to have." Until the fears are realized on the conscious plane, a person continues picking unsuitable emotional partners and limiting the possibilities of a warm and sensitive relationship with someone who promotes growth and maturity.

When Mars opposes the Sun, it's advisable when beginning something new (in first trying to work with the energy in a constructive fashion) to consider every new move carefully, to evaluate what the move means in terms of what is to be accomplished. If the impending action won't add anything constructive to the overall life scheme, or if it may offend the overall scheme, we need to let it go if we want to grow. Once the energy level changes, healthy reactions can be established. Instead of self-hurt responses, it becomes easier to incorporate positive action into the life style. This difficult aspect then becomes an asset.

SUN–MARS QUINCUNX. The quincunx represents a strain, and wherever it appears there is a conflict between two approaches to life. The Sun is the essential spirit; Mars represents "I act." When the "I am" principle is in a strain aspect with the action principle, the person experiences a constant feeling of unspoken apprehension or insecurity. An example: an Aquarian Sun with Mars in Virgo. The Aquarian is an unconventional type, has a father-dominated background, is a little unsure about parental history, looks to make a mark in the world, is interested in humanitarian ideas, statesmanship and in bringing a new consciousness to himself and to the world. The Mars in Virgo is a critical one—"I act critically" or "I act in an intellectual, rational, well-thought-out manner." Or "I act on statistical information," for Virgo planets are the supporters of the concept of statistics. If this Aquarian is to bring *new* ideas into consciousness, how can he be involved in statistics? By definition, statistics is a compilation of data based on past experience. Franklin D.

Roosevelt was an Aquarian, and in a time of national stress he brought programs into being that helped people survive. He couldn't have done that if he had criticized his every move (and Mars in Virgo tends that way). FDR had Mars in Gemini, by the way.

The quincunx of Mars to the Sun serves as a stymie. The strains in behavior have to be worked through, with the understanding that action must take place in respect to the Sun or a feeling of isolation, loneliness and lack of purpose will eventually take place.

SUN–JUPITER ASPECTS

These planets in aspect indicate an emphasis regarding how the individual is programmed to relate to the self (the inner values, the personal needs). Jupiter symbolizes how we relate (see Chapter 6 in this section) to the concept of self, family and the universe around us. If Jupiter is favorably aspected, it generally implies that our early family experience was open, and that we saw or felt our parents accepting bounty and good feelings, so we can do it too. When there are hard aspects between Jupiter and the Sun, the child saw the relating principle as a difficulty. This can indicate an adult problem with relating in general. The hard aspects often indicate an inability to diagnose the needs of the self. When talking about childhood experience, these may be the people who swear they had a wonderful childhood environment, when the aspects in the chart say they didn't.

Jupiter afflictions are hard for us to accept within ourselves. They create a subconscious aversion to looking within, but it's important to do so. We cannot receive what we need if we don't know who we are. To know that "I am" and to know that "I exist" are important to share with someone. The relating ability includes friends, lovers, families, children, as well as a feeling of being a part of the universe and feeling excited about being alive in the world around us.

SUN–JUPITER CONJUNCTION. This is an exciting configuration. It represents the well-born in some way. These children are born at a time when the father feels good about himself and the family is doing better than other families in the neighborhood. If they are born in a poor neighborhood, their family is the most successful around. If they are born to a professional or wealthy family, the environment is comfortable. But the comfort usually expresses itself in financial terms rather than in emotional terms; so, the child may be well fed, well educated and well cared for, but the sense of happiness, or emotional comfort may not be there. It brings an energy to the child that attracts money, prestige and trust as the child matures. Because people trust them, any venture that these individuals undertake will probably go well, unless there are other aspects to the Sun–Jupiter that cause a problem.

When the father feels good about himself, the child absorbs an inner sense of well-being and brings to maturity the ability to cooperate with authority figures. The child born in a masculine sign will always do better than the child born into a feminine sign for the Earth/Water sign child gives more emphasis to the aspects coming from the mother's side of the family. In order to develop the influence from the father (the Sun sign) the mother-blocks must be released. Then the energy is free to flow.

SUN–JUPITER SEXTILE. This indicates children who are born into a family that has a great deal of confidence to give them. When the energy of the sextile is released, these individuals have the ability to draw benefits that come from a career that cooperates with tradition, authority and works with established groups. As far as self-development is concerned, the Sun–Jupiter sextile acclimates itself to growing in a positive direction, and there is an ability to understand the innate needs of the self. In relationships, these people are able to express the self as well as to listen to others. This facility may not show much before the age of twenty-eight, but unless Mars, Venus or the Moon are heavily afflicted, these individuals are interested and able to work through the relating problems that are involved with the various maturing cycles.

SUN–JUPITER SQUARE. Here the child is born into an environment where the father does not relate well to himself. He doesn't like what he does, or he doesn't like the position he holds when the child is born. The chances are that Dad doesn't handle his problems maturely. Because the father doesn't relate well to himself, the child doesn't learn how to relate well to himself either. The child may not care for or communicate well with his father. He absorbs an environment (or family habit experience) that teaches him not to relate to his personal needs. If the child is born into a father-dominated atmosphere (positive Sun sign), then he may not care for the father, may not be able to communicate with him, and may not be able to relate to him. In some cases the father disappears during the childhood.

If the child is born into a mother-dominated family, Mother rules the universe and Father takes a passive role. The father is less respected because the child doesn't like the man. This individual can grow up to have a bad attitude toward men in general, and these feelings come into conflict in general dealings with men.

If the person with Sun square Jupiter is a male, he has difficulty working cooperatively with any male authority figure. He may not relate consciously to his own needs and he may not have a perspective of himself, for he has not been taught that he has a right to develop such things. If the person is a female, she may resent men. This can manifest in homosexual behavior (if the rest of the aspects in the chart warrant it), or she may become involved with heterosexual relationships with men who don't express themselves well, for she doesn't expect much of men. She, too, is unsure of who she is and what her needs are. Her sense of self is often poorly developed, or she has little perspective of the qualities represented by the signs and aspects active in her chart. These are the people who say that astrology doesn't work for them.

These individuals grow to have a limited concept of their personal needs. They are difficult to reach for they have developed reaction patterns that don't consider their inner needs. There may be no conscious sense of self, or any real understanding that they have a RIGHT to satisfy the needs of self. They are often motivated by the idea of excess, they blame others for the dilemmas they are in, and they don't spend much time at real self-analysis. The surface characteristics of the aspect seem to be selfishness, but underneath there is a bigger problem to be worked out.

If a child learns NOT to consider inner needs, he can easily be led away from using the energy symbolized in the natal chart. Metaphysically, the energies take on a life of their own, and the person with this aspect is not really in control of his personality. Unhappiness is a result, and when he is unhappy for too long a period of time, the body may become seriously ill. The illness is the body saying "I can't stand the life style anymore."

In order to solve the aspect, these individuals need to be encouraged to love themselves, to understand that they have a right to exist in the universe, and to begin to understand that if they will take responsibility for their actions, the universe will comply and begin to work with them instead of against them. There is no "awful" chart; there are only unhappy people who don't understand the purpose of their existence. Mother Nature's laws teach us that there is a place for all of us. We give better when we understand our own needs, for then we can share our needs with someone who not only understands us, but whom we can understand. That is truly relating.

SUN–JUPITER TRINE. This aspect is similar to the Sun–Jupiter conjunction. However, life comes more easily to a trine, and that doesn't always promote growth. When the trine exists, it should be considered in the light of the signs. For example, a woman with Sun in Virgo trine Jupiter in Taurus may be a very critical woman with a strong mother-dominated background. She may have been raised in an economically comfortable atmosphere and expect to be taken care of. In one case, this type of woman has had several homo-and heterosexual relationships. She misused her lovers, threw them out, and got financial assistance and possessions that she was not "given." In this particular case, an ex-lover stored some antiques in her home while in transition from one location to another. The lover never got the stuff back! Since nothing was put in writing, it would have become a legal case where it's the word of one against the other, and the lover didn't think the stuff was worth the legal hassle. Here is Jupiter trine the Sun at work—the owner of the aspect gets material assistance in life, but sometimes one thinks that one *deserves* assistance that is not ethical.

Jupiter trine the Sun acquires. But each of us must decide for ourselves if the method we use to acquire our material "goodies" is ethical. The reason a Virgo Sun and Jupiter in Taurus is acquisitive comes from the *signs*. Virgo tends to criticize any partner, and often gets into relationships where anger and resentment are directed at the lover. Taurus likes to collect things of value. When a person with this setup is unaware of the sign dilemma in the chart, he tends to use more negative energy. Had this been a Gemini person with Jupiter in Aquarius trine the Sun, the above situation would not have occurred. An intellectual disagreement might have taken place between the lovers, but the furniture would have been returned. Earth signs tend to like material possessions better than Air signs. The Air signs will want a piece of the "mind."

SUN–JUPITER OPPOSITION. This aspect is a difficult one, for the child must work through two basic environment problems. First of all, the father doesn't relate to himself. If the child is father-dominated, the lack of relating ability is picked up from the father's reaction to the environment. If the child is mother-dominated, it must be determined whether the child feels overwhelmed by the mother, or whether he picks up his mother's strengths. Sometimes mother-dominated children hate their fathers, sometimes they side with them. The father and child sometimes gain strength by aiding each other, they are the two "losers" who side with each other for protection against the power of the mother. If this is the case, the Sun–Jupiter opposition becomes even more pronounced in the mother-dominated child. Essentially it makes the child give up relating to its needs.

Early in the life the values of the Sun, the needs and the qualities of the Sun, are dismissed or disapproved of by the power parent. The relating principle (seen by the aspects to Jupiter and the sign it is in) wins out over the expression of the "I am" principle. The child becomes an adult who doesn't know his own needs. The constant suppression of personal needs causes much internal tension, and the adult may eventually become ill as a physical reaction to the emotional or mental turmoil. Astrology can be helpful here for one can evaluate the Sun sign needs and learn to handle the compromise.

One client who is working through a Sun–Jupiter opposition has been in psychotherapy, has had the disease cancer, and is now beginning to look at herself analytically. She has Sun in Cancer, Jupiter in Capricorn. All her life she suppressed the Cancerian part of herself: the emotional needs, the desire for affection, the need for emotional warmth and emotional reactions. She tried to place her life values and her reaction to life on the Capricorn traits. If she had been able to compromise or combine the qualities of Capricorn (the traditional stiff-upper-lip stuff) with her emotional needs, she would have been ok; but her emotions were suppressed. She used the Cancerian virtues of the Big Momma complex but did not take care of her own need to be held. Her emotional nature was suppressed to such a degree that she had to maintain a constant "control" over her life. In order to stay in control she had to eliminate laughter, tears, honest compassion and empathy—for these are spontaneous feelings. In the face of trauma and disillusion, she couldn't let the emotion out; she upheld the traditional attitudes toward the world, her family, her husband and her children. The disease cancer developed. She says that because she is now allowing herself to feel, to be, the freedom she feels within is tremendous. She never thought that she deserved to be herself!

This happens often to Jupiter as it affects the Sun, for the individual has suppressed the ability to look within on a feeling basis. The cure is beautiful, once the reality of the psyche and the self has been faced.

SUN–JUPITER QUINCUNX. This aspect creates a strain. Jupiter indicates how we relate to the world, and the Sun represents what we are. The strain usually exists because our relationship abilities conflict in some way with our inner needs. For example, I have a Cancer male client with Jupiter in Aquarius quincunx the Sun, who has strong Cancerian traits: he's emotional, intuitive, possessive, sensitive, and needs lots of emotional reassurance. He relates on an unorthodox level, and people who don't know him might think he is the last of the great experimentalists. He's open, questioning, and tries to present himself as a person interested in the unorthodox. This approach carried over into his love life, and he found himself in the midst of an "open" love affair because his lover suggested that they see other people openly. The Jupiter in Aquarius relates as an unconventional type, but the Cancer Sun needs emotional reassurance. He's facing the situation with great bravado but doesn't feel comfortable inside, for he thinks "if my lover needs other lovers, what's wrong with me?"

The qualities of the two signs conflict and the owner will feel discomfort. They have to both be worked into the life pattern, they both need expression. If this particular Cancer person can understand the needs of his Sun and can share his needs verbally by telling his partner that fidelity is important to him, the qualities symbolized by the signs and the planets can be liberated through discussion. If he can learn to tell people "I may seem unconventional, but I'm really a prude about this relationship, and I don't want to share you," then the Sun needs will be expressed.

Generally speaking, Jupiter–Sun afflictions represent a certain barrier to personal growth. If we can't really relate to who we are, how can we really share ourselves in a relationship? In the spiritual sense, Jupiter and Saturn are the planets that get us from this plane to the others, for they are the qualities that permit consciousness to expand. Referring back to the ancient houses, Jupiter and Saturn rule the ninth, tenth, eleventh and twelfth houses. These are the areas that represent consciousness expansion. If Jupiter or Saturn afflictions exist in the chart, they should be the first planets to be understood.

SUN–SATURN ASPECTS

When the Sun and Saturn are linked together the spiritual self is combined with a process of restriction. In order to grow with these aspects, we need to understand Father Nature, the masculine half of Mother Nature! Saturn represents how the father may psychologically influence or hamper the growth of his child. In a general sense, Saturn contacts involve the concept of restriction or a feeling of "lack" in the personality. However, because we tend to give more attention to our lacks, they can become our strong points.

SUN–SATURN CONJUNCTION. This is both a good and bad aspect. In terms of childhood experience, the father is an influential person in that he does something to prohibit the child's development. If the Sun sign is positive, the child will be more seriously affected by his relationship to his father, for he will adopt his father's mannerisms and life reactions more so than the positive Sun sign child without this Saturn contact.

This configuration seems to encourage the person to "act like the father" every time it's decision time. Individuals with this conjunction seldom act spontaneously. The value system is patterned after the father's, and the qualities of the Sun sign have difficulty manifesting. It is often said of this type, "You don't *seem* to be a Gemini," etc.

When Saturn conjuncts the Sun in a feminine sign, the paternal influence is lessened because the child is born into a mother-dominated home. The father will restrict the child and cause the child to have resentment toward him; but, the way in which the resentment will manifest depends on the signs involved in the conjunction. When the Saturn influence involves the passive parent, the child's development is restricted by a parent whose power is "second rate," which can cause even more resentment toward that parent. An example of this would be a mother-dominated child born to a hard-working mother and an alcoholic, violent father. The child sees the mother run the universe because she has to, and sees the father not only being passive in his role, but destructive to the children or to the mother, or to the entire family. The behavior of the father causes resentment in the child, for the kid can see, and perhaps feel, the results of Daddy's behavior. Other Saturn influences are more subtle, and when the effects of the conjunction remain in the subconscious they become more difficult to cure. A lack of worth may come into play, and astrological symbolism can help to discover how to build a sense of personal values.

As far as career is concerned, this type functions well for Saturn conjunct the Sun can be read in keyword language as "I take myself seriously." However, this advantage can outweigh the more personal side of the individual's life because the joy of living is often absent, the sense of humor is often satirical (which is fine in its place) and spontaneity is lacking.

Often the physical health is not all that it can be, for in the process of imitating daddy, the individual doesn't have a chance to express his own feelings, and the physical body rebels.

It's important to consider the Sun sign when reading this aspect, for the aspect restricts the development of the Sun sign potential. It inhibits self-assuredness. The self is offered to the universe more carefully, and the natural creativity is not considered worth much by the owner. If the child dislikes the father, he often dislikes himself more. A concept of self-worth must be developed.

Saturn conjunct the Sun in Leo, for example, may be an outwardly rigid, pompous type, who imposes a code of ethics on others. The life style may include a large portion of righteousness, whereupon the native judges all that he or she sees and hears. It's hard to please this type, for it finds fault with everyone while posing as a meek and sweet person. Proper respect is demanded at all costs, and indignation occurs when respect is not properly offered by all, even when it isn't deserved. This personality can appear to be stuffy and supersensitive, and if the aspect is not handled well, the person can be what is known as a pompous bore. On the other hand, when the Saturn influence is understood, it makes for a serious Leo who wants to develop a serious career along traditional lines, who wants to work in management, and who wants to participate in some idealistic profession—like the helping professions.

In a personal sense, a counselor may find that this person may be self-sacrificing, self-effacing and highly self-critical. Leos have a perfection complex. They take being "perfect" seriously because of the Sun-Saturn conjunction, and they may place limitations on themselves because of it. As children they take Daddy seriously, and as adults they react to the various life crises that arise as Daddy would have, or as they think Daddy would have. Every new move is carefully considered, for it's difficult to fail when you're a Leo, it's difficult to appear imperfect, to lose approval. They eventually learn that inner peace is more important than the career goal that's reached because of Daddy's influence. The inner values don't often manifest before the individual is thirty-five.

The person with Saturn in Virgo conjunct the Sun will be far less righteous, for the qualities of Virgo will be restricted rather than the qualities of Leo. Virgos have a rough time developing self-confidence; they feel that they must "crawl through the mud on their bellies" before deserving anything! With Saturn conjunct the Sun, the Virgo has even less self-confidence. The critical abilities that can be useful in separating the wheat from the chaff cannot develop as they should, because the critical ability of the mind will more often be spent defending oneself by criticizing others. When we criticize others excessively, we are really saying, "I'm not so bad, look at them." Even though Virgo is a mother-dominated sign, the Saturn–Sun influence here indicates that the child identifies with the father. If the mother rules the universe and the father is a loser and the child identifies with the father, you can draw your own conclusions! This child has to pull himself up by the bootstraps in order to develop the confidence to express himself.

Regardless of the other favorable aspects present, the energy will not manifest positively until the native copes with the Daddy imitation. Opportunities may be present throughout the life, but if Daddy was a failure, the child will be too. The incredible change in these people occurs when they realize that they can use their energies any way they wish. As soon as they become conscious of the pattern they are imitating (by going back into the childhood and remembering the father's pattern, and learning to see how they imitate him), they can kick the habit and use this conjunction for strength. Wherever Saturn sits, it represents the part of yourself that you regard with caution. After the first Saturn return (approximately age twenty-eight), we get better and stronger by using our Saturn.

SUN-SATURN SEXTILE. The early environmental conditions encourage the child to develop. This child learns to work with authority figures because the father presents no harsh influence; and as the child matures, it functions well within the social structure. Management, traditional forms of expression will take place without too many problems. Sextiles indicate talent, so the child will manifest its particular energies best through traditional methods. As the child matures, the sextile will lend itself toward slowly opening and expanding consciousness; surefootedness develops. This person tends to enter the spiritual life after the age of fifty, for the mind is ready at that point to accept the universal laws. The father provides a healthy model for the child.

SUN-SATURN SQUARE. The child is born into an atmosphere in which the father does not like himself. The Sun represents "I am," it also indicates the type of physical father. Saturn indicates where repression comes from. It also indicates the psychological influence of the father on the child. It can also be used to indicate how the father's father was—for when Saturn squares the Sun, it indicates that the grandfather was influential in developing the behavior pattern of the father, who in turn influences the child.

Saturn runs in seven-year cycles, and the Bible is full of references to heredity and the sins of the fathers being visited on the sons. This metaphor can be interpreted as the influence of a parental behavior pattern on the children born into a family. When this aspect occurs it can mean that the father is feeling sorry for himself when the child is born, or he resents his fatherhood, his career, his life style, his responsibilities, his neighborhood, etc. The child born at this time will inherit or learn Daddy's behavior pattern. The learning process is an unconscious one; the parent may not even be aware that he can influence his child in this manner.

The life pattern that the child develops will be described by the signs that the Sun and Saturn are in. Again, the child born into a positive sign may be antitradition, antifather, antimen, anti–organization. This energy can be used for accomplishing either good or bad, for world changers go against tradition but so do rabble-rousers. How one wishes to use this energy is a personal decision.

When the child is mother dominated, the Saturn affliction may affect it differently. The male child has to garner a sense of self-worth in a world he feels is balanced against him. Mothers rule the universe, he thinks; men have no value, he doesn't care for his father, and eventually he may manifest symptoms of not caring for himself. If the child is a girl, this aspect will affect her relationships with men, for she will have to work through her dislike of them. Here is the setup for the homosexual woman, or for women who marry in order to castrate men, or for women who become passive and select men who destroy them, for what else do men do?

Often the Saturn square Sun children have a father who leaves them. This is particularly important for girls, for some of them subconsciously expect any man they love to leave them since Daddy did. One never knows how the energy of the early environment affects the mind; but we can begin to understand when we listen to a client's problem and begin to tie it into the chart. Because we don't remember our early childhood impressions, sometimes the only way to unearth them is by trying to understand the language of the symbolism contained in astrology.

Sun-square-Saturn people carry with them an aura of resentment toward any authority figure, including the boss. People in management dislike personnel with this aspect, for although the employee does his job, he often does it with an "attitude." These people are sometimes better off self-employed or working at the management level, for they don't work well with others. In order to get into management, however, one has to do some time on the obedience level. Once a job is well learned, or if we have a talent to offer, we can advance our status. It's important that these people receive the training necessary to free them from subordinate positions.

The aspect also doesn't make for enthusiasm in the school system, for teachers represent a form of authority too! Young people with this aspect need to learn to work with the Saturn energy long enough to turn it into a friend. Once the energy is disciplined, they can be world changers, for they methodically plod through reams of ideas and can decide which ones will be most productive. They have energy that allows them to stick to a commitment long enough to complete it.

On the self-awareness level, since the father negatively influences these children on a psychological level, and this influence is rarely conscious, they need to develop feelings of self-worth. They have to convince themselves that they have a right to invest time in themselves, to build a sense of self. When one has no sense of self-worth, one even feels guilty about asking for help, so it's difficult to go into therapy.

These individuals may project all their problems onto others—it's the world's fault they aren't successful—and they may sound rather paranoid. A relationship that doesn't go well is their partner's fault; and all the ills in life happen because of other people. However, they aren't able to put much into a relationship until they *like* themselves, so healthy people may leave them. Understanding the attitude alleviates the problem. Learning that we all have a right to do something to help ourselves can lead these individuals into the right path. When we are on the right path for ourselves, we can feel it in our guts. We begin to *feel* good!

SUN-SATURN TRINE. These children are born at a time when the father's influence serves as a calming one. The family atmosphere teaches deliberation and thorough thinking. Any contact from Saturn to the Sun brings a more serious note to the personality; it becomes less frivolous. The family influence, especially that of the father, gives these children a "handle" on how to deal with the world and authority figures, and teaches a positive and deliberate self-expression. They can become adults capable of working with those in authority, with traditional systems, and with organizations and management. If these individuals wish to accomplish something important, they have the universal vibrations in their corner to help them. If they need help from organizations or those in power, it will not be difficult to attain. Any problems that they encounter will come from other aspects in the chart; but, this aspect will always be their "ace in the hole."

As far as spiritual evolution is concerned, these people (along with Sun sextile Saturn) will do more growing after the age of fifty. They usually choose to follow more traditional lines. They either become involved in the Judeo/Christian movement, or may at some point choose one of the more orthodox forms of Oriental thought.

If they move in the right direction according to the chart, they can expect longevity. Karmically speaking, this aspect indicates an ability to work through the line of heredity, or family ties, to change and build the social structure. As Jung expressed it, the collective unconscious incorporates what the species attains over the many centuries of development. These are the people who have a chance to help humanity move in higher directions.

SUN-SATURN OPPOSITION. This aspect works much like the conjunction or the square, with the special qualities of restriction placed on the child by the psychological influence of the father. It also indicates the possibility of the loss of the father, either on a physical or an emotional level. Some form of separation takes place. The father's position in life forces the child to give up the concept of self and places even greater restrictions on self-expression than the other afflictions of Saturn to the Sun.

As the child matures, he needs to learn how to live in the universe without feeling oppressed. He tends to see life and himself in terms of restriction, and feels that in order to accomplish anything in life he must fight for self-expression. Little does he realize that most of the restriction is psychological in nature; by exploring the circumstances of the early childhood environment with an eye to the effect of father, he can remove the feeling of restriction. When the negative influence is removed, the aspect becomes an asset to career and gives the ability to follow through on projects.

A male born with this aspect feels that men, authority and law are all against him personally, that he is doomed to failure. The female with this setup feels some problems with self-expression in "this man's world." If she doesn't understand the father oppression, she will tend to choose men as partners who oppress her, feeling that it's normal for men to be oppressive. Both sexes feel a lack of self-worth and find it difficult to invest money in their personal rehabilitation. In the very negative sense, this aspect can indicate a lawbreaker, one who has no respect for authority and resents the system. It doesn't matter which system they are born into, for they will resent *any* system. This sometimes makes for the hopeless revolutionary who fights empty causes merely for the sake of fighting a system. When this aspect is tied into a chart full of idealism, it can indicate a person who takes the energy into himself, and rather than becoming a revolutionary type the energy implodes, causing great stress to the physical self. Eventually, the stress causes the body to break down and chronic ailments occur.

The failure to express the self in any positive way is basically an imitation of the father in this case. In situations where the father died or left the family, it is difficult to unearth the personality of the father, for it is often shrouded in mystery and awe. Once the individual gets under the veil and remembers exactly what the father stood for, he can begin to erase the power of the opposition. The father may have been a man who was set on destroying himself. He may have had personal reasons for wanting to fail, but a child doesn't understand such things. The individual can redirect this energy once he understands the message from the father.

The Father archetype represents universal law, and a failure to understand universal law can cause personal failure. Everything exists for a reason, and one of the reasons that the Oriental masters teach philosophy in such vague terms, and ask students such vague questions, is because they know that understanding the universe is personal. We each must find our own answers. People with Saturn opposing the Sun attempt to establish their own universe before they learn how *this* one functions. Often they want to make changes merely for the sake of change. Altruism has shown itself to be destructive; when one doesn't understand what one is doing or protecting, the altruist often does more damage than good. For example, an altruist in New England decided that killing deer was bad. What he didn't realize is that the land feeds only so many deer, and during the winter snows when food is hard to find, the wild dogs hunt the deer. Because the deer are starving, they have no energy to run in the snow. As a result, farmers find deer in the snow, half-eaten and still alive since the dogs eat the hind quarters before they kill the deer. Eventually, a new law was instituted to establish a doe season. Hunters can kill doe, which keeps the deer population down. Mother Nature and Father Nature need a balance that good-hearted universe-changers just don't understand! Altruists decided that booze was bad, and so we got prohibition—which gave the Mafia, and subsequently the drug industry, capital to invest in other businesses that hurt people. We now have pending legislation on cigarettes, and soon the cigarette smoker may be buying contraband cigarettes, much like the potsmokers bought contraband marijuana in the 1960's. Each righteous decision feeds the underworld, and we find doctors and lawyers and respected citizens supporting the black market or the underworld. When we try to create our own universe, we set ourselves at odds with nature. This energy would be better used in furthering an understanding of the inner abilities inherent in the individual, and express-ed for the common good.

When Saturn opposing the Sun is taken to its extreme, and the chart has planets in signs that bestow the qualities of righteousness, the individual may develop a god complex. He thinks he's right and everyone else who has gone before is wrong. The overall effect of the father, and the father's inability to encourage the child, turns into a restriction of the child's healthy energies. This restriction of energy causes anger that is often sub-conscious, and the child later rebels. The lesson, on a karmic level, is to learn that restriction or boundaries can be helpful when the energy is used constructively. When we stop fighting authority for its own sake, then we can work through it or as part of it and accomplish new goals from a dif-ferent point of view.

SUN–SATURN QUINCUNX. Here the father influence is not downright negative, but it causes a strain to develop in the child. The strain concerns the "I am" principle versus the tradition of the day: "Which do I follow?" Father disapproves of the child's behavior in a vague way or of the child's existence, but not in a violent way. When this child becomes an adult, the problem will manifest as a compromise bet-ween feelings of self-worth versus restriction. The feel of lack caused by Saturn will subtly undermine the expression of self. By using the keywords of the signs, planets and houses, the energy can be manifested in a positive way.

SUN–URANUS ASPECTS

Any contact between the Sun and Uranus tends to influence the person to be a more unconventional rather than "normal" sign type. It signifies unusual parents and an unusual childhood environment, but how these things are "different" is an unknown. Unusual behavior can range anywhere from unorthodox on a healthy level, to all kinds of perversity. The childhood environment can be determined by looking at the rest of the aspects in the chart.

Uranus is a generation planet, affecting thousands and thousands of people in one sign. When someone has Uranus conjunct the Sun, for example, many people born in that sign in that year will have the same aspect. Uranus generally affects the behavior pattern of a generation as well as the spiritual, religious and humanitarian cults that spring up around the world. It has to do with liberation, consciousness expansion and an increase or change in the world awareness. When these aspects occur, the very life of these individuals is bound up in the problems and thoughts of their era. They have an opportunity to use the energy in a profound way, or it may be used to develop the eccentric type. As these people experience life, they are much like the mustard seeds that fall to the earth to grow or fail, depending on the environment they land in. They are free to use the energy as they wish, although the early childhood environment is out of their conscious control. It's interesting to observe children born with these aspects for they are the bringers of the new age. People who don't have Uranus aspecting the personal planets are not as involved with the movement of the masses, but are more caught in the middle of the experience.

SUN–URANUS CONJUNCTION. These people are honorary Aquarians. The qualities of Aquarius are added to the Sun sign characteristics. These are the people who have chosen to be a part of the new age, for they are involved with the uplifting of the consciousness of the sign type. The sign lifting consciousness now (when this book is being written) is Scorpio, since Uranus by transit is traveling through that sign and will be there for several years. Then we will have a generation of children born in Sagittarius with Uranus conjunct the Sun, and the Sagittarians will evolve to a new height. Pluto is several generations behind Uranus, patiently following and uprooting the people on the Sun-Uranus conjunction! These lifetimes are profound, for they are full of opportunity. For those who believe in reincarnation, these are the people to watch, for their lifetime is a crucial one. They are the bringers of the new age; they are each a part of the "new Christ spirit," so to speak. This responsibility is awesome. The energy forces a particular soul to grow, to transform itself, to become conscious.

The life will be unusual, perhaps erratic, perhaps eccentric, as they look for the right path to walk. The influence of the father is important, for he is an unorthodox and unusual man in some way; he sparks his child's growth because of his effect on the personality. The father is forced out of his particular "rut" when this child is small, and his child will be forced out of the rut of his sign type. Karmic astrologers say we choose our lives; this choice includes the evolution of the sign type characteristics.

The person with Sun conjunct Uranus has to learn to channel the energy of the aspect or he will be controlled by it. One of the problems here is an unorthodox approach to life that may not be understood or appreciated by folks who don't have it. Parents have problems raising this child, for the child picks up the father's unorthodox behavior and ends up harassing the parents by being difficult to manage, hard to train, and stubborn and eccentric even early in life. This is a highly independent child. In certain atmospheres, the child will or can be overwhelmed by the stronger parent, sometimes by sheer force, for the child doesn't fit acceptable childhood patterns that the parents require.

As the individual learns to use the energy, the interpreter of the chart can evaluate the circumstances with an eye to the growth of the personality, and help this energy to manifest itself in a constructive way. The possible effect is the chance to be a far-reaching Aries or Taurus or Scorpio—to grow and be different from those who have come before.

SUN–URANUS SEXTILE. This child comes into a constructive but "different" type of atmosphere. The personality can be quite creative and innovative as an adult. He understands the changing ethics, morals and needs of the masses, and can help bring these changes about. The energy needs to be developed, but he seems to be karmically here to help carry out the best of the ideas brought here by people born with the conjunction.

SUN–URANUS SQUARE. Because the Sun represents the self and Uranus represents the behavior pattern of a generation, the square is not easy. During the individual's childhood, the father is stubborn about his eccentricity. He may be a "thwarter" in the social structure, or he may resent the social structure of his day. He may be a religious or political dissenter. But, in some way, this father reaches out to make some changes in his world. He may do this from a positive or a negative point of view—and end up by being productive or merely stubborn and eccentric. The father probably finds his child's behavior difficult to cope with as well.

The aspect works differently according to the sex of the individual and the dominant parent situation. A male with a positive sign Sun will be a radical; so will the female. The person coming from a mother-dominated family will resent the father's radical position. The mother-dominated male may have problems accepting his own unconventional attitudes; or he may be unconventional at the cost of getting to understand himself. The mother dominated female will have an unorthodox attitude toward men since she resents her father's position. She will draw an unorthodox male, and perhaps will not develop her talents because of such relationships.

The unorthodox factor will be present throughout the life, but one can choose to be unorthodox-productive or not, as one wishes. As we mature, we find via the system of trial and error that certain energies can be used productively or not. When a woman chooses an unorthodox mate (or a controversial one) and plans to have a family, she may end up with a mate who refuses to take the responsibility of fatherhood. This eventually limits her growth, since she may be forced to support her children rather than being in a situation where she gets help. When she is twenty, she can't see this—therefore the trial and error!

SUN–URANUS TRINE. Here the personality chose to evolve in a positive way during this lifetime. The child arrives in an atmosphere that gives it a chance for growth. The parents enjoy being unusual, or unconventional, and the child is exposed to new ideas. If the person chooses to grow in a happy, productive direction, the attitudes of the generation that he is born into will help direct his ideas as an adult.

However, the trine aspect will bring this person into whatever behavior pattern exists at that time within the attitude of the masses. This can mean that he can offer productive ideas to the communicty, or he can flow with the tide and become a part of the generation problems that exist; i.e., the drug cult, etc.

Obviously the creativity and inventiveness of this aspect will only show if the energy is used. Old programs can be modernized, tradition can be restructured when this aspect is directed into a career. On a personal level, the owner of this energy is innovative and interesting, for the mind is capable of walking many paths.

SUN–URANUS OPPOSITION. The behavior patterns of the father are not productive at the time this child is born, and the child is caught in the unproductive pattern. The father presents himself in such an unorthodox way that the subconscious mind of the child develops a pattern that includes "unsureness" of self. The father causes the child to undergo some kind of hardship; perhaps the life situation or hardships that confront the father are taken out on the child when Dad comes home. Whatever the case, the child assumes that life should not be easy! When one believes this one usually draws the life experience one expects.

Relationships are often difficult for those with this aspect, for they present themselves to others in a manner that is difficult to understand. The generation they are born into may have an adverse affect on them. They may also become involved in the exclusive idea of being "different." Unconventional or eccentric people can be either interesting or self-destructive. When we pursue the unusual merely for the sake of being unusual, either to get attention or to bother someone else, we seldom stop to see if our eccentricity is productive. Because each individual is free to choose how he will live his life as an adult, it's impossible to predict the behavior patterns of people born with this aspect. The Uranian type is either ahead of or behind the times, which adds to the difficulty of predicting behavior patterns for this individual.

It seems as if the father does not provide a dependable image for this child. If the child is born into a positive sign, he may suffer through his experience with Dad, dealing with some form of physical violence, or perhaps some kind of emotional violence that serves to develop a quality of insecurity. If the child is born into a mother-dominated atmosphere, the father is even more unorthodox, although probably less productive, less mature and less concerned with his responsibilities as a father.

Yet, the aspect brings with it a transformational quality, and because the child is exposed to unusual behavior patterns, it is capable of developing new avenues of thought as an adult. These can be the individuals who evolve consciously, who become the contemporary philosophers of their generation, for Uranus lifts up the sign type. However, the uplifting experience seldom takes place until they get over hating Daddy or feeling self-pity because of their childhood circumstances.

A Taurus, for example, born with Uranus in Scorpio opposing the Sun, will have to incorporate the transforming qualities of Scorpio with the qualities of Taurus. This opposition combines selfish sensuality with transformational behavior: learning to do things for oneself as well as doing things for others; transforming self as well as others. This will be an unusual type of Taurus, for it cannot build only on Taurus qualities. It denotes an unusual life style and an interesting mind. Before the mind can develop, the family resentments must become both conscious and released.

SUN–URANUS QUINCUNX. The child born with this aspect has to work harder to attain consciousness than the child with the other Uranus aspects. The attitudes of his generation don't affect him as overtly, but they bother him. The Sun has to incorporate the values of the Uranus sign placement into the life style. "I am," says the Sun, "I behave according to the sign Uranus is in," says Uranus. Perhaps the incorporation of the qualities of this aspect is easiest in the career. Much time can be wasted, for the values that need to change are different from the life path, but not strong enough to cause enough dissatisfaction to force the owner of the aspect to take action. This person can either stagnate or grow.

SUN–NEPTUNE ASPECTS

The "I am" principle is affected by inspiration or delusion when these two planets are in aspect. The Sun indicates who we are, what we are growing toward, the qualities we will learn to work with. Neptune represents the world of dreams, the inspiration as well as the delusion in the universe.

The Hindus call the life experience "Maya" for the material world is full of illusion, and our consciousness allows us to view this illusion any way we wish. The person with Sun–Neptune configurations will learn to incorporate delusion/inspiration with the qualities of selfhood. This can be an extremely creative aspect, or it can indicate a person lost in fantasy.

SUN–NEPTUNE CONJUNCTION. This is a powerful conjunction. These individuals are influenced by a strongly spiritual father image. They have chosen to develop a spiritual consciousness this lifetime, and this consciousness may be hard to discover.

They are born with insight that may not be appreciated by the family. Much of the insight is derived from something picked up from the father image. However, these individuals usually get some kind of distorted father image later on in childhood and don't later remember what the father stood for. Because they can't consciously relate to what they intuitively feel for the father, they get caught in self-doubt. With Neptune affecting the "self" energy, the personality is influenced by fantasy. This aspect indicates an intuitive, creative potential that can make these children unwelcome in the household, for they see and know things that make parents uncomfortable. Much like a Piscean, the intuitive facility is well developed. These children may live in two worlds: the world of parental authority and school systems, and the world of fantasy and illusion.

If properly guided when young, they can develop into tremendously creative and intuitive types, being drawn to the more creative aspects of life—the classical ballet, classical music, the arts. If the early environment doesn't provide this insight, they may begin to wonder if they are living a lie and wonder what is real. Depending on how the rest of the chart is aspected, they may become adults who muddle through life until they find some form of creative expression; they may develop into adults who have trouble dealing with what the rest of us call reality. These individuals may be so sensitive that they retreat into a world of drugs or fantasy or both, in order to avoid facing the more harsh aspects of the living experience.

One interesting aside in connection with the Sun–Neptune conjunction (and also with Neptune conjuncting the Ascendant) is that the individual may look "dumb." Many times doctors think a patient with this conjunction is a drug addict or "on something." In office situations, other employees think this individual is not quite "with it." For a woman, this aspect can be a lot of fun, if she knows she has it. Women who look "dumb" can muddle through life doing very well; if Mercury is not tied into the conjunction, she can plan her moves and not "threaten" anyone. People who are more obvious, who look "smarter," usually are more harassed on the way up the corporate ladder than those who are working with the Neptune aspects.

These people need stability, and the conjunction does not give them that. Because the world of fantasy is just behind the blink of an eye, it's easy to wander off in the mental realms of delusion, illusion or creative imagination. As the mind wanders far from home, the personality may periodically become suicidal, especially when the Sun is under heavy affliction by transit. Most people are unaware that many philosophers have considered the prospect of suicide before becoming more impersonally involved in the structure of the universe. When we consider suicide, we are at first feeling very sorry for ourselves because we haven't gotten our way about something. "If you don't marry me, I'll kill myself!" has been said more than once. After we get tired of feeling sorry for ourselves, we begin to question *why* we are alive. When we get more comfortable with the question, we then move on to the question of why *anybody* or *anything* is alive. Shortly beyond that comes the "I am" principle and we begin to sound like Plato or Descartes! As we begin to observe life patterns, which happens after we wonder why a tree is alive season after season, we begin to tune into the pattern in the universe. We can then begin to see Mother Nature at work, especially in the spring. As we begin to accept Mother Nature, we begin to think about Father Nature and life becomes an exciting prospect. Many people are afraid of the word "suicide," but it merely is a conscious contemplation of life and death. As soon as we are born we are approaching death. As the Aquarian Age comes into being in the next few centuries, people may return to the ancient customs long enough to begin to understand death from a positive point instead of the fear with which we now view the event.

People born with this conjunction (as well as the square or opposition) will walk many different paths on the way to spiritual enlightenment. This can be an exciting trip. The blocks on the path are often caused by misunderstanding the father. He was looking for something and he may not have found it. He, too, was trying to find himself, in his own way. If he sold out, if he gave up his quest, if he left home or happened to die when these people are young, they may have great difficulty sorting through the family history so that they can get at the truth about the father. But armed with the knowledge that Dad was searching for something, the mystery becomes clearer, and the questions can be asked better. If relatives other than the mother are available, they may be more helpful, for in some cases the husband or wife may know less about the spiritual crisis of a loved one than would the friends or brothers and sisters.

SUN–NEPTUNE SEXTILE. The father brings the child along a road that encourages the development of talent, creative endeavor and spirituality. But the encouragement is subtle, and the child only expresses talent based on his or her childhood environment. A talent coming from the sextile aspect must be developed, so this talent may remain latent during the lifetime. It's possible that this individual may just view the various spiritual movements going on in the world, or may move from religious fad to religious fad. But if this individual chooses to work to develop talent, it manifests in a positive way after the age of thirty. Neptune always brings intuitive creativity into the conscious mind. Used properly, this person can work creatively in any chosen situation.

SUN–NEPTUNE SQUARE. Here the child is born into an atmosphere that *requires* spiritual development. The father tries to develop spiritually, tries to find himself in the universe, but it seems that he misses out on the spiritual awareness that is necessary for his own particular form of spiritual growth. Perhaps his interest in religion is rather perverse, and his religious trip (or antireligion trip) prohibits him from developing as he needs to.

To illustrate, the father of a Sun square Neptune child may be a "holy-roller" Protestant, one of those people who gives up smiling and loving and compassion in the pursuit of his God. Some people view religion as a process of giving up all pleasure, thinking that God is angry and demanding. The God-consciousness can develop any way that it wishes. The various religions of the world really define the God energy as the creative essence—something bigger or more meaningful than accidental life, something that signifies an order and a meaning in the universe. When a person with the Sun square Neptune is born, it's necessary to explore the God-consciousness in this life. If the father got lost on some fanatic trip, of if he got lost on some atheistic trip, this person may assume that all interest in so-called religion or philosophy must be "crazy." If the father was an atheist, the person may be afraid to pursue his interest in religious development, for his father may have shut all doors to this area.

People with this aspect are often presented with an image of the father that is not altogether accurate. For example, when parents divorce, one parent may have harsh feelings toward the other. A mother may tell her children that she ended the marriage because the father was incompetent. The truth may be that she drove the man out with her temper and unattractive personal characteristics. When there is a Neptune–Sun aspect in a person's chart, it's wise to become suspicious of the mother's reports of the father. He was either better or worse than she describes him. It may be that she didn't understand the man—he may have been listening to a different drummer.

Parents can influence or confuse this child's personal concept of reality more than they realize. The Sun–Neptune child is intuitive and knowledgeable. When he questions his parents, he tends to believe the answers given, and he may then begin to doubt himself! He knows what he saw, but Mom said that wasn't so. This affects his future decision making ability, his concept of reality, even his inner convictions. When a child feels unsure of reality, he grows to become an adult who is unsure of himself. This is apt to make him prey to anyone who has a good spiritual "game" together and he may be inclined to support all kinds of strange religious movements.

Because people with the Sun–Neptune square often live in a "strange reality,'' they lack perspective. Their aspirations may be muddled because the foundation of the personality is not understood. The Sun represents our essential spirit, it's the part of us that enlivens the body, and it's the essential spirit that leaves the body as a shell when we die. The Sun, then, can be considered the foundation of personality. Through the ages, the symbolism of ''building on a rock'' is mentioned in literature. If the Sun represents the foundation of personality, then the Neptune affliction can blind one to the essence of the personal structure. The aspect can be worked through as the individual realizes that many conscious memories have been ''fed'' to him, that he must establish a way of life for himself in the conscious sphere. Once this is accomplished, the energy within can be used on a constructive level. This energy can be extremely creative.

SUN–NEPTUNE TRINE. People born with this trine have the privilege of using their spiritual insights in a positive fashion. The spiritual evolvement of the father can be used to their benefit. These people come into a family where the father is pursuing some ''spiritual'' goal for himself, but the goal may not be apparent to a child.

The father's path, or the father's choice may not be the choice of the child, for the child needs to walk the path of his sign type. Once this is realized, the person can manifest this energy creatively in his own way. If the creativity is not apparent in the early life, look to see what aspect is blocking the person from using the talent.

Talent may be a gift from a previous incarnation, say the karmic astrologers, and the talent needs to be expressed in this one. The problem associated with the trine is caused by the need to balance the spiritual life with the physical. If the personality forsakes the physical body because it chooses to live completely in the mind, the energy cannot express at its highest level. The physical body is the temple of the soul. All the human emotions should be felt and lived in harmony with spiritual development or the energy cannot express itself as it should. The body actually presents a balance, for it helps the mind function on the plane of experience.

The father offers the child a pattern, or help, early in life; if the child doesn't get too caught up in the dreams of her generation, the pattern is the key to self-expression. The only thing to remember is that patterns do not have to be imitated, and each person must find individual self-expression.

SUN–NEPTUNE OPPOSITION. This aspect functions much like the square or the conjunction, except that there is a feeling of loss and a need for compromise added to it. The father of this child is so involved with his own spiritual trip that he ignores the child. The child doesn't understand why the father is so removed. When questioning the parents, the child probably is misinformed, for Neptune opposing the Sun often indicates that the father is either romanticized or aspersions are cast in his direction. The child is confused as to who Daddy is and therefore who he or she is. The world of fantasy, creativity, illusion and delusion are delights for this child. The tendency to go off into a dream world is sometimes hard to avoid. The sense of the individual's personal reality is distorted in some way—the child feels she is living a lie. This opposition also makes the child fantastically intuitive and psychic. It's difficult for others to understand these children.

Since these people don't know what is expected of them as far as social behavior is concerned, forming love relationships can present difficulties. Communication with others may be delivered on a "mental plane" rather than by verbal communication. Expectations about relationships may be unrealistic, for the expectations may be full of fantasy. This in itself may prevent relationships from developing, for their feelings are hurt by too many people too often. There may be discomfort in working with the physical body, so the physical-emotional relationships may be difficult to consummate on the "grosser" levels since love is a spiritual experience.

Much of the difficulty can be traced back to the father, for when this person is young, the father lives in his own private world. The boy child grows up to be like his father, and the girl child grows up to think that all men should be like her Dad. Both are surprised to find that other adults don't act and react in a manner similar to their Dad's. When the energy is understood, the aspect can be extremely creative. Like the conjunction and square, the opposition produces people who are in seventh heaven when they find the right outlet for their creative energy; they love their work, they love to work with their ideas, and their enthusiasm is delightful.

SUN–NEPTUNE QUINCUNX. This aspect is less noticeable in terms of personal insecurity. The child has an internal battle going on, for the self is interested in one thing, yet the creative or spiritual urges send it in another direction. The aspect causes unproductive daydreaming. The energy of the Sun must work constructively with the Neptune energy and is best expressed via career.

SUN–PLUTO ASPECTS

When these two planets confront each other, two portions of the personality are interacting. The Sun represents the "I am" principle in each of us. Pluto is a generation planet that affects masses of people whenever it makes an aspect. Carl Jung talked of the collective unconscious, and the inner growth of the human mind. Pluto can be considered a planet that represents great transformations, for its rulership was designated to Scorpio, the sign of reform, transformation and rebirth. As these two parts of the personality relate to each other, they involve the principle of personal growth, much like that of Uranus but from a different point of view. Pluto brings obsession, the ability to control and manipulate, as well as the energy of transformation. As long as we hang onto our present life style and our present consciousness, we reach out more often to control others as well as the universe around us. We think that "control" will guarantee that our personal universe will not change. However, the "catch 22" about Pluto aspects is that we *must* transform ourselves. The effects of Pluto seem to tie in with the feeling of being uprooted, or overwhelmed by something or someone much larger and stronger than ourselves. We have to learn to trust in the universe before we can let go—and when we let go of control or obsession, we are beginning our rebirth.

SUN–PLUTO CONJUNCTION. This is a creative aspect, for it puts the personality in touch with the collective unconscious as it is defined in the Jungian concept. This contact can be an easy, creative talent once it's channeled.

The physical father plays an important part in the child's development, and how important this is depends on whether the Sun is in a positive or negative polarity. The positive signs indicate the father is an overwhelming personality who is able to completely control and manipulate the child. This child will become an adult who automatically imitates the father because he doesn't know any other set of "normals."

This is a person who thinks he must totally control his environment. So he enters adult relationships with this attitude and doesn't consciously know what he is doing. The people around him resent being controlled and manipulated and pull away as soon as they can. As relationships fail one after another, this person becomes more apprehensive and therefore more controlling until he attracts only people who are weak enough to be manipulated. This aspect needs to relate to strong people in order to develop balance; there is a general feeling of discomfort when he becomes attached to weaklings.

When this aspect occurs to a child from a mother-dominated background, the mother and father are often involved in a great power struggle. The child sees no other way of life, no other form of relating. The battle that goes on between his Mom and Dad is the one involving the power of the strong versus the power of the weak. The child doesn't really know who's winning, so he doesn't know which role to play. As he becomes an adult and attempts relationships, he too will try to control those relationships any way he can. He can be strong one day and completely neurotic the next, whichever tactic will win the war.

Care must be taken when trying to determine power in a personality, for power can be that of the strong dominating the weak, or the tyranny of the weak in an attempt to manipulate someone who is physically or mentally stronger. A person who feigns a heart attack or other forms of illness in order to control a family is just as Plutonic as someone who wields a mighty fist!

People with Pluto conjunct the Sun do not want to feel out of "control" in any situation. They overwhelm others any way they can. One can't really blame them, for they were taught how to do this early in the childhood. They can overwhelm with love, caring, concern, guilt, problems, solutions, or with anything else one can think of! If you find yourself becoming resentful of someone, if you feel you have no "space" or you can't breathe, you may be feeling what it's like to be around a strong Pluto type. The energy causes others to become defensive, for they feel that their very essence is being invaded.

This conjunction brings great energy, but first the owner must become conscious of the power. Some people become righteous, some have all the answers, some are obsessive. Often they are not conscious of their obsession with an idea or a person. They can be so intense that they are considered "psychic vampires" for they take energy from everyone around them. They don't always know what they are doing or saying; the unconscious need to control just seems to burst forth in the personality. If the energy is channeled, this person becomes a transformer, a powerful and helpful person in the universe.

SUN–PLUTO SEXTILE. If you must have a Sun–Pluto aspect, this is a nice one to have. Rather than the Sun being overwhelmed by the power of Pluto, the sextile indicates that the native has a talent for developing groups, for working toward goals that benefit the masses. With proper training and experience, this talent can be developed to constructive use.

The parents were helpful to this child. They taught it how to work with a cooperative attitude; the family may have been concerned with current, national or world events; they may have been working in some cooperative situation when the child was born.

SUN–PLUTO SQUARE. This aspect indicates the child is exposed to a father who is not interested in relating to the mass consciousness. The power of the collective unconscious, according to Jung's definition, is an integral part of this person's life. It's important that he understand the spiritual and social evolvement of the species and work toward integration of the unconscious. His father is a man who doesn't like groups, who doesn't like his peers, and the child will grow up thinking that Dad's behavior is normal. The child may alienate himself from his peer group in school. Although the child participates within his peer group, he may never feel that he truly belongs. The interests of his peer group may bore him, he may be so antigroup that he avoids groups of any kind. This type is uncomfortable in crowds for he fears a loss of control.

This aspect requires these individuals to maintain a controlled environment. In relationships they tend to try to maintain a constant control over what happens. They can be obsessive about the people they love or care for. They can be a bit paranoid about their social position. The irony is that in order for Pluto to transform, the obvious forms of "control" behavior have to go, for these people must learn the order of the universe. Folks with this aspect say, "I just want to know where I STAND." Unfortunately, each individual must determine from within where he stands, for no real determination can be made by basing one's life decisions on someone else's reactions. When attempting to force others to make decisions for one, the result is dissatisfaction anyway! The games we play in order to control others never build inner security, for we know that we cheated at the game!

SUN–PLUTO TRINE. Here is a soul on a constructive trip. This aspect tends to manifest on two levels: either the individual is going along for a ride in this life, a ride that allows one to enjoy all the things of the contemporary culture—the suburban home, the color television, the joys of mass-market entertainment, etc; or the person has the energy and talent to work cooperatively with traditional managemental concerns dedicated to doing something for humanity. In each case the personality is capable of expressing the Sun sign energies in a constructive way as long as he is involved in some form of group endeavor. Any kind of mass-media communication will be successful and fulfilling for there are natural talents for it in the chart.

This is a child who is born into an atmosphere where the parents are able to teach him or reach him. The father is a cooperative individual who presents the child with an image of an authority figure communicating in a warm way with other authority figures. When Dad returns home from work, he doesn't present a negative picture of the work world, he doesn't feel isolated as a father; therefore, the child feels more secure. Other aspects may offset this, and the energy may not be free to flow until the "blocking" aspect is cured.

SUN–PLUTO OPPOSITION. This child has a chance to go through profound transformations in this lifetime, if the circumstances of the life lead in the necessary directions. A strong psychic energy is present, tying this person's subconscious to the material of Jung's collective unconscious. Without really trying, the child will be drawn to information that concerns the occult, or the soul-searching depths of analysis familiar to Jungian students. If the child is not raised in an environment that leads it to transformational knowledge, the underside of Pluto may manifest: a strong desire (on the subconscious plane) to be in total control of everything in the environment.

This child is born into a highly manipulative atmosphere. If the Sun is a Fire or Air sign, the father exerts influence that overwhelms the child. The most difficult kind of power game for a child to comprehend is that of mental or psychological manipulation. When a child is abused physically, he knows it, at least when he reaches a certain age; but Plutonic games are not always physical. Sometimes they are mentally coersive, and the child's mind becomes submerged in the power trip of the parent.

When the child is born into an Earth or Water sign, the father has a passive control game going, for the mother rules the marriage. The father resents her, and he may use any means necessary to control the environment—it may even be called love, for love covers a multitude of sins! "I only did it because I love you and want the best for you," and other control games of a similar nature.

At any rate, the child gets caught in a series of "what is good for you's" and can't fight free of what he can't see. This energy works much like it did on the German public when the country was taken over by Hitler. The general populace went about its business, not really noticing what was going on, until they realized one morning that they were trapped. There are many stories about what happened to those German citizens who did not agree with Hitler's regime. They couldn't talk to other citizens for fear of being reported; in order to work for the German underground they had to move very carefully. The Hitler takeover is an example of negative Plutonic energy at work.

Adults with this aspect may attempt to control everyone around them, through love or fear or hate. The point is that they drain others—of their talent, their hopes; for the drain is insidious. They complain that their friends and loved ones have no initiative, and they are right: they drain all the initiative out of everyone they know! They can make others feel physically tired because of this energy drain. Pluto types try to control their environment and, like the Pluto–Sun conjunction or square, they want to "beat" Mother Nature. They are unconsciously driven to think that they must make and control their universe—it can't be shared, it can't be spontaneous, for this is what they learn is "normal" when they are children. They can become obsessed with those they love or those they want to control, thinking up little games to play to make sure they are still in command. Most of this energy and game playing goes on at the subconscious level. Seldom does this aspect work in a negative sense from a conscious point.

When this energy is channeled into constructive use it can accomplish great things. Pluto always represents the mass consciousness in an impersonal sense, and this indicates how one can work in a cooperative way with groups and organizations that are dedicated to serving the masses. Any major political or social work, or any humanitarian endeavor will involve the Pluto or Uranian energies in the chart. Since Pluto rules Scorpio, and Scorpio represents things of a transformational nature, the personal transformation that can come out of the Sun–Pluto opposition can be intense. In a personal sense, the hardest thing for Pluto types to learn is to let go—to let creative energy work through them, to learn to let the body and mind be a channel for creative energy, to let ideas "flow." My clients who are working on this aspect tell me that this is the most difficult thing to start.

Before the energy is free to operate productively, the person needs to understand and fight free of the parental domination. Throughout mythology, the child has to fight the parents for freedom. Pluto aspects indicate that the freedom fight is a tough one and it has to be handled on both an unconscious and conscious level at the same time. It can be an exciting experience!

SUN–PLUTO QUINCUNX. This aspect produces a strain, for the values of the generation, the values of the "masses," conflict with the values of the native's father, or the inherited values. In the search for selfhood, how does one proceed when the father disagrees with the movement of the times? These are the children who are born to people who want to return to the "good old days." The irony here is that the child's health will suffer until he or she is old enough to decide which road to travel.

II-2: MOON ASPECTS

THE MOON INDICATES HOW WE RESPOND EMOTIONALLY, how we react to our world experience, how we react to emotional experiences directed toward us, what we respond to in terms of love as well as poetry and politics. The Moon represents our physical mother; the Moon sign and aspects will tell how our mother was feeling about herself and her life when we were born; it indicates the kinds of physical energies and reactions to life that she transmitted to us when our personality was forming. A female will garner her concept of womanhood, femininity and motherhood from her mother's reactions to these concepts. A male garners a sense of "woman," how he expects the women in his life to feel and react, from his mother. We also determine our emotional nature from the Moon placement. Many astrologers say that the Moon is a subconscious influence, but it seems more to reflect the feeling-intuitive process within the individual. The feeling-intuitive nature often has been confused with the subconscious, but feelings are a part of the conscious personality. Consciousness is ascribed to the intellect, to the rational process that takes place in the ego-centered consciousness—and this comes from the Sun–Mercury placement. The Moon energy is subjective and irrational but feeling, and equally as important in the development of a well-rounded personality.

The relationship between the Sun and the Moon is very important in the chart, for it determines how comfortable we are with ourselves. The Sun represents the physical father and how he feels about himself at the time of our birth, and the Moon represents the physical mother and how she feels. These two positions in our chart will tell how our development has been influenced in terms of the male and female polarities (see Section I, Chapter 3 for further details). The Sun also represents the essential spirit, the life drive in an individual. The Moon not only houses the spirit (our physical manifestation), but symbolizes our capacity to respond emotionally to influences both inside and outside the self: the interrelationship between the

Sun and Moon fixes our own personal pattern—it establishes the sense of self we have, how comfortable we are being "me."

The parental image is important to our development, for we get a concept of mind and authority from Dad and a concept of feeling and caring from Mom. In real life our parents may not be able to provide the image that is called for in the psyche. The image of Mom and Dad in the psyche teaches us how to combine the masculine and feminine principles. These two energies meld together and cause us to feel either comfortable or uncomfortable with the inner self. If we are lucky enough to be born with easy aspects between the Sun and the Moon, we feel comfortable with our ideas and emotional reactions to them. If not, we have to learn how to become comfortable by overcoming the squares and oppositions, by developing perspective, and by freeing ourselves from the past, from the bonds that keep us miserable. The concept of inner peace comes from the Sun–Moon relationship. If we don't have it at birth, we can develop it by attaining consciousness.

The Moon represents how we feel about the world, how we respond to every life situation thrown at us, our response to the neighborhood, our response to our loved ones, our children, our dearest possessions. The house placement is important, for it indicates where feelings are apt to be overemphasized. Our emotional responses can be a weak point when the life activities represented by a certain house are handled only from an emotional level and not from a rational point as well.

For example, the Moon in the first house combines the house symbol for the body (the first house) with the planetary symbol for the body (the Moon), and this person is both physically and intuitively sensitive. People with this Moon placement have usually built a tough exterior to cover their sensitivity by the time they are twenty years old. In early childhood, they were so sensitive to their surroundings and the people with whom they associated, that they had to become more self-protective than the rest of us (they wouldn't have made it past third grade if they hadn't!). They are highly intuitive, psychic if you will, sometimes a bit paranoid, because they are so sensitive to the vibrations around them. They respond to the world in a very personal way and may be considered selfish. But they aren't really. It's difficult for them to understand the editorial "you" for they respond personally to every life situation. When they are told about a friend's illness, they feel it too. As they begin to understand their overly personal response, they can alter it a bit and learn to stop reacting so intensely. When we know people with a first house Moon, we should try to be more considerate when presenting information to them, for they tend to overreact. A person with a fifth house Moon will not react the same way, even though the Moon sign may be the same. Rather, the excessive emotional response will be directed toward creative endeavors, children, lovers and the emotional life.

The Moon's aspects show the effect of the mother on the child, and the effect of life in general on the child's mother. When the Moon is afflicted, the person comes from a difficult childhood environment; it can give a sense of emotional bleakness or a lack of joy in the childhood.

Usually, people with extremely difficult childhoods block their memories, retaining only what was pleasant and forgetting any experience that they can't handle emotionally. I recently talked with a client who couldn't remember any childhood experience before the age of ten. She underwent hypnosis and, after several sessions, became aware of the fact that she had been raped by her father. Hypnosis revealed the unpleasant memory for her. She also learned it had been blocked after she discussed the incident with her mother, who had refused to accept her story and told the child to stop imagining. My client understood, as an adult, how hard it may have been for her mother to accept such information. The mother had three children and was in the hospital giving birth to the fourth when the rape occurred. After hypnosis she understood her "unreasonable" fears about sexuality. When a client has a background like this, therapy can be a great help—for the emotional reaction must be worked through before the emotional life can be lived with any real comfort.

The day, month and year of "Sybil's" birth is presented in the book by the same name (by F.R. Schreiber, Warner books, 1974). The solar chart shows several probable afflictions to the Moon. Because her mother couldn't cope with the environment, she abused Sybil. And because Sybil couldn't cope with her mother's cruelties, she developed sixteen different personalities. Our unpleasant aspects doubtless will not cause the miseries that Sybil endured. However, we tend to avoid looking at uncomfortable aspects to the Moon, for we may see more of what really went on in the early environment than we want to discuss, or perhaps face. Whether a child is exposed to physical or emotional abuse, the end result is similar—the emotions become blocked. The person born with an afflicted Moon has undergone emotional pain and trauma early in the life, and those hurts will be taken into the adult environment on a subconscious level. They keep us from being warmly emotional and spontaneous, for they create various complexes. Working through these blocks helps us to have better emotional experiences in the future. We can burst forth from our emotional blocks (the emotional bondage created by family experience), much like the butterfly bursts forth from its cocoon, to become conscious and beautiful. The Moon afflictions should be understood, worked through and let go so we can be free.

MOON–SUN ASPECTS

See Chapter 1 in this section.

MOON–MERCURY ASPECTS

Any tie between these two planets emphasizes the need to express the emotional self, to discuss personal emotional reactions and requirements. It can indicate a person who goes into emotional tizzies—babbling on about every reaction to life. When the hard aspects occur, the energy can be used creatively in the subliminal sense, for the emotional and communicational blocks force the individual to express feelings in diverse ways.

The Moon represents our mother—how she physically reacted to us. Mercury indicates how we communicate. Ties between the two planets can indicate a close relationship with the mother, an ability to share emotions with her. It suggests she was influential in the development of the ability (or inability) to communicate.

MOON–MERCURY CONJUNCTION. This conjunction indicates a person who talks a lot about feelings, one who is interested in communicating what he feels, and one who talks when he is emotionally involved. The reaction to life experience will come from the sign in which the conjunction takes place. For example, if the Moon and Mercury are in Scorpio, the person will feel strongly about transforming and regenerating people; it will be a regular topic of discussion. On the immature side, the Scorpio Moon will have difficulty forgetting a slight or a hurt and might respond to hurt feelings by zinging people. Because the conjunction takes place in Scorpio, hurt feelings may be responded to with harshness. The Moon in Scorpio indicates a mother who (during the native's formative years) feels unsure of herself, who controls her environment, who perhaps feels unwanted in her marriage situation. The native will feel emotionally rejected, and may therefore be emotionally defensive for fear of the rejection that he assumes will take place. "I'll reject you before you have a chance to leave me!" may be the key phrase here in emotional relationships.

The same conjunction taking place in Capricorn will be very different. The Moon in Capricorn indicates a traditional type of mother, one who is austere, and perhaps cold and harsh when she deals with those around her. Children born with a Capricorn Moon want to be in control of their emotional involvements; they feel uncomfortable when they have a "crush" on someone; they don't like the spontaneity of emotional reactions, and they like well-ordered emotional lives. They respond to the qualities of Capricorn, admiring traditional things, enjoying the more traditional forms of entertainment, etc. This type will communicate with others in a traditional manner and will express feelings and reactions in a more traditional way than the conjunction in Scorpio.

The conjunction can indicate a closeness to the mother and an ability to communicate with her, unless the conjunction is afflicted by other planets. This person is a "gut-reactor."

MOON–MERCURY SEXTILE. The sextile aspect indicates talent. The Moon in sextile to Mercury indicates a person who can develop talents that combine the art of communication with feeling, subjective experience. Emotional reactions can easily be discussed, for the mother teaches this child how to communicate feelings early on. In the area of relationships, this aspect is obviously helpful. As far as career is concerned, the tie between the intuitive-feeling process, represented by the Moon, and the mental processes and ability to communicate, represented by Mercury, can help this individual communicate in a nurturing, responsive manner. This aspect may be wasted in pleasant conversation if not trained properly.

MOON–MERCURY SQUARE. This configuration indicates a child who grows up in an atmosphere where his mother doesn't discuss her feelings. She has great difficulty talking about herself, her needs, her wants in life. When she does discuss her needs, she usually explodes after she has taken all the pressure she can handle, so the child and the rest of the family are forced to cope with her venom and anger. The child imitates what he sees, so he may grow to be an adult who cannot easily express opinions or feelings. This person will have difficulty in emotional relationships because he can't share his feelings, can't talk about reactions easily. Explosions occur when he can't stand any more emotional pressure, but he doesn't discuss emotional upsets or hurt feelings under the boiling point. The scenes can be unpleasant and the aspect can cause one to feel guilty, for the explosion is unplanned. This person may go from lover to lover for he doesn't feel he's being understood. The problem with this type is he doesn't share his feelings, hurts and responses until he becomes excessively negative. Anger is healthy, but it should be expressed as each little hurt occurs so that it doesn't come out representing five years of hurt feelings. People with this aspect also don't communicate easily with their mothers.

The signs in which the square takes place gives a good idea of how the energy works. A Cancer Moon square Mercury in Aries usually is supersensitive and possessive; it reacts to every feeling situation in an overly sensitive and emotional manner. Mercury in Aries talks intellectually, rationally, idealistically. When one *talks* sensibly but *reacts* intuitively or possessively to every life situation, neither the Aries energy nor the Cancer energy is being satisfied. The Mercury tries harder and harder to be rational; the Moon in Cancer feels more and more suppressed. If the Sun is also in Aries, one may be quite angry with oneself, for the emotional nature is unpredictable. Inner peace is not easily achieved.

I met an Aries Sun square Moon in Cancer person who was so self-conscious about being rational that she covered her face every time she laughed spontaneously, as if to hide the reaction. This happens when the divergent energy is not understood. When it is understood, the Mercury in Aries can become the spokesman for the Cancer feelings—the concept of sensitivity can be expressed as well as the possessive needs, the need for sensitivity and the need for emotional security. Then the Moon won't be "making a liar" out of Mercury!

MOON–MERCURY TRINE. The trine indicates a mother who easily communicates her feelings and is interested in dealing with her child. This produces an adult who enjoys relating, who enjoys the social graces and sharing both thoughts and feelings. It bestows an intuitive creativity, an interest in expressing the emotional self.

However, this aspect can be outweighed by afflictions from stronger planets to the Moon. For example, if Mercury trines the Moon but Saturn squares it, the Saturn aspect will be the stronger one, especially in the early years. This type of combination will indicate the child had a good talking relationship with the mother, but not with the father.

MOON–MERCURY OPPOSITION. This aspect indicates a difficulty in expressing feelings that is similar to that of the square. The opposition tends to make these people feel that they must give up either communicating or feeling. The mother figure was a person who vacillated between reacting and talking, and not. There may be a lack of honest self-expression when this occurs, for these people assume that a compromise is necessary.

For example, consider the Moon in Aries and Mercury in Libra. Moon in Aries is an emotional idealist; one who responds quickly to ideals, to the underdog; one who gets easily angered, who is protective of the one he loves, who is opinionated and basically very honest. Mercury in Libra wants to placate everyone with words, to soothe an unpleasant scene, to be diplomatic in tense situations. With this opposition, the person is caught between the qualities of the two signs; the idealism and straightforwardness of Aries on the one hand, and the diplomatic tendencies of Libra on the other. In order to work this through, the owner has to understand the qualities of both Aries and Libra and decide how he wishes to manifest the energy.

If the opposition is owned by a woman, she may not be open in her romantic relationships because she has difficulty expressing herself. She doesn't easily share her emotions because Mother didn't share hers. This type of woman may blame her unhappy marriages or love affairs on the men she chooses, yet she chooses men who won't listen to her or men she won't communicate with, for she never saw her mother do it well. (When we don't see our parents relating emotionally, we don't know how to do it ourselves unless we consciously make a commitment to learn.)

A man with a Moon–Mercury opposition will not assume that he can easily share his feelings with women. Because his mother periodically burst forth in anger, he will expect any woman he loves to do the same—"Don't all women?" he asks. He may assume that women are unreasonable, or he may assume that he can't really share his feelings with anyone because they won't listen. He may not feel comfortable talking about his emotional reactions since he did not see it done in his childhood environment.

MOON–MERCURY QUINCUNX. Any quincunx in the chart shows strain. The strain is not a big tense feeling like the square or opposition, but it is worrisome. Because the strain is subtle, or gnawing, it eventually affects the health. When Mercury doesn't express the feelings of the Moon, the internal self is not at peace. The qualities of the signs need to be understood; one tends to favor one sign and suppress the other, but both qualities need to find expression.

MOON–VENUS ASPECTS

These aspects are important in diagnosing the relationship to the mother. The Moon represents the physical mother and how she reacted to life when the child's personality was forming. Her response to life will influence the child's. Her attitudes will be picked up by the child and applied to the concepts of caring and nurturing. The sign the Moon is in will tell *how* the mother responded. Venus symbolizes the *psychological* effect of the mother: that is, how she affected the child's psyche. Venus also symbolizes the concept of love and the type of affection that the person is willing to give and receive. Attitudes toward women, motherhood, the feminine biological system, the appreciation of affection, even fears about childbirth and the general status of women, can all be determined by examining the signs and aspects involved with these planets. Any unpleasant training from the early childhood experience can be reprogrammed once the original program has been understood. For a female, it's important to understand the interrelationship between these planets in order for her to develop a good sense of what "woman" is; for a male, in order to develop healthy relationships with women he must first understand the feminine influence in his own personality.

MOON–VENUS CONJUNCTION. If the Moon represents the emotional reaction to life and love, and Venus indicates the ability to appreciate love and beauty, the interaction between these two planets is very important in terms of emotional relationships. Venus can also represent the psychological impact of the mother on the child's psyche. The Moon represents the mother in a physical sense. When these two planets are conjunct, the person has an overwhelming tie to the mother that may seem insurmountable. In order for this person to break away from the family and mother ties, he must go through many more internal changes than the rest of us.

This aspect in a woman's chart represents the daughter who can't leave Mommy, who goes into a marriage and lives on the next block and talks to Mommy on the phone every day. Or, the girl who can't have a love relationship inasmuch as she can't share herself with another person because the ties to her mother are too strong. If the rest of the chart agrees, this aspect may indicate a homosexual female. Often, the lady she falls in love with is fifteen to twenty years older than she, since she may be looking for a mother substitute. She has difficulty considering the idea that she may be tied to Mother in some kind of incestuous manner.

We usually consider incest in terms of the opposite sex—the daughter is in love with her father, etc.; but we have trouble diagnosing when the daughter is too close to her mother. Often these desires are not faced on a conscious level, for they are socially unacceptable. If a woman is homosexual and the rest of the chart doesn't look like she has reason to be, this is one aspect that may help to find the key to *why* she is the way she is. However, when Venus conjuncts the Moon, it's difficult to talk to her about her relationship with her mother. She doesn't want to hear anything negative about Mom. Even if the rest of the chart shows difficult family influences, perhaps even an abusive childhood, she will defend her mother until the end.

Often, these children have been hurt more by the mother than the father, yet they see the father as the reason for all their failures. It's a hard aspect to work through, and for an astrologer it indicates a difficult client. This aspect should be approached with tact, gentleness, and diplomacy by the astrologer. If this conjunction carries other hard aspects, the client may be helped by entering therapy of some kind; it is not an easy aspect to handle in one counseling session.

When a man has a Moon–Venus conjunction, the effect of the physical and the psychological mother influence is overpowering. This man is emotionally close to his mother—usually too close—and it can manifest in many ways. Sometimes it indicates a love-hate polarity with the mother; the son may literally hate or love her. If the man is father dominated, he may have a lot of guilt about his feelings toward his mother. If he is mother dominated, he may be angry with her, or estranged from her, or he may be completely possessed by her.

For example, a Virgo male with Venus conjunct the Moon will either hate his mother or, on a subconscious level, feel so close to her that he cannot have sex with another woman. The Taurus male also doesn't react to this conjunction easily. He will feel somewhat guilty about sex, and the guilt can manifest in several ways: it can bring confusion regarding love and sex and motherhood, so that he grows up to be homosexual; subconsciously there may be guilt about being unfaithful to Mommy, which can manifest in feeling guilty about heterosexual relationships, or it may drive him toward the "freedom" of homosexuality; the Oedipal problems may occur, for he may be physically attracted on a subconscious level to his mother. In the case of the Taurus male, the quandary often stems from a confusion between affection and sexuality; both seem mingled together and are not easily separated in the mind of a child. A grown man may overreact to the feelings stirred up by the mother image and may therefore try to cut her out of his life. The other aspects to the Moon and Venus have to be taken into consideration when reading this aspect.

Once the mother ties are recognized, the individual can begin to use the energy another way. Venus conjunct the Moon can be used to understand how we appreciate and respond in love situations. The energy of the sign can be used constructively for our appreciation of love (Venus) and our feeling responses (Moon) can work together because they are in the same sign. The blind spots will be caused by an overreaction to the influence of the mother. Again, therapy can be helpful in working through the unpleasant ties in order to free the constructive possibilities. We are not meant to remain as a child tied to our mother forever. The Moon represents our feelings and Venus indicates how we appreciate love. We can separate these qualities from the mother in a physical sense and begin to listen to our own responses.

MOON–VENUS SEXTILE. This aspect indicates a mother who had a healthy psychological impact on the native. These people are able to enter the adult community without heavy relating problems. They will go through the ordinary pains connected with growing and maturing, but the ability to love and to appreciate love is a natural asset. This aspect indicates an ability to appreciate creativity, to appreciate the arts, the artistic community, to express artistically through and with the emotional self.

The problem in expressing artistically, however, comes when endurance becomes necessary—often the great artist is emotionally blocked, being unable to give or receive any other way than through his or her work—and the greatest artists come from difficult emotional backgrounds. The sextile indicates individuals who are capable of giving and receiving love in a personal way rather than sublimating, so they may not produce as much as one might think.

MOON–VENUS SQUARE. The Moon represents the physical mother and how she reacts to her life at the time of our birth, and how she reacts to us emotionally. Venus represents the psychological effect of the mother's concepts of femininity and love that is retained in our psyche. The square between these planets represents emotional stress absorbed in the childhood. This square indicates excessive feelings of resentment regarding the biological role women are forced to play; it therefore indicates that the mother had certain resentments about the responsibilities of motherhood when this child was born. She may have grown out of these feelings, she may have adjusted to the role of motherhood later on in the marriage. But when this child was born, the mother passed on a feeling that women had to justify or prove their existence, that a woman was a second-class citizen.

When this aspect occurs in a woman's chart, it often indicates a deep-rooted feeling of insecurity about her femininity, feelings of insecurity about motherhood, feelings of resentment about the biological role that women must play. The resentment is directed toward the dedication that is deemed necessary in order to raise children, for a woman with this aspect doesn't like the drudgery involved in caring for children. Women with this aspect may not marry because they are often afraid to admit that they don't want children of their own. They may not feel that they are really womanly or feminine; they resent the freedom they think men have; sometimes they function on a homosexual level in order to avoid pregnancy. If they have little exposure to the concept of femininity on any level these women may even be prone to hysterectomy, for they are *subconsciously* willing to give up the physical symbols of femininity. It's very difficult to get mature women to talk freely about this aspect because our culture programs all women to "enjoy" motherhood. Until recent years, if a woman didn't want children, we thought there was something wrong with her. Until now, a woman who didn't want children had to avoid discussing her feelings about the matter; she simply would avoid marriage, for example. She might have dated only noneligible ne'er-do-wells, enabling her to "righteously" avoid marriage, since it makes no sense to marry an alcoholic, a drug addict or an unemployable. (Her friends and family merely deplored her taste in men!)

There are many ways this aspect can defeat the feminine function. A woman may fall in love with a married man, but the relationship obviously cannot be consummated with children. Or, she may avoid all relationships. Or, she may function on a homosexual level; everyone is so busy diagnosing her "homosexual problem" that they never look into the underlying cause—a fear of motherhood, a rejection of the biological role.* Women who have children in spite of this aspect are often pushed into motherhood by the social pressures engendered by friends and family. They seldom enjoy the early years of motherhood and resent not being free to have a career. Sometimes this resentment is taken out on her children. How much resentment may be directed toward her children will be shown by the other Moon or Venus aspects in their charts. This aspect is seldom discussed with her children, for she often feels guilty about her attitude toward them and later pretends that she "loved" her children always.

If the woman with the Moon–Venus square understands that she is afraid of motherhood, as well as the feminine side of her nature, she can then begin to consciously open up to allow herself to examine the "woman" experience. A "woman" doesn't have to be our mother's con-

---

*In view of recent debates regarding homosexuality, I would like to mention that I feel homosexuality can be diagnosed from a chart, but that reasons for homosexual behavior can vary greatly. Not all homosexual women are avoiding motherhood. Determining homosexual behavior is at least as complicated as determining heterosexual behavior. The subject is too vast to be discussed with any clarity here.

cept of womanhood—especially in today's culture. Today's woman is free to explore her femininity; literature is available about the women's movement, the mythology of woman, the positions held by women in ancient religions, the female goddesses and the emergence of women-consciousness.* These doors are closed to her if she cannot first accept that there is a problem to be worked out. Many women think that if they recognize Mom's problem, they have to hate her for it. As we mature and as we begin to experience our own life crises, we begin to understand that we, too, may have a child in the middle of a growth cycle and that our growing pains will affect our child as well. When we understand this, we can no longer hate a mother who gave all she was capable of, for she could give only what she knew. If we consider that a chart can be read five minutes after birth, then maybe there's some karma here. Perhaps both the child and the mother learn something from their relationship to each other.

The male born with Venus square the Moon has a different problem because he is a man and not a woman. His mother didn't like her biological role, she resented being stuck with diapers and the two A.M. feedings, and she probably didn't get enough understanding or help from her husband when this child was born. The mother may have given up all hope of a much wanted career.

The male with this aspect has a different dilemma than the female who has it, for he will have to make peace with the concept of his emotional worth, or his values regarding women, or both. When he grows up, the chances are he won't expect a woman to be in his corner, and he may have a closed attitude about the possibilities of any love relationship. If his Moon is in Taurus squared by Venus in Leo, for example, he responds like a Taurus—sensually, emotionally. The Venus in Leo says that one should be respectable, one should love a woman that the world (or the community) will approve. So the battle is on between caring for a woman he likes versus marrying one who is more socially acceptable. He is affected by his mother's lack of respect for "womanhood" in general. The square indicates his Mom didn't like or respect other women, and if she's a woman and *she* didn't like women, why should he?

His image of woman is not healthy. He may dislike his mother intensely, for if Venus indicates the psychological influence of his mother, the square indicates that the influence was not constructive. Venus (the concept of love) works against (square) his normal emotional responses (Moon). He is apt to be confused about love situations. In order to further understand the possibilities of this particular configuration, look at the other aspects to Venus, the Moon and Mars. This will give a picture of the odds as to how he will choose to express himself emotionally. This can be

---

*I recommend the books by M. Esther Harding—*The Way of All Women, Women's Mysteries, Psychic Energy.* See Bibliography.

the chart of a man who chooses to express himself homosexually because he really dislikes his mother as well as women in general. This may be a man who overreacts whenever he has contact with women. This aspect can indicate a man who doesn't appreciate (Venus) his own feeling nature (Moon).

MOON–VENUS TRINE. This aspect indicates a mother who was able to give this person a sense of emotional self. The emotional needs will be determined by the signs involved in the trine. Whether or not the person *values* this gift will be shown by the Sun sign. If the power parent is the father, the individual will not value the mother's gift as much as if the power parent were the mother. This energy, in any case, can be drawn upon in later life once this person understands the other configurations in the chart.

Other aspects to the Moon may cause emotional turmoil; but once that conflict is resolved, the Moon–Venus trine indicates that any work done to establish emotional awareness will be rewarded. If the chart doesn't have Sun or Moon afflictions, this aspect will help a child to become a warm and emotionally responsive person. The mother of this child enjoyed being a woman, she didn't resent her role of mother. This doesn't necessarily mean that the mother had a happy marriage, only that she did not resent being a mother.

MOON–VENUS OPPOSITION. This aspect is analogous to the square. There is a dichotomy between the physical mother and the psychological effect that she has on the child. There is sometimes a loss of the mother, or of some aspect of the mother's love. Sometimes the child spends time with a grandparent or an aunt in the early years, for the mother may be busy doing something else, or she may be ill, etc.

This aspect works differently in the chart of a woman than in the chart of a man. A woman will be forced to consider her own concept of self-worth as a woman. A man will have to cope with his relation to his anima and how that relationship affects his attitudes toward the women in his life.

The opposition, as does the square, indicates the problems a woman has accepting her biological role: it indicates a susceptibility to women's diseases (hysterectomy or uterine/ovarian problems that can occur in later life). Metaphysically, these types of illnesses can be avoided if she works consciously to develop a sense of self-worth as a woman. If she comes from a generation that faced social pressures regarding marriage and children, she may be difficult to counsel because she may not want to face the fact that she did not or does not enjoy the role of mother. She may often relate better to her children after they are grown. If a young woman wants to work with this aspect, she must be willing to cope with her fear of being abandoned, for many times the Venus–Moon afflictions occur in charts of children raised by mothers who were abandoned by their men, or who were married to irresponsible men and, therefore, emotionally abandoned. The child carries a subconscious memory which produces a fear that she may be abandoned if she becomes pregnant. Such women seldom encourage relationships with men which might result in pregnancy. I've seen this aspect work in charts of women who married men with children from a previous marriage. A woman may seek a man who has gained custody of his children by a previous marriage, since a man who has custody of his children obviously cares enough about children to help raise any she may have by him. When these women avoid the biological role, they sometimes marry much older men who are not likely to want children. Or, they pick men who have had children by other women; they can then become honorary mothers. They may adopt children so that they don't have to go through the birth trauma.

A man with Venus opposing the Moon has been affected emotionally in an adverse manner by his mother's influence in his early childhood. His feeling responses are inhibited because his mother pushed something on him when he was very young. What that "something" was varies from family to family. Venus indicates the psychological influence of the mother, so this is the planet to diagnose first since it functions on a more subconscious level.

For example, the Moon in Capricorn and Venus in Cancer: the Capricorn Moon indicates a mother who was serious and traditional, and who attempted to control the family. She was austere and apprehensive of spontaneity, for the sign Capricorn indicates controlled reactions. Venus in Cancer indicates the concept of love that the mother passed on to the child. It indicates a person who wants a warm, emotional relationship. Venus here wants to own the loved one; it is jealous of sharing the loved one and indicates the sensitive lover. But the opposition causes an internal problem: the Moon sign wants to be in control of emotions, the Venus sign wants to be spontaneous. The Moon wants to be serious and traditional (a traditional response to love would be to marry the one loved, not live together); it wants to dedicate itself to the person to whom it's committed. Venus in Cancer wants to be sensitive, wants to rant and rave about whatever the concern is at the moment, wants to be jealous of any contact that the loved one has with the outside world. People with the Moon–Venus opposition don't really believe they will ever have what they want from a love relationship. In order to satisfy their own emotional expectations, they feel they must compromise themselves. This setup indicates a man who wants a wife but who also wants to be free to gad about, but his wife won't let him. Or a woman who wants a stable marriage *and* a career, but the only man she can find to love wants her at home and won't allow her to pursue the career she so desperately longs for. The compromise can be worked out, for the opposition is an easier aspect to work through than the square. The square always operates in excess, while the opposition temporizes the opposite sign. The cure requires acknowledgement of the needs of both sides of the wheel. In this case, the Cancer-Capricorn opposition compromises tradition and warmth, control versus spontaneity, rationality versus intuition.

The man with the Venus–Moon opposition expects that relationships must be compromised; he expects that he can't satisfy his feelings in a relationship with a woman and secretly resents his mother for making him feel this way. After the age of thirty, the compromise can be more easily worked out from a conscious point.

Emotionally, both the male and female with this opposition have difficulty in relationships. Until the opposition is understood, the female will bring her insecurity about her femininity into her relationships. She will defend her womanhood to the 'nth degree. One such woman criticized me for making a cup of coffee for a male friend. "He can do it himself, you're not a waitress!" she snarled. I laughed and asked her to think a bit. "If I can make a cup of coffee for you—my lady friend—why can't I make a cup of coffee for him? I like him, too!" We only become defensive of something we don't possess, for when we know we have it (perhaps a sense of self-worth), we don't need to attack others to defend our position.

This aspect may lend to women a proclivity toward picking lovers who really don't like women; lovers who may have had severe problems with mother as well. When a woman with this opposition decides she is no longer a second-class citizen, she will choose a different type of man. When men haven't solved the mother-hate problem, they usually pass on their injurious feelings to the wife or girlfriend.

The male with this aspect is uncomfortable on two counts. He doesn't really like his own emotional nature; he doesn't really like his mother, and he therefore doesn't really feel comfortable with women. This dislike of women can manifest in homosexuality or in the abusive treatment of women. In more sensitive souls it can indicate a man who must feel totally "on top of" an emotional involvement, fearing the female take-over that he expects to happen at any moment. This can produce the male chauvinist, the guy who won't be understanding of his wife, who may treat her as though she were "the enemy."

His emotional nature makes him feel uneasy as well, but this is an internal problem. For example, Moon in Aries opposing Venus in Libra. He responds aggressively and he responds to idealistic ideas and a sense of fair play. Yet he wants to be a member of an elite group (Venus in Libra). He appreciates the art and beauty of Libran qualities. Aggressive feelings are not diplomatic. Fairness and idealism cannot be present when one wants membership in an exclusive club, since exclusivity is seldom fair! The dilemma in his emotional nature causes inner tension. It's painful, but with conscious understanding comes a release from the pain.

MOON–VENUS QUINCUNX. This aspect implies a strain. Again, the quincunx always indicates health problems since it causes a strain to take place in the individual's psyche, but the stress is not as noticeable as with the square. It causes the person to "grit his teeth and bear it" rather than talk about it or handle the problem. The strain can be worked out intellectually. If Venus indicates what we want from a relationship, what we want in life, and what we appreciate as far as the arts are concerned, as far as love is concerned, then the conflict is easy to diagnose.

For example, Moon in Cancer quincunx Venus in Sagittarius suggests sensitive emotional needs; there is a need to nurture, mother, develop intuition; there is spontaneity, and excess of feeling attributed to the Moon. Venus in Sagittarius wants to be free. How can one be free if one is mothering everyone in sight? How can one be nurturing (Cancer) if one also wants to be a revolutionary (Sagittarius)? The conflict can be resolved by putting certain qualities to work in certain situations and other qualities to work in others.

MOON–MARS ASPECTS

The Moon represents the physical mother in an individual's early childhood environment. The child imitates her emotional reactions to life, and develops according to the Moon sign and aspects. Mars indicates how the child acts physically, how it will react to external stimulii, what kind of action will be taken whenever an attempt is made to start something new. Mars can be used to diagnose how a person will function sexually as an adult. The interaction between Mars and the Moon can help us to understand how an individual will act in regard to emotional issues. The Moon represents the physical body, and Mars aspects to the Moon can indicate how an individual will take action to protect his body, to care for it. Sexual conflicts can come from Moon–Mars aspects, for the aspects and signs will tell the story of emotional needs that may not conform with a particular sex drive. In order to really understand the emotional/sexual needs, Venus should be considered in relation to the Mars and Moon aspects. The aspects and signs involved in these three planets will tell the story of the emotional life.

MOON–MARS CONJUNCTION. The Moon represents the physical body; the physical mother of the early childhood years; the emotional nature of an individual and his responses to life experience. Mars indicates how one acts, how one expresses sexuality.

The early childhood experience reflects an emotional mother; a mother who nursed her hurts, who reacted to her husband and children when her feelings were hurt. This child learns to respond in a similar way. The adult with this conjunction will be easy to anger, will act on hurt feelings, will act out emotional upsets rather than thinking them out. He may be seen as self-destructive because he seldom considers his own safety while in the midst of an emotional trauma. As he matures, and as he experiences physical pain because of his emotional reactions, he will eventually learn to think before he acts, but this behavior will be *learned*.

The conjunction can indicate a person who has a great deal of anger to cope with. He either explodes and takes out his anger on someone else, or he implodes and takes out his anger on himself. The conjunction can operate either explosively, implosively, or both ways. Rather than suppressing the anger, *it is more important to understand it*—to allow oneself time to work through it (writing letters that aren't mailed, sitting on reactions for several days prior to doing anything about a situation, getting a perspective from someone else) in order to learn how to channel the energy. Mars energy is creative, anger is merely the undisciplined tip of the iceberg.

The conjunction will express differently in each sign. In diagnosing the energy, the Mars energy will intensify the sign qualities of the Moon. When the supersensitivity is understood, when the overreaction to the environment is understood, this energy can be used creatively.

MOON–MARS SEXTILE. The sextile indicate a mother influence that was constructive to this person. The action taken by the mother harmonized with her emotional needs. This person therefore will be able to cope with emotional needs and sexuality in a constructive manner. The Moon represents the emotional response-ability, and the Mars sextile indicates that action taken will complement the emotional nature. This person is drawn to healthy, constructive relationships. The chances are he will enjoy his work as well, for he cares (Moon) about what he does (Mars).

MOON–MARS SQUARE. Here the influence of the mother was not particularly helpful to the child in the development of healthy emotional reactions. The child will have to learn to do this as an adult. The Moon represents the emotions, Mars represents action, the square aspect represents excessive or unconstructive use of energy. In keyword language it reads "I act (Mars) against (square) my body (Moon);" "I act (Mars) against (square) my emotional needs (Moon)." Sexually it indicates "I sex (Mars) people against (square) my emotional needs (Moon)." Sexual relationships may not be emotionally fulfilling.

This person has similar traits to those of the Moon–Mars conjunction or opposition, for the action taken often stems from an overly emotional response to a situation. It may be that the person with this square is exposed to physical violence or to violent explosions of temper in the childhood years. The mother may be emotionally distraught for reasons known only to her. She may be living a life that is either uncomfortable or unhappy. The child emulates this emotional response for he knows no other.

Because Mars (as well as the sign of Aries) indicates anger, the person with this aspect is easily angered. He can react with anger and violence to unpleasant situations he encounters; or he may suppress his anger and implode, causing much internal stress and tension. Implosive energy causes weight problems and other delicate health problems to manifest. The emotional patterns need to be examined, for this person is apt to pick partners who are emotionally ungratifying or he may even become emotionally involved with violent types of people. (It seems that when there are hard aspects between the Moon and Mars and the individual is not physically violent himself, he chooses a partner who is.) A woman may express the Moon–Mars square by choosing to live with a man who beats her; a man with the same aspect might beat his wife and children. Both the male and the female may choose a partner who doesn't satisfy their emotional needs.

For example, the Moon in Leo square Mars in Taurus: the sexual needs of the individual are governed by Taurus (it is sensual, selfish, self-gratifying), and there is a strong physical need for sexual expression. Moon in Leo wants respect and approval. A woman with a Leo Moon may find a gratifying lover but one who doesn't respect her enough. Or he doesn't earn the respect of her community. A man with the same configuration may meet a woman he adores and respects, a woman who approves of him, who is supportive of him—but she isn't sexually satisfying for him. He can't get the physical love that he wants or needs.

The excess of this aspect tends to make one angry, and the anger is eventually vented on the loved one. One client with Moon in Leo square Mars in Taurus has had several affairs. She married a man she didn't love but who was socially acceptable and emotionally good to her, but the sex wasn't there. She left him and had an affair with a man because the sex was great, but her family and friends didn't approve (and with good reason). She is now attempting to have both—to find a relationship that is emotionally satisfying, sexually enjoyable, shared with a mature individual. This client is working with a Moon–Mars square and another self-worth problem which is shown elsewhere in the chart.

MOON–MARS TRINE. The mother influence on this individual is a healthy one. If the child is mother-dominated, or has a chart so aspected that he can accept what the mother has to offer, he grows to be an adult who can receive emotional relationships in a positive manner. He is receptive emotionally, he enjoys relationships, and looks for healthy emotional involvements. He is that lucky person who picks a lover who is good for him!

He is able to participate emotionally in the work he does, enjoys the interaction between fellow employees, and participates in life from a full viewpoint. Action taken will support his emotional needs. Creative action will be full of joy. Because his emotional and sexual needs are easily expressed, he can be supportive and helpful to those he loves.

MOON–MARS OPPOSITION. The key here is compromise. Any opposition indicates a compromise to be made, and the Mars–Moon opposition indicates that action taken may be compromised because of the emotional reaction to what is being done. The mother of this individual feels sexuality is restricting, that her personal needs are different from her professional needs and that she can't have both. She has difficulty expressing her emotional needs, and she may have violent emotional outbursts. Action taken may be ill-planned or have unhealthy results. She may make foolish decisions based on hurt feelings. The child sees this reaction to life as ''normal.''

The Mars placement indicates how we act, how we develop our career, how we function sexually. The Moon indicates our emotional needs, our emotional responses. The conflict of the opposition is expressed as a compromise between the professional action at the expense of personal relationships or vice versa. Or the sex drive (much like the Mars square) is at odds with the emotional needs. Consider the opposition between Moon in Leo, Mars in Aquarius. Mars here is unconventional, interested in the unorthodox and an open or experimental sexuality. The Moon in Leo looks for approval, wants proper respect and an idealistic love relationship. The Mars acts erratically and may pick an unusual type of lover, one who may not play Sir Galahad to the Moon or one who may not be approved of by friends and family. What happens if the Mars in Aquarius is too open sexually, of if the sexual needs are disapproved of by the partner—how will the Leo Moon react to this?

People born with a Mars–Moon opposition may compromise several ways. The work (Mars) may be separated from the emotional life (Moon); the lover may satisfy the sexual needs (Mars) but not the emotional/affectional needs (Moon); they may choose a partner who shares affection (Moon) but is sexually unsatisfying (Mars); an overreaction to emotional needs may take place; the energy can express in violence.

Men and women use this energy differently. A man with the opposition may take out his anger on women; a woman with the opposition may take out her anger on her self-regard as a woman by becoming involved in basically unhealthy relationships. Both can be physically violent or draw physical violence to them in some way.

The aspect causes so much emotional sensitivity that much time can be wasted blowing minor issues out of proportion. The misuse of energy takes place because, as a child, this person saw no other approach to life. The energy can be rechanneled whenever the underlying causes are understood.

MOON–MARS QUINCUNX. Here the subtle argument between the emotional needs and the activity or sexual needs is harder to diagnose. The quincunx represents a strain similar to that of a nagging toothache, one that is not painful enough to go to a dentist about. The emotional needs, the emotional responses to universal energies and the love requirements are not fulfilled either by the action taken or the sexual expression chosen. The emotional needs may drive one to spend time with a person who is not sexually satisfactory; the sexual needs may drive one to spend time with someone who cannot fulfill the emotional needs, and the problem is often not discussed or even consciously faced. A hint of aggravation remains. If our actions (Mars) cause us grief, the aspect needs to be worked with. Both qualities of the signs need to find expression.

MOON–JUPITER ASPECTS

The Moon represents our physical body, how we respond to life around us, our need for affection, the mother as she responded in the early childhood relationship with us. Jupiter indicates how we open up, how we expand our consciousness. When Jupiter ties into the Moon, it indicates that a gut-level awareness will take place when something new is envisioned or learned, for the opening up will be received in a physical sense as well as in other ways. If Jupiter represents how we relate, its tie to the Moon will indicate how we relate to our emotional needs and reactions, how we relate to our physical body and its needs.

MOON–JUPITER CONJUNCTION. This conjunction often indicates someone who relates effusively in the manner described by the sign involved in the conjunction. The mother of a child with this aspect is indulgent; she indulges in emotional reactions, she indulges her body in some way. The child will too. This indicates a person who may have a close rleationship with the mother, who may stay close to her long after the other siblings have left home. This may be a person who indulges in the physical appetites and therefore overdoes in some way—too much food, alcohol, etc. This individual is open emotionally, open to feeling each new experience, open to relating how he feels to those he knows, open to sharing what he has.

This conjunction often denotes a generous emotional nature, and how the generosity will operate will be determined by the sign as well as the other aspects to the conjunction. This person may want to do so much for the mother that he never leaves home to develop a personal life.

MOON–JUPITER SEXTILE. The mother feels good about herself emotionally when this person is born, and provides her child with a healthy and warm atmosphere. The child learns to relate to others because he cares about them. He learns to relate his feelings to others in an open fashion. The aspect brings a sense of personal generosity, an ability to share emotional experience.

MOON–JUPITER SQUARE. This person is raised in an atmosphere where the mother does not relate to herself or her needs. She may be playing a role; playing the role of mother or wife first and being a "person" second. She doesn't express her emotional needs easily, and when she does, she probably overreacts or overrelates. She may not spend time doing anything for herself. Because of this, the child grows up assuming that people don't consider themselves when handling obligations, and this aspect can cause a disproportionate development of emotional needs.

People with this aspect may feel that consideration of emotional needs, needs for affection, a physical caring for the body, is an overindulgence. Consideration of these factors is not a part of their early childhood environment. So these individuals may jump into emotional involvements and then jump out; they may jump into a relationship without considering their own needs; they may feel guilty about asking for equal time; they may not understand what their emotional needs are. Often, needs for affection and caring are confused with sexuality. These people may burn the candle at both ends, for there is little regard for the physical needs. If Jupiter represents the way in which relating is handled, the square aspect indicates that the relating principle is at odds with the emotional development—responsibilities may be taken on without regard for the inner self.

This aspect can cause certain health problems to manifest because the diet may not be considered. The body may be overfed or fed food that it doesn't need; it may be wined and dined on rich foods that cause more harm than good. If reaching out is difficult (for Jupiter indicates how we reach out, how we open up to others) the difficulty may be handled by using alcohol or drugs. This individual may reach out one day and turn off the next without really understanding why, but Mom did it. Over- or underrelating must be curbed so that the excess caused by the square aspect can be channeled into healthy and productive relationships.

MOON-JUPITER TRINE. This aspect indicates the mother is a happy woman during the formative years of this child's life. She's able to share, to open up with her children as well as those who visit the family. The child is taught to cope with emotional needs, to relate to the feeling nature, to express the feelings and affections in a warmly generous manner. A mother-dominated child may pick up more of this energy from the mother, may place more value on the childhood environment than will a father-dominated child. In either case, this aspect gives generosity, effervescence, warmth, the ability to reach out to others, to share emotional responses, to share caring and affection. Because the aspect is easy, and because the energy flow is easy, it may not be appreciated and may be taken for granted by the individual.

MOON-JUPITER OPPOSITION. During the early childhood

experience of this person, the mother withdraws from him; she may not be relating her needs as a woman; she may feel that women's emotional needs are not considered by others. This child will pick up her attitude; and, like the square or the conjunction, he will be too involved with the mother for one reason or another. As an adult, he will have to learn how to relate to his personal emotional needs as well as to the needs of his body. There may be too little emphasis placed on personal needs and too much placed on those of others. Emotional responses are not easily shared, relationships may be considered from a point of compromise and tensions in these areas may be assuaged by an overindulgence in food or alcohol.

Relationships may be started with little consideration for the future; the career, friendships formed, or even love relationships may not be developed easily for there is a tendency to play a role. This can be the person who works hard at the wrong job, the person who has friends who don't really know him, the person who marries and has children with someone who never knows how he or she really feels.

For example, consider Jupiter in Taurus opposing the Moon in Scorpio. The emotional needs (Moon) are enormous, for the Scorpio Moon needs a lot of love and affection. This person needs affection, but may feel unwanted or unworthy in some way. The love needed will be the kind that includes a transformation, a growing process shared with another individual. Jupiter in Taurus can be materialistic, intensely practical and can relate in a sensual manner. Often, Jupiter in Taurus relates in a common sense manner, it seems to be practical. When the feelings are hurt, this individual may not handle the situation based on the feeling needs, but rather on the practical needs of the situation. For example, hurt feelings may not be discussed because it's more practical to worry about the kids. Or a person can become involved in only a sensual relationship, leaving the personal needs for self-transformation unsatisfied.

MOON–JUPITER QUINCUNX. The quincunx implies a strain, but one that is not intense enough to cause much action to take place. There is a vague discontent that occurs; the relating ability, the need to reach out, to open up, to expand the consciousness, is hampered by an emotional reaction to it. For example, Moon in Leo, Jupiter in Pisces: the person reaches out like a martyr or with sensitivity and compassion. The Moon in Leo wants to be properly respected, needs approval from others. When one relates to the underdog, how much respect does one get? Can one be approvable or respectable when one relates to those inferior to one? Is suffering (Pisces) approvable (Leo)? Both energies need to find expression in some way; perhaps the house placement will provide the key to the mystery.

It's important for this individual to learn to consider the real needs of the self. There are certain benefits from being selfish—''honest'' selfishness indicates a certain amount of sincerity. For example, when we really love ourselves, we are better able to share ourselves with another, for we are able to give more. A person who doesn't love himself cannot give nearly as much because he harbors resentment.

MOON–SATURN ASPECTS

The Moon indicates our emotional responses to the various aspects of life; it represents our physical mother during childhood; it indicates how we react emotionally to those close to us. Saturn symbolizes restriction, feelings of lack, inhibitions, attitudes of self-denial. It also indicates the impact of the father on the psyche. When these two planets interact with each other, they indicate the mother and her emotional reactions to her environment and how they are affected by the attitudes of the father during the native's formative years. Whenever there is a contact of the Moon and Saturn, the person feels that emotional reactions cannot or should not be displayed; that all authority figures (the father, other males introduced later in life, as well as any person in authority) can restrict and restrain the emotional nature.

Generally speaking, the hard aspects between Moon and Saturn can indicate a depressive influence for they bring on melancholia—these people tend to view life "through a glass darkly." The irony here is that in the natural zodiac, a natural opposition between the Moon (Cancer) and Saturn (Capricorn) takes place. Perhaps the Moon–Saturn aspects need to learn to express emotions in a constructive manner and that emotional involvements also include joy as well as the sorrow that is all too often found.

MOON–SATURN CONJUNCTION. This aspect is difficult to work through, for it symbolizes a childhood that was less than ideal. The energy manifests in early childhood illness or emotional deprivation or both. The mother of the native is suppressed and restricted by the father in some way. This child is suppressed and restricted by the father as well. The mother's emotions are thwarted; she may not be able to have friends; her "causes" are put down; her life style may be completely hampered by marriage responsibilities. The mother may feel depressed, emotionally unfulfilled, and the child absorbs her attitudes and responses. Because the mother is unhappy, the child assumes that this reaction is "normal.' Sometimes this aspect occurs in marriages where the mother is a brood mare—raising babies and taking care of a family. There may be no relationship between the parents other than the father being the provider and expecting to be fed at six o'clock sharp. The mother may resent it, but she may not be strong enough to change her situation. Her reasons may be myriad—she may have too many children, she may not have skills or, like the heroine in "Dr. Jekyl and Mr. Hyde," she may be psychologically overwhelmed by the power of the Mr. Hyde personality. Each time the mother reaches out emotionally, responding to someone or something spontaneously, the father "dumps" on her.

This child picks up the emotional deprivation and brings the following characteristics into his adult life: a tendency toward melancholia, quick mood changes that are psychologically or subconsciously based, a basically unhealthy attitude regarding relationships. If this child is female, she will enter into romantic relationships assuming that she cannot share her thoughts and feelings with her loved one; she doesn't expect men to be nice or considerate or understanding, so she will tend to share her innermost feelings (and druthers) with her friends rather than with her lover or husband. In the chart of a male, the ability to respond emotionally will be restricted, for the father restricted this male's emotional development. This aspect also affects his relationships with women, and he may feel that no woman will ever care for him. He forces himself (often subconsciously) to barricade his emotional self, sometimes expressing himself harshly. If his father was physically or emotionally abusive to women, he may be too. He may be drawn to women who cannot give anything emotionally. In the case of the female, if her father was physically or emotionally abusive, she will expect the same kind of treatment from the men she chooses and will stay in unwholesome situations far longer than someone who doesn't have this aspect.

The aspect seems to place restrictions on the body in some way. Saturn symbolizes restriction, and the Moon represents the physical body. Children with this aspect sometimes have skeletal deficiencies or are prone to chronic ailments. The adult with this aspect has a harder time shaking colds or chronic maladies. These people should contemplate preventive medicine, for they can ward off illness by keeping healthy.

MOON–SATURN SEXTILE. Any contact from Saturn to the Moon brings slowness, apprehension and seriousness to the emotional self. The father of this native was not a debilitating influence on the mother and did not restrict her ability to nurture the native, but he did take life quite seriously.

People with this aspect can use it to establish steady feelings; once an emotional commitment has been made, it will be taken seriously. They are responsible people. The aspect's energy can be used in careers that need a steady hand and a level head.

MOON–SATURN SQUARE. The father of this person definitely thwarted the mother's personal expression. He may have been the kind of person who took delight in restricting and limiting the female. This person, in his early years, sees that mothers don't have a chance to do what they want to do, can't pursue anything that interests them without being harrassed by fathers. The subtle psychological games going on between the parents are not lost on the child. The father often thwarts the child as well as Mom, pouring cold water on the childhood enthusiasms. As the child reaches maturity, he will approach life with the expectancies inherited from the childhood experience.

A male with this aspect feels that women are not to be trusted, that emotional responses are not given freely, that one doesn't respond spontaneously. The father's attitudes and gestures toward the mother prevent this male from developing easy emotional relationships. He may feel that it isn't "masculine" to care, to be emotional, to be responsive. In adult situations, he will offer love and then take it back; the woman who loves him will find that he opens up, responds to her and then withdraws. He doesn't let loose with his emotions because he is trying to barricade himself against being hurt.

A female with this aspect has a different set of problems. She draws emotional relationships to her that serve to reinforce her subconscious childhood expectations. She thinks that since Dad restricted Mom, all men restrict all women. She will probably only accept men in her life who place restrictions on her in some way: either he won't let her work, or have friends, or he doesn't care about her emotional needs. She usually thinks that when a woman falls in love she has to give up a part of herself. Often, it's her friends who really know her rather than her husband or lover, for she doesn't easily express her "druthers" to a lover. She feels that her man only wants to hear certain things, that he doesn't want to hear how she feels anyway, so she gives responses that she thinks he can accept. When love relationships are formed on a "giving up" of something emotionally important, bitterness and resentment eventually occur. She feels lonely in her relationships for she chooses men who seldom allow her to develop and grow.

Whether a man or a woman, this is a hard aspect to break. In order to have a meaningful relationship, these individuals must understand that they draw relationships similar to that of their parents. Depressions and melancholia are associated with relationships, as well as suffering and a lack of emotional fulfillment. Emotional needs are not to be confused with sexual needs here, for these people may be involved in satisfactory sexual relationships, but their emotional needs are unfulfilled. Their partners are usually incapable of understanding them. They may choose mates who are either far above or below them in terms of education or from a different cultural or economic background. The lack of understanding caused by too great a difference in social background may cause hurt feelings, and barriers begin to develop in the relationship. The partner often feels the disparity between the two of them more than the Moon–Saturn person will. As said before, the aspect causes one to feel that one has to give up something in order to have a relationship, so the Moon–Saturn expects to marry beneath itself.

This type of problem can be cured when the Moon–Saturn person understands that he often chooses (on a subconscious basis) to repeat the pattern established by his parents. Although he cannot see it at the time, he ends up with similar results: unhappiness, emotional depression, a feeling that he cannot have what he wants. Saturn–Moon afflictions cause a lack of joy. Life is seen as difficult. Joy needs to be nurtured.

In a more mundane sense, the Moon–Saturn square can be read using these keywords: "The restrictive influence of the father (Saturn) works against (square) my emotional needs (Moon)." This translates into individuals who have difficulty pursuing the needs and feelings associated with the Moon sign and expect emotional needs to go unsatisfied. "My apprehensions, my fears, my feelings of lack (Saturn) work against (square) my physical body, or my feelings (Moon)." The legitimate fears represented by Saturn can restrict the development of the nurturing-caring-feeling ability: these fears can even affect the intuitive ability until the Saturn qualities are considered consciously.

Saturn is the weak point in our horoscope. When we are young, it causes us to worry a lot about that part of our life so that as we mature, it becomes one of our stronger features. Saturn can turn into a friend. When the Moon–Saturn aspect is understood, it can develop into a quality used to foster mature relationships.

Going back to Jungian psychology, the Saturn–Moon affliction (either the conjunction, square or opposition) tends to hamper the development of the anima/animus function. Because of the possible distortions of these images, it may be that the feeling-intuitive process is restricted; the individual has more difficulty using anima/animus to increase or quicken the development of personality.

In a man (because the anima function may be restricted from growing due to the strong influence of the father) female companionship seems to stay on the youthful anima level; women are chosen as companions because they represent the young anima in a physical sense (the billowing dresses, the flowing tresses); the sweetness associated with her is projected onto a woman. Such a man allows his woman to mature very slowly; she may have to fight him in order to retain her own consciousness or identity.

In a woman, the animus function seems to restrict her overall development, and she may even have to fight her father to gain a sense of her own femininity. The fight may not be a conscious one: she may find herself in the middle of a family holocaust and discover that she is not participating in a mundane disagreement but that the underlying causes of the disagreement involves her wresting her sense of female self away from her father. Because her father is able to de-feminize the mother, he will also try to do it to the daughter.

Most of the de-feminization takes place on a subtle level, it's seldom a conscious harrassment on the part of the father. In one case I know of, the father didn't want to allow the daughter any of her mother's possessions after the mother's death—he was saying in essence, "You can't have her, you can't have any of her things—they are mine." In a case where the mother dies early in the female child's life and the father holds on to all that his wife owned, never sharing it with his daughter, sometimes never speaking of his wife to his daughter (because he doesn't want to share his "private" memories), the child feels completely left out and also completely unfeminine. It's as if Daddy is saying, "You're not good enough to be a woman." This kind of energy will not always be present in the Saturn–Moon afflictions, but the potential for it is there. This is not the kind of information that one would readily share with a twenty-year-old, but a thirty-year-old would be old enough to begin to deal with it.

MOON–SATURN TRINE. People born with this aspect will not be as frivolous as those born without it! However, they are not as depressive as those born with the Moon–Saturn afflictions. This child arrives in an atmosphere where the father works cooperatively with the mother and vice versa; the parents present a united front, even if it is a rather somber one. The child learns to work through emotional problems; he offers himself carefully in a relationship, for emotions are not treated lightly. The chance of starting a relationship that works through all the possibilities, that leaves no stone unturned, that explores all its potential, comes out of this aspect.

As far as career is concerned, this aspect makes for a careful thinker, someone who is reasonable in crisis situations, a person who doesn't fly off the handle in spontaneous reactions. This is a diplomatic personality.

MOON–SATURN OPPOSITION. The child born with the opposition comes into a home environment much like that of the conjunction or square, except that depression and melancholia are often associated with a loss. This may involve the loss of a parent early in the life, either through death or separation. The child may keep both parents, but the atmosphere may be so somber that he feels a deprivation on the emotional level. The father (Saturn) influences the mother (Moon) in a restrictive sense; he inhibits her in some way so that the normal nurturing and caring that the child learns from the mother is missing.

The father may not be a violent person, but he may have a lousy attitude and therefore inhibit his wife from doing anything she is interested in pursuing. The atmosphere of coercion can be violent (obviously or subtly) to the child, depending on the rest of the chart. Sometimes the financial crunch does it—the wife wants to work, the husband won't let her. The wife wants to see a special movie, the husband takes her the day after her movie leaves the theatre. The husband may figuratively throw buckets of cold water on any idea his wife may have. The child picks up the reaction, and even though the father is not physically abusive to his wife, the child feels the depression and hurt the mother feels. When this child grows up and prepares to enter into an adult emotional relationship, he is programmed (on a subconscious level) to expect that he won't feel happy about it.

A male with this aspect is afraid to give of himself emotionally (especially if he lost his mother early), for he feels he will lose any feminine influence that matters to him. Some of these men marry women they don't love and carry on their love affairs outside the marital relationship, for they don't wish to establish a secure marriage with a woman they love. The attitude seems to be based on the fear of a loss of love. Some men feel they cannot demonstrate love on an emotional level; contact with women is merely sexual since Dad didn't love Mom and, therefore, they cannot love either.

A woman with this aspect often draws a man who resembles her father as far as personality is concerned. She finds someone who won't listen to her or care about her emotional needs, although he may take care of her sexual needs. He may not be supportive of her endeavors, whether it is redoing the house or finding the right job. She assumes that all men are like this. She assumes that she must suffer some loss in order to have some love. Because of this assumption, she tends to pick (on a subconscious basis) a man who doesn't have the same qualifications for life that she has: she may marry beneath her station or into a family that doesn't relate to her.

One of my clients with this aspect married a South American man and found it difficult to live with her new husband since she didn't speak Spanish and his family didn't speak English. The family expected her to live with them while her husband went off to graduate school. She was miserable; she had no friends, she didn't speak the language, she was not free to leave the family home, she couldn't help out in the house because she was a guest. Her mind stagnated, and she began to show symptoms of a nervous breakdown. She came back to America for treatment. It was hard for her to understand that she was being emotionally mistreated because she thought *all* marriages were difficult. It turned out that her husband married her because he loved her "American" freedom, her openness, her interest in developing a career—but after the marriage took place he didn't want her to have those interests anymore. The love affair was fine but the living together was difficult!

People born with the Saturn–Moon opposition must teach themselves about self-worth. All their unproductive relationships need to be consciously analyzed in order to determine the pattern of behavior that determines the lack of self-worth. Fear of confronting another person in regard to their emotional needs and the fear of being put down when they reveal their goals should be considered. (If someone really loves us, he or she can't ignore our needs.) Loving involves giving—not giving up. A mutual sharing takes place when a love relationship grows. The tension and depression of this aspect can be alleviated when the effect of the father is understood. A sense of joy needs to be cultivated. Life is not gloom and doom unless we make it that way. When the childhood environment is released, a mature joyful person can emerge.

MOON–SATURN QUINCUNX. The Moon represents our emotional reaction to life; it symbolizes how the mother teaches us to respond when we are young. Saturn represents the effect of the father on the mother and his effect on our ability to express emotions. When the quincunx aspect appears, it indicates a strain that eventually takes its toll on health, although symptoms rarely show up before the age of forty. The energy needs to be worked into consciousness, for the quincunx is the kind of aspect that more frequently plays itself out like a small toothache—it isn't important enough to take to the dentist immediately.

The sign qualities of the Moon and Saturn need to be worked into a relationship that allows them both to express. Saturn says "I lack," the Moon says "I feel." Moon in Leo, for example, feels sensitive to the world's approval and judgment. It feels or responds to ethics, proper behavior, a sense of fairness. Saturn in Capricorn is indicative of a fear or a lack of social position; a fear of power, a lack of power, a fear of losing face. Such fear can cause one to do something in a career sense that may not be approved of by the Moon. The Moon wants to get to the top the right way, Saturn just wants to get there. The dilemma may not be noticed by others since it involves internal tension. Often, the symbolism of astrology can bring the tension to the attention of its owner so it can be worked out.

MOON–URANUS ASPECTS

The Moon symbolizes the way we respond to our environment. We respond to life in general, to our family, friends and loved ones according to the sign the Moon is in at the time of our birth. The planet Uranus symbolizes our behavior and the behavior of our generation. Spiritual astrologers say that the three outer planets (Uranus, Neptune and Pluto) denote parts of the unconscious that can be used to attain a higher consciousness or wisdom, as well as to free the soul from the bonds of the material universe. When the Moon and Uranus make contact in the chart, it indicates that we have unusual, eccentric, erratic, or different types of responses than people born with the same Moon sign. There is more of a chance to grow because Uranus brings an opportunity to evolve the consciousness—to perceive different kinds of emotional reactions, to perceive different kinds of relationships. It can be difficult to own a Moon–Uranus aspect for it is a requisite to becoming more self-aware, more self-responsible; otherwise, our relationships may be unhappy or unpleasant.

MOON–URANUS CONJUNCTION. The Moon symbolizes our emotional responses to life, the responses we learned at an early age from our mother, and Uranus indicates a behavior pattern that is connected to the generation we were born into.

If the word "erratic" can be associated with Uranus apsects, we may surmise that we have erratic emotional responses with this conjunction. The chances are that the mother of the person with this aspect responds to her life in some erratic or eccentric fashion during the individual's childhood. It may be that the mother doesn't respond emotionally unless it's in the form of an emotional outburst; the child may have difficulty determining whether Mom is happy, angry or upset; here the emotional tirades come out of nowhere.

The adult with this aspect tends to make sudden and abrupt emotional decisions that sometimes offend others, for decisions of an emotional nature are seldom discussed before they are made. The emotional responses or reactions may be unpredictable. This can be both good and bad. It gives the individual a close tie to his generation and creates an affinity with peer group goals; so, it often indicates a person involved in healing or social welfare. It indicates a person who responds so suddenly and so strangely to emotional relationships that he leaves a string of broken hearts behind him as he rejects one lover after another, rarely working through relationship problems.

If the rest of the chart warrants, it can indicate individuals who draw violent relationships. For example, a woman with this aspect can be involved in sudden breakups; this may result in an angry lover trying to break down her door. If these women want to avoid violence, they must consciously learn to share their feelings and hurts before coming to a decision about a relationship. They need to learn to discuss their feelings, for this is the only way a man (or anyone) can understand how they feel. The constructive behavior pattern will have to be learned, for the child didn't see the mother making reasonable or considerate decisions.

In the case of a man, it tends to indicate an individual who doesn't commit himself to one relationship, who may leave in a huff when the situation is not going his way. He goes from one love to another, or one marriage to another, rather than sharing himself with the person he says he loves. Rarely is he physically abused, since men usually are not physically attacked by women; but it sometimes happens. Should this male be homosexual, however, he may suffer from physical violence in his emotional involvements until he learns how to share his feelings.

MOON–URANUS SEXTILE. The emotional response-ability that the mother shows this child, because of her reaction to life, is extremely positive for the child's emotional development. This aspect indicates a person who can work through emotional crises, who has original ideas, who can understand many other patterns of reaction than his own, and who brings much positive energy to the environment. Bless 'em!

MOON–URANUS SQUARE. This aspect resembles the conjunction or the opposition in that the mother of this individual plays an eccentric role when the person is a child. If the Moon symbolizes the mother and how she reacts to life, and her reactions inspire her child to react, to develop an emotional response to all life situations; and if Uranus symbolizes the behavior pattern of a generation, as well as how we handle ourselves with others, then this square shows a person who is apt to abruptly end a relationship of any kind, for Mother taught the pattern. This person feels that it's normal to end relationships abruptly, and that it's normal to make relationship decisions before discussing them with the other person. This produces brusque behavior with friends as well as lovers, family members and co-workers. This person can leave a job suddenly, or impetuously change his feelings about his present career. So, it can possibly indicate a person who has several careers over the years.

The most difficult part of this aspect manifests in personal relationships, for this individual doesn't give his partner an even break. When his feelings are hurt, he often plays the situation through in his head, and by the time he gets around to discussing the unpleasant situation with the loved one, he's really made a decision to end the relationship: any conversation regarding it is merely a polite form of speech. This aspect makes for lots of misunderstanding in all types of relationships; the eccentric life reaction was learned from the mother because she was eccentric in her own way. If this person can remember the mother's relationships, how she handled her husband and friends or the rest of the family members, the behavior pattern can be broken. (Did she have a friend one year and not the next?) When he understands where he got the pattern from, it can be easily resolved. In order to develop relationships that other people will understand, this individual needs to recognize when his feelings are hurt, when animosity is *beginning* to build, so that the unpleasant life situations can be worked out instead of cut out. The alternative is to leave every unpleasant situation and start over and over again with new friends and new lovers. This doesn't help him handle the various cycles in life in a mature manner, for he never stays with anyone long enough to work through a crisis or a cycle.

Part of our development as we move from young adult to "Wise Old Man or Woman" is the growth caused by facing unpleasant situations and the working through of differences in personality, so that we can truly understand how someone else can "listen to the beat of a different drummer." In order to develop compassion or understanding, this awareness should be brought into consciousness.

The aspect gives potential for understanding, much personal growth, a chance to raise the consciousness to a high point, to break old family patterns. When the creative energy bursts forth, the square becomes more productive than the trine.

MOON–URANUS TRINE. The child born with this aspect comes into a home where the mother understands the attitudes of the younger generation. The Moon symbolizes the mother and how she responds to life when the child is small. The child learns emotional responses, how to care, how to nurture, how to feel and respond, from the mother. Uranus indicates the behavior of the generation; it also indicates our point of eccentricity or willfulness. This child's mother is willing to work with her environment in a positive manner, and her children will imitate her creative response to life in their adult relationships.

The only problem coming from this trine can be that of too much permissiveness—perhaps too much support given to people before understanding their goals and purposes. For example, a woman with this trine gave a great deal of support to a juvenile group in her neighborhood. The kids wanted a club house and needed adult support in order to get it. She gave them her endorsement, only to find out later that the club house was a center for drug activities and was even used for violent situations—several children were physically abused there, one young girl was raped.

This aspect can be called the aspect of "positive" eccentricity! It indicates that the individual has a creative bent that bestows an ability to be emotionally involved in any career chosen. It also indicates an unusual emotional nature, one that may enjoy "new age" relationships.

MOON–URANUS OPPOSITION. Here the child is born into an environment where the mother doesn't give it a healthy emotional pattern to follow. The Moon symbolizes the mother and how she reacts to life when her child is small. Uranus opposing the Moon indicates that the mother behaves one way and feels another. It's hard for the child—or anyone else—to know how she is going to react ahead of time; she may suppress her emotional needs while favoring eccentric reactions to situations; she may be extremely willful, eccentric, erratic, the kind of person who "cuts her nose off to spite her face." When a child is exposed to a mother who doesn't discuss her feelings before reaching a conclusion, when the adults in the family make erratic or eccentric emotional decisions as a matter of course, this child will become an adult who does the same thing.

The adult with this aspect can be irresponsible, for the feelings are always changing, the response to others may be eccentric or erratic and perplexing. The general behavior (Uranus) operates against or apart from (opposition) the emotional needs, the ability to nurture, care or respond (Moon). For example, it can indicate the type of woman who has one affair after another. Each time a man hurts her feelings, she gets ready to leave the relationship rather than talk out the situation to make sure that he is conscious of having hurt her feelings. She goes from one lover to the next, or one husband to the next, until she walks out on a man who won't take "no" for an answer; or she ends the relationship so abruptly that she really hurts his pride and he indulges in physical violence. When relationships are ended abruptly, the injured partner can respond with anger. This is not the only way that a difficult aspect expresses itself, but violence can occur from time to time.

The aspect tends toward the inability to see a situation through to its logical conclusion. In the matter of love, when two people disagree with each other (as two people always will because we are all different), the differences can be compromised or worked out, or at least understood! If the differences are so great that no compromise can be reached, that becomes clear after a while. But if two people are willing to compromise, the relationship can continue. Uranus opposing the Moon often makes a person unwilling to compromise (as does the square) due to a personal eccentricity or due to self-will learned at home.

The aspect is stronger in the mother-dominated types and is easier to break in the father-dominated types. In either case, if the energy is rechanneled, it indicates a person who is unusual, unorthodox, one who can transcend the Moon sign type, who can bring the humanitarian values from Aquarius into the realm of feeling and caring. It develops the intuitive ability so that the individual can become extremely creative. One side effect of the opposition is that it brings a great deal of nervous energy to bear on this person; when the energy is not used constructively, the individual may appear to be emotionally hysterical. Emotional hysteria attached to this aspect indicates the talent available is not being used constructively. Decisions are probably not made well, for the emotional needs are not being considered.

As an example, consider Uranus in Taurus ("I behave practically," or "I behave sensually," or "I behave like a materialist"), opposing the Moon in Scorpio ("I feel unwanted, I feel like a transformer, I become emotionally involved in the transformational process, I feel strongly about the needs of other people," etc.). How does one handle practical behavior on the surface when one really feels hurt and unwanted emotionally? Consider a business situation where this type of person wants to be regarded warmly, whose feelings become easily hurt, who needs the affection of fellow employees, but who behaves in a practical manner? The chances are that most of the time the personality will manifest in a Taurean manner, only to lash out from time to time to protect the emotions in the manner of the Scorpio Moon. Fellow employees may not understand the abrupt personality changes. Meanwhile, the individual who owns the aspect feels uncomfortable because he is projecting two different types of energies.

The tension absorbed into the system because of the misunderstood opposition may manifest in an hysterical manner. If the personal needs are understood, the energy no longer needs to manifest in this way.

MOON-URANUS QUINCUNX. The physical influence of the mother is indicated by the Moon sign of the child. When Uranus quincunxes the Moon, Mom's reaction to emotional tensions and life in general is hampered by the qualities of the sign Uranus is in. The aspect indicates a strain, so she had trouble relating emotionally but it wasn't big trouble. The child will pick up her habit pattern and will have vague feelings of emotional disturbance that eventually take their toll in terms of health. The aspect can be worked out by understanding that all the qualities in a chart need to be expressed in some positive manner.

For example, Moon in Gemini, Uranus in Scorpio—an aspect that affects many babies born in the late 1970s. Moon in Gemini responds to life via ideas; it responds emotionally to ideas about education and spiritual development; it responds to love through poetry, prose and wonderful intellectual words. Uranus in Scorpio says that this child is born into a generation that needs to transform in a spiritual sense, and one that may believe in "an eye for an eye." Retaliation over hurt feelings may take place. If retaliation is not manifested on a physical plane, it may manifest internally by allowing the body to build up toxins in the intestines or reproductive organs. The Gemini Moon is a free spirit, but the Uranus in Scorpio indicates a generation that may "behave" by telling others what to do! It may be that this generation will establish orders and patterns regarding groups of people that may or may not be good for everyone. When Uranus entered Scorpio, religious groups appeared that judged others harshly; people made decisions about other people's abortions, about other people's beliefs in God, etc.

With the quincunx aspect, the emotional needs of an individual may not set well with the peer group requirements, and some comfortable middle ground will have to be found.

MOON–NEPTUNE ASPECTS

The Moon represents the physical mother at a time in life when the child develops patterns of emotional reaction and response. The Moon symbolizes how we care and nurture and how we feel, and the pattern is formed by the time we are three years old. Neptune is the planet that represents our inspiration-delusion-creativity function, and it becomes extremely important to us when it touches our personal planets. Neptune represents spiritual development, creative urges, universal or impersonal love; it also represents how we delude ourselves.

When Neptune connects to the Moon, it sometimes indicates that we associate spiritual urges with emotional responses. When this occurs, some confusion usually exists as to how to express the emotions or who to express them with. The Neptunian delusion causes strange concepts to develop regarding feelings. Because of Mother's state of mind, Neptune–Moon aspects indicate that intertwined with feelings are vague spiritual awarenesses, a concept of unearthly love, perhaps even a veil of delusion about Mother herself.

MOON–NEPTUNE CONJUNCTION. The Moon represents the individual's physical mother and how she reacts to life when the person is very young. Neptune represents some characteristics of delusion or inspiration, or it clouds the mother issue. In an adult, the Moon indicates the ability to respond to life, and its sign indicates how it will be done. When Neptune conjuncts the Moon, it clouds the feelings, covers them, puts a veil around them, and it may also cloud the image of the mother so that much of her affect is confused or unclear. This makes it difficult to evaluate the mother's actions and it deludes the individual about woman issues: how a woman should act, how a woman is expected to behave, what are "nurturing," "caring" and "feeling?" The aspect affects males and females differently.

In a man, the aspect often clouds his emotions and veils his concepts of what a woman should be, so that when he enters into a relationship with a woman, it is often with strange expectations. He thinks women are different from what they are in reality, and he is usually disappointed in their behavior. This man doesn't want to know that "women go to the bathroom," or wear hair curlers, etc. His mother taught him illusions and delusions, so he is eventually forced to determine from a conscious point what adult female behavior is all about.

He is also extremely intuitive; he will have intuitive feeling responses that he may not consciously understand. This can be both a blessing and a curse. If his body is so sensitive that he picks up too many vibrations from the environment, he may not know "who" he is feeling—himself or those around him. He may be unsettled because of his intuitive response, for his sensitivity may not match his conception of a two-fisted, hairy-chested male. If he is mother-dominated, his mother can do no wrong; he seldom sees her for what she is, always covering her with a shimmering cloud of perfection. If he is father-dominated, he often bases his idea of what a woman should be on a fairy tale image of Cinderella/Sleeping Beauty attributes. He has trouble separating his anima function from his wife or girlfriend because he often projects his anima onto her personality. His girlfriend's actions may not be akin to his anima image, so he is constantly disappointed. If he is mother-dominated, his girlfriend seldom acts like his mother told him "good" women should.

When a woman has her Moon conjunct Neptune it indicates that her mother misled her as far as the behavior of woman is concerned; therefore, she often has a distorted image of what a woman should be. The image of Woman is frequently associated with martyrdom and unrequited love. She falls in love with a person on a spiritual basis and sometimes doesn't notice that the one she has fallen in love with is a hopeless alcoholic or has psychotic disturbances. She feels guilty about sexual involvements and consequently may pick a partner who cannot relate to her sexually, or she can't relate sexually to him. She may find herself in perplexing predicaments, for she doesn't know what earthly love is. The problem stems from the fact that she doesn't know what a woman should be and how she as a woman should react. The result is often too much phoney spirituality and a lot of hurt feelings. Confusion surrounds the nurturing, caring and feeling functions.

Both sexes have some kind of problem expressing their feelings of love on a sexual level. Sometimes it's easier to be sexy with someone you don't love, for love is such a "spiritual" experience that physical sex can "defile" it in some way. Men with this aspect sometimes have a woman they love and a woman they sex. Or, they have trouble with erections if the Moon is in a Fire sign, for their sexuality is limited because of their idealism. Women with the aspect tend to choose spiritual relationships that may be emotionally painful—the man may mistreat them, or he may not be able to perform sexually. Sometimes this aspect appears in the charts of women who fall in love with homosexual men, so the relationship is close but the unrequited love aspect is there.

The aspect is an intuitive and sensitive one, and its owners may have many interesting psychic and intuitive experiences. It can sometimes indicate people who have a great deal of healing ability; they become involved in the mental, spiritual, physical healing of others. They are intuitive enough so that they can manifest on a creative level as well, and this source of energy is never ending once they learn to tap into it. The creative potential cannot be completely realized until they learn to share their feelings with another human being. This can be a most productive aspect. The blind spot toward the mother can be emphasized by other aspects in the chart; she may be the one who stands between this person and his freedom—and he can't see it.

MOON–NEPTUNE SEXTILE. The child with this aspect is born into a family that presents a constructive emotional environment. The mother is symbolized by the Moon placement in the chart, and the Neptune energy is handled in a positive way with this aspect. She teaches her child, through her own example, to respond to a creative atmosphere: she works well with her search for spirituality, she moves in a direction that involves her personal spiritual development. The child may not grow up to understand his mother's spiritual interests, but because she had them, the child will be free to develop his own as he matures and discovers his direction.

The Moon sign indicates how the child will respond emotionally, the Neptune sign indicates the child's creative bent. The house placement of the sextile will indicate the area of creative response.

MOON–NEPTUNE SQUARE. The energy of this aspect manifests much like the Moon–Neptune conjunction, except that it is less productive. The Moon indicates how we respond emotionally, and this response is learned from the mother during the first three years of life. Neptune indicates creativity, inspiration and delusion. When this planet squares (or works against) the Moon, it usually indicates that some delusion is at hand. The circumstances of the delusion are an unknown factor of the childhood. The delusion can range from the fact that the mother "played around'' but told everyone that she was a ''goodie-two-shoes'' to the fact that family members lied about her. At any rate, the child born with this aspect is misinformed either by the mother herself or by the family members. (When a client wants to figure out the family circumstances that caused the personality disorder or discomfort, the Moon–Neptune square is the place to start.)

This aspect is difficult for it means that the person doesn't have a clear picture of his mother image and cannot see how she did or didn't influence his childhood. If the person is mother dominated, he may blame the state of his emotional problems on his father because Mother told him he should. The other aspects in the chart will either verify her story or show the individual that Mother needs to be investigated in order to gain freedom from her influence. In the case of the father-dominated person, the mother is not so important and the father may be favored, or the role Mother played may not be considered as important. In either case, the individual needs to understand the mother in order to develop the feminine function, the feeling and intuitive side of the self.

One of my clients with this square had a difficult time discovering who her father was, and was able to do so only after having a reading. It's especially important to understand the truths of our early childhood when we are unable to live adult lives free of parental influence. If we go from one unproductive situation to another, the root cause is often within ourselves: and it is by determining what kind of ''normals'' we absorbed as children that we can ultimately let go of the problem. The investigation of family patterns will not be successful when pursued with vengeance. As we mature, we begin to understand that misunderstandings created between children and parents are done by accident.

MOON–NEPTUNE TRINE. This aspect indicates a child born into a home where spiritual development is important to the mother. The mother needs to relate to something in a spiritual sense, and the child sometimes avoids developing spiritually because he thinks that he must walk the same spiritual path Mom did. This person needs to learn that we each find our own paths and determine our own values.

The trine aspect fosters energy for spiritual insight. The individual needs to be creative, needs to learn to meditate, needs a chance to grow spiritually. Out of a meditative mind comes new ideas, inspirations that are received on a feeling-intuitive level. However, creativity is limited as long as the body will not permit emotional relationships. Since the body is the ''temple of the soul,'' it needs to be nourished and loved as much as the soul it houses. This aspect can cause a person to be so involved with spiritual or universal love that he forgets to live in this world!

The mother was a productive influence in the childhood and both males and females with this aspect are looking for a spiritual type of personal relationship. However, they may not be prepared for a close relationship, one that involves caring and sharing both mentally and physically, because love may have been reserved for an ethereal plane.

MOON–NEPTUNE OPPOSITION. This aspect works much like the Moon–Neptune conjunction or square except that the opposition seems to also include a feeling of loss. The Moon represents the physical mother and how she responds to raising us during our formative years. We learn our emotional response from hers. Neptune symbolizes the creative instinct, inspiration and delusion. When Neptune opposes the Moon, it indicates that a veil of illusion or delusion clouds our perception of our mother. Either we were told stories about her that weren't true, or she told us she was something that she wasn't.

Men get a distorted image of what a woman should be when they have this aspect. This is the man whose mother tells him "a good woman doesn't do that," and he believes her. Her description of what a "good woman" is will influence his response to the idea of "woman," and it also influences his ability to care and feel in his own life. He may be constantly disappointed in the women with whom he comes in contact, for none of them seem to match his mother's description.

A woman with this aspect is not quite sure of what a "good" woman is. She also doesn't know how to respond emotionally as a woman. The aspect usually sets her up for involvements with men who are unproductive or unkind; or she cannot see that the man she loves is not what she thinks he is. Again, this can sometimes indicate the woman who falls in love but the love affair is not consummated in the sexual sense, or she marries a man who doesn't want to have sex with her after the marriage takes place.

Both the male and female can be drawn into strange spiritual groups and become victims of the "professional guru" who takes their money and leads them down a path that doesn't get them anything. They both need to determine who they are; they need to define "woman" and what she is, relationships and what they are, so that truly creative energy can manifest. If they have emotional problems that need solving, this aspect gives a clue as to where the problems originated. When children have been presented with distortions at the formative stages of development, it's difficult to shake the delusion. The aspect indicates a kind of emotional confusion that can be most frustrating, but it also gives an intuitive ability and a creative sense; and a drive for spiritual growth and awareness that can be most exciting.

MOON–NEPTUNE QUINCUNX. There is a strain between the feelings, the emotional responses and the creative urges with this aspect. The Moon represents the individual's physical mother and how she responds to her child. Neptune indicates the creative inspiration or delusion of a generation. Neptune quincunx the Moon adds a strain here: the need for spiritual development and the dreams and goals in life are often different from the feeling function. The intuitive awareness that comes from Neptune disagrees with the emotional responses symbolized by the Moon.

When this person listens to intuition, he may hear two voices, neither of which are strong enough to outweigh the other—just strong enough to create suspicion within himself. Ideals interfere with emotional needs, and the two kinds of energy need to be expressed in some constructive way. The keywords of the signs and planets can be of help in understanding this dilemma.

MOON-PLUTO ASPECTS

The Moon represents the physical mother and how she reacts to life while the child's personality is forming (age 0-3). She responds a certain way emotionally (indicated by the Moon's sign) and the child imitates her response because it is "normal." When Pluto aspects the Moon, it brings a transformational kind of energy to the emotional responses of an individual: it brings all the possible energies created through Pluto into focus with the emotions. Because of this tie, the focus is on concepts of cooperation, coercion, obsession, a need to manipulate, as well as the idea of transformation or helping others transform themselves. There are healing energies at play here, and an ability to research the intuitive and feeling capacities. Pluto-Moon configurations are strong and productive if handled consciously. If not, they can represent obsessive personalities that tend to attempt to control others in order to insure their own safety in the environment they attempt to create.

In a more profound sense, Pluto aspects involving the Moon can symbolize the emotional transformation that must take place in order to free the individual from the powerful tie to the mother. Because the mother is the first person who really cares for us, holds us and supplies our needs, it is difficult for us to become free of the mother because she is so special. She may embrace all the love and hate polarities possible; we may not appreciate the manner in which she nurtured us; yet the tie is mythic in its importance, and the pursuit of consciousness (our own personal Hero's venture) encompasses the need to free ourselves from both the personal and the mythic parents. The hard aspects to Pluto from the Moon indicate the need for this transformation or else we may become swallowed up by the archetypal mother image in the psyche, which can be confused with the physical mother image also in the personal subconscious.

The quest for freedom gives us the opportunity to work with the energies of the psyche in most creative ways, but we have to earn the power first. If we don't understand the energies at play within us, they often manifest on less important levels, such as the need to control others. When the energy is used on a mundane level, we are not free to use it in the most profound way. The choice to pursue this knowledge and ability is ours to make when we are old enough to explore the depths of consciousness. (See Chapter 10 in this section.)

MOON–PLUTO CONJUNCTION. The Moon represents how the physical mother teaches the child to respond emotionally. Pluto represents the unconscious motivation of a generation. When it ties to the Moon, it usually indicates a manipulative and controlling mother type. This aspect should be read after considering the other aspects to the Moon, for the combination of aspects to this conjunction will tell the story of *how* the child is overwhelmed by the mother's energy. She is a strong woman; a woman who may be obsessed by something that is going on in her life during the time this child is influenced. The sign involved in the conjunction is important in determining what kind of energy is available.

The conjunction is overpowering; emotional reactions are usually formed in the subconscious rather than in the conscious mind. The aspect indicates a person who responds emotionally (via the feelings, or the responses in the physical body), although the cause of the emotional reaction is actually subconscious. By way of compensation, the individual with this aspect feels that he must be in control of all his responses all the time. He will keep a tight rein on his own emotional responses, and will attempt to control any emotional situations around him in order to avoid being surprised or shocked at his own reactions. This can indicate that his mother controlled her environment completely and manipulated everyone around her. This person will become an adult who has difficulty responding spontaneously in any emotional relationship involving family, friends or lovers. He can obsess on any relationship and may surround himself with people he can control. He may surround himself with inferior types in order to maintain control; he may play all the control games possible, from excessive gift-giving to "smother" love. This aspect may describe the "smother" love syndrome which causes the person to produce the same kind of emotional responses when he reaches adulthood.

The root of the distortion is control. This is the underside of Pluto manifesting itself; when it is understood, the transformational process can begin. Jung talks of the collective unconscious, that part of the psyche in all of us that remembers all that has happened to the species up to this point. The collective unconscious can be likened to Edgar Cayce's Akashic Records, though Jung interpreted it in much different terminology. When the Moon is attached to the energy of Pluto, it gives a person a chance to be tremendously creative, to tap into the wealth of information and ideas that lurk below the surface. This type of creative energy can be called intuitive for it comes from the subconscious. The person has to develop the skill of letting the intuitive energy flow. It cannot be developed as long as the feeling nature is controlled.

Various metaphysical and religious organizations sponsor classes which teach trust in the God-self and how one can get in touch with the creative center that exists in all of us. Trusting the personal creative energy of this aspect has to be learned, for it is hard to let go of early childhood experience. The circumstances of the childhood and examples of the mother's manipulation and control techniques must be understood so that the individual can evaluate the kind of game absorbed from Mom. With a little effort, anyone can begin to recall early childhood memories. Memory becomes difficult only when trauma occurs to block the mind channels, for we don't like to recall something that offends our ethics. The ethics can be determined from aspects in the chart and read from planet and sign. This conjunction gives the individual great creative energy. Powerful as it is in the creative sense, it can be as powerful in a hurtful sense.

When a man has this aspect, he attempts to control all his emotional relationships with women: the aspects to the conjunction should be checked to see if there is violence there. A woman with this aspect can draw men to her who are physically violent if the signs are right, or if additional aspects to her Moon indicate the potential for this kind of behavior. An astrologer can warn her that indiscriminate behavior may bring emotional difficulties into her life, but the words should be carefully chosen.

This aspect gives great intuitive and healing ability. The charts of healers and psychics often have Pluto–Moon configurations, and the hard aspects seem to confer more power. These individuals are so empathetic to the feelings of others that they may even assume symptoms of other people's illnesses. When they become aware of this ability, they can learn to channel it; after all, who wants to walk around with someone else's headache? Eventually they may learn that not only can they pick up information from other people without asking for it, but they can heal the hurts as well. Those who don't wish to pursue the occult forms of healing can find an outlet in the multiprofessional field of medicine: many physiotherapists have strong Pluto–Moon aspects.

MOON–PLUTO SEXTILE. The Moon represents our physical mother as she presents herself during our early years. It symbolizes how we will respond emotionally to friends, to politics, to feeling/caring needs. Pluto represents the mass unconscious; it indicates the unconscious motivation inside each of us, so it indicates how we cope with feelings toward our fellow man on both a conscious and an unconscious plane. Pluto represents coercion, control and the manipulation of others in all its forms.

When these two parts of personality are tied together by sextile, it indicates a constructive energy flow. It means the mother's actions demonstrate to the individual how to work cooperatively with groups, and how to cooperate with others. The sextile is a talent aspect; it indicates that talent is there, although it needs to be trained. Any career involving contact with unions, great numbers of people or the spirit of community effort will bring pleasure. The sextile gives a certain amount of intuitive ability that can be developed over the years, but probably not until after age thirty-five.

MOON-PLUTO SQUARE. This aspect has much of the same energy that is present with the conjunction, except that it may be more excessive or obsessive. The Moon indicates how the mother responds emotionally to her environment when the child is developing his emotional responses. Pluto represents the transformational energy symbolized by Scorpio: on the one hand it indicates the ability to transform the self; on the other hand, the energy of the square usually manifests in a subconscious urge to control others, to manipulate life so that one always knows where one stands. The low form of the energy shows more readily in the hard aspects.

In order to channel this energy for constructive use, the formation of the original pattern must be consciously understood. The mother of this individual needs to manipulate her universe; she controls her husband, family, friends and neighbors, and this child assumes her response is "normal." The area of emotional control can be determined more fully by the house placements and signs involved in the square. In order to be free of oppressive energy, this person needs to understand how he imitates his mother in his own personal life, how he manipulates those around him, and the manner in which he attempts to control others. He got the pattern from his mother. The person with this aspect can be obsessive about people he loves. He needs to learn spontaneity, for he often plans everything in his life and becomes upset when his plans don't work out. Creative and intuitive energy comes out when manipulation and control stop.

Pluto was in the sign of Leo for many years. A person born with Pluto in Leo square the Moon in Scorpio, for example, can be described in the keywords "I am unconsciously motivated by respect and approval," and "I respond to the world as though I am unwanted." Combining the keywords creates the description of an individual who feels emotionally rejected. The chances are his mother felt rejected when he was very young. The child learned her response pattern. Feelings of being unwanted, feeling a need to defend oneself because one expects to be uncared for, become "normal." A young person with this aspect will probably have several unhappy love affairs, for he may not be drawn to love someone who makes him feel wanted—it isn't "normal" for him. The Pluto square indicates that this person will be extremely sensitive (perhaps on a subconscious level) to those who do not respect or approve of him enough. This is a defensive placement—the individual will be apt to respond defensively to life experience.

Because his mother controlled her environment, the chances are he will try to insure emotional safety by placing controls in his environment as well. "Control" may indicate the selection of inferior types as lovers (for you can't lose a loser); choosing friends he takes care of (because then they owe you); overgiving to people, for giving gives him a certain amount of power. This may indicate a person who helps everyone in his social circle—and that gives power as well, for your "friends" owe you and have to be eternally grateful.

It is a sensitive position. The transformational quality of Scorpio may be expressed as a rigid code of ethics which often appears in people who have planets in the signs Leo and Scorpio—these are strongly ethical signs. When avoiding personal transformation, these people often impose standards and ethics on others such as "Do as I say, not as I do!"

Owning this aspect isn't easy. The individual doesn't feel sure of himself emotionally, for the Pluto often operates on a subconscious basis. When it is tied to the Moon, the body responds emotionally to subconscious stimuli. So his feeling response may be overly sensitive, and he may feel he must establish controls. Because Pluto is in Leo, the person feels it's important to be respected, to be approvable: so a certain amount of sensitivity manifests when any new relationship is started, for he may be looking to be rejected. In this individual's psyche is a memory imprint of a woman (his mother) who felt rejected and who imparted her feelings of rejection to her child. She may have ignored him, or provided for his comforts but let his need for emotional support go untended; so, the child feels emotionally insecure—and the adult will as well. The combination of Leo and Scorpio planets indicate that this individual needs a lot of emotional support; yet he won't trust it, for it is not a "familiar" feeling. The control, the need to be ready for anything that might strike at any time, brings this person a great deal of inner tension.

At the same time, the aspect is tremendously creative for it can give emotional and intuitive insights and feelings. Emotional ties have to be built consciously, and those who have to *learn* to feel are often as exuberant about their new-found feelings as religious converts are about religion—they appreciate it more because they didn't always have it! The trauma of working the aspect into consciousness is definitely worth it.

Each sign will alter the interpretation, for the above description has been based on both the aspect and the signs involved. Each possible square between the Moon and Pluto can be discovered by working with the planets and the signs involved in the square. Each of us must discover the interpretation for ourselves, remembering that the aspect looks like one thing to an outsider and *feels* very different to the person who owns it.

Consider Pluto in Virgo the Moon in Gemini: the mother symbol comes from Gemini—this is a woman who influenced her child at a time when she was responding to life with Gemini characteristics—she responded to emotions with her mind, she intellectualized her feelings, she did not feel comfortable expressing emotion with her body. Her child picked up that response as "normal."

Pluto in Virgo says that the child is unconsciously motivated to pick up Virgo characteristics, so the psyche will be sensitive to criticism (abnormally so), and there may be some doubt regarding the intellect. In order to control life situations, these individuals will be self-critical, critical of others, and may unconsciously find themselves criticizing those with whom they are emotionally involved.

The house placement of the square comes into play for the emotional responses (other than love) that will involve the critical Pluto energy can be described by the houses holding the Moon and Pluto. Any square between the Moon and Pluto will be similar in that the mother controlled her universe the best way she could and her child will imitate her. The person with this aspect will hesitate to embrace new emotional involvements, for he wants to maintain control. The differences in interpretation will be the kinds of emotional responses and kinds of control involved in the aspect, for these adjectives come from the signs.

A woman with this aspect may appear to be cold, or she can obsess over any new emotional involvement. A man with this aspect often manipulates his relationships with women and plays all kinds of subtle control games. Anyone with this aspect who is not yet conscious of it can make others feel emotionally drained; sometimes the Moon–Pluto square loses out on relationships because they won't give the loved one breathing space.

MOON–PLUTO TRINE. Like the sextile, this aspect is a blessing. It indicates that Mom demonstrated a warm, open and cooperative emotional outlook during this person's formative years. Through her actions, she taught him how to work with others: how to work through problems with authority figures, friends and family members. The child will be sympathetic to the needs of his generation, for Pluto also represents the mass consciousness of the era. This can be both good and bad, for it indicates that the child will be receptive to his peer group as he is growing up.

Those children born into the teen-age drug culture were open to their friends who were selling "grass" in the suburbs! They may have become a part of the teen-age drug culture, or the teen-age smoking clique, or the teen-age alcohol group, merely because they wanted to join their peers. (Look at the aspects to determine *why* a child participates in contemporary peer group fads, for then it can be seen whether a child is rebelling against his parents or just joining the fad of the day.)

As this person matures, the energy gives him a natural "in" with the media, mass communication, politics, social work and related careers that help service the masses. It can be a creative aspect, for the development of intuitive insights is easy.

MOON–PLUTO OPPOSITION. The Moon symbolizes the physical mother, how she reacts to life when the native is forming his or her emotional self. The mother is not comfortable with her environment when this child is very young, for the Pluto opposition indicates that the mother feels she has to control everyone. A lack of spontaneity, feelings being manipulated, outsmarting the rest of the family in order to maintain control—these are the symptoms of the opposition.

This child learns manipulation and control because it is done to him—so it must be "normal." The mother may feel that raising a child is an overwhelming responsibility. She may be in the throes of an unstable marriage, not knowing where she stands. Whatever the cause, she smothers those around her. The child becomes an adult who "smother-loves," who obsesses over people and feelings, who falls apart emotionally when he feels the reins of control slipping away. One can't truly resent a person with this aspect, for the actions taken on an emotional basis are seldom conscious, and the person who smother loves doesn't know any other way to behave. He must consciously learn new behavior patterns, for he doesn't know how to respond emotionally without the Pluto controls.

Pluto also represents the mass consciousness and it usually remains in the psyche on an unconscious level. As the opposition energy develops, it can result in disassociation from the peer group for it hears "a different drummer." This person may avoid groups and crowds because he doesn't feel in control of himself in a crowd. A fear of crowds, a fear of being trampled by the masses, pertain to all the hard aspects (conjunction, square and opposition) of Pluto to the Moon.

Before one can use the creative energy of the Pluto–Moon opposition, the control and obsessive needs must become conscious and released. It's important to learn to love people without helping them so much that they become helpless. Obsessive love patterns need to change. If other aspects in the chart warrant it, this individual may draw a partner who is also controlling and who also drains him. The battle of the two strong individuals is interesting to watch.

When we give up, when we let go, the creative self can emerge, and we no longer have to live our lives guarding the "Boulder Dam" of our emotional selves. When we realize this, the Pluto energy brings wonderful blessings.

MOON–PLUTO QUINCUNX. Pluto quincunx the Moon brings the subconscious drives into touch with the emotional nature, but the energy is strained. There is a subconscious pulling or tugging that affects the feeling ability. The energy is not as disruptive as the square or opposition, but the feelings are out of synch with the inner self. The interplay can be solved by examining the signs involved and considering how the discomfort will manifest within the personality.

Consider the Moon in Capricorn since it is in a quincunx aspect with Pluto in either Gemini or Leo. Examine the keywords and synthesize. Both energies need expression somewhere in the life. The Moon in Capricorn responds to life in a traditional manner, yet Pluto in Gemini is unconsciously motivated by exciting controversy. And, if the Moon in Capricorn is traditional and realistic, how does that work with Pluto in Leo? Leo needs approval and yet is motivated by idealism. How will idealism work with the "reality" factor?

MERCURY WAS CALLED THE "MESSENGER OF THE GODS" in ancient mythology. It moves around the heavens quickly, always staying a sign ahead or behind the Sun or in the same sign. Gemini and Virgo are the mercurial signs in the zodiac: Gemini symbolizes the presentation of ideas, mental curiosity, the development of the mind, the concept of the new, and the Logos. Virgo represents the feminine side of Mercury and, as with all the feminine signs, symbolizes the ability to apply what has been learned on mental levels to the world of actual being.

Mercury in the personal chart indicates our five physical senses (touch, taste, hearing, sight, smell) and how they work, as well as how we communicate. Blocks in communication indicate that we are unwilling to share, or we may be afraid to share, or we may not be able to hear. The aspects to Mercury suggest the communication difficulties that may have occurred in the early life; they also suggest the difficulties we may have as adults because we never learned to discuss things properly, or fairly, or at all, in our early childhood environment. Stress is laid on the parental influence because we are a species of imitators. When parents don't communicate, children don't have a chance to see how others communicate. When there are blocking aspects to Mercury, communication will be an experience that a child may have to learn if he wishes to share experience with others.

If the Sun is in Taurus, Mercury will have to be in either Taurus, Aries or Gemini. The different Mercury placements will express the energy of the Sun sign in various ways. Taureans with Mercury in Taurus will have the archetypal energies and personality of Taurus and will express in an earthy, practical manner. When they talk, these people will be more apt to express themselves honestly, for both Mercury and the Sun are in the same sign. They "talk what they are" so to speak. Taurus people with Mercury in Aries will express differently. They will have the same Taurus early childhood experience, but they will discuss it differently. Such people may be observers, or writers perhaps. They are more apt to think before doing, for they look to past experience in the learning process. They may be more outgoing than the average Taurean, for they will be more aggressive when they speak; Taurus qualities will be expressed from an Aries point. They may seem to be more idealistic than they really are, for their speech reflects Aries but the Taurus practical and scientific approach may be hidden. Rather than voicing their problems, they are more apt to discuss their ideas of what they *should* be.

Those with a Taurus Sun and Mercury in Gemini will express in quite a different way. The Taurus base is the same, the childhood circumstances are the same, but the speech will be colored by Gemini qualities. These people may be effervescent, mentally curious, and may even appear to be flighty, covering the Taurus qualities. These are the therapists who work with new approaches to therapy; the people who want to build a growth center to help bring new ideas into consciousness—this is building (Taurus) the new (Gemini). The stability of Taurus is still there, but the approach is different.

When counseling people with Mercury in a sign different from the Sun, it may be wise to keep in mind that what they say they need may not be what they actually need, or even what they really want. However, because Mercury is in a different sign than the Sun, there may be an excellent chance for personal awareness to take place, since the personality includes the varying qualities of the different signs. When the Sun, Mercury, Venus, Moon and Ascendant are all in different signs, there is diverse energy within the individual. There is the possibility for greater understanding because all the different qualities of the different signs are expressed in the personal planets. With the chart of a specialist (a bundle of planets in one sign), there's a tendency to see a great part of life through the eyes of that sign, leaving little room for introspective questioning.

Mercury may be what Jung calls a part of the "trickster" mechanism in the unconscious. Our mind asks us questions and argues with us. Sometimes there seems to be a "little person" in our heads, someone who argues with every decision we make. Sometimes that "person" leads us astray, sometimes it is a valuable critic. We have to determine its place in our life. Some have called this "little person" the conscience. Perhaps it is, but it is mercurial.

MERCURY-SUN ASPECTS

See Chapter 1 in this section.

MERCURY-MOON ASPECTS

See Chapter 2 in this section.

MERCURY–VENUS ASPECTS

When these two planets are tied together by aspect, it indicates that the mother of the person has had an influence on the ability to communicate. It can indicate a person who enjoys communication, who may be involved in the arts, in literature, in appreciating the beauty in the world. It may also indicate a person who loves to talk!

MERCURY–VENUS CONJUNCTION. The childhood environment of this person includes open communication: the family talks about what it wants. Although the words may not be intellectual, the child is exposed to conversation. This may produce a ''wordy'' child and, consequently, a ''wordy'' adult! It may be a person who talks too much about nothing or it may indicate a prolific writer, depending on the rest of the chart indications.

Venus suggests the type of affect the mother has on a child's psyche. When the conjunction is afflicted by another planet, it may be determined how the person is hampered by the mother's influence. This individual will enjoy using the senses, and will enjoy some art form related to the sign in which the conjunction takes place.

MERCURY–VENUS SEXTILE. This aspect happens on those rare occasions when Mercury goes retrograde and allows Venus to catch up to its position via the sextile. With this aspect, the background of the person is more shy than with the conjunction, but it is productive when it receives proper training. Talent emerges that connects communication and the arts. An art appreciator, a communicator in the arts, someone interested in the classic art forms, or someone interested in the large-scale merchandising of beauty items may emerge.

This tie between Mercury and Venus indicates the person's ability in childhood to talk with and easily relate to the mother and her concept of femininity. Other aspects that may tie into this one will clarify the picture more.

MERCURY–MARS ASPECTS

These aspects are fun to work with once they are understood. Mercury indicates how we communicate, how we use our five senses; Mars symbolizes the action we take to express ourselves in a career and in our personal life. Mars also represents sexuality. When Mars ties into Mercury, communication becomes tied to action. If the aspects are easy, the result is constructive. If the aspects are hard, one must learn to listen before one acts!

MERCURY–MARS CONJUNCTION. Mercury is the symbol of our ability to communicate, the ability to hear others as well as to talk with them. Mars symbolizes the "I act" principle. Mars energy includes anger, violence, harshness and thoughtlessness in certain signs. People born with Mars–Mercury aspects emphasize verbal interaction. They may act on words—they hear, they speak, they act. They may speak impulsively, may react impulsively to what they hear; they may not listen to others. The mind works quickly, jumping to conclusions, skipping the necessary steps when learning good work habits in school or on the job.

Children with this aspect usually have trouble learning multiplication tables or division—they don't want to waste time on the rudiments. They don't listen easily because they are ahead of most people they talk with—but this doesn't make them smarter; it just makes them impetuous. The conjunction may imply a quick mind, but sometimes the tortoise wins the race! The environment is verbally volatile when these people are young, making them quick to explode, and quick to use or misuse words when they are older. The manner of verbal expression will come from the sign in which the conjunction takes place.

MERCURY–MARS SEXTILE. This aspect bestows the ability to act with reason; the mind and the action taken can be coordinated in time. These people can be creative producers. The childhood atmosphere encourages the discussion of problems and circumstances, so they can easily discuss their difficulties as adults. The imagination is fertile. Although it isn't as fertile as a Neptune aspect will be, it is fertile in a productive way because this individual is likely to act on constructive thoughts.

MERCURY–MARS SQUARE. This aspect is the symbol of a quick mind that is often improperly used. The square brings tremendous creative ability, but the creativity won't manifest until the anger and tendency toward being judgmental is channeled. The mind functions on several levels at once. People with the Mars–Mercury square see a lack of communication in childhood between the parents, and much in the family situation is not discussed. There are endless misunderstandings, and the child thinks that misunderstandings are normal aspects of adult behavior.

These individuals grow up jumping to conclusions. When knowledge or information is presented to them in a manner they disapprove of, they won't listen. They judge the veracity and capability of others on how they look; if one doesn't have the right credentials, they won't listen to more than three words of conversation. These people would put down "God" if IT isn't dressed right! They can go off half-cocked before they have heard the whole case for the opposition. They cause problems in their relationships and careers because they don't listen. The problem can be overcome, if they learn to develop a sense of humor and a bit of humility.

MERCURY–MARS TRINE. This aspect signifies an open household during the individual's childhood as far as certain kinds of communication are concerned. The most value from the aspect comes when it is applied toward career, for it is a prolific communicator: the mind is always working and is capable of being extremely productive. The aspect will only work if it's free, so look to see if it carries hard aspects from other planets.

This mind can be lazy, for the gift hasn't been earned in this life. When the talent is a natural one, when the person hasn't struggled to "earn" it from a conscious point, he may overlook its importance or even its existence. This can indicate a person who procrastinates.

MERCURY–MARS OPPOSITION. Words pop out of the mouth and, in spite of himself, this individual has said something he could have held in. This aspect has the power of the conjunction and the square, but it's easier to learn how to handle. The compromise will be indicated by the signs in which the opposition takes place.

For example, Mercury in Cancer, Mars in Capricorn, added to a Leo Sun, will need to balance the qualities of Leo with those of Cancer. The Sun communicates its sense of ethics (Leo) through the warm and nurturing attitudes of the Cancer Mercury. But Mars in Capricorn wants to act in a traditional and powerful manner. The goals need to be determined in conjunction with this individual's age. Goals change as we enter each new epoch in our life. Mars must cooperate with Mercury in order to satisfy the needs of the Sun. Some compromise will take place between the warm and encouraging words and the actions that seem so formal and traditional. The Leo Sun needs dignity in his life, and the Mercury–Mars opposition will have to learn to be noble enough to listen to others.

MERCURY–MARS QUINCUNX. This aspect always causes a strain to take place between the words and the deeds. Using the keywords of the planets and signs involved in this aspect, the strain can be understood and alleviated.

For example, Mercury in Gemini, Mars in Scorpio: the conversation is controversial, but the deeds are transformational. Or, the words may be contrary and the deeds revengeful if the energy is used in an unevolved manner. If one wants to reform, transform or search out life experience (from Scorpio), the Mercury in Gemini has to be curbed. Research won't get done if one is busy blabbing to everyone around. And controversial attitudes (or contrary ones) developed as attention-getting devices won't help reform. A positive synthesis of ideas and concepts must take place to satisfy both sides of the equation.

MERCURY-JUPITER ASPECTS

When these two planets are linked together, the ability to use the senses, to communicate, to use the mind, is combined with the relating principle. In order to have a relationship, we must be able to talk about it with the person with whom we are trying to relate. The easy aspects indicate unconstrained energy at our disposal; the hard aspects indicate that some lessons need to be learned. Jupiter represents how we absorb the atmosphere around us, how open we are to receiving new life experience. Mercury can indicate how we *listen*. During the Hero's venture (the process of individuation), we must be able to read the signs along the road. How easily can we do this?

MERCURY-JUPITER CONJUNCTION. If the Jupiter placement is the bridge to higher consciousness, and if Mercury is the messenger of the gods, once this person gets past the overindulgence in words, he will be able to indulge sensibly in ideas. He relates to words, ideas, and he enjoys communicating. The kinds of ideas he's involved with are indicated by the sign involved in the conjunction. If the energy is not being used well, this may indicate a person who talks profusely.

MERCURY-JUPITER SEXTILE. This indicates a person who is well-born, for the communication in his childhood environment is positive and uplifting. The ability to relate through the power of words (the various media, writing, film) grows with the years and with proper training. A sextile indicates talent that must be developed. This individual has the capacity for being open, he can expand his consciousness using the energy of the sign qualities involved in the aspect.

MERCURY-JUPITER SQUARE. The aspect indicates that the individual is raised in a home where words are not used well, the mood of the childhood environment is somewhat excessive, and people are hurt by words—they aren't supportive of each other. The family finds communication difficult; the family members are more involved in role playing than relating. The child absorbs this attitude and assumes that relationships are normal when words are difficult.

The aspect needs to be worked through if this individual ever wants to truly communicate and share his thoughts and feelings with another person. The power of Jupiter, the ability to expand the consciousness, to receive new ideas, cannot take place when one's words are not received well by others. This person has difficulty talking openly once a relationship has been established. He may not relate honestly, he may not listen, he may not hear what others say, he may even destroy relationships by misquoting what he thinks he heard. The ability to communicate can be learned if he thinks it is important enough. Excessiveness can be curbed and understood, for excessive or angry communication only hurts others.

The dilemma can be understood by examining the qualities of the signs involved in the square. For example, Mercury in Gemini, Jupiter in Virgo: "I talk controversially, yet I relate critically." This may indicate a person who says anything he pleases but criticizes others at every turn—a dilemma!

MERCURY–JUPITER TRINE. This aspect bestows natural talents. The childhood environment of this person is open, progressive and supportive of him as far as relating is concerned. He feels encouraged by his parents; his mind develops. This person is willing to share knowledge with others. As an adult, sharing thoughts in a relationship will be relatively easy. He enjoys communication and listening to the other person. The most profitable kinds of communication can be diagnosed from the houses and signs involved in the trine.

Because the trine is considered an easy aspect, it may not be noticed since we tend to give more attention to those aspects with which we are forced to struggle. The aspect can be wasted on prolific conversations, procrastination, etc.

MERCURY–JUPITER OPPOSITION. This person comes from a childhood in which the family doesn't relate to him. The power of the trine can be developed out of an opposition, but constructive use of the energy will have to be learned—early childhood experience doesn't provide the training.

Friends and opportunities may be lost because of a poor choice of words. The opposition causes a compromise between the relating ability and the need for communication. It can express in an excessive manner—one day relating nicely, the next not, or words can come out in a tirade. The feeling is that if communication is honest (according to the sign Mercury is in), then relationships can't happen. These feelings create inner tensions; eventually resentments develop because real communication isn't achieved. The aspect is a powerful one. The resentments will go once the individual learns how to express the compromise in a profitable manner. This can be learned once he realizes that he was not shown how to do it by his family.

For example, Mercury in Aries, Jupiter in Libra: the Aries Mercury is outspoken, idealistic, helpful of the "underdog." Jupiter in Libra wants to relate in a beautiful and socially acceptable manner to only the "right" people. The Mercury in Aries needs to learn diplomacy, and Jupiter in Libra needs to leave some room for ideals. The opposition can be compared to the needs of the Sun archetype and then worked out.

MERCURY–JUPITER QUINCUNX. Mercury symbolizes the communication abilities, and Jupiter represents the relating principle. The quincunx adds a strain, so the relationships formed may contain some remnants of role playing rather than direct or open communication.

Each facet of personality needs expression, and the key that unlocks the condition can be found by examining the house placement and the signs involved.

MERCURY–SATURN ASPECTS

Mercury is the messenger of the gods, the symbol of outgoing communication, the mind, the ideas, the five senses. Saturn represents the law, tradition, the psychological influence of the father, our ideas of caution based on apprehensions that we may have absorbed from the early father image.

When these two planets are bound together it indicates that we take communication and words seriously, that inhibitions or traditions taught to us by the father will affect our ability to communicate. It places restrictions on our confidence regarding our ability to communicate, even when the aspect is soft. This tie indicates a person who is serious, dependable and often hardworking. A certain kind of loneliness may be conferred, for when communication is restricted, limitations may be placed on the ability to share thoughts.

MERCURY–SATURN CONJUNCTION. This aspect causes the person to feel restricted by the father in some way during childhood. On a subconscious basis, the individual will carry the father's effect into his adult life, for it seems that Dad inhibited the child's expression. It may be that Dad resents the child, or that the child's crying makes him angry. If the mother tries to shush the kid because Dad doesn't like the noise, the child with this aspect will develop an inhibition regarding communicating with his father. This will only happen if the father is angry in the child's presence. Other aspects will confirm the father-child relationship.

Because of the early influence of the father, the child will not respond easily to the learning process that takes place in grammar school. He may avoid recitation or answering a teacher's questions. He may not be able to hear well; there may be some dysfunction, or he may be so tense that he "can't hear" because of his apprehension. Under pressure, he may not be able to receive instruction or follow directions.

As an adult, words come with difficulty, and he may sound harsh while trying to get his point across. The harshness may be caused by a subconscious fear that any authority figure will reject what he says, so his conversations may be tactless and too much to the point. A great deal of resentment may take place before he feels strong enough to talk about his feelings.

Once the energy is understood, this aspect can be turned into a strongly constructive one, for it gives the ability to follow through on details, to work to the finish, and to seriously express the needs of the self.

MERCURY–SATURN SEXTILE. Even the good aspects between Saturn and Mercury seem restrictive. The sextile places some restriction on the person's ability to communicate; the family atmosphere in childhood is usually precise and somewhat serious.

These individuals have orderly minds, and they can apply themselves to involved and detailed tasks. The aspect indicates thoroughness.

MERCURY–SATURN SQUARE. This aspect is similar to the conjunction, but with the square the quality of excessiveness is added. The psychological influence of the father (Saturn) impedes the ability to communicate and, therefore, produces adults who find words difficult. They have problems communicating what they want to those around them. During childhood, somehow the father created some block or fear that the child responded to. It brings apprehension regarding self-expression. In order to overcome the aspect, this person will have to work through the block set up years ago because of the relationship with the father. Once that has been accomplished, this person can teach himself to communicate in a sturdy and diplomatic manner. Until the aspect is understood, however, the words may come harshly, or in some authoritarian manner that seems designed to offend the very people he wants to talk with.

This aspect can restrict relationships, for the core of any relationship is the sharing of one's thoughts and feelings. Mercury rules the mind, the thoughts, the ability to express one's thoughts to others, the ability to hear what is being said. When a father feels that a child should be seen and not heard, he may have no idea of the limitations to creative expression that he places on the child born with this aspect. He may have other children whom he raises the same way, but, without this aspect, the other children will not react in the same manner.

Along with turning this energy into consctructive expression, this person will have to develop a sense of self-worth. If other aspects in the chart also indicate self-worth problems, he may need to seek therapy in order to transform the energy. Before one can confront authority figures in life, the inner self has to decide it is worth something.

MERCURY–SATURN TRINE. This person is exposed to a father image that helps him learn to communicate, even though the family communication tends to be serious. Because of the attitudes absorbed in the early environment, such people can follow through on details, work well with the general public, and have well-ordered minds.

Any contact between Saturn and Mercury will lend a serious note to the personality. Since Mercury rules the mind and Saturn represents tradition, authority and so forth, this contact will shape traditional attitudes.

MERCURY–SATURN OPPOSITION. This person is born into an

environment where communication is restricted. The father's influence keeps family members and others from saying what they want; communicating is done carefully. The child will be inhibited by attitudes of coldness or disapproval. Every time he reaches out to talk about how he feels, he is shut off, so he assumes that people always will reject his communications. The father may have difficulty handling the child's teething problems, or one of the childhood illnesses may cause a fretfulness that Dad can't cope with. Perhaps the father can't contend with the child's "why" stage. At any rate, the child becomes apprehensive about speech, so the grammar school years are difficult; he may avoid recitation, answering questions, or any verbal communication with teachers or authority figures.

As an adult he may have to learn how to communicate with others; he may have to teach himself to no longer assume that he will be disapproved of by those in authority. If a sense of self-worth hasn't been established, it becomes even more difficult to express feelings. His words are uttered harshly, they seem to offend people, others feel he is officious, pompous or power hungry, when in reality he's merely uncomfortable and unsure of himself.

Some compromise must be made so the planetary energies involved in the opposition can be expressed. Once the energy is transformed, the aspect indicates a thorough worker, one who handles details well, one who has a great deal of perseverence.

MERCURY–SATURN QUINCUNX. This aspect produces a strain involving verbal expression and inhibition. It can manifest in many ways: the Saturn restrictions may indicate some limitation involving the five senses—minor eye, nose, ear, taste or speech problems that are hampering. The causes are indicated by some kind of confusion in the childhood—a confusion that causes the child to respond to authority figures with difficulty. The father influence (Saturn) causes a strain or a frustration (perhaps he silently disapproved of the child).

This aspect denotes a "private" person because it is difficult for him to communicate his thoughts and feelings to others in a comfortable manner.

MERCURY–URANUS ASPECTS

Mercury rules the mind and the sign it is in tells us how we communicate best; it also tells us how we use our five senses. Uranus generally represents the Aquarian part of ourselves, how we expand our consciousness, how we develop our minds. It can also indicate how willful and eccentric we are, and how we behave. When these planets are in aspect, the mind is activated, and creative energy as well as nervous energy will be added to the qualities of Mercury. Mental tension and mental activity will be increased.

MERCURY–URANUS CONJUNCTION. The person born with the conjunction is exposed to an early family atmosphere that includes mental chaos; no one says anything that makes sense, words are used in all kinds of strange ways, and the child responds to the stimuli. As a result, when these children are admitted to the school system, they are not interested in learning thought patterns or the rituals involved in thorough work habits. As adults, they seem to be erratic and undisciplined.

Communication is unusual. Personal relationships may be difficult because conversation may be erratic or impulsive. In the creative sense, Mercury represents the possible concepts of consciousness. As messenger of the gods, it represents a part of the wisdom-learning process. If Mercury asks the questions and Uranus represents the heights of expanded consciousness, the conjunction combines these energies and the creative possibilities are enhanced.

If the energy is not properly channeled or trained, it may not operate constructively. When it isn't, the adult may be highly erratic, eccentric or nervous. The combination can create such a quick mentality that the individual appears to be "flaky." When this aspects is set off by transit, the individual needs to become involved in some personal creative endeavor so that the energy can be brought into focus. Painting, writing, making pottery or stained glass, or similar activities help the creative energy channel itself.

MERCURY–URANUS SEXTILE. This aspect is much safer than the conjunction for it isn't as strong. The environment during this individual's formative years is healthy for mental development; some effort is made to cope with the concept of spirituality in his family. The child is used to hearing rather unconventional forms of communication and can therefore grow to be a creative, innovative and productive adult.

The sextile indicates talent that can be developed, although it may not manifest until after the age of thirty.

MERCURY–URANUS SQUARE. If Mercury represents the ability to communicate and Uranus represents the ability to expand the consciousness, then this aspect indicates a person whose spiritual development may be hampered in childhood by mental confusion. The mind is bright, witty and quick but not thorough. Work and learning patterns are not solid because this child is easily and quickly bored. Brilliance will show through periodically, but it can't be counted on until the energy is properly channeled and trained.

Uranus indicates erratic and eccentric behavior as well as willfulness and expanded consciousness. When the hard aspects apply, one tends to use the lower energy first—this is a child who is raised in an atmosphere which doesn't share thoughts and ideas. Decisions are made, words are said without regard for the feelings and needs of the rest of the family members.

Because this kind of energy is present in the early life, the aspect produces adults who don't consider others while talking, who may speak impulsively or erratically in relationships or on the job. Once they start talking, the words just flow out, and under stressful situations they may say things that they may later regret.

However, when the energy is properly trained, it becomes creative. These individuals will have to train themselves to talk about their needs before they explode, to consider discussing situations with others before arriving at decisions, and to choose words more carefully in business situations.

MERCURY-URANUS TRINE. If this aspect is utilized well, it indicates people who have a proclivity to apply a heightened state of consciousness in their daily lives. It indicates a brilliant mind. When these people are young, their thought patterns may not be orthodox. Teachers may find them a trial to teach for they question everything they learn. The early family environment is open, interested in pursuing unusual ideas of some sort, and open to searching for new paths in life. These children develop quickly, and they may be innately wise and mature for their years. If the environment is not protective, they may not be able to use this energy constructively before the age of thirty.

Because the aspect is easy, these people may not be consciously aware of the gift of creative thought. Ideas come easily, communication is easy for them, and the media, arts or new sciences may appeal to them. Mental instability may be felt from time to time and will indicate that mental energy is not being used correctly; pursuit of any creative endeavor will bring the energy into focus.

MERCURY-URANUS OPPOSITION. This aspect works much like the conjunction or the square, except that a compromise is added to the energies. The person is born into a family that doesn't communicate easily or constructively. The power parent (See Section I, Chapter 5) tends to make decisions based on eccentricities or willful attitudes. Feelings and thoughts as well as decisions involving family members are not discussed before decisions are made. When the family does discuss an issue, it's only a polite formality since the decision has already been made. Because the child doesn't see the power parent sharing decisions, he becomes an adult who makes his own impetuous decisions without consulting those he's involved with. The areas of life most affected by the aspect will be indicated by the house placement of the opposition, as well as by any other apsects made to it.

Impetuous speech, poorly thought-out programs of mental endeavor, conversations that sound irrational to others, all come from this aspect.

Once the fountain of the mouth has opened, the owner of the aspect may be as surprised as anyone else about what comes out! One thing may be said one day, its opposite the next. Jerry Ford has this aspect; reporters loved to discuss his conversations, for Ford often said things that he probably didn't mean. It can indicate someone who blurts out all they know, or one who babbles inanely at the wrong times. It can be conditioned, however, and the qualities of the signs involved in the compromise (caused by the opposition) can be channeled constructively.

Any aspect between Mercury and Uranus indicates a sharp mind, a quick wit and creative ability. Consider Mercury in Aries, Uranus in Libra: an Aries Mercury is outspoken, idealistic, aggressive in an intellectual way, aggressive with words. Uranus in Libra wants to behave diplomatically, and behavior will include the social graces. If one wants to be graceful or socially acceptable, one must curb aggressive speech, for people will respond to it. The energy can rather be used in some creative manner. The pursuit of metaphysics, philosphy, the ability to write, can be nurtured here. (The written word can be edited until it says what you mean!)

As far as the personal life is concerned, if relationships are important enough, rash statements and erratic conversations can be edited when it is understood that this type of communicating can harm the potential of the sharing experience.

MERCURY–URANUS QUINCUNX. This aspect brings some form of mental strain. The family members seem to circumlocute when discussing important family matters, and the individual grows to feel disconcerted and unsure of himself.

However, the lack of communication is not as obvious as that involved in a square or opposition. The quincunx brings a nagging dissatisfaction regarding efforts at communication. Once the qualities of the signs involved are understood, it will be easier to channel self-expression.

MERCURY–NEPTUNE ASPECTS

Mercury represents how we communicate, how our five senses operate within us; the sign it's in tells us how we will use our words. Neptune represents the creative part of the self, our fantasies, our dream goals, the part of us that dreams of being far away, the part of us that can be deluded, that can live in an illusory world. When these planets interact, the energy can be extremely creative and imaginative. In some cases it must be channeled before it can be used constructively, for we may dream our lives away.

MERCURY–NEPTUNE CONJUNCTION. Mercury indicates the state of mind, the natural interests on the mental plane; Neptune affects the mind with its fantasies, dreams, delusions, etc. This can be a most creative aspect and it makes for an unusual type person. Neptune can represent the search for the truly spiritual, and Mercury tied to it indicates that the mind may be on some wonderful spiritual search that others don't understand.

Children with this aspect are born into families where a search for some sort of spiritual identity is going on. The search may not seem obvious to the outsider, or even to the child; but after a thorough investigation, it is discovered that one or both parents have some "strange" ideas about religion—religious attitudes can be orthodox or unorthodox. Often, the spiritual philosophy is hidden.

The aspect indicates that the mind may be "clouded." This child may daydream into maturity. Communication between the parents is nebulous and vague; the child learns to communicate with others the same way. He may not know how to share himself or his ideas with others, for he may live in his mind. In the mundane aspects of day-to-day living, he will communicate strangely; he may start sentences and leave them unfinished, or he may start a sentence in the middle and leave you to figure out the beginning. (If you don't have a Mercury–Neptune aspect, it can be trying to live with!)

However, it is a tremendously creative aspect, for the mind is capable of reaching into the depths and heights of creative endeavor. The aspect becomes dangerous when the child is born into an environment that doesn't encourage creative thought, for then the energy can use him—and may manifest in various forms of psychic phenomena that are not readily understood. Because of the spirituality of Neptune, this aspect can evince the religious fanatic, one who talks with God, one who hears voices, or who has frightening prophetic dreams.

Once the energy is used creatively, once the intuitive energy common to the aspect is comprehended, it's a wonderful one to have. Misunderstood, it frightens the person who has it because he doesn't know how to use the energy effectively. The study of the occult, a pursuit of metaphysics, theosophy, religion in some form, will also help the owner to expend his energy constructively. It can be fun!

MERCURY–NEPTUNE SEXTILE. This aspect represents a creative potential that can be developed during the lifetime, especially after the first Saturn return (at age twenty-eight or so) has taken place.

This person sees people communicating creatively during his childhood years. There is some interest in spiritual development or a spiritual consciousness in the family as well. As this child grows, he can readily draw on the creative energy of the Neptune function.

MERCURY–NEPTUNE SQUARE. The square is much like the conjunction, except that more misunderstandings are likely to take place.

The energy can be more excessive, more forceful, for the square aspect serves to stimulate the mental dilemmas. It's easier for the unhealthy energies to manifest because the childhood environment couldn't or didn't teach the child how to focus since his family was unfocused. A need for spiritual development is indicated, and the child may suffer because of the family's adverse reaction to religion. There may be strong orthodox religious ties, or some feeling against religion that hampers the child from exploring his consciousness on his own.

This child sees life differently than others will for he is extremely intuitive. He has a natural grasp of extrasensory perception, and can live in a fantasy world and daydream his life away. Historical novels, books about strange lands and strange people, different cultures, may fascinate this child. One parent usually has some secret occult interest, which may not be discovered until the child becomes an adult. Because the occult interest, or the spiritual interest, is not discussed with the child, he feels lonely and left out, not understanding where his curiosities come from.

Incomplete thoughts occur with this aspect and, like the conjunction, sentences are begun midstream or left half-finished. School may become frustrating, for term papers are unacceptable when the introductory paragraph is left out. This individual may not present all the facts of any situation, for he may feel that since *he* knows what he's talking about, so does everybody else. Others feel they aren't "connecting" with the person who has this aspect.

In order to use the energy, the intellect must be harnessed, interests must be developed and followed through on; metaphysics and other forms of spiritual development will help. Even the study of parapsychology can release the tension. Because of the extrasensory perception, this individual may fear mental instability. The symptoms will disappear once the mind is used creatively.

MERCURY–NEPTUNE TRINE. Often, the person with this aspect is interested in some form of spiritual development. During his childhood, the parents often force him to follow in their spiritual footsteps—and their religious attitudes can range from orthodox church going to heavy antireligious attitudes that become a religion in themselves. This influence can keep him from pursuing his own goals. The power parent (see Section I, Chapter 5) will be determined by the Sun sign, and the individual will react most strongly to that parent's influence.

People with this aspect who were raised in an atheistic home feel guilty about the need to pursue spiritual insight because of a fear of being laughed at by their parents. At any rate, the aspect bestows creative energy which can be used in the development of a career as well as for the pursuit of spiritual ideals. Neptune brings a "bottomless spring" of creative energy that won't run dry. The ideas are usually ahead of the times and the masses may not understand. Along with the creative expression is a need for spiritual identity.

MERCURY-NEPTUNE OPPOSITION. This aspect works much like the conjunction or the square in that it gives the individual a strange, ethereal outlook on life. Thoughts range from inspirational to delusional, and the mind needs to be directed into something creative and constructive.

People born with this aspect grow up in an atmosphere where the parents are privately and/or peculiarly spiritual, keeping their spiritual interests away from the child. These children may be extremely intuitive and seldom discuss their extrasensory experiences with anyone for fear of being misunderstood. Privately, they may consider their mental stability with misgiving. If they don't understand the intuitive or psychic experiences, they can be frightened by them. They either assume that *everyone* is as psychic as they are, or they fear that they are not really psychic, they're just crazy. The energy may use its owner if it isn't channeled and understood.

In my work with therapists, psychologists and others who work in the professions associated with the insane, this aspect is not uncommon among disturbed clients and patients. Often, the delusions that take place are tied to some strange religious experience. For those who feel they don't need religious or spiritual experience in their lives, this aspect is a difficult one to understand. Stability and understanding often come when parapsychology, metaphysics, philosophy, Jungian analysis and mythology and related subjects are pursued. As this person reaches the age of thirty, the creative energy can be put to use, for the aspect brings insight, intuitive reasoning and mental ability. The ideas that come through may be far ahead of the times.

As far as relationships go, this aspect causes some hardship; ideas are not fully related to others, subjects are left out of the sentences, conversations are begun in the middle or started and never finished. This person may appear to be untruthful to others when he is merely being Neptunian! It can be fun to work with—but include a sense of humor! People with this aspect need to associate with other creative people, for it can be too lonely attempting to live in a mundane community with this mind type. As the creative energy is used and shared with others who can understand it, this individual will stabilize beautifully.

MERCURY-NEPTUNE QUINCUNX. The creative or spiritual energy is present with this aspect, but the mind is not as well ordered as it could be. This person may spend most of the day dreaming and fantasizing about what life could be, or what experience could be. This indicates a person who thinks a great deal but who doesn't do anything about his thoughts. An internal argument is taking place for he feels confused about his creative urges.

Consider Mercury in Aries quincunx Neptune in Virgo: the Aries Mercury wants to talk, to accomplish, to consider life on an idealistic level. Neptune in Virgo dreams about perfection, dreams that it might be organized one day. Aries wants to accomplish as quickly as possible; Neptune in Virgo wants to work out all the details. By the time the surroundings are right to get some work done, the day or even the idea may be gone. Conversations may be cluttered with extraneous details, or details can cloud the main issues in life. The energy needs to be channeled, and the person will have to spend time considering profitable thinking.

MERCURY–PLUTO ASPECTS

When these planets meld together, they combine the functioning mind with the powers of the collective unconscious, transformation and creative insight. The less evolved manifestations of the energy have to be worked through before true creativity can express itself. Pluto, as it manifests on the lower levels of consciousness, represents obsession. There is a need to control all thoughts when it ties into Mercury. Pluto also represents the power of transformation, transfiguration, growth.

The phoenix has been used to symbolize Pluto, or the Scorpionic energies—it's the bird that rises out of its own ashes, the symbol for rebirth. In order to be reborn, we must first become conscious of our motivations. For the mind (Mercury) to be free when it is aspected to Pluto, we must give up control in order to gain insight into different levels of consciousness.

MERCURY–PLUTO CONJUNCTION. If Pluto can be called the symbol of the collective unconscious in the chart—Jung's definition of the intuitive history of the species since time began; that part of ourselves which transmits knowledge over generations; that part of ourselves which combines instincts with conscious development—then this aspect can understandably be a powerful one.

In everyday activities, the person with this aspect doesn't always know what he is talking about, for the words come out before he knows what he is saying. If he uses this energy constructively, he has the beginnings of a great writer, a great social commentator. The childhood experience with the family may be an overwhelming one in terms of communication; words are controlled, or words are used to control others. The power parent (see Section I, Chapter 5) is the most controlling influence, unless the aspects indicate otherwise.

For example, when a child is born into a mother-dominated household and Mercury conjuncts Pluto, it can indicate that the father attempts to stay in control, but from a passive controlling point. Passive control can be called the tyranny of the weak, and if this is the case, the conjunction will have strong or hard aspects to the Sun or Saturn. If so, the child will attempt to control from a passive point as well. The child with this conjunction is controlled and manipulated by his parents and his investigation of new ideas may be suppressed. When the child becomes an adult, this energy will place limits on relationships because his conversation may not be spontaneous. Manipulation via words can be used in career; copy editors often have this aspect!

MERCURY–PLUTO SEXTILE. The person with this aspect is born into a family that cooperates with the neighborhood, with family members and with new ideas. The family enjoys the status quo. Conversation may be cooperative or team oriented. The child is taught to relate to the needs and interests he is born into; he can cope with the system of the moment; he doesn't have blocks that keep creativity from developing.

The sextile indicates a talent that needs to be developed. As the talents indicated by the signs and houses involved are developed, this individual can function in a cooperative manner.

MERCURY–PLUTO SQUARE. This person is born into a family that finds the status quo difficult to cope with. Something is wrong with the surroundings, and people born with this aspect are convinced early in life that they cannot cooperate with their peers, and that communication is not a part of the family life. Malicious or sadistic humor may be directed at these children. The dominant parent (see Section I, Chapter 5) will fight the recessive parent for control.

Words come in anger without forethought. As the energy is understood, people with this aspect can learn to communicate with peers, omitting their hidden motives. The energy can then become fertile and creative. When the energy is used improperly, the square can obsess a lot—conversations may be obsessive and they may be manipulative. This conversation pattern is learned in the early family environment; it can be changed by merely becoming conscious of its existence.

These people can overwhelm others: they get their own way because others find it easier to agree with them and then get away. This can inhibit the development of sincere relationships because conversation and thoughts are not shared.

MERCURY–PLUTO TRINE. Like the sextile, this aspect suggests a person who is born into a family that enjoys the status quo. The child with this aspect may be too interested in the "fadism" of his generation. The family is cooperative in the neighborhood and receives new ideas in a positive fashion. Consequently, the child readily cooperates with authority figures and with the needs of his generation.

The aspect can give this person an "in" with the writing market, for often people with Mercury trine Pluto write about contemporary problems. The area of politics, labor movements, civil and equal rights and related subjects are good for this writer.

The aspect bestows creative energy, but it may not be valued by its owner because he doesn't have to go through any spiritual transformations

in order to work with it, as do those people with the squares and oppositions.

MERCURY–PLUTO OPPOSITION. The early family atmosphere
of this person shows constant manipulation. One parent tries to control
the other. As an adult this individual will attempt to control those around
him as his parents did; he may manipulate conversations or use words to
keep tabs on the environment he thinks he must create for himself.

The aspect can make relationships difficult because conversation is not
spontaneous, ideas may be highly controlled, and the mind is not free.
However, if the Jungian concept of the collective unconscious is considered—if Pluto can represent the creative depths or heights of consciousness—perhaps that knowledge alone will convince the owner of this
aspect to let go of the controlling influence in order to get at the creative
energy lying dormant below. Once that path has been started, this person
will realize that relationships just "flow" and he'll see the glory of spontaneity.

The energy can be used in the creative process, producing the "bottomless spring" of creative possibility. Unchanneled, it can represent the
person who is righteous—the one who imposes his new-found information
on others before getting permission to do so. The habit is learned at home,
and it can be unlearned.

MERCURY–PLUTO QUINCUNX. With this aspect, the unconscious energies work against the mental functions; the mind is not as
free to be as productive as one might wish. Will the mind be free to explore new ideas or not? Is it ok to be undisciplined? Can one be spontaneously creative? Does one have to maintain control over conversations,
or is one weak for not doing so?

The strain or tension caused by this aspect is not as profound as that of
the square or opposition, but it can create an atmosphere of mistrust, and
the mistrust may be of the self. The energies of the two planets need to be
understood so they can merge in order to release the strain.

For example, when Mercury is in Taurus and Pluto is in Libra, the tension will be caused by conversation of a practical and scientific nature being
influenced by a subconscious need to be socially acceptable. What if one is
blunt and practical but needs to feel that one is gracious? How can the two
energies of the signs involved meld to solve the problem? Each of us must
find our own answers.

VENUS IS A PLANET THAT IS NEVER TOO FAR FROM THE
Sun. It can't square or oppose the Sun, it can only amplify the Sun's
energy. Venus represents our ability to love; not sex love, but the art of
loving in its intellectual sense. Venus symbolizes our ability to appreciate
being loved and how we appreciate affection. The sign it is in indicates the
kind of affection we will accept versus what the Sun sign is willing to give.
The type of earthly beauty that we wish to be around, our taste in furniture and clothing, the things we collect, our attitudes about loving, all
come from Venus. It can represent the person we *want to be* and causes a
dilemma when the Venus placement is different from that of the Sun.

The Moon indicates the physical mother, how she carries herself, how
she copes with emotions or her emotional needs at the time the child's personality is forming from birth to the age of three. Venus, on the other
hand, represents the impact the mother has on the child's psyche and it is a
more subtle thing. Each mother has her own attitudes regarding the concept of motherhood, the responsibilities of rearing children, and view-
points regarding self-value. If a mother has poorly developed concepts
regarding the feminine principle, if her self-esteem is low, if she thinks that
women (or the feminine) have little value, these concepts will be passed on
to her child. Hard aspects to Venus can indicate if she affects her child
adversely because of her state of mind at the time. Because a child is influenced during the first three years of its life, the effect on the subconscious may be difficult to self-diagnose. The mother may change,
mature, become self-aware, develop self-esteem later, and the individual
won't remember the early pattern.

Venus operates differently in a man's chart than in a woman's. Everyone
has an intellectual concept of what love is, but *how* we direct the concept
will be based on our sex. When a man has Venus afflictions, it often means
that his mother affects his concept of love on a subconscious level; he may

unknowingly project that image onto other women. His mother may have had little regard for women or even for herself when his personality was receptive to her attitudes. If she instilled the idea that "women are no good," he may subconsciously carry that attitude with him when he approaches women. He may have a double standard regarding matters of affection; he may feel uncomfortable about receiving love or maintaining a love relationship. In short, he may subconsciously project unhealthy attitudes toward women while feeling uncomfortable about his own need for love, or his own feeling capacity.

When a woman has hard aspects to Venus, she responds differently. She is receptive (during the formative years) to the attitudes projected by her mother; but unlike the male, her response to the mother's influence is directed at herself. She may feel like a second class citizen, she may feel that women have no rights, and she may have little sense of self-esteem. She may be apprehensive regarding the role of the biological female; all phases of the reproductive and mothering process may be affected in some adverse manner, ranging from avoiding motherhood to overcompensating for her dislike or apprehension regarding the child-rearing process.

In contemporary society, she may be involved with women's liberation for all the wrong reasons. She may be defensive of herself and her rights, not seeing clearly that those ideas could be better established within. If she has no regard for her femininity, she may respond to love and affection with difficulty—it may not seem natural to her. She may reject men who are nice to her, for when a woman regards herself as second rate she will be suspicious of anyone who likes her. As she becomes conscious of the limitations of the hard aspects, she can cure them and thereby enter into more satisfying relationships.

The aspects to Venus tell whether or not we can easily handle emotional relationships, whether or not we really feel comfortable in an emotional situation or whether we have to work at being able to become receptive to the love vibration in the universe. Some astrologers feel that Venus indicates our interest in pleasure; it does, but the emphasis is on how we will receive it.

VENUS–SUN ASPECTS

See Chapter 1 in this section.

VENUS–MOON ASPECTS

See Chapter 2 in this section.

VENUS–MERCURY ASPECTS

See Chapter 3 in this section.

VENUS–MARS ASPECTS

Venus symbolizes the intellectual concept of love and how it relates to being able to receive sexual experience. Mars symbolizes how we act out our sexual needs. Sometimes an examination of the mother's values will help the person to understand what he picks up from her. When these planets are in aspect, the individual often is so close to the mother that the ability to have a close emotional relationship with another person is inhibited by the relationship with the mother.

The easy aspects between these planets indicate a natural ability to love and to appreciate love. Action taken will be considerate of the needs of others, and caring will be appreciated and well received. The aspects are important when diagnosing the inherent emotional problems motivating an individual's action.

VENUS–MARS CONJUNCTION. If Venus represents the concept of love and Mars represents the way we sex someone, then one may rationally assume that this conjunction is an easy one to live with. However, it has been noted that many people who own it have trouble opening up sexually. Women are often nonorgasmic, and men have either potency problems or problems with premature ejaculation. There may be difficulty with sexual expression; either it is taken too seriously or there is a need for total commitment before getting involved. It seems that the sex drive is tied up with some subconscious mother influence. Other aspects to this conjunction and the Sun sign needs for expression may give a clue as to how the conjunction is working. The aspect indicates that the individual receives sex with difficulty. As a result, the sex partner becomes apprehensive about the relationship and begins to wonder if he or she is loved. The partner becomes insecure; the person with the Mars–Venus conjunction absorbs that insecurity and becomes insecure too. It can be a difficult aspect to work out because even more tension is caused by any serious discussion of sexuality.

This conjunction is often the mark of individuals who have fantastic crushes on people they admire; and in the midst of a yet untried love affair, they are thinking of marriage and commitment. They fall in love quite often—men sometimes propose before they have even necked with the lady. In some instances, it represents people who are so tied to Mother that they may express love only homosexually or maybe not at all.

At any rate, the two planets influence each other in a difficult manner, for the Mars heats up the Venus and makes it harsh, while the mother's influence softens the Mars expression. Various Sun signs react to this aspect differently, depending on the influence of the dominant parent. In order to relieve the tension caused by the aspect, the mother's affect on the psyche must be explored. A double standard may have been evoked, for there is sexual confusion. A culture may rule that commitment (or marriage) must be coordinated with sexual involvements, but Mother Nature does not. The individual may have responded to the mother on some forgotten sexual level, therefore creating a subconscious guilt complex that confuses loyalty, mother love and sexuality. (This aspect still surprises me and it would be nice to get some serious feedback from the readers.)

VENUS–MARS SEXTILE. The sextile indicates that the mother of this individual has a healthy attitude toward sexuality and femininity. This person can go into emotional relationships and easily combine the emotional and sexual needs. Relationships can be enjoyed.

The sextile indicates that an appreciation of beauty is inherent; often this person becomes involved in the arts, or employment may be obtained in the art field. Career action taken will include an appreciation of other people's needs.

VENUS–MARS SQUARE. The square implies a complication regarding the area of love and relationships. Venus indicates the concept of love, the kind of love one is looking for intellectually, and the ability to appreciate love when it is offered. Mars represents the physical action taken in life; it indicates how an individual physically reacts to the environment; it indicates how the sexual needs are expressed. The square aspect indicates hardship for the energy cannot express easily.

Consider Venus in Aries square Mars in Cancer: Venus in Aries is ardent, idealistic, tending to look for a knight in shining armor or a maid in gossamer as a lover. Mars in Cancer acts either possessive, moody, emotional or sensitive; it acts on feelings and responds physically to feelings. Venus in Aries responds to wonderful poetry and flowers but doesn't feel comfortable about acting in a possessive manner for that kind of action is not idealistic. Sexual relationships may bring a feeling of discomfort for the mother influence (on a subconscious level) may include a feeling of guilt regarding love. The guilt may confuse the "ideal" love with the physical manifestation of it.

Consider Mars in Taurus square Venus in Leo: the Leo Venus indicates a search for an ideal love situation, the knight or the maid, the poetry, the cloak flung over the mud puddle; added to this is a concept that one must be "properly respected" in a love relationship at all times! Mars in Taurus acts sensually and at the same time reacts to life in a practical manner. When these two energies combine, the sensual Mars wants to wallow in some warm emotional sexual experience and the Venus says that "one doesn't do that—it's not proper!" The Mars in Taurus wants to express in a practical or reasonable way, the Venus in Leo wants to chase some ideal, wants to appreciate some of the finer "lost causes" in the universe. The energy works against itself.

When considering the influence of the mother in this aspect, it seems that Mom was against sexual expression in some way, and she unknow-ingly encouraged her child to look upon sexual activity with apprehension or frustration. The mother may have been frustrated herself; her emotional and physical needs may have caused her pregnancy. At any rate, this person grows up to have mixed feelings about sexual expression. On the one hand he wants to be in love, and he often falls in love at the drop of a hat. But, he feels uncomfortable in extended love relationships. He may run from one love to another, or one marriage to another, or he may deal with one relationship with great inner stress. Much of the compromise or frustra-tion felt by the owner of the aspect may be projected onto the lover, for "they" are creating the problem. Once it is understood that the emotional turmoil comes from within, the two kinds of energies manifested by the signs can be incorporated comfortably into the personality. If the mother felt apprehensive about sex, and although her attitudes may have affected the child during his formative years, those attitudes can be altered by an at-tempt to develop consciousness.

The negative or unproductive expression of the energy most often manifests in the adult emotional sexual experience rather than in the work environment. This energy can be turned around and put into action: Mars represents action, Venus indicates what we want to be, what we ap-preciate. Thoughtfully used, this energy can be applied to achieving goals. Once the needs of a relationship have been consciously thought out, the unproductive patterns can be released and more satisfying ones developed.

VENUS–MARS TRINE. The mother of this individual is a healthy influence during the childhood from a psychological point. What a person wants, desires, appreciates in life, what a person expects from a love rela-tionship, is shown by the Venus position and sign. It is complemented by the Mars energy, for Mars enables one to act in a manner that helps the goal manifest. When the trine takes place, the personality reflects a great capacity for love and giving. If there are other relating problems indicated in the chart, this aspect can help give confidence to the "worthwhileness" of working through them.

Mars represents action and Venus symbolizes what we appreciate, what we want from a love relationship, what we want to surround ourselves with in life. This interaction can be a beneficial one if used for accomplish-ment on the career level. However, any trine should be examined in con-text with the Sun, for trines can indicate a different dilemma. For example, a Fire sign trine here might be too idealistic, and the idealism may cause an overly sensitive reaction to the normal day-to-day relating problems.

VENUS–MARS OPPOSITION. This aspect is similar to the square, but it seems easier to solve. For some reason, it's easier to compromise through the opposition aspect than to work through the frustration of the square. Here the mother has some subconscious influence on the native during the formative years, and the affect concerns the ability to love. The mother's problems are an unknown factor, but she will act (Mars) in a manner that causes her to compromise her femininity, or her concept of "female." She may be sexing someone because her physical desires are so strong that they outweigh her convictions regarding what women should do. She may be angry that she has physical desires. Her child absorbs her fear or apprehension or feelings of self-disgust or discomfort. When the aspect affects the adult life, the circumstances or relationships formed between the ages of twenty and thirty will establish the pattern and give a clue to what the fears are.

It will be difficult for this person to coordinate loving someone with relating on a sexual level. A certain amount of discomfort may occur when the young adult is in a sexual situation. This person will have difficulty acting out (Mars) his desires, for Mars says "act one way" and Venus appreciates something else. It makes for confusion about life goals and about what one wants from a love and sexual relationship. This person may feel uncomfortable loving someone, or combining sex and love in the same relationship. Some of my clients have loved one person and had sex with another.

Consider Venus in Aries opposing Mars in Libra: Venus in Aries is aggressive and lusty but highly idealistic. Mars in Libra symbolizes a person who takes diplomatic action. Venus in Aries is idealistic and direct—Mars in Libra is often diplomatic rather than idealistic, and tends to suppress anger rather than vent it openly. If Venus in Aries wants an ideal intellectual love relationship with knights in shining armor or maids in gossamer going off into the sunset in some special wonderful way, and Mars in Libra wants to fight, especially in the sexual area, how does one feel comfortable loving the person one loves? Mars in Libra can act diplomatically, but it can also be quite belligerent in a diplomatic and intellectual manner.

Venus in Gemini opposing Mars in Sagittarius indicates a person who desires to be controversial, intellectual, different, maybe contrary; a person who wants an unusual kind of love relationship. But, the Mars in Sagittarius values freedom and independence. The compromise takes place when one determines the rub between controversy and freedom. By mere definition, controversy needs an audience. Freedom and independence cannot easily be acted out if the need for an audience is there. This particular opposition will cause a determination of the love values to take place, for this individual has the capability of being interested in love from a more intellectual point of view than the average person. Once love and love-making get into the intellectual bracket, people have more difficulty expressing the physical side of love, for it becomes more and more spiritual—even platonic.

VENUS–MARS QUINCUNX. This aspect implies a strain between the concept of love and the ability to physically act out a personal love relationship. When a person appreciates being loved, he may appreciate different values than his sexual needs signify. A strain exists, for the partner may be sexually satisfying but not emotionally gratifying—or the reverse; the emotional needs may be fulfilled leaving the sexual side of the relationship somewhat unfulfilled. When this aspect occurs, it's important not to settle for just anything—for once the emotional needs are determined, an arrangement can be worked out with an appropriate personality.

The confusion stems from the mother and her misapprehension regarding the combination of love and sex. She may have second thoughts about her own life when this person is young; her personal standards and the morals of her generation will bring some answers to how her dilemma may apply to the generation to which this personality belongs. We all take our mother's problems and apply them to some related feminine concept, and the root problem is often very similar from generation to generation.

VENUS–JUPITER ASPECTS

Venus symbolizes how we appreciate love, our intellectual concept of love, the kind of warm and loving relationships we want to have (such as friendships), the kind of entertainment we prefer, our concept of the "perfect love affair," our predilection for comfort, our appreciation of art objects, etc. Jupiter signifies how we relate—how we reach out or open up to the universe around us, and how we relate to those we love. Where Venus describes what goes on in our heads, Jupiter describes how we reach out to get it. Venus shows how the mother image affected the psyche and, therefore, the concept of the feminine. This is an important placement for a woman for it tells how she feels about being one. When Venus aspects Jupiter, it tells what the chances are for easy growth and maturity, and it indicates how easily an individual can relate to what he needs, what he wants and what he loves.

VENUS–JUPITER CONJUNCTION. The mother brings an exciting, open and straightforward influence to this child's concept of expectancy. This influence can be somewhat moderated by the signs in which the conjunction takes place, and the aspect should be read with the signs in mind. Other aspects can mitigate this interpretation, for the energy will not be free to operate until the mitigating aspect is rechanneled.

Venus conjunct Jupiter in Aries indicates a person who is idealistic about love (Venus), who relates generously (Jupiter), and who is lovingly aggressive (Aries). This personality may be lovingly aggressive when young, and may have many lovers—an abundance of them; as maturity takes place the appreciation of beauty may be developed instead. These people tend to be lucky in love for they are exuberant and others enjoy their companionship. However, a square from Mars in Cancer added to the conjunction in Aries gives a horse of a different color! Here the qualities of Mars color the

Jupiter and this person may not be so exuberant, or the exuberance may be more surface than heartfelt. The relating ability will be there, but the additional aspect adds complication to the energy that a therapist would consider as a complex.

As another example, Venus conjunct Jupiter in Capricorn indicates a person who wants to be a Capricorn. Pretend that this person has Sun in Aquarius with the Capricorn conjunction. This configuration indicates the Aquarian archetype who wants to be a Capricorn (Venus), who appreciates the traits and the qualities of Capricorn; who relates (Jupiter) in a traditional Capricornian manner. It indicates a more serious Aquarian type, someone who will mature to enjoy stable, traditional forms of entertainment, furniture, art; one who will enjoy the kind of position in life that a Capricorn would seek. One might say of them, "They don't seem to be Aquarians." When diagnosing the riddle of life for this person, the dilemma felt by the owner will come from the father-dominated Aquarian archetype (see Chapter 5, Section 1) and the affect of Venus (mother image) on the drives and goals.

The conjunction aspect is helpful for it indicates the capacity to relate to what is wanted, to pursue what is wanted, and if the aspect is unafflicted the energy can indicate a go-getter. If other aspects inhibit this one, or if the chart is undeveloped, the aspect can indicate a person who is merely self-exuberant or selfish.

VENUS–JUPITER SEXTILE. The sextile indicates a person whose psyche is constructively affected by his mother for she shows him that relationships can take place, that one can reach out and be favorably received. Metaphysically speaking, we all get what we expect. Some people are naturally able to reach out—to respond to others, to ask for what is needed because the early childhood environment was encouraging. This individual will have an inner sense of security that will enable him to have the confidence he needs to pursue his goals.

For a woman, this aspect indicates a predilection for comfortable emotional relationships, and she will pass her responsiveness on to her children. For a man, the aspect indicates an interest in relating to his children; he can encourage them to respond and relate. The trine aspect will also encourage this kind of attitude.

VENUS–JUPITER SQUARE. Venus symbolizes how the mother affects the child's psyche as far as the concept of love and/or femininity is concerned; Jupiter indicates the ability to relate. When these two facets of personality are square to each other it indicates a person who tends to be excessive. Jupiter denotes our ability to open up, to expand, to reach out. The concept of love developed from the qualities of the Venus sign will not correspond to the relating qualities. This person may fall in love in an instant and fall out of love the next, or may overreact to every nuance in the relationship.

When this aspect occurs in a female's chart, she may be excessive about her femaleness, she may feel unsure of herself as a woman and therefore attempt to overrelate to anything she loves. This can indicate a superficially feminine woman who is all hairdo, painted fingernails and make-up, one who appears at her door at 8 A.M. looking like she's ready to go to a party; a woman who is overly sensitive to any slight she feels may be directed toward her femininity, who has to prove that she's affectionate, who may seem a bit shallow. This is an overreaction to the concept of the feminine. It means that her mother presented an image during the formative years that neither she nor her daughter could relate to. A concept of self-worth will need to be developed.

The man born with this aspect may be a bit afraid of women, for his image of mother is unpredictable and he may have unconscious memories of her reactions to life that were formed by the time he was three years old. He tends to project this uncertainty on the women he meets; he may have difficulty taking love and marriage seriously. He may enter a relationship from a role-playing point so that he can play "Daddy" and she plays "Mommy." He may wander from one love affair to another, for like his female counterpart, he can fall in love at the drop of a hat.

Here the relating principle doesn't agree with the concept of love: one reaches out to grab the brass ring on a merry-go-round that one doesn't really want. When loved, this person may not be able to relate to or appreciate being loved by the person who cares. When one can't relate to what one wants, the riddle of life becomes more and more mysterious. This person really doesn't know what's good for him.

The aspect can be understood when it's broken down by sign and keyword. The concept of love can be interpreted by sign. The relating principle can be intellectually understood by sign. Relationships can be analyzed so that previous relating problems can be used as the key to avoiding the same situation in the future. Once the frustration of the square energy is comprehended, the aspect can be rechanneled into a productive pattern similar to the trine.

VENUS–JUPITER TRINE. Many people think that this is a creative aspect, for Venus indicates an appreciation of beauty and the arts, and Jupiter indicates our ability to expand, and it sometimes indicates abundance. When the two are in trine aspect, it implies that the mother of the native is able to relate her concept of femininity and feeling in a constructive manner. She demonstrates the ability to give and receive love easily when this person is forming a personality (age 0-3). The individual learns to respond to works of art, to beauty, and to relating in general. This usually is the mark of one who falls in love with a constructive person, who enjoys a lovely home, literature, the classics. This individual is able to appreciate the love given to him, and can graciously accept any favor or gift.

Such people are inspiring to be around for their enjoyment of life is obvious. However, the impact of the aspect will be curtailed if the Moon is afflicted.

VENUS–JUPITER OPPOSITION. This aspect indicates that the mother of the native does not relate well to her femininity; she may be going through a period in which she considers herself a second class citizen during this person's formative years. Jupiter indicates how open we are, how we receive love and beauty, the capacity to relate to others. Because Venus represents how the mother thinks of her femininity and how she is able to perceive love and affection, the opposition between Venus and Jupiter indicates a person who is extravagant and excessive when beginning a love relationship, but the energy is seldom long lasting. It is a response to the loving-relating function that was learned early in life. It may cause a feeling that love is a compromise, that one's ideals and "druthers" cannot be fulfilled while relating to another.

A female with this opposition will learn not to accept love easily, nor will she expect that any woman can be appreciated for herself. She may not even appreciate herself. A male will have little feeling for the feminine principle; often this aspect indicates a male who doesn't appreciate what his wife does in the home to make it attractive; nor does he really appreciate the fact that she loves him, if she does. He may fall in and out of love as does his female counterpart, for he turns on and off. These people bring an expectancy of loss into their love relationships. If they can understand that this attitude can be changed, that they can develop their own expectancies, that the universe is metaphysical, that it gives what one expects, if they understand that the pattern was learned from the mother at a time when she was relating poorly, then they can teach themselves to change. Sometimes this aspect develops a selfishness that needs to be overcome, for it indicates a tendency to want immediate satisfaction to all wants.

This aspect can be analyzed as follows: the Jupiter (relating potential) opposes Venus ("I want" facet of the personality). This can be interpreted as "I don't relate to what I want," and can be the basis for forming individual relating patterns that are brought about because the person thinks he is able to appreciate his surroundings when in fact he is relating discontent. The aspect can indicate a confusion of goals, and some signs may indicate an inability to reach the goals desired. For example, Venus in Aries opposing Jupiter in Libra: "I want to be aggressive, idealistic, intellectually involved in causes, romantic about love," versus the Jupiter in Libra—"I relate intellectually and in a socially acceptable manner." This energy can lead to discrimination conflicts. Venus in Aries wants to be "fair" and Jupiter in Libra wants to be accepted in the right circles—people who don't fit into the "proper" social category may be rejected by the individual, causing an inner conflict for him. This can inadvertently cause a bigoted attitude.

The same opposition taking place between the signs of Cancer and Capricorn will involve, not discrimination, but power struggles. Venus in Cancer wants to be emotional and sensitive and wants to love as innocently as a "little boy/girl" using the power of the child over the parent to attain the wants of life. Jupiter in Capricorn, on the other hand, tends to relate to love and friends from a more traditional point or a more powerful and Saturnian point. The conflict comes when this person cannot be a manager (Capricorn) and a child (Cancer) at the same time. The trick to working with the energy is learned when the different phases of life are understood so that both sides of the opposition can be expressed in the appropriate time and place.

VENUS–JUPITER QUINCUNX. Venus represents the effect of the mother on the person's psyche, and Jupiter basically represents the ability to relate to others. When the quincunx aspect ties these facets of life together, the resulting strain eventually has an effect on the health. It causes indecisiveness to occur, for the "I want" part of the self disagrees a little with how this person will relate to others. The aspect can be resolved by understanding the signs and the houses involved. If it remains unconscious the "I wants" are never really satisfied and relationships are not all they could be.

VENUS–SATURN ASPECTS

When Venus and Saturn are in aspect, major phases of personality are forced to consciousness in order that we may mature. These contacts have not been easy ones in the people I've observed, for the energy tends to restrict the part of the self that reaches out for self-satisfaction.

The Venus position indicates how our mother affects our psyche in regard to the feminine function; it indicates how she influences the development of a concept of womanhood, the concept of self-gratification, and in a personal sense she influences our ability to love and appreciate being loved. Saturn represents our father's impact on our psyche during our early years. The Saturn placement is traditionally interpreted as a restriction; some astrologers explain it as "I lack," and it certainly represents an aspect of personality that is the least confident. The Saturn influence indicates the concept of self-worth, and, as maturity occurs, self-confidence can develop in this area because Saturn becomes the strong point in the chart as the cycles of life progress.

The combination of these two facets of life indicates how we view our capacity for self-worth and how confidence affects career accomplishment and personal relationships. The hard aspects between these planets sometimes cause an individual to pursue only career goals, for the emotional life may be repressed.

In order to overcome Venus–Saturn aspects we have to re-establish personal values as adults. If we become a victim of the aspect we often create the same relationship problems that our parents had; we project our parents' values onto those people we love, and we may develop an extremely pessimistic attitude about loving. When pessimism is rampant, it usually indicates that all the energies are put into the accumulation of money, for money is a "trustable" commodity.

When people with hard Venus–Saturn aspects are successful in terms of career, it usually indicates that they have not been successful or fulfilled in the love department, for that part of themselves remains undeveloped. At some point in life it is important to experience love and affection; it's easier to reach a higher consciousness when we can allow ourselves to be vulnerable in a feeling situation. If we cannot "put out" on a personal level, our philosophy of life is only a theory. A higher consciousness cannot be thought, it must be felt. When loving and appreciating being loved is restricted, the possibility of spiritual attainment remains only an interesting concept.

VENUS–SATURN CONJUNCTION. When Venus and Saturn are conjunct it indicates that the mother and father of this individual presented a united front that placed certain restrictions and limitations upon his psyche during his formative years. Venus indicates the effect of the mother's attitudes regarding her femininity, and these images will help form the concept of womanhood, the feminine function and the concept of love in later life. Saturn represents the area of restriction; it also shows how the father influenced the psyche. The combination of these planets indicates a strong tie to the mythic Mother and Father image—these archetypal images can easily be confused with the physical parents.

The aspects between the Sun and Moon indicate the parents in their *physical sense*; and how they responded to their lives when the personality of the individual was forming. The Saturn–Venus placement affects the concept of giving and crystallization in the psyche and is a more difficult concept to comprehend. The conjunction of Venus and Saturn implies that the individual was restricted or restrained from having what he wanted during the first three years of life. This may not mean that he was abused (although I would not entirely dismiss the thought) but that he may have lost his favorite toy or his "Linus" blanket; or he may have been fed according to some scientific theory rather than when he was hungry. This person grew up to view affection as something that is coupled with loss. He may be a pessimist in love relationships and may be apprehensive of romance. He may marry out of common sense: in other words, he doesn't marry someone he loves, he marries someone who will logically make a "good" partner. Or he falls in love with someone, and ends the relationship after the first argument because he feels the relationship is over. Or he withdraws into years of hurt feelings and never trusts the loved one again.

People with this aspect are extremely interested in guarantees—one must constantly prove to the Saturn–Venus types that one loves them. Ironically they don't offer the same guarantees. They can be takers and have great trouble giving. They don't know how to give because they did not see their parents giving to each other; when children don't see this during their formative years, they have to make a conscious attempt to learn how to do it as adults. These people also think the grass is greener on the other side and often wonder whether they might do better in another relationship—so, sometimes they can be seen as flirts.

When the individual becomes aware of this aspect, it's a good idea to start practicing how to give—not how to buy someone, but to give. Learning how to give a part of the self is the hardest thing for this person to do. Because the parents' marriage was not a model of a healthy relationship, it is hard for this individual to learn how to have one. My suggestion would be that any activity in a relationship that is inspired by the memory of "that's what Mom and Dad would have done," is probably *not* what needs to be done. Sometimes we learn what we want by beginning to understand what we don't want!

VENUS–SATURN SEXTILE. Any contact between Saturn and Venus is a sobering one. It always establishes a somewhat serious personality, but here the parents' influence on the individual was serious but not destructive; the parents worked well together. The Sun and Moon signs and the aspects involved will give a clearer picture of the early childhood.

The sextile aspect indicates a natural talent waiting to be developed. This person will cautiously and seriously approach what he wants, will cautiously develop a strong love relationship, and may have a solid sense of the arts as well as an appreciation of them. This aspect indicates a steady worker and a steady lover—he will steadfastly stay with the person he finally decides to love.

VENUS–SATURN SQUARE. Here the mother and father present an influence to the individual during his formative years that makes it difficult for him to develop any sense of self-worth. In order for an adrogynous personality to develop—a personality with the masculine and feminine principles in balance—the parents must offer an image that can help build the concept. A feeling of self-worth is created by the constructive union of the masculine and feminine principles. The square aspect indicates the images are at odds.

Venus indicates the effect of the mother and Saturn that of the father on the person's developing psyche. When these two planets are in a square aspect, the parents are at odds with each other and the effect on the person during childhood is a weighty one. People with this aspect don't know how they feel about men or women, warmth and affection (Venus), or authority and the ability to execute a personal sense of order in the life (Saturn). "Is love frivolous?" they ask. "Or, are men against women and vice versa?'' This person carries an unconscious memory of Mom and Dad against each other, and this puts a feeling of apprehension in every relationship. Many internal or even subconscious apprehensions about relationships may occur because the parents didn't express affection in a healthy manner. These people often get into role-playing marriages; they merely live with the partner but don't really share emotionally.

The aspect can cause a lonely feeling; pessimistic thoughts about love are similar to the Venus–Saturn conjunction. Here again we see the person who was deprived of the kind of love he needed, or one who was deprived of possessions that his parents didn't understand his attachment to. These people do not enter into relationships easily nor do they work well or cooperatively when relationship compromises must be handled.

When attempting to break the power of the aspect, the individual has to stop looking for guarantees; he must learn to give confidence to his partner as well as look for it from the partner. More comes from a relationship when the "insurance policy" ideas are abandoned. Any personal behavior that seems to be motivated by "my parents handled life this way" should be questioned because it may be an imitation of an unhealthy family pattern that will also create the same problems in the children he parents.

The person born with this configuration comes from a bleak childhood. He didn't have a chance to learn how to give or how to receive, for it wasn't done by the parents. The aspect can be overcome by deciding to learn how to give, how to appreciate, how to take a chance in a love relationship, how to work through a compromise without a feeling of loss. When these things are learned, then the hardness of the aspect goes. It is much like taking a course in French or German: you start at the beginning and learn the subject!

VENUS–SATURN TRINE. These individuals don't have the same difficulties as do those born with the hard aspects—for Venus (the effect of mother on the psyche) trines or works constructively with Saturn (the effect of the father on the psyche). The parents work together, giving the person a chance during childhood to see two serious people working at the role of masculine and feminine. Neither the male nor the female will have problems understanding their sexual role or feelings as ''men'' or ''women'' in terms of self-worth, for each is given a sense of worth—even if the Sun and Moon are afflicted.

The aspect indicates a serious personality since any contact between Saturn and Venus tends to make one more somber. The "I want" nature as well as the ability to appreciate love, to give love and to receive love are taken seriously.

These are the individuals who are naturally able to give others credit where credit is due. They can instill a feeling of confidence in others for they are able to recognize another's worth and, as a result, function easily in the position of teacher or counselor. When they decide to love someone, the love is steadfast and sure. This is a nice aspect to draw upon—I wish I had it!

VENUS–SATURN OPPOSITION. Here the energy is similar to the conjunction and the square, but there is an additional feeling of compromise or loss (or both). Venus symbolizes the effect of the mother and Saturn represents the effect of the father on the individual, and the images are confused. One parent may leave when the person is a child; but even if the loss of a parent doesn't occur, the person feels like a victim between the two parents who are each throwing a different vibration into his developing psyche. What is a man? What is a woman? How does one treat men and women, how does one feel about oneself and one's relationships with members of the opposite sex?

This often represents an individual who has losses in love because the psyche is programmed to lose; this individual may fall in love with someone who is unavailable or with someone who dies or who makes him intensely miserable. The parents removed the objects that the person was attached to during his formative years. The "love object" may have been a favorite toy or a security blanket, or the affection of one or both of the parents. One parent may have been harsh to the other; one parent may have suppressed the other; the child saw the parents disliking each other in some way. So the image in the psyche carries a message that men and women are against each other—each must make the other compromise in some way.

The ability to love is harshened or lessened, and frequently authority is resented. When Saturn opposes Venus, the father is harsh with the mother because Saturn is a stronger planet than Venus. It makes the person suspicious of his own desires, unnecessarily hard on himself, willing to give up pleasure, and ready to turn away from love.

The mother didn't value herself, and this person will absorb her feelings: women have little value; love can hurt or love can be a harsh experience. This individual grows up to be very cautious about developing relationships, and it is this feeling of caution that makes him look for the love insurance policies that are unattainable. This is the type of personality that doesn't give of itself or gives only of the material self, or one who unconsciously picks someone to love who is taken from him. One of my clients has fallen in love with three men, all of whom died before she was able to marry any of them. She came to me because she thought she was putting "death spells" on people. We discussed the possibility that her psyche or her unconscious self didn't think that she deserved to have a long-lasting, good relationship. She has since changed her approach to life, and the men she is dating are still alive.

It's important to understand that there are no bad aspects or awful destinies in astrology, but rather that we tend to seek what we have been programmed for even though the program is unconscious. The psyche is powerful; the power of the subconscious is far stronger than that of the conscious mind. There is no argument going on between the subconscious and the conscious. Once we are able to diagnose an unhealthy program, we can begin to change the way we use our energy and rid ourselves of the negative influence of any energy source that we call an aspect.

VENUS–SATURN QUINCUNX. This aspect symbolizes a strain or a mild struggle between the "I want" part of the personality and the "I take seriously" or "I fear" part. This energy serves to inhibit in the sense that it becomes difficult to manifest an appreciation of love, to pursue the "druthers" because the restrictive effect of the father serves to inhibit emotional concepts. The signs involved should be examined for they will give the key to overcoming the energy block. This individual's parents weren't actively standing in each other's way, but they tripped each other occasionally.

Consider Venus in Aries quincunx Saturn in Virgo: "I want to be fair, I want to be romantic, I want to be intellectually aggressive, I want to be idealistic," says Venus in Aries. And Saturn says, "I fear the intellect, I fear intellectual criticism, I take practicality and service seriously." The two thoughts produce a standstill.

The father did not approve of the mother's interests and, therefore, authorities will not approve of your Venus interests, or men won't or your partner won't—or, conversely, your partner won't appreciate or understand what you fear, or won't understand the aspect of life that you regard with caution. If this quincunx sits in the money houses, your partner may not take your financial problems seriously and may spend money that you aren't making! It can manifest on petty mundane levels as well as the bigger psychological ones.

VENUS–URANUS ASPECTS

Venus symbolizes our intellectual concept of love, how we appreciate beauty, how we receive love, how we approach our "wants" in life. It tells us something about the concept of femininity that we absorb from the mother during our formative years. Uranus is more of a generation symbol having to do with our behavioral urges, our eccentricities, our more willful behavior, as well as an attitude toward consciousness.

When these two facets of personality combine, the concept of love becomes more farsighted, perhaps more unusual or unorthodox. If Venus is in Aries, for example, the person with the Venus–Uranus aspect will express very differently than will one who has no tie to Uranus. The tie between the planets will symbolize those who look at love in an unorthodox manner, who have unusual expectancies about the giving and receiving of affection. The concept of femininity may be different from what is considered usual. If the tie is not understood on any conscious level, the owner of the aspect may have difficulty in being understood by partners.

VENUS–URANUS CONJUNCTION. When these two planets are conjunct it indicates some kind of tie between the psychological effect of the mother and the behavior pattern that she manifests during the individual's formative years. It is indicative of some kind of eccentric or erratic behavior on her part. She may have been tremendously creative or self-willed. The Uranus–Venus conjunction indicates that the mother presents herself to the native in some sudden and erratic manner which the native cannot relate to; even so, the native forms a similar behavior pattern because of the mother's behavior. This behavior pattern affects the part of life that has to do with the intellectual concept of love, how one is able to appreciate love, to receive love or to communicate it to others. This tie can bring out unusual talents as well as unusual perceptions of what love is, so it can either manifest in creative energy or in an abrupt attitude regarding affairs of the heart. This individual may make impetuous decisions and cause unnecessary pain to those around him. He will have to learn how to "play fair" since his early childhood experience taught that decisions are made before talking things over with the partner.

The aspect indicates that this individual may fall in love impetuously and fall out of love the same way. The concept of love will be unusual, unorthodox, and the lover may seem to be a very different type from the norm. Because the image of woman in the psyche is an unusual one, the loved one may be an unusual Uranian type who may not seem suited to this individual's outer personality. This conjunction may signify a lack of communication for all decisions regarding love may be made in an abrupt manner and without consulting anyone else. When a relationship problem needs to be solved, the person with this aspect thinks it through, makes a decision, and when any discussion of the problem takes place it is merely a social courtesy, for as far as he is concerned the decision is done. Relationships are ended with no warning and the partner may be left in a state of shock.

Men with this aspect may leave a woman with little idea or no feeling about the emotional trauma caused to her. Women with this aspect may be an enigma to the men they are in contact with. The aspect is harder on the female than the male because she may reject her biological role. The mother may have resented the responsibilities of motherhood when this person was young and the memory in the subconscious mind recalls some plaguing fear about childbirth, or distaste for the responsibilities of child raising to such a degree that this woman may avoid ever getting pregnant. The biological role can be reconsidered when the aspect is analyzed from a conscious point. She is not required to be like her mother or to have the attitudes of her mother. The damaged image in the psyche can be healed through good counseling or therapy.

VENUS–URANUS SEXTILE. Here the mother affects the individual's psyche in a constructive manner. Venus represents the intellectual concept of love, the ability to appreciate love, and Uranus represents the behavior pattern that affects one's generation. The sextile indicates that the mother is able to give this person a far-reaching or modern concept of love and can teach him how to appreciate being loved. Since Uranus rules the sign of Aquarius it encompasses development on a humanitarian level as well as new concepts in scientific research. The energy is exciting for it uplifts or lifts the desire nature to heights that Venus probably would not reach all by itself. The aspect represents talent, and as this individual matures the influence from his mother will benefit the consideration of new ideas, new possibilities—and that's a healthy pattern for creative expression.

VENUS–URANUS SQUARE. Venus represents the ability to love (the intellectual idea of what love is) and how one appreciates love, how one is able to give and receive affection. When Uranus is in a square aspect to Venus, it indicates that the ability to love is influenced on some psychological level in an unfavorable manner by the mother, for she must have presented herself to the native during the formative years (0-3) in an erratic or eccentric manner that the native could not comprehend. This produces an adult who jumps into love affairs and who jumps out just as quickly. Because the mother didn't really discuss her feelings and didn't share her ideas before making decisions which involved other people, the native will learn to do this too.

It can be a painful aspect, for the person is drawn into romantic situations with strange types of lovers, or with people who may not be able to fulfill the emotional needs signified by the Moon placement in the chart. A man with this aspect may turn off and on like a water faucet and sometimes his partner is shocked by his behavior. Women who have been unfairly abandoned by him become hurt and angry, and he doesn't understand why. Women with this aspect may attempt to get rid of men who don't want to be gotten rid of and thereby end up in the middle of sometimes violent situations when the man won't accept the end of the love affair. All the hurt feelings will stop when these people learn how to discuss their feelings before making final decisions about relationships.

Sometimes people with this square are willful or inconsiderate of others' feelings and bring unpleasant conditions into their lives. They are merely imitating the mother's behavior. When the aspect is consciously accepted much can be done to change the behavior pattern.

VENUS–URANUS TRINE. This is a lovely aspect; it is much like the sextile. Venus indicates our ability to appreciate love, our "druthers," our "I want to be's," and Uranus indicates our behavior pattern. The

Venus placement shows how the mother influences the individual from a psychological point. The trine to Uranus denotes that she is a broad-minded woman who is receptive to growth, change, ideas from the younger generation, and that she is able to give the child a similar image to imitate. This individual will enjoy exploring humanitarian or new-age interests, sharing with others and supporting future generations and their ideas. If the chart warrants, this may be a person who will make an excellent teacher or counselor, for he can be supportive of his students or clients; it can indicate someone involved in the art world, for he is looking for new forms of expression.

As far as love is concerned relationships may be unusual or unorthodox but meaningful. The elements will express this energy differently for this trine in Water signs will indicate a much different person than the trine in Fire. The Water trine will be extremely sensitive and intuitive, looking for a very special relationship. The Fire trine will be looking for ultra-idealism. The energy is best used when the needs of the signs and elements are incorporated into what is looked for in life, and those needs should be tied into the qualities described by the Sun.

VENUS–URANUS OPPOSITION. Here the talent in the aspect has to be worked for because the individual arrives in a difficult family atmosphere and absorbs some unproductive behavior patterns from the mother. Venus indicates the affect of the mother on the child's psyche. Her influence will affect the formation of the child's concept of what a woman is as well as the concept of affection, love and the ability to receive it. Uranus indicates the behavior pattern of the generation the individual is born into, and the sign and house placement will show areas of willfulness and erratic or eccentric behavior.

When the opposition takes place it indicates that the person is subject to some kind of loss in childhood; the aspect may or may not be as severe as Saturn afflictions to Venus. The rest of the chart should tell whether or not the mother was cruel—look at the aspects to Moon, Sun, Ascendant and determine the effect of the fourth house in order to further understand the affect of the mother. She may or may not have been cruel to the person, she may have just not been involved or not cared.

The aspect shapes an adult who jumps in and out of love affairs and doesn't know what he wants, for Venus represents the "I want" nature and Uranus makes that erratic. This person may jump from one relationship to the next, or one job to the next, or even jump in and out of career training programs for he changes his mind a lot. He doesn't know what to expect from his own emotional nature or how to receive the love given to him. He may be warm and affectionate one minute and gone the next. The fear of relationships may have something to do with the fact that his mother had an erratic personality; she may have been unpredictable when he was a child. No matter how stable she is later in life, the individual still fears a trusting relationship.

The female has more difficulty with this aspect than the male for it alters her concept of the biological female role and she may not feel comfortable coping with children. (When the childhood is extremely unpleasant the adult may subconsciously avoid creating any similar circumstance. This can put a damper on relationships.) Men react differently—they may not trust women, some may avoid women altogether thinking women are just too unpredictable; some enter into either homo- or heterosexual relationships which include hurting the partner. I suspect that these individuals (both male and female) were physically or mentally abused in some way when they were children.

If the data I have is correct, the solar chart of Sybil (a woman with sixteen personalities, from the book of the same name)* shows a Uranus–Moon conjunction squared by Venus. Her mother was excessively cruel although no one in the community knew about it. Sybil was unable to accept the conscious realization of the cruelty so she blocked the awful memories and the mind gave birth to multiple personalities. In years to come students can research the possibility of child abuse when a Venus–Uranus conjunction, square or opposition also involves the Moon.

In order to break the power of the aspect, unhealthy or erratic behavior patterns must become conscious. The abrupt handling of emotional relationships can be altered by analyzing past relationships, especially in a therapeutic setting.

VENUS–URANUS QUINCUNX. Here the individual feels the strain between the ''I want'' nature and the ''I behave'' nature. The trick to overcoming the aspect involves a conscious compromise, for if you don't behave in accordance with your needs you won't get what you need.

Consider Uranus in Gemini, ''I behave controversially,'' and Venus in Scorpio, ''I want to be transformational, I want to research,'' or in a personal sense, ''I want to be needed,'' or perhaps ''I want to be unwanted.'' The Scorpio planet indicates a lack of emotional warmth from the mother when this person is a child. Adding the Uranus quincunx from Gemini, the person may behave in a contrary, controversial manner; he may appear to be capable of discussing anything with the loved one, seem to be interested in open or perhaps experimental relationships, while the Venus in Scorpio needs to be loved and reassured.

The quincunx is not as strong as the square but it does cause tension, and at some point so much long-term minor stress may be present that medical problems may develop. In order to relieve the tension, a conscious understanding of the different energies at play needs to take place. Each energy needs to manifest in some appropriate manner. The question is: how can both best express the Sun needs?

---

*Sybil, F.R. Schreiber, Warner Books, 1974.

VENUS–NEPTUNE ASPECTS

Venus represents the psychological influence of the mother, the way in which she influences the native's ability to receive and give love, to appreciate kindness, to appreciate art; it represents the intellectual concept of what love is to each individual, what he or she is striving to attain. In a mundane sense, it represents the little instant gratifications that we like, the comfortable homes, pretty clothes, etc. Neptune symbolizes many aspects of creativity; it indicates inspiration, delusion, dreams—those dreams that represent "If I could only;" it represents love in its spiritual or universal sense.

When Neptune afflicts a planet it tends to bring out the more detrimental energy that Neptune represents; when it's involved in a so-called easy aspect, it brings out a more beneficial or socially acceptable kinds of dreaming or even delusion. Any of its aspects can indicate creative ability. The dream world, the world of Maya (illusion) and the separation of external reality from inner vision is represented by Neptune. Before the more creative aspects may be realized, the individual may find it necessary to push away the veil attached to Neptune in order to more clearly see so that the dreams can fit into the contemporary environment.

The combination of these two facets of personality generally combine the world of fantasy with the concept of love. Since Neptune indicates spiritual or universal love, the concept of love may be depersonalized or lifted to such heights that satisfaction may be difficult to attain. Love may become universal or so spiritual that mere earthly lovers are not understood. The love attachments may be formed because of some strange ethereal tie, and the more practical issues in life, like jobs or the necessity to financially support a family, may be overlooked.

VENUS–NEPTUNE CONJUNCTION. There are many ways to look at this conjunction. The Venus placement indicates the psychological influence of the mother, and when attached to Neptune it indicates that this influence or the impact on the psyche is clouded, unreal. It may be difficult to consciously realize just how Mom influences this person; or how or what she does that keeps him from being comfortable with the outlook on life that is developed. The aspects to the Moon and other aspects to Venus may give a clue as to what the emotional disorder may be, for usually more than one aspect will describe serious conditions in the emotional life.

Venus indicates how we appreciate love, our ability to give and receive affection, warmth and love; it represents our intellectual concept of what love should be for us. When Neptune conjuncts, or influences, this part of life, it becomes cloudy, veiled, deluded or overly spiritualized. We could say that this conjunction gives a person an unrealistic concept of love in some way—many times this shows up as a tendency to spiritualize sex, to make a love affair so special that it condemns everyone else's as not being as good. People may become involved in spiritual love affairs that are not consummated sexually, for they feel that sex and the physical expression of emotions is too animalistic. It confuses religion or religious piety and love relationships. A Venus–Neptune conjunction once said, "I have lusted in my heart." Love is not dirty, only people are. However, the Venus–Neptune conjunction can develop many kinds of sexual phobias depending on the gender of the owner and the additional aspects to either Mars or the Moon in the natal chart.

A woman with this aspect may look for a great spiritual relationship, sometimes being drawn into the soul-mate syndrome, and usually the soul-mate is a homosexual or a married man with five kids and a happy wife. She sees the potential in someone's soul and can be drawn to relationships with an alcoholic or drug type. At any rate, she seems to be drawn to unhealthy people—and the problem is caused by the fact that she relates to them from a spiritual or ethereal point of view and sees something there that no one else can. This situation makes it difficult to grow in a relationship for the person she is attempting to relate with is not capable of giving anything back and she may become very lonely, or make up a life for herself.

A man with this conjunction puts women on a pedestal and may feel guilty about expressing love physically. His mother projects a quality onto women that doesn't add up—for she presents women as a special group of people who are excessively good. The male's guilt about his own sexual and emotional needs can come from the fact that he was taught that "good women" don't like sex, so he feels guilty when he wants it. This conjunction can go so far as to force him to be unfaithful in a marriage for he can't defile the woman he loves; he would rather defile a stranger. A woman with this aspect doesn't know what she wants from a love relationship, and most of her insecurity about what a woman should want comes from the mother figure.

For some reason, there seems to be a cloud of illusion/delusion around the mother as well. For her own reasons, the mother presented an unusual or delusory image of what women are, along with a cloudy picture about her own history. This untruth gives the native a strange image in the psyche that will affect his adult relationships. The mother may have good reason to delude her child, for she may be hiding something about herself. Sometimes the reason for this misrepresentation seems ridiculous later but it doesn't seem so at the time. The psyche drives us to live out the dreams and delusions held on that level, and if we want to change our circumstances, we must know why we have created the unhappy ones in the first place.

As I mentioned in an earlier chapter, a client whose mother lied to her about her father's identity was so upset that she became involved with hard drugs because she didn't know what was real in her life and what was not. The mother was hiding her first husband from the child, and that man was the child's legal father.

The mother may have had her own reasons for hiding what she was, or what women are, for the aspect indicates that she had her own ax to grind; and later in life this ax may not be important to the Venus–Neptune conjunction. The ax is only important to discover so that the power of the aspect can be diminished and we can each be free to establish our own values.

VENUS–NEPTUNE SEXTILE. Venus indicates the image in the psyche having to do with the intellectual concept of love. It is absorbed from the mother while the individual's personality is forming (age 0-3). Neptune indicates delusion and creativity. Since this is an easy aspect, it indicates a creative talent that can be diagnosed by observing the signs and houses in which the sextile takes place.

The mother influenced this person in a constructive manner and gave him a healthy dose of interest in the arts, in creative expression in general, and an interest in developing on some spiritual level. The talent has to be developed. This aspect signifies an individual who is capable of appreciating other people's talents and who enjoys the beauty that is described by the signs and houses involved in the sextile.

VENUS–NEPTUNE SQUARE. Here is a similar configuration to the conjunction, except that it is a bit more difficult to work with, for the square brings with it a tinge of excessiveness. The mother presents some kind of an untruth about her status to the native, about who she is or what women are in general, or what women should be. The influence prohibits this individual from developing a clear picture of the concept of love. The ability to give and receive love is clouded and misty, for it is difficult to differentiate what is wanted from a love relationship. Along with the square goes all the side effects such as sexual guilt, difficulty consummating a love relationship, perhaps the separation of sex and love. The aspect denotes a strange interest in occult or religious matters. This person may be drawn to explore the self and may find the occult or other related matter fun—for pleasure is attached to spiritual development.

On a creative level, the ideas about self-expression may be muddled, and it is possible that the individual may "want to be" someone that he can never be, for the career training and the life's desire may be different.

The problem most often associated with the square is that of religious fanaticism. These people may get involved in a religious sect that feels strongly antisexual, that sex is somehow dirty and a union with God is the only thing that will clean it up. They may project personal values onto others and like to force their morality on others. This may be the "good boy" who goes around killing the painted girls because Mommy taught him that painted girls were bad, etc. Obviously the rest of the chart will have to warrant the decision to express in this manner. The ordinary person with this aspect combines spirituality with sensuality and may feel guilty about his everyday reactions to life or may fluctuate from celibacy to sensuality. Women with this aspect sometimes become involved with dating ministers!

The cure ties into investigating the lie or the delusion the mother presented in order to get started in re-evaluating what a woman is as well as what the concept of love should be. Both men and women have to work this out if they expect to have healthy relationships, and it can be worked out in an analytical situation quite easily. The thing to remember is that this individual needs both love and time to develop spiritually. Any religious or philosophical pursuit should avoid the practice of celibacy if that practice intimates that physical love is dirty or that love can only be expressed on a spiritual plane. All forms of love are beautiful and one is no better than the other.

VENUS–NEPTUNE TRINE. Venus represents the psychological effect of the mother on the native. Neptune symbolizes the creative ability, the aspirations, delusions, illusions in an individual. When these two planets are trine each other, the mother influences the individual's creative ability. She gives this person a generous gift and he matures into an adult who likes art and appreciates the efforts of others. This person may love the arts so much that he wants to be an artist, but the aspect more often indicates the art appreciator than the artist. This person can appreciate love and will look for the kind of relationship that encompasses both a spiritual and physical involvement that allows two people to grow together.

The aspect also indicates that there is a need for spiritual development. One hopes that those with this aspect will not become prey to concepts which separate sex and love; for they can become victims of such propaganda. When we evolve in a spiritual sense it is a more complete evolvement when we can live in our body in a healthy way and open our mind to a greater consciousness as well. The body doesn't need to be repressed in order to develop spiritually; the mind will work as the body works. These people have a strong need for metaphysics, the occult, or religious philosophy. They become jaded and hurt when exposed to groups that offer the more traditional forms of religious expression, especially if the groups also include political jostling for power. These individuals may end up exploring religion alone, making their own decisions about spiritual development.

VENUS–NEPTUNE OPPOSITION. This opposition ties into the symptoms also available to those born with the conjunction or square. There is a loss attached to the mother influence here—perhaps the mother deprives the native in some way, or the native is deprived of her. The aspect doesn't indicate death, but some kind of separation. It may indicate a working mother, or a mother who is ill or absent for some reason. At any rate, Venus symbolizes the mother's impact on the native's psyche when the concept of love is being formed. Neptune indicates that this influence will hold some distortion of truth or reality. The distortion must be understood in order to use the energy of the opposition in a creative way or to its fullest creative potential. Because this person cannot express wants and wishes easily and may not understand how to appreciate or express love in a physical sense, he may have a great deal of talent to offer the world for often our most creative people have been repressed emotionally.

The problem caused by the aspect is the distortion of the definition of what a woman is or what a woman should be. It tends to combine guilt with love; it creates an individual who has unclear concepts of what he wants. A male with this aspect expects a woman to be what Mother told him they were. He can be hurt when he finds that women do not behave the way he thinks they should. A woman with this aspect has an unclear definition of what she should be as a woman and what is expected of her. She may alter her actions and desires to accommodate not only the sign Venus is in but the Neptune aspect as well. She may be difficult to live with for she may set impossible standards for herself.

VENUS–NEPTUNE QUINCUNX. This kind of aspect brings another sort of dilemma. The mother of the native influences his psyche about womanhood according to the sign Venus is in. Neptune brings a vague feeling that this idea is all wrong.

As far as the desire nature is concerned, Venus represents what we desire in life and the kind of love relationship we want; Neptune represents what kinds of goals and dreams we work toward. The two are not working together when quincunx. It may be that the aspect provides the kind of strain or discontent that ends up stagnating the efforts of this individual; that the person may end up drifting instead of creating. The qualities of both signs need to compromise with each other in such a way that both the signs can be expressed in the life.

VENUS–PLUTO ASPECTS

Venus symbolizes the intellectual concept of love; the regard for the feminine or the feminine principle. The attitude affecting a woman's self-worth and her response to her biological role comes from this placement for it indicates the attitudes of the mother in regard to her own nature when the individual's psyche is able to absorb those feelings. For men, this position indicates the images formed in the psyche that function on a subconscious level in regard to his attitudes toward women and the biological role of woman. It can indicate the key to problems affecting his intellectual concept of love for he absorbed those attitudes from his mother.

Pluto can be identified as the unconscious motivation of a generation as well as symbolizing the portion of the collective unconscious that holds the mythic archetypal images of humanity. When this symbol is not understood consciously, it can reflect an aspect of personality that is less spectacular but more commonly recognized as forms of personal control and obsession. The hard aspects to Pluto will require that the individual move from obsessive responses to transformation and regeneration. The hard aspects may in fact cause more growth potential than the easy ones.

When Venus and Pluto come together it is obvious that the effect of the combined energies will influence the personal capacity for love. The range of feeling experience is phenomenal for one can easily cooperate with the mood of the generation, changing the patterns of social custom in a manner complementary to previous traditions, or one can function in a highly controlled manner.

In the personal sense the combination reflects the possibility of including manipulation in the life experience. Because Venus is involved, the manipulation or obsession or control/power game comes from the mother influence. A person who is exposed to power games in childhood will develop into an adult who thinks he must control everyone as well—because a child can only imitate what he sees his parents doing. The facet of life that has to do with love and affection will be the area of heaviest manipulation.

In order to use the tie to the collective unconscious (symbolized by Pluto) the more obvious misuses of the energy will have to be rechanneled. When an individual takes responsibility for his actions, when he can recognize the control games that he plays, he can let them go. When this occurs, the energy becomes creative and exciting. The ideas are new, the fountain from the collective unconscious never runs dry. The struggle is worth it.

VENUS–PLUTO CONJUNCTION. Venus represents the psychological effect of the mother on the individual, the ability to appreciate love, as well as the intellectual concept of what a love relationship is. These feelings will be altered in some way by the presence of Pluto. It seems that during the individual's formative years the mother was convinced that she had to control her universe through her "womanhood." In some way she was able to overwhelm this native on a psychological level, and the resultant adult is a person who has to protect himself from the unseen influence, the image of Maya-Kali, the devouring mother. The mother is an overwhelming influence. This produces a male who feels he has to control his relationships with the female, and perhaps even subconsciously he will be attempting to control any relationship that he forms. He may obsess over relationships or obsess over his desires, but the most harmful part of the aspect in the subconscious is a fear of the power of woman. It means that rather than relating he must manage everyone and that does not make a relationship smooth or happy.

The female with this aspect was taught early in her childhood that in order to survive as a female one must control all relationships. One must know where one stands in any relationship that is formed or it may be lost. This woman will attempt to have a "grip" on everything around her; otherwise she thinks she will lose her position. Often the aspect works subconsciously. She may be vaguely aware that she needs to determine edges, for rarely is a hard Pluto aspect really conscious of the maneuvering it does. She may pick men that she can manage and then resent them for being manageable. She may want to end relationships when this conjunction is being transited by other planets, for the energy may bring her insecurity into focus. She may be afraid of her mother or resent her mother from childhood on into adulthood.

The aspect can indicate a person who has obsessive desires. Additional configurations in the chart may indicate how much so and what area of life is affected by the aspect. If Pluto represents transformation, or if it represents the collective unconscious of humanity, then the tie between Pluto and Venus is a "biggie" in terms of human growth potential. If Venus represents our appreciation of art, culture and beauty, then the conjunction will intensify that appreciation and enable the owner to transform the art world, or to gain understanding of potential art forms. Because Pluto symbolizes the archetypes of the collective unconscious, personal transformation and/or insights can be developed when the lower manifestations of the aspect are comprehended.

VENUS-PLUTO SEXTILE. Here the mother influenced the individual in a productive way, enabling him to develop patterns of reaction that can be used constructively and cooperatively with others. Venus represents the concept of love; it indicates the mother's psychological influence over the native. Pluto represents an individual's ability to cooperate, to work with groups, to understand the needs of the masses, to understand the needs of a changing social environment.

If this talent is developed, if the influence from the mother is put to use, and if the rest of the chart indicates that the individual will consider the mother's influence important (for a father-dominated child may not), then this can be a most helpful talent.

VENUS-PLUTO SQUARE. Here the mother provided an unhealthy atmosphere for the native for when he was forming his reactions to the "female" part of the world, when his psyche was developing an ability to love, and to appreciate being loved, the mother was responding to her life in a Plutonic manner. For some reason the mother of this individual felt that it was important to control all the people she loved and she may have drained her family. This created a feeling in the individual that all women drain one, that all females are out to manipulate. If the Pluto influence was a physical one it will be more comprehensible in later years; but if the mother used the manipulative power of "smother love," this person may be forced to confront her at some point and his guilt over having to do so may inhibit his capacity for solving the aspect.

This aspect tends to unconsciously attempt to control others. One way for the individual to become aware of how he does this is by observing others' reactions to his manipulation games. Strongly self-contained people will avoid him for he tries to manipulate them, and manipulation is usually an indirect action. Some people resent controls being placed on them by the person with the Venus–Pluto square, for his energy makes them feel cornered, unfree, unable to breathe around the Plutonic personality. The person with the aspect is often totally unaware of what he is doing, for he knows no other way to be. For the male, it creates an unconscious need to control the women around him because he believes they will manipulate him like his Mom did if he doesn't do it first. The female with this aspect feels she must hold on to her position for all it's worth or she won't have one.

When Pluto aspects are strong in the natal chart it indicates a powerful personality with lots of potential for growth, but the energy must be used consciously or the individual tends to be used by it; the individual may be a victim of his own energy. When the individual can trust the natural power within, the inner self can guide him and he begins to allow things to happen.

We cannot make anyone love us; we can "make" them act politely toward us, but love is always a voluntary experience. When giving up controls, we have to confront the fact that love cannot be forced, not made to happen. When this is understood, the transformation is easy. The prize at the end of the rainbow is the chance to really experience an open and warm relationship with none of the insecurities that come from trying to make it happen. We can control with power, prestige, money, or our manipulative abilities, but we can never have inner feelings of security if we are living that way. When the inner confidence comes, so does the creativity!

VENUS–PLUTO TRINE. Like the sextile, the trine aspect between these two facets of personality indicates that the individual is exposed at an early age to concepts of cooperation and shown how to enjoy working with his fellow man. The aspect gives its owner a good basis for working in a career that helps the masses, that involves public cooperation, social issues, media and mass communication, etc. However, when we have the trine we sometimes don't appreciate it, for it has been given to us rather than developed with a struggle. The person who has this aspect may be struggling to solve less easy aspects in the chart, forgetting about this one.

On the good side, the influence of the mother helps the individual to appreciate love, the arts, culture: human expression may well be uplifted so that a larger scope of personal feeling may develop than the Venus placement would ordinarily encompass.

If the personality is not particularly developed, the creative energies of the aspect can be overlooked. This individual may ride the crest of the wave describing his generation. Since Venus also represents personal gratification, the trine may indicate a person who becomes a victim of the media, who strives for only the material comforts available to him.

VENUS–PLUTO OPPOSITION. The psychological effect of the mother on this individual's developing psyche was a profound one. This person feels the need to compromise as well as control. The mother managed the native's development. She may have decided what was good for this person, enforcing her decisions by not allowing him to make any decisions for himself. Because she may have had such an overwhelming personality, the individual develops a resentment toward her and other women over the ensuing years.

The concept of love includes management, and this individual may attempt to develop love situations with partners who are easily managed. The male will resent women, often subconsciously, and will be cautious and careful in any involvements with women. The female may fear her own femininity and may feel that in order to keep a man around, he must be manipulated. Both sexes will more often get into role-playing marriages than good relationships, for they won't allow themselves to be spontaneous in love situations.

As with the square and the conjunction, Pluto aspects inhibit the capacity for letting go of the urges to control. The person has known no other way to approach life. Because Pluto symbolizes the collective unconscious and the mythic archetypes of human expression, the mother image can become distorted and confused. The personal mother may become confused with the mythic mother image, giving the personal mother a power that she doesn't recognize she has over her child. The resentments caused by this confusion may be difficult to let go until the confusion is consciously recognized.

In order to free the energy so that it can be used creatively, control games must be analyzed. Personal responsibility, morality and ethics regarding those we love must be established on the conscious plane. We cannot make anyone love us, we cannot make the future of those we love; no one is dependent on us for survival. We cannot be responsible for anyone else. For example, the woman who loves an alcoholic may want to "make" him stop drinking rather than exploring the idea of why she is with him in the first place. Letting go is hard. Losing at love is hard. These people need to learn that sometimes you win "yourself" when you lose someone else. The hard aspects can be more productive and more transformational than the easy ones, for more energy is released in the struggle.

VENUS–PLUTO QUINCUNX. The influence of the mother is strained by an unconscious control pattern that this individual absorbs from her. The concept of love may be marred by a subliminal feeling of doubt regarding decisions in this area. The Pluto placement can indicate a sensitivity on a subconscious level that may elicit a reaction to love that involves retaliation or control.

The energy can be understood by examining the signs involved as well as the house placement of the planets so that the areas of life implicated in the aspect can be determined.

THE PLANET MARS IS THE SYMBOL FOR TWO BASIC expressions of the life force: it symbolizes the kind of action we take to express our Sun sign qualities; it can also be used to determine how we "act" sexually. When looking at the planet Mars, it should be considered in relation to the Sun and Moon: the Sun (the "I am" principle) and the Moon (the "I respond" principle) are compared with Mars (how "I act" this out). Mars is the symbol of how we will use the creative energy given to us; it indicates how we will manifest who and what we are, what we have, what we think, what we feel. Mars can be used as an indicator of how we will function in a work situation; the sign, house placement and aspects can be used as determining factors when giving career guidance. It also symbolizes how we will "act out" our feelings of love when we consider this planet with Venus, the symbol for our intellectual concept of what love means to us.

Mars enlivens the quiescent creative Sun nature as well as the possibilities of consciousness that are inherently within each of us. The qualities of the Sun cannot be expressed if we don't use our Mars energy to express them. Unconscious libido (Mars) may interfere with Sun creativity. Webster's New Collegiate Dictionary defines libido as follows:

> 2. Psychoanalysis. Energy, motive force, desire, or striving, either as derived from the sex instinct or from the primal urge to live.

Jung mentions that the libido is more than just the sex drive, for it combines the sex drive and the life force. This energy can be interpreted as a part of the psyche—psychic energy. When this is considered astrologically, Mars can be considered the horse that carries the rider (the Sun). The rider won't get where he's going if the horse doesn't take him. The two energies work together, one needs the other.

In the natural zodiac, the ancient rulerships ascribed to Mars were those of Aries and Scorpio. Aries is the action sign: it symbolizes the pioneering spirit, the adventurer, the explorer of the undiscovered. Scorpio is the sign of reproduction, death, and one's potential for self-transformation; it's the sign of conscious rebirth. The life/death enigma symbolized by Scorpio has been difficult to understand, but life and death function together, because of each other. Without darkness we can't see light, and without life there is no death, and vice versa. In the symbolism of the house system, the first house (the Aries or Mars house) stands for any new endeavor, any new action taken. The eighth house (the Scorpio or ancient Mars house) indicates the reproductive system, the reproductive ability, and here Mars has to do with rebirth as well.

Staying with the astrological symbolism, and considering the ancient philosophical edict "know thyself," can the chart show the dilemma caused in each of us when we struggle with "I am" and "I act?" The action principle comes from the first house, which can be called the persona, the masquerade of personality, our "best foot forward." The Sun is the ruler of the natural fifth house, and it symbolizes the creative self, which may never really be expressed in a lifetime. The fifth house can be read as the house of children, and many people have worked toward achieving immortality by being remembered through children and their children's children. However, Mars energy can conceivably activate the consciousness as well as our reproductive organs. But in order for that to happen we must become responsible for our *actions*.

If Mars represents the libido, the sex drive, and represents our ability to transform as well, then Mars can be called the symbol upon which our chance for consciousness rests. The occult philosophies all say the same thing—the Buddhist, Hindu, Egyptologist and the alchemist all talk about changing consciousness. The alchemist was interested in changing base metals into gold (or something of value). The Mars energy represents action; it can also represent anger. When angry energy is rechanneled, it becomes "gold." It provides the energy that enables us to raise the Sun sign potential to the highest levels possible in a lifetime.

As Mars interacts with the other planets in the chart, the action energy becomes more and more complicated and exciting. Each nuance of unconstructive energy must be looked into and developed if the Sun is ever going to become expressive of its full potential. Because Mars rules both Aries and Scorpio, it seems that our sexual decisions will affect our conscious growth, for if we cannot express ourselves in a healthy or happy manner, we slow down our Sun—the eighth house squares the fifth in the natural zodiac. In the Oriental philosophies, one hears about the "wheel of life," and everyone involved is trying to get off the wheel, not to stop living, but one must stop being unconscious in order to become conscious!

In the personal sense, the Sun indicates our personal archetype and the family environment that existed when we were forming our personalities. As each child manifests the "I act" principle, that energy becomes recognized in the family. If the child has difficulties with the parents, the difficulties will show up because of the aspects between Mars and the Sun, Moon, Venus or Saturn. The child's action principle, as well as the development of sexual concepts, will be affected by the parent appropriate to the aspect. When Mars is afflicted, it means that the facets of life described by the planets involved will need to be consciously changed in order to allow maximum inner contentment.

MARS–SUN ASPECTS

See Chapter 1 in this section.

MARS–MOON ASPECTS

See Chapter 2 in this section.

MARS–MERCURY ASPECTS

See Chapter 3 in this section.

MARS–VENUS ASPECTS

See Chapter 4 in this section.

MARS–JUPITER ASPECTS

When these two planets interact, physical action is combined with the ability to relate. The sexual and relating concepts are combined. Physical action is a physical-acting experience; when Mars combines with Jupiter, often excessive action results. If the aspects are not easy ones, Jupiter can overexcite the Mars.

The Jupiter placement shows how we relate to our own needs, to the universe around us, to those we love, to those we work with. When Jupiter is afflicted, we don't relate easily, we overcompensate. Jupiter indicates how we open up, how we reach out, how we expand. The aspects between these two planets indicate how the parents were relating sexually during our childhood, how the family related to action taken in the household.

MARS–JUPITER CONJUNCTION. Mars represents "I act" and Jupiter symbolizes "I relate, I reach out." When these two energies are together, the "I act" principle combines with the ability to expand, to reach out; the energy will be described by the signs in which the conjunction takes place. It can bring exuberance in the Fire signs, oversensitivity in the Water signs, etc. Mars conjunct Jupiter in Aries in keyword language says, "I act aggressively and I relate aggressively," or "I act intellectually, from an intellectual point of view, and I relate as an intellectual." Or, "I act rashly, I'm always in a hurry, and I relate hurriedly as well." This conjunction in Aries may indicate a person who is not careful before becoming involved in new situations.

When Mars conjuncts Jupiter in Capricorn it expresses differently. "I act in a traditional manner, I relate in a traditional manner, I may present myself in a Saturnian way, for I seem serious to others." Or, "I take my sexuality seriously, and I may use it to control my relationships, for I relate in a controlled manner in the sex department."

The Mars–Jupiter Conjunction can indicate an exuberant person, one who jumps to conclusions, one who has boundless energy, one who may overrelate or overreact. The aspect by itself is not harmful, for it generally indicates an open person who acts in a straightforward manner, expressing the energies of the sign involved in the conjunction. It can indicate a tendency to overcommitment or a person who works too hard. It's important to note the other aspects to the conjunction in order to determine how they will affect this one, and to also check how the Mars placement will affect the expression of the Sun archetype. In matters of love, both the Mars and Venus position should be considered, since these two principles work together.

MARS–JUPITER SEXTILE. The sextile indicates a person who has been raised in a family that related to each other, so he is able to relate to the action he takes. He also can relate to his own sexuality. He can enjoy both work and love. The sextile shows a family that took constructive action. This energy can be applied to career situations in adult life.

MARS–JUPITER SQUARE. The square indicates that the relating principle and the action principle are at odds. Mars represents the action taken on any physical level, including sexual expression. Jupiter represents the relating principle and how one opens up to new experience. The square indicates that this person may not relate to the action he takes, and therefore may be accident prone for he may expose himself to unnecessary risks. He may not relate well to career decisions either; he may not understand the actions he takes regarding his job responsibilities. On the sexual level, he may not relate to his own sexual needs, he may have excessive needs, depending on the additional aspects in the chart.

Consider Mars in Aries square Jupiter in Cancer: "I act aggressively, I act rashly, I act intellectually, I may sex in a hurry," versus the Cancerian qualities as they apply to Jupiter—"I relate from a sensitive point of view, I relate as a little girl/boy, I relate from an intuitive point." Action is presented one way, yet he relates from another. This can be a drawback in career for others don't understand the image. Sexually, it can mean that he chooses a partner that satisfies one side of the square and not the other. He may relate from a possessive emotional point and "act" like a fair and idealistic person. The lover gets a mixed vibration. Or he relates from an emotional caring point (Cancer) yet sexually he's in a hurry—which may not make his partner very happy!

Any square between Mars and Jupiter indicates a setup for excessive action, and when things don't go as planned, this individual often overreacts. The aspect indicates a childhood environment that was excessive during the formative years. If the square also ties into the Sun or Saturn (father) or the Moon or Venus (mother), we can see which parent helped form the reaction pattern. Because Mars indicates action and sexuality, the square to Jupiter indicates a problem relating sexually, as well as an overrelating in other aspects of life. If the square doesn't tie to any of the parent symbols, *everyone* in the family was functioning that way during the individual's formative years. Overreacting sexually may be indicative of a parent who *only* relates on a sexual basis, or one who is confused about sexual attitudes. The individual picks up the reaction and makes this response a part of his or her adult experience.

Because of the square, one form of expression that happens is that of not relating to the partner after a sexual relationship has been established. Sex is separated from the relating experience. One of my clients who has the square was told by her husband that she related better to her friends than she did to him. The complex can be cured by examining the needs of both planets by sign and function. Combining the energies in some constructive manner can be learned. Examining old relationships may be of help in discovering the relating pattern, so that new ones can be established.

MARS–JUPITER TRINE. The trine between these two planets indicates an individual who was presented with a family atmosphere that encouraged positive and constructive action. This individual had someone around in childhood who encouraged him, and he was shown (through other family member interactions) that one can relate to what one does and that one can be open about action taken. The two energies express well together.

This usually indicates an individual who enjoys sex and enjoys loving, unless the Mars placement is in turn involved in some other hard aspect.

MARS–JUPITER OPPOSITION. The opposition is similar to the conjunction or the square, for it indicates a person who may not relate to the action taken. The individual may be raised in an atmosphere of law and order, but with little explanation as to *why* one does what one does. It indicates a person who feels he must compromise his actions or his sexual needs in order to have a relationship. This attitude is learned in early childhood. It can help develop an excessive attitude, and the person may push to have his own way; he may overreact to life situations and take excessive risks. He may act before he thinks, he may generally be an over-responder to many life situations presented to him. This can indicate poor judgment as far as career moves are concerned. It can indicate the type of person who is in love with someone new every three weeks, for the exuberance is rarely lasting, and as one exuberance fades, another comes along.

In order to rechannel the opposition, the compromise must be understood, and overreactions have to be checked. Individuals in the process of overcoming the aspect are forced to think out every move, and they may spend months evaluating every decision. "Will this action be good for me six months from now as far as my overall goals are concerned?"

The cause of the frustration comes from either the family environment and the ethics or traditions espoused, or from one or both of the parents. If the opposition also ties to the Sun or Saturn (the father) or the Moon or Venus (the mother) the parental influence can be determined so one can see where the pattern comes from. In order to develop consciousness we must each take responsibility for what we do, and that is difficult as long as the opposition causes us to function without regard for actions taken or our sexual needs.

MARS–JUPITER QUINCUNX. The quincunx indicates a strain wherever it exists and here a strain is indicated regarding the action taken in life and the ability to relate to what is being done. There may be feelings of a vague discontent regarding the sexual needs versus the relating needs.

In career situations, the action taken may not complement the manner in which this individual relates to fellow employees. Both planets need to express and the qualities of both signs need to find an outlet.

MARS–SATURN ASPECTS

Generally speaking, Mars represents the action principle and Saturn represents the influence of the father on the individual's forming psychic images (age 0-3). Saturn indicates feelings of lack and restriction within the personality because the father inhibited the native in some way. Saturn hardens anything it touches, makes it brittle, restricts responses, or indicates a cold attitude. When the two planets interact with each other, the action principle is directly tied to the concepts of Father Nature, or natural law as illustrated by either Father Time or the Wise Old Man archetype image in Jungian psychology. Saturn can be a teacher or it can be the Grim Reaper. We have many choices as to how we wish to use this image.

Because Mars represents the libido, the sex drive, the life force, any contact with Saturn implies a need to understand how the life force functions, how one fits into the overall scheme of things. If we don't understand, the action taken will always be influenced by the Father archetype. As the energy becomes conscious, we can begin to understand that the mythic Father image in the psyche has its place and the energy can be used with a new perspective. Obviously, people with the easy aspects will have less trouble than those with the hard ones.

MARS–SATURN CONJUNCTION. The "I act" principle is affected by the influence of the individual's father. Mars indicates the ability to act out the energy of the Sun. The conjunction indicates that the actions may be limited or restricted because of something the father does while the individual's personality is forming (age 0-3). This influence inhibits the person's ability to react constructively and to feel confident about the action he takes. The conjunction usually has some effect on the sex drive.

Saturn says "I take seriously," and conjunct Mars means "I take my action seriously." This can serve to inhibit or restrict any action taken; it can indicate harsh action, for Saturn symbolizes the concept of law in each individual, causing this person to act out (Mars) the law (Saturn). This energy is sometimes used for law enforcement and can indicate a person who will enjoy a career that involves enforcing the law. This energy can create a sure-footed, slow moving individual who moves cautiously in life; or an extremely hard individual who becomes an enforcer of the law regardless of the circumstances. It is wise to consider the other aspects to this conjunction for it will give a broader picture of how the personality will operate.

In a personal sense, the conjunction can indicate a serious outlook regarding sexual expression. It can limit sexuality, cause one to avoid sexuality, indicate symptoms of frigidity in both the male and female, make one afraid of sexual expression, or cause one to attempt to force sexual standards on others. The Mars–Saturn conjunction indicates that the father inhibited the individual's sexual concepts or perhaps his early sexual expression in some manner. *What* he did is an unknown factor, but he did something. Other aspects to the conjunction may tell more about what happened.

My clients have had a wide variety of sexual reactions to this aspect, ranging from difficulty with orgasm or erection to marriages with no sexual fulfillment. It seems that this type of individual is rarely chemically attracted to another. The sexual difficulties cause guilt, and then the conscious mind decides to have a sexual relationship because the prospective lover will be "good for me." Or, because the individual is so rarely physically attracted to another, when the chemistry does happen he jumps into bed without going through the normal courtship period. Then the guilt begins because he feels he responded too quickly. This individual can respond sexually to the right person but he finds few people appealing.

The father may have had his own guilt about his sex drive; the father may have had a harsh attitude as the small child explored his body as all small children do. The rest of the chart will help tell the story. The pressure of the aspect can be relieved when this person investigates the relationship between sexual expression and universal law. Sex is not unhealthy, only people are.

MARS–SATURN SEXTILE. This aspect indicates that the individual was encouraged by his father. The action principle is treated seriously by this person, and all actions are weighed in some way, but this energy can become useful. The individual may be a careful planner, a careful coordinator, and one who has a natural talent for organizing group action. The career may involve large groups or general business, for Saturn is the ancient business symbol.

On a sexual level, this aspect indicates a person who does not rush into foolish romances, one who has some realization of sexual responsibility.

MARS–SATURN SQUARE. The "I act" principle conflicts with "I take seriously," or "I regard with caution." The father's influence on this individual's psyche built an atmosphere of mistrust or fear—he did not encourage the individual's actions. Authority seems to be the "thing in the way" of personal action. The person often feels that all authority figures (Daddy, teachers, bosses, men in general) are against whatever he may be trying to do. As an employee he can appear as a subversive type for he may develop a strong anti-authority complex. The aspect can indicate a rebel, a rabble-rouser, or someone who works to change the status quo. The energy has to be directed, for action must be taken from a constructive point. As a youth, this person may be so negative to authority figures that he "cuts off his nose to spite his face."

As far as sexuality is concerned, there is a seriousness to it that is unwarranted, and self-imposed restrictions on sexuality are the result of a subconscious fear caused by the father early in life. Men have been traditionally expected to enjoy sex with many women; we have been trained to think that men should enjoy any sexual contact. Men with this aspect seldom do, however, for they find few partners pleasing, and when they do, they fall deeply in love. The female reacts the same way, and depending on the freedom of the generation she was born into, her sexual enjoyment may vary considerably. In this day and age, many women are experimenting with sexual freedom, and some women with this aspect are shocked, since few men appeal to them. Some of the women married early, have had a family, a husband, and no sexual pleasure, for they married before trying sex.

The aspect doesn't completely restrict sexual feeling, but it's difficult for these individuals to find a pleasing sexual partner. Once that is understood, people who have the aspect can cease judging themselves so harshly. The original sexual restriction had something to do with the father and his influence on a small child. Sometimes analysis can help get to the root of the problem, sometimes self-diagnosis can do it. At any rate, this aspect indicates serious and loyal people, for once they make an emotional or sexual commitment, they mean it.

MARS–SATURN TRINE. All contacts between Mars and Saturn

bring a serious note to the nature and this aspect is no exception. What happens is that action is seriously considered, well thought out, not particularly restricted, but this individual will seem very mature at an early age. He was taught to think about what he did more than most children were. These are people who make dedicated and loyal employees, who make careful decisions, who are highly organized, and who do well in traditional management or big business. They make good investment counselors; they are highly rational and orderly in any profession.

Since Mars also represents the sexual energy, the Saturn trine will restrict sex as well, but in a mature way. This person doesn't rush into relationships "where angels fear to tread." He relates only after having carefully thought out the possibilities of the situation, and then he will slowly move toward his goals. It indicates an individual who tends to be loyal sexually and emotionally, who feels a strong bond of responsibility regarding sexual relationships.

MARS–SATURN OPPOSITION. This tie between sexuality and responsibility is one that is difficult, for it involves a compromise regarding either sexual expression or action taken, or both. Mars symbolizes the "I act" principle and Saturn indicates the restriction caused by the image of the father in the psyche. Mars is "I sex" and Saturn is the restricting influence from the father because of views he had about sex when this individual was young.

It can seem that Father Time, or the Wise Old Man, is universally against any action attempted, for every action is tested for its merit. The individual who lives with this energy may become resentful and feel that too much is asked of him. He may rebel against society, authority or his father. If this energy is used constructively, the rebellion against the father can establish a personal ethic that causes this individual to become involved in changing cultural conditions that need it. If not, it can indicate an individual who may be harsh, who wishes to become a law unto himself.

In the sexual sense, it may be that the Saturn opposition controls the sex life, that there are losses connected with sexual expression; it may be difficult to establish long-lasting relationships. It may be difficult to find an enjoyable sexual partner. In this case, check out Venus and Moon aspects as well for that may tell the story more completely.

As far as career is concerned, the Mars–Saturn opposition can cause restrictions on any action taken; so movement may be stagnated, or the individual worries too much about what he does. The aspect may indicate a person who doesn't handle crises well, for any crisis demands immediate decisions and immediate action. He may be restricted because of ideas and concepts learned from the father. As this energy is worked with, it can develop a slow and careful decision-maker, a steady worker, one who is precise and deliberate.

MARS–SATURN QUINCUNX. Here the activity of Mars is influenced subtly by the restrictions of Saturn. The psychological effect of the father on the individual, the limitations within the psyche, are present but not obvious.

Action may be taken with gritted teeth and others don't see this internal dilemma. Sexuality may be inhibited in some way for an image is retained in the psyche that says one shouldn't do that.

MARS–URANUS ASPECTS

Mars represents the action principle; it indicates how we will activate the energy of the self qualities symbolized by the Sun archetype. Uranus indicates the behavior of the generation into which we are born. It also indicates that part of the personality which is self-willed, stubborn or eccentric. Uranus can symbolize creative energy, for it rules the sign of Aquarius and indicates how we will crystallize our ideas about consciousness.

Mars–Uranus aspects can indicate a certain kind of genius, for the person is motivated to action that is based on unusual insights. When the energy is misunderstood, it can cause erratic or eccentric action to take place, but these manifestations are more often tied to the hard aspects.

MARS–URANUS CONJUNCTION. If Mars represents the ''I act'' principle and Uranus represents the erratic or self-willed tendencies of the personality, the combination may be indicative of an individual with a ''short fuse.'' How this energy will manifest depends on the sign placement, for a Mars–Uranus in Aries may signify a person who is abrupt, erratic, quick to act on impulse, perhaps one who acts thoughtlessly.

The Mars–Uranus conjunction in Pisces functions from a watery response to life and may implode instead of exploding. So, the energy manifests differently in each sign. The conjunction in Aries is outgoing and direct, but it may express in Pisces as some form of suffering. If the conjunction is in Leo, one may observe a person acting impulsively when spurred by a lack of respect or approval. Each of the Mars placements will function differently and should be interpreted according to sign.

The energy level is usually high. People born with this aspect are aware of the inherent energy level, and by the time they reach their twenties they have learned something about channeling it.

In a sexual sense, the conjunction can indicate a strange, unusual or unorthodox sexuality, which can manifest as a slightly eccentric conditioning as well as include all forms of what is considered sexual perversion. The aspect should be synthesized with the other aspects involved in the conjunction; the Venus, Sun and Moon placements should be considered before determining that a Mars–Uranus conjunction is unhealthy. The aspect indicates precociousness, impulsive sexual reactions, as well as impulsive physical reaction in general. This person may jump into emotional or sexual involvements without considering all the factors necessary in a relationship. This aspect can cause relationships to develop with partners who are unusual types.

Because Mars represents the action taken to express the Sun potential in each individual, it's important to become conscious of the energy here. Uranus involves erratic behavior and one can take erratic action. The concept of self-will may need to be considered, for action may be too impetuous to accomplish what is desired on an overall level. The conjunction bestows a creative genius that may not be expressed until the less evolved qualities are disciplined.

MARS–URANUS SEXTILE. Mars represents the "I act" principle and Uranus indicates the behavior of the generation we are born into, as well as the part of us that expresses as self-will before it evolves consciously.

The sextile indicates that the action patterns formed by this individual in childhood were well received by the parents. The early environment demonstrated the ability to act (or sex) in a manner that expressed the will, allowing the child room for being "different" so that he could form his own particular value system. The value system can be diagnosed from the signs and houses.

MARS–URANUS SQUARE. Mars is the indicator of the action principle and how the qualities of self reflected by the Sun archetype will be expressed. Uranus indicates the overall behavior of the generation we are born into, as well as how eccentric or self-willed we are.

The square indicates that the peer interests or behavior patterns of the individual may keep him from taking action that reflects the interests of his Sun. Action taken may be more impulsive than well thought out, and impulsive action is sometimes somewhat self-destructive. The goals, the overall scheme, the best laid plans can be totally forgotten in a moment of anger. The early childhood environment reflects parents who may have impulsively put a stop to the individual's activity in some way. This aspect can indicate some form of abuse toward the individual, either physical or emotional in nature. If the square also ties to planets that symbolize the mother and father, the source of the abuse can be determined.

On a sexual level, the individual may bring a great deal of anger into relationships. The aspect is sometimes found in adults who have some need to hurt either themselves or others because of the sex drive. The energy will manifest differently depending on the signs involved. For example, Mars in Cancer square Uranus in Libra may be read as "I act emotionally, I act possessively" and "I behave democratically." This individual may (depending on the sign the Sun is in) publicly display a gentlemanly demeanor but in private circumstances he may be a violent and possessive lover.

A woman with this square will function a bit differently than a man will, for she may get into a self-destructive situation apparently caused by the kind of lover she chooses. Consider a female with Mars in Gemini square Uranus in Virgo: "I act controversially" but "I behave critically." This can indicate a woman who normally behaves in a rational way but who occasionally acts in such a contrary manner that she confuses or angers those around her. When the aspect is set off by transit, she may be illogical, impulsive and excessively angry. It may be that the anger is projected onto others but is really directed at herself.

The energy can be creative once it is channeled properly, but that has to be learned. Part of the learning process includes taking responsibility for one's actions, learning to see how behavior patterns conflict with what one wants. Because Uranus represents the behavior pattern of a generation, this can indicate a person whose action conflicts with that of the peer group, and the conflict can manifest either in a constructive or destructive manner. The choice is ours. If this energy is rechanneled it brings out the creative genius that lies buried under the anger, for this aspect can indicate a brilliant mind.

MARS–URANUS TRINE. An astrology teacher once described this aspect as the mark of genius. Uranus indicates erratic, unconventional behavior; Mars indicates action. If the action taken is unorthodox or unconventional and constructively applied, this individual can bring new ideas into his generation. However, if the ideas or behavioral attitudes are merely unconventional, the aspect may reflect a person who *thinks* he is creative only because he is "different."

In order to determine whether or not the aspect is functioning creatively, the rest of the chart must be synthesized, for the creative energy expresses better when action is taken because we like ourselves. If either the Sun or the Moon is afflicted, perhaps the creative energy will not manifest until this person becomes conscious of the need to bring body and soul into context. Once the Sun and Moon energy find appropriate expression, this individual has creative energy at his disposal.

MARS–URANUS OPPOSITION. The action principle essentially describes the action taken (through Mars) to represent the Sun sign archetype. Uranus indicates how the generation behaves as well as the kinds of eccentricities to which an individual is prone.

When the opposition is in effect, the action taken by the individual is compromised or colored by the behavior pattern; he may not relate well to his peer group. This individual may take self-willed or erratic action rather than make necessary compromises in life. In some cases he may be violent when angered or threatened. Because the will is involved in the action aspect, this individual may be overly willful and want immediate satisfaction because constant internal pressure is at play. The childhood environment was unpredictable, and this person may have been so repressed at home that high anger levels are considered "normal."

Mars in Taurus opposing Uranus in Scorpio can involve the following: "I act in a practical way, I act in a sensual manner," but "I behave like a reformer." In other words, "Do what I want you to do, because it's good for you." Sexually it can translate into "Have sex with me now for I need it and it will transform you." On the one hand this individual acts out the Taurus qualities; but when the will comes into focus, the action may become overly forceful.

When people act one way and feel compromised by their eccentric needs, the action taken may not only be unproductive but these individuals feel internally angry with themselves. If the anger is projected onto others, if others are blamed for the mistakes created by those who have this aspect, then the energy is destructive. They will have to learn to act in such a manner that any eccentricities within the nature also have a chance for constructive expression. When the anger is neither directed at the self nor at others, the energy is free to express creatively.

When attempting to determine where this behavior pattern comes from, check the planets that reflect the affect of the mother or father. This person may have been abused as a child. If so, much resentment may be harbored toward the parent, along with guilt because one is not supposed to hate one's parents. It's important that the anger be understood and not suppressed, for until the energy is free to flow, the creativity cannot be released. This person may wish to undergo analysis in order to get help breaking the old pattern.

MARS–URANUS QUINCUNX. Mars represents "I act" and Uranus indicates "I behave." The combination here brings a subtle strain that can be interpreted via the signs and houses involved.

Mars in Aries quincunx Uranus in Virgo indicates aggressive action and either critical or logical behavior. How can both manifest? How can one express the spontaneity of Aries when one's behavior indicates an analytical type of personality? Other people won't notice the problem, but it causes some inner consternation to those who own the aspect. Both energies need to manifest, and find appropriate expression.

MARS–NEPTUNE ASPECTS

Mars represents the action principle, the physical action taken to represent the self as it is symbolized by the Sun archetype. Neptune is the planet that symbolizes inspiration, creative fantasy, delusion. When these planets are joined together, creative fantasy and action are combined. We can take action to express our creative ideas; we can take action to express our ideas of spiritual creativity as well. Actions may be inspired by some ethereal creative urges, or our actions may be inspired by an illusion, or we may delude ourselves and our actions will be colored by our particular delusion.

Because Mars represents the sex drive, the Neptune contact will influence the sexual attitudes. It may add inspiration and spiritual love to the sexual expression, or it may warp the desires. It may veil sexuality with a cloud of guilt, or may help develop imaginative techniques that can be most enjoyable. The easy aspects are more productive than the hard aspects.

MARS–NEPTUNE CONJUNCTION. Mars symbolizes the action principle; Neptune adds fantasy, illusion or delusion to any facet of the action principle. In one sense this conjunction can indicate inspired action; it conveys creative activity. It may also indicate a person who doesn't know what he's doing!

Since Mars rules sexuality, the Neptune influence indicates one full of fantasy and delusion, and that fantasy can manifest in myriad ways. It can indicate the person who must have a spiritual and inspired sexual relationship; it may reflect the person who wants to live out all his sexual fantasies. To determine whether or not the conjunction suggests those who may have unprofitable or strange sexual relationships, one must check the other aspects in the chart to see if sex is viewed as something abnormal. If so, the conjunction will support that abnormality; if not, the conjunction will reflect a person who may be at least an interesting sex partner. Sexual dysfunctions will be indicated by other aspects to Mars, Moon or Venus. If the Sun is afflicted, the person may have an unhealthy self-image and therefore take sexual action that reflects his self-image.

This particular conjunction must be interpreted according to the additional aspects to it, for the energy will syncretize all the planets involved. If the individual develops a sense of self-worth and becomes trained in metaphysical principles, the energy can be indicative of brilliance.

MARS–NEPTUNE SEXTILE. Action taken to express the self will be aided by the creativity that comes from Neptune. The fantasy that enables him to create, the dreams he holds in his heart, the fantasy that stimulates his action combines the energies of Mars and Neptune in a highly creative manner.

The only obstacle that might come from the sextile aspect is that associated with an overly optimistic illusion regarding actions taken.

MARS–NEPTUNE SQUARE. Here the action principle works against the creative energy within the individual. Neptune inspires or deludes one, and in the case of the square, the tendency is to take deluded action or action that is not carefully thought out. In terms of expressing the qualities of the Sun archetype, the Neptune influence may serve to confuse the action taken; the Sun–Mars energy may not be operating in a clearly defined manner. Maya, the veil of illusion or delusion (as described in Hindu symbolism), often takes over the action principle. This can be a creative aspect, however, but the creative energy tends to be disorganized. The tension of the unexpressed creative energy can cause too much fantasy, too much imagination, and this individual may resort to alcohol or drugs if he doesn't know how to release the energy any other way. He may find the physical universe unpleasant, he may be uncomfortable coping with the realities of his day-to-day environment.

This individual may be prone to spiritual misinformation, he may search out all the groups that lead him down a religious path merely involved with religious theory and little practice. It's important that he discover a life philosophy that he can live, a life philosophy that he can put into practice in his daily experience. As he examines his previous actions, as he examines his previous ideas, he can begin to determine what is illusion and what is a creative fantasy. The energy of the hard aspect can be rechanneled into highly productive activity, but it won't just "happen," he has to make a conscious effort.

The Mars–Neptune square influences sexual expression as well. These people may have sexual fantasies, and depending on the other aspects in the chart, will use the fantasy either constructively or destructively. Neptune adds a spiritual flavor to anything that it touches, for it has to do with the concept of spiritual love. Spiritual love and sex don't always express well together until the conflicts between the two ideas have been consciously understood. Feelings of guilt may interfere with normal sexuality.

A female with this aspect may feel so guilty about "the animal nature" that she becomes frigid. A male may have potency problems, or have difficulty making love to a woman whom he spiritually loves. Guilt can also manifest in an unhealthy expression of the sexual nature, for this person may attempt to live out sexual fantasies, or become involved in sexual relationships with people he or she doesn't love.

The conflict can be dispersed when the concept of sexuality and the concept of spirituality are explored. If this person was taught that sex is "dirty," those teachings need to be re-examined, for Mother Nature is not "dirty." The cultural or religious teachings that propagate such misinformation could be better examined. A healthy and comfortable expression of the love nature can be developed.

MARS–NEPTUNE TRINE. Like the Mars–Uranus trine, this energy is extremely creative. The individual is gifted or blessed with a creative ability that can be put into action with ease. The inspiration and imagination of Neptune combine with the action principle.

Because a trine is a gift, we sometimes don't appreciate it. We are often more tuned into our difficult aspects because they cause us pain. When we become aware of the trine, it can be used to great advantage in career situations; the action taken is creative.

MARS–NEPTUNE OPPOSITION. The urges for creative expression (either illusion, delusion or inspired creativity) must be compromised by the action taken. The "I act" principle expresses the Sun archetype and the actions may be confused or muddled. The spiritual nature or the creative imagination is at odds with the action principle—causing guilt or even the development of misplaced loyalties or attitudes to interfere with action contemplated.

There may be some difficulty in expressing sexually as well, for sometimes the sex drive is confused with spirituality. This may indicate a person who has confused ethics regarding the person he loves. Either the conjunction, square or opposition can indicate sexual fantasies that don't hurt anyone. However, if this individual was raised in a family that held "narrow" religious convictions, the energy may become warped; rather than developing an imaginative sexuality, the reverse becomes true, and the sexuality is viewed as something to be ashamed of. If this individual leaves the home and family traditions, it's possible that he may become immersed in the exploration of his fantasies and get stuck there, wandering from one sexual experience to another, becoming more and more jaded and disappointed. On the other hand, this same individual can develop an extremely personal and special love relationship in which the loving can be imaginative. The sexual union can be lifted to such spiritual heights that the exploration of Tantric yoga may be enjoyable.

If the world seems too harsh, or if this person has no constructive outlet for his creative energy, or doesn't understand that it needs expression, he may be drawn to alcohol or drugs. If he isn't actively involved in the drug or alcohol scene, his partner may be.

The creative energy cannot express properly until the energy is directed, and some conscious effort to understand the energies symbolized by these planets will help the rechanneling process.

MARS–NEPTUNE QUINCUNX. This indicates muddled action: Mars represents "I act" and Neptune represents "I dream." The dreams and aspirations may be confused because the qualities of the two signs involved don't work well together.

The strain is not an obvious one; it seems to reflect an internal confusion. It's a confusion between the creative aspiration and the action taken to support those dreams.

We talk about our squares and oppositions whether we know astrology or not; the astrological symbols merely give us a formula to use when discussing problems that we know exist. But the quincunx is just there, annoying, but not annoying enough to do anything about. The energy needs to be consciously directed.

The qualities of the signs involved and the house placement of the aspect will indicate the area of life most affected. Both energies need expression; the solution can be found by discovering how to use both energies.

MARS–PLUTO ASPECTS

Mars represents the action principle; it symbolizes the kind of action we take in order to express the qualities of the Sun archetype. Pluto indicates the possibility of transformation or regeneration; it may represent what Jung calls the collective unconscious, for it seems to reflect the unconscious motivation of the generation. When these two energies merge, an unconscious motivation for action may occur; action may become transformed, uplifted; action may be taken to express the concept of regeneration or transformation in the personal sense.

When the energies are expressing on undeveloped levels, the Mars energy can indicate anger, and that anger can be directed into one's actions, or into one's expression of sexuality. Pluto can manifest as a coercive force, as an impetus to control the events occurring in the environment. People with undeveloped Pluto energy are only imitating a pattern taught to them in the early childhood environment. They saw one (or both) parents controlling everyone in sight, and assume that this reaction is necessary for survival. (To determine which parent created the pattern, check the aspects between Mars or Pluto and either the Sun, Saturn, or the Moon, Venus. If both parents were involved in the game, the chances are the individual will imitate the stronger parent, which can be determined by the Sun sign polarity.)

When trying to break an obsessive attitude, the definition of obsession—"persistent and inescapable preoccupation with an idea or emotion"*—might be kept in mind. Obsessions preclude any spontaneous action, so our obsessions keep us from sharing many delightful and unplanned experiences. A Pluto-caused obsession is a subtle attempt to *control* in this case. "I love you, therefore I must have you regardless of how you feel about me," is one Plutonic statement. The energy can be better used in a constructive manner, for the action taken can be uplifting to others. A cooperative attitude can be consciously brought into our daily activities.

MARS–PLUTO CONJUNCTION. The "I act" principle may be overwhelmed by the power of Pluto's energy as described above. This may indicate an individual who takes "controlled action." Action may be manipulative of either self or others, or both. This individual may be unconsciously angered, for Pluto indicates unconscious motivation and Mars can symbolize anger. It may be that this individual is influenced by the symbols of the collective unconscious, that the images in the psyche interfere with any physical action taken. It indicates (because of the energy coming from the psyche) that action taken can be inspired by the mythic images of the collective unconscious. Action may be extremely creative.

---

*Webster's New Collegiate Dictionary.

Before the creative potential can really be expressed, however, the anger must be worked out.

Consider Mars conjunct Pluto in Leo: The Leo keywords indicate a need for proper respect and approval as well as a sensitivity to fair play. If someone doesn't give this individual enough respect, a lot of anger can be generated. Mars conjunct Pluto in Cancer indicates action may be taken because this person is too emotionally possessive. The conjunction doesn't always work consciously, for the Pluto position indicates our unconscious motivation. Action taken based on an unconscious motivation may not be responsible action, and it might be harmful to others. Action may be caused by anger or control needs.

If this person has other aspects that indicate problems expressing sexuality, this conjunction may indicate a setup for sexual violence. Sexual violence may range from having sex that hurts self or others, or it can indicate the rapist, the masochist, the person who may draw sexual violence to him.

An astrologer once told me that Mars–Pluto combinations are the mark of Christ-consciousness, that hard aspects between them implied a need to develop conscious responsibility for action taken. She recommended the study of metaphysics.

MARS–PLUTO SEXTILE. Mars represents the action principle used to express the Sun archetype. Pluto indicates the collective unconscious, the unconscious motivation that may underlie our actions later in life.

If Pluto represents the masses, then action taken by this individual may be beneficial to the masses. This person was exposed to the idea of cooperation in the early family environment. The sextile indicates an individual who can develop a talent that is marketable as long as the action taken coordinates with the needs of groups: so, media, communication, politics, etc., would be a good direction to follow.

MARS–PLUTO SQUARE. This is a difficult energy level that needs to be channeled and understood before it becomes productive. A square indicates that the planets involved in the aspect are working against each other. In this case it indicates that Mars (I act) works against Pluto (my unconscious motivation). It signifies a person who takes action that may be spurred by negative input from the psyche, or a person whose need for control works against his ability to take action. For example, Pluto in Leo square Mars in Taurus: "I act practically, I act scientifically, I act sensually (in the sexual sense)" square "I am unconsciously motivated by pride, approval, or respect." How can one act rationally if one is motivated by pride? How does one respond to a sexual rejection if Pluto in Leo is unconsciously motivated by approval? Would this person interpret a sexual rejection as a "put-down?"

Anger may be confused with sexuality when this aspect is present. This individual may use sex to control other people. The Pluto–Mars square requires that an individual control the action taken, and when his universe crumbles, anger takes over. Blind rages can surge up from the unconscious. Because the rage can be so intense, those who own this aspect are aware they have it! They are usually afraid of their own anger. They may not be willing to admit that the anger exists, for these are often people who implode—they push the anger far down into the depths of the personal unconscious because they are afraid of expressing it. People born in Fire or Air signs usually suppress this aspect, for anger is not considered "spiritual." Folks who've attempted some form of spiritual development don't want to admit to having this anger, for they are not proud of it.

However, in order for the aspect to become productively creative, the anger has to become conscious and channeled into other directions. Anger is merely unchanneled creativity. This person needs to become aware of the Plutonic sensitive points so the anger can be consciously let go. Anger usually manifests when we are either afraid of something or our feelings are hurt. When the fears and hurts are understood, we no longer need to be angry.

MARS–PLUTO TRINE. Mars represents the action principle; when it trines Pluto, (our unconscious motivation), it indicates that the energies can merge in a productive manner.

This individual was encouraged in childhood to express himself, to cooperate with groups, to act for the common good of the family. The collective images in the psyche may influence actions that are taken, but in a constructive manner. The creative facet of the aspect may not be used early in the life, for this individual will be coping with the more difficult configurations at that time.

MARS–PLUTO OPPOSITION. The action principle, or the action taken in life, works against the images coming from the unconscious. The aspect indicates that action may be forced, the individual may not be cooperative. Usually hard aspects between Mars and Pluto indicate an individual who avoids groups, who doesn't care for crowds because he feels out of control there. This can cause certain kinds of claustrophobia or ochlophobia.

Some kind of compromise has to take place between the action principle and the sensitivities from the unconscious. The unconscious motivation represents an influence (or a sensitivity) developed in the early years that will work against constructive action. The difficulty with Mars–Pluto aspects is learning how to control anger, how not to act or react because of anger, how to diffuse the anger when one is out of control.

Before the benefits (the creative action potential) can manifest, the aspect must be understood. Anger is so intense that the individual more often implodes than explodes. This person may not even be conscious of the anger he is shoving down into his personal unconscious. Until the anger is recognized it can't be rechanneled. Anger is usually caused by hurt feelings and/or fear. The hurts or fears can be handled intellectually, they can be reasoned out. When hurt, fear, or anger appears, one can ask "Why am I hurt? What am I afraid of?" The answers will reflect the needs of the Sun or Moon, plus the signs involved in the Mars–Pluto aspect. The next key will be the Pluto position, for it indicates an unconscious influence. Was the person who has Pluto in Leo disapproved of or made fun of as a child? Is this why he is so sensitive now?

Once the anger becomes conscious it can be worked out. The power of the aspect shows management ability as well as the potential for creative group action. It's worth the work.

MARS–PLUTO QUINCUNX. This is not a heavy aspect. It indicates a strain between the action taken and unconscious motivation for it. For example, Mars in Pisces says "I act like a martyr," and Pluto in Leo says "I am unconsciously motivated by (or unconsciously sensitive to) a need for respect and approval." If the quincunx exists, the sensitive action of Mars is mitigated by a need for approval. Could this person be a martyr as long as it's approvable? What happens sexually when the sensitive Mars reaction is not understood by the partner? Does this cause an overreaction based on pride? If so, the problem can be analyzed consciously and reasoned out.

WHEN WE ARE BORN, WE LOOK TO THE MOTHER FIGURE to give us our food and care. Our first attempt at relating to someone else comes from our own survival needs. A baby yells for food and the food appears; a baby needs care and after a cry or two, the care appears. When a baby reaches out to another person, the reaching out is motivated by "need." The childhood years teach us how to relate with people who are not our parents; we usually learn how to do this because of our relationship with brothers, sisters and/or playmates. We want their toys, we have to learn to share. We go to school and learn something about team play or teamwork. If we have problems learning to relate as young people or if we still find it difficult to relate as adults, some Jupiter affliction may be prominent in the chart.

Many astrologers have called Jupiter the expansive planet: it indicates our "good luck," problems with weight gain, and it indicates abundance. Jupiter may symbolize all of those things, but if we are looking to discover what motivates a person, what the blocks may be when attempting to communicate with others, the problem may be diagnosed from the sign and aspects that are involved with Jupiter.

Jupiter can be called a generation planet because it sits in a sign for about a year, and it takes twelve years to circle the zodiac. This means that many people have Jupiter in the same sign. Jupiter cannot be considered a really personal planet unless it aspects the Sun, Moon, Mercury, Venus, Mars or the Ascendant in the chart. The personal planets describe personal attributes, and Jupiter describes the beginnings of relating self to the outer environment. Some call the process of relating self to environment the microcosm-macrocosm relationship. At any rate, those rare people who have no strong Jupiter aspects will relate according to the qualities symbolized by Jupiter's sign. Relationships may not be as important or as problematic to these people; they may be content with the roles designated by the social structure of that time period.

When Jupiter is afflicted, the individual is born into a household where attitudes regarding the concept of relating are not well developed. This child sees a set of "normals" which imply that people do not consider each other's needs, or perhaps the family members don't listen to each other, etc. As an adult, he may reach out to relate and find he's lapsed back into the patterns he observed as a child. He may express himself in an unconstructive manner, getting into those dilemmas fostered by "I want it anyway;" he may relate excessively, he may overexpand or overrelate; he may pursue whims that are not based on common sense. He may not have any conscious idea of what he wants from life. He may not know how to examine his personal needs because he never was allowed to do so as a child, or he may not have seen his parents doing it.

If we wish to experience more than just a role-playing relationship, we each must learn how to relate our feelings, our thoughts and our personalities to someone else. When Jupiter is well aspected, the individual is taught healthy relating procedures in the early home. When Jupiter is afflicted, the ability to relate to another person must be consciously learned. As we each explore consciousness, if we wish to develop a well-integrated personality, Jupiter symbolizes one of the stepping stones in our development, for it gives us the key to how we are functioning in the relating department.

If we wish to go further in the process of evolving consciousness, Jupiter symbolizes the need to integrate the knowledge we learn into our daily lives. The knowledge that we assimilate must be kept in perspective. The learned person may use his knowledge to set himself apart from others, to maintain a position above others, to remain untouched by those with whom he comes in contact. We hear the phrase "he has a large ego," but more often than not the individual with the purported large ego has no ego at all. Because he has a poorly developed sense of self, he has a need to make others aware of his importance. Relating, on the other hand, is a whole different thing, for it includes sharing, being a part of, while at the same time maintaining a sense of self. This means the self must feel pretty secure, for we can't really share it until we have a healthy self image! Relating to another person can be illustrated by thinking of a pebble thrown into a pond. It makes ripples. Every ripple is free and also a part of the water in the pond. We are each free to do our own thing, yet we, too, are a part of a "pond."

In the personal sense, Jupiter indicates how we each will relate ourselves to others. Some people may feel that Mercury would better indicate relating potential, but Mercury symbolizes how we think and talk. We can talk an awful lot without relating or allowing ourselves to be open or receptive to share with someone else. The aspects to Jupiter will indicate how the Sun sign potential can be shared with others—friends, lovers, family, as well as how the personality is integrated into the environment.

JUPITER–SUN ASPECTS

See Chapter 1 in this section.

JUPITER–MOON ASPECTS

See Chapter 2 in this section.

JUPITER–MERCURY ASPECTS

See Chapter 3 in this section.

JUPITER–VENUS ASPECTS

See Chapter 4 in this section.

JUPITER–MARS ASPECTS

See Chapter 5 in this section.

JUPITER–SATURN ASPECTS

Jupiter and Saturn were the generation planets of the ancient astrologers. Jupiter spends a year in a sign and Saturn takes two to two-and-a-half years to move through one sign in the zodiac. Because of the slow motion of these planets, they symbolize a trait, characteristic, or quality that is common to a large group of people.

Jupiter simply indicates how we will relate—to ourselves, to our environment, to our friends and loved ones. Jupiter also symbolizes how we will naturally open up to new ideas, new information, and how we will expand our consciousness. Saturn represents how the father may have affected us psychologically during our formative years; the house placement and sign indicates what we are cautious about. Saturn also represents Father Time and/or Father Nature, so this symbol can indicate how we crystallize our life experience, how we cope with being tested. When these two planets combine they describe how we withstand being tested as we reach out to relate to others. As we relate to the changing life cycles, as we approach each new perspective in life, Saturn makes our relating abilities crystal clear, because they are tested.

Any combination of aspects between Jupiter and Saturn indicates a personality that will benefit from the process of individuation, or the process of becoming self-responsible. The hard aspects signify that the attaining of consciousness (or self-responsibility) will not necessarily be easy! Once the aspects are understood they are not difficult to work with—as a matter of fact, they are far easier to work with than are some of the more personal squares and oppositions.

Going back to the natural zodiac, Mercury indicates how we *talk*, how we communicate, what we say and think. It symbolizes the mental functions, and Mercury rules the third and sixth houses and the signs Gemini and Virgo. The ancient astrologers ascribed the rulership to the ninth and twelfth houses (Sagittarius and Pisces) to Jupiter. Jupiter *opposes* both Mercury in the third and Mercury in the sixth in the natural wheel, so it seems that the opposition temporizes or causes a compromise between the relating abilities and the communication needs within the individual. Some interplay must take place between communicating and relating to others. We may assume, then, that because the symbols appear in opposition in the natural zodiac, this kind of temporizing of personality is normal.

Saturn, as crystallizer, opposes both the Sun and the Moon in the natural zodiac. The Moon rules Cancer (fourth) and the Sun rules Leo (fifth). In the symbolism of the natural wheel, Saturn opposes both these facets of personality because it rules both Capricorn (tenth) and Aquarius (eleventh). If the Moon symbolizes our emotions, then Saturn opposing the Moon may be interpreted to mean that immature emotional reactions to life will be restricted by Saturn. The Sun represents the "I am" part of the self, and in the fifth it symbolizes the creativity of an individual. The opposition to Saturn in Aquarius may be interpreted to mean that creative expression must be responsible. Creativity cannot exist for long unless it serves a purpose—the person must function within the framework of universal law.

So, in the natural zodiac Jupiter opposes both functions of Mercury and Saturn opposes the personal functions symbolized by the Sun and Moon. The Jupiter–Saturn aspects in the natal chart may then be interpreted to indicate a special emphasis on an individual's need to take responsibility for the self, to understand the relationship between macrocosm and microcosm. Individual freedom in a philosophical sense doesn't imply the freedom to do as one pleases. It means that one is self-responsible. One doesn't leave Mom and Dad to be taken care of by the big government in the sky. In order to be a free adult, each person must assume responsibility for his or her own survival. When we reach out to receive new knowledge and experience we also assume responsibility for understanding what we learn, for the information or experience must be absorbed in perspective. That is what most of the so-called spiritual philosophies are really talking about. And that is what Jupiter and Saturn symbolize in the chart, if one is looking for long-range explanations regarding the life pattern.

JUPITER–SATURN CONJUNCTION. This aspect is interpreted on many levels of experience. Jupiter symbolizes how we relate to others, Saturn symbolizes restriction in some way. The sign of the conjunction is important for it lends its qualities to the aspect. Jupiter symbolizes how we open up, and Saturn symbolizes the restrictions placed on us at an early age because of our father's attitude toward us, or our response to his influence. In a mundane sense, the conjunction means that the individual has a tendency to open up (Jupiter) and close up (Saturn) at the same time! He may reach out to share some new experience and be afraid to do it because there is an unconscious memory that authority figures or Fathers don't like him doing that. It may mean that the father is a restrictive influence when this individual is learning how to relate; maybe the father can't relate easily either.

The conjunction will indicate a person who takes relationships seriously, one who may work too hard on developing all the potential in a relationship. It may indicate a person who takes relationships so seriously that he or she is afraid of making a commitment, or even starting a relationship at all. This person may have relationships that are similar to the kind the father created, and the pattern can be determined by exploring memories of the father's friendships over the years. Once the pattern is understood, the father's influence is diminished, and the owner of the conjunction is free to pursue the kinds of relationships he wants to develop for himself—although he will approach the subject seriously.

In order to reach the fullest possible realization of life potential, in order to develop consciousness to its highest point, the individual with this conjunction will have to develop a perspective on both how he reaches out to relate as well as understanding the restrictive influence from his father—and both aspects of personality will develop at the same time. As he begins to view his cautions, as he faces his fears and the feelings of limitation and frustration caused by Saturn, his opportunity to open up, to relate to new experience, will also be developed. This person will then have an above-average perspective for he cannot relate fully until he takes responsibility for himself.

The aspect will be further influenced by the sign of the conjunction as well as the house placement. The conjunction taking place in the twelfth house seems to be the most difficult because this house signifies that part of ourselves which can remain the most unconscious. The aspect is not threatening in the twelfth, just harder to bring into consciousness. The karmic astrologers say that because it is more difficult, it's also more important. The person who investigates the twelfth house conjunction will learn the reaching out (Jupiter)-reaching in (Saturn) process at the same time that he also begins to view other secret depths of personality.

JUPITER–SATURN SEXTILE. The sextile between Jupiter and Saturn indicates a pretty healthy home environment. The relating principle is not adversely affected by the individual's father. The sextile indicates that the father's influence probably helped the individual to view the reaching out and opening up process as normal. Authority figures were not damaging to the development of this person's relating ability.

Although the aspect may not be appreciated until after the age of thirty-five, the later years bring a maturity and a consciousness to the concept of relating that this individual can use to better develop the potentials of the Sun.

JUPITER–SATURN SQUARE The square indicates that the individual is raised in an atmosphere that prohibits or restricts the relating principle. The father places restrictions on this person, and these restrictions will be carried into the adult life on some subconscious level, causing the young adult to feel inhibited about relating, or he may relate excessively periodically and then withdraw.

Jupiter indicates "I relate," it indicates how we open up and allow new experience in our lives. It indicates how we will relate ourselves to another human being through the bonds of friendship or love. The Saturn square indicates a restriction, a holding back in the relating department. It can also indicate a person who turns on and off in a somewhat unpredictable manner. These people may feel apprehensive about taking chances on new relationships. The apprehension can even undermine personal confidence to the extent that they are uneasy about accepting new jobs, new responsibilities, etc.

The square can be understood if the father's relating values are examined. The early childhood years can be explored again in order to decipher any pattern that can be an indicator of the influence. If the father adversely affected the individual's relating ability, if he restricted the individual, if he encouraged apprehension or fear in regard to new undertakings, that pattern can be reasoned out and let go.

In personal relationships, this individual may be drawn to inferior types or may choose people to love who are unable to help him through relating problems connected with the relationship. Personal cautions and apprehensions will have to be looked into consciously. The individual will have to take responsibility for his relationships and relationship conditions. As that happens, he will find himself drawn to more healthy relationships in the future.

JUPITER–SATURN TRINE. This aspect indicates an individual born into a family with a generally healthy perspective on life. As this person reaches out to relate, to bring in new life experience, his parents are supportive. The father image is healthy and it gives this individual a sound psychological basis from which to work as he approaches new situations in his life. Authority figures are not frightening, there is an innate sense of responsibility for actions taken, and chances are any commitment will be thought out carefully. Relationships will be regarded seriously, and any attempt at developing them will be considered from a responsible point.

As this person matures, as he passes through the various cycles relating to the maturation process, he will discover that he opens up and expands his conscious awareness at a similar rate to his letting go of Saturnian cautions and fears. This aspect indicates a steady growth, steady maturity and, therefore, the growing process may be more difficult to discern. The person with the Saturn–Jupiter afflictions will grow with leaps, bounds and fallow periods. The trine will move from one level of awareness to another from a more circumspect point.

The trine between Jupiter and Saturn will not outweigh aspects indicating personal conflict. It can be used to indicate the available inner strength needed when working through other difficult aspects in the chart. An individual may have developed such an intense dislike of the father during the early childhood years (the dislike being based on other aspects in the chart) that he may be unable to see any constructive father effect in his life. Understanding the Jupiter–Saturn trine may give him new insight into the early experience with the father.

JUPITER–SATURN OPPOSITION. Jupiter indicates the relating principle; it tells how the individual will reach out, open up to new experience, how an individual will attempt to relate himself to his universe, his friends, lovers, family. Saturn indicates how the father influences, hampers or restricts the individual when he first attempts to reach out to the world around him. The influence may be physical or it may be merely that the father has a disapproving attitude.

The opposition suggests that some definite restriction was placed on the individual early in life. Whenever he reached out for something new, his father disapproved. This subconscious memory will remain for many years, and every time effort is made to open up, a fear symptom may be set off, causing this person to reach out with great caution. He may reach out and then run away—he may be open and receptive one minute and closed and cold the next. He may have difficulty relating to people he considers to be authority figures—teachers, supervisors, partners, etc.

If these individuals pursue the drive for consciousness, if they believe in self-responsibility, the personal qualities symbolized by Jupiter and Saturn will have to be integrated. Often, these people grow with leaps and bounds followed by severe fallow periods between growth cycles. The concepts of relationship possibilities will have to be explored at the same time that a confrontation of the fears and apprehensions caused by Saturn takes place.

If Jupiter represents how we assimilate the universe around us, the opposition indicates that every time we have a new idea it will be tested by Saturn. Our mettle will be tested and molded, our character developed, the Hero venture intensified. The universe doesn't hurt us, but the untested warrior is no warrior. As Jupiter develops, the personality becomes more secure in itself because it has been tested by Saturn.

The opposition also signifies a break with the father, a break with the tradition of the family. That doesn't mean that the individual must leave home forever, but unhealthy family traditions can be left behind.

JUPITER–SATURN QUINCUNX. The quincunx aspect is not as strong as the square or opposition. It causes a strain that can eventually affect the health if it's left untended.

Jupiter indicates the relating ability and Saturn represents the area of caution or apprehension in the personality. The strain between the two qualities indicates that the effect of the father on the individual may not be consciously understood. Relationships may be unfulfilling because of an experience absorbed in the early childhood. There will be some conflict between pursuing relationships and remaining closed to them.

The aspect can be handled when the signs involved in the quincunx are understood intellectually. Both facets of personality need to find expression.

JUPITER–URANUS ASPECTS

Jupiter indicates our ability to relate. It symbolizes the kinds of personal qualities (because of its sign) that we bring into our relationships. It symbolizes how we tend to see ourselves as a part of the universe around us. Uranus is a generation planet that affects masses of people. It symbolizes our behavior pattern. It symbolizes our erratic or self-willed tendencies.

When these two planets tie together they show a combination of the energies—and relationships may be unusual, erratic, inspired or impaired because of a strong sense of self-will. These planetary ties can indicate a person who responds to unusual, unorthodox or unconventional relationships; or a person who needs to develop consciousness to its highest level—this may only happen if the aspect is also tied to the personal planets.

JUPITER–URANUS CONJUNCTION. The relating principle is influenced by the unusual qualities of Uranus, or the individualistic qualities, etc. The sign the conjunction takes place in will be important to the diagnosis of the energy. Since Jupiter represents how we open up to new experience, this conjunction may indicate a person who opens up erratically or impetuously. Ordinarily, this conjunction signifies a person who enjoys unusual relationships—and it must be remembered that "unusual" can be either constructive or destructive.

If this individual takes responsibility for himself, the conjunction will have to be considered seriously; for no relationship happens without his consent. He may form relationships without considering the consequences or choose partners who do not make him feel good about himself, because he didn't think before he opened up. In this case, check the Saturn placement to see how Saturn can help the conjunction take responsibility for itself.

Uranus can be of help when the energy is understood, for as Jupiter determines perspective, Uranus adds the potential for increased awareness, even awareness that can bring new philosophies into being. If the conjunction also involves the personal planets, it can help to develop an unusual and exciting personality.

JUPITER–URANUS SEXTILE. The relating principle is unusual and unorthodox, but in a healthy and constructive sense. New approaches to relating, new concepts or innovations regarding the relating principle are at this individual's fingertips. The behavior pattern doesn't impede a developing relationship. This individual's eccentricities won't stand in the way of his relationships. It's a steadying influence.

JUPITER–URANUS SQUARE. Jupiter represents the relating principle—it indicates how we reach out to the world, how we relate to those we like and love, how we relate as an employer or employee. It indicates how we see ourselves in perspective to the universe. Uranus indicates a behavior pattern, how we are eccentric, how we are different, or how willful we can be.

The square aspect indicates a frustration, a problem, an excess of energy. The behavior pattern or personal eccentricities may be working against the relating principle. Impetuous decisions may be made regarding the beginning or the ending of any relationship. This individual may be open one day and excessively stubborn the next. He is imitating a family pattern. The picture becomes clearer when the aspects from either Jupiter or Uranus are tied in to the personal planets; it can then be seen just how the energy affects the personality.

Because Uranus indicates a humanitarian consciousness, the aspect may cause a somewhat warped perspective to develop in regard to this person's place in the universe. It therefore may indicate someone who doesn't relate to Father Nature or universal law, or one who feels he is beyond it. Selfishness, abrupt behavior involving other people, a willful attitude about partnerships, and similar kinds of behavior will have to be let go of if this individual wants to get the most creative potential possible from himself.

JUPITER–URANUS TRINE. Jupiter indicates the relating principle while Uranus indicates how eccentric or willful we can be. Uranus indicates a behavior pattern that can affect relationships. The trine aspect indicates a person born at a time when his family was exploring some new concepts regarding the relating principle; this individual was encouraged to try new and different approaches.

His general behavior will not interfere with developing relationships for he won't be giving conflicting messages to his partner; he can work through relating problems without extra stress. He may have unusual ideas about what a relationship is, and he may choose unusual or unorthodox people as partners.

As Jupiter represents the perspective we have of ourselves in the universal flow, this perspective will be influenced by Uranus, but in a positive manner. This person has the potential to raise his consciousness to different heights than those attained by the average person; he may even become a philosophical leader when he is old enough and thoroughly tested!

JUPITER–URANUS OPPOSITION. Jupiter indicates the relating potential, the concept of what a relationship is, how the individual will put himself forth to the people around him. Because Uranus opposes this concept, relationships may be impetuously started or finished; the behavior pattern is at odds with the relating needs.

For example, consider Uranus in Cancer opposing Jupiter in Capricorn: Uranus in Cancer says "I behave emotionally, I behave jealously, perhaps possessively, I behave in a sensitive manner." Jupiter in Capricorn says "I relate in a traditional way, I'm relating that I want stable traditional relationships, I relate in a controlled way, for I want to know where I stand, or I relate carefully and slowly, as the sign Capricorn suggests." The opposition causes tension, for the person expresses two different energies. If he jumps into a relationship he'll regret it, for the Capricorn part of himself will be suspicious. If he is too cautious, he'll feel uncomfortable because he's suppressing his emotional reaction. Both energies need to be expressed.

Relationships cannot be entered into impetuously, for in order to relate, one must listen and receive the other person. Serious relationships must be built, stone by stone, word by word. Because the early family experience showed this individual that relating is a sometime thing, he will attempt to relate the same way. If he lets the Uranus energy pull him into poorly thought-out schemes, he'll suffer. The universal perspective can be learned and then the Uranus tie will help him become more innovative. The qualities of Cancer and Capricorn can be balanced and used in a constructive manner.

JUPITER–URANUS QUINCUNX. The quincunx causes a strain that eventually affects the health because the strain is not painful enough to face and conquer, or even to face and let go.

The behavior pattern is at odds with the need to relate. It brings feelings of apprehension into any attempt at relating, and it also may cause the partner to feel unsure of where the relationship is going. For example, Uranus in Aries says "I behave in an aggressive and idealistic manner." It is wordy aggression that combines with a sense of gallantry or chivalry. Jupiter in Virgo relates critically. The behavior is aggressive and straightforward, but the relationships are handled in an excessively analytical manner. Self-observation may help this individual so that he can quit being so critical. The intellectual energy of Virgo can combine quite nicely with the intellectual energy of Aries. However, criticism of the loved one doesn't help win any popularity contest.

JUPITER–NEPTUNE ASPECTS

Jupiter symbolizes the relating principle and Neptune symbolizes the creative dream within us. When Neptune aspects Jupiter it brings a wonderful veil of illusion or delusion with it, and relationships can be clouded with dreams of perfection, or spiritual love. The combination indicates that we may choose relationships that we don't understand, or seek what we cannot find.

When the energy becomes more conscious, it can indicate the possibility of relationships that are inspiring or especially creative, or relationships that can be lifted out of the realm of the ordinary.

JUPITER–NEPTUNE CONJUNCTION. The conjunction between Neptune and Jupiter is not a personal aspect, for it will be present in all the charts of people born when Jupiter is transiting the same sign that Neptune is during a given year. The aspect indicates a group of people who will view relating from a more spiritual point than those born in the same year.

Neptune clouds the Jupiter position, causing many different kinds of personality traits. These traits can range from an overly spiritual or cosmic-love approach to all relationships down to the mundane setup for too much sugar intake. Neptune symbolizes the creative dream as well as universal or impersonal love. When a person reaches out to relate (Jupiter) and his relationships are colored by too much "universal love," the individual with this aspect is more prone to be hurt when the relationship doesn't stay in the lofty spiritual heights that he expects it should—thus a withdrawal into the personal universe full of love that can be made more sweet by the addition of candy, starchy foods, or even alcohol.

On the other hand, when this individual realizes that he tends to see relationships through rose-colored glasses, that he may project too much Neptunian dream-world spirituality onto his relationships, he can begin to reconstruct the way in which he approaches other people. When the reaching out or relating principle (symbolized by Jupiter) gains perspective, he can then use his Neptune energy to uplift the kinds of relationships he forms, but from a conscious point. He can recognize the qualities he brings into his life, or the qualities he needs in order to feel complete when he looks for companionship. The energy is thereby transformed, and he can proceed to develop very special ways to share his personality with his fellow man. The aspect implies that a spiritual awareness, or a need for discovery of the man-universe relationship is important.

JUPITER–NEPTUNE SEXTILE. The sextile energy is easier to use than that of the conjunction, square or opposition. The energy doesn't really manifest until the middle thirties, for it is a latent talent that needs development. The individual is taught to accept his own creativity when he reaches out to relate to his childhood environment, and that encouragement develops certain unconscious ideas about creativity and relating that can be used in later life.

This aspect will be outweighed by any hard aspect involving Jupiter because the hard aspects need to be taken care of, reassessed and rechanneled before the Neptune sextile can take affect. The conjunction indicates the possibility for sugar addictions; the sextile does not for it isn't strong enough or threatening enough.

The sign and house placement is important in diagnosis, for they show the qualities and the areas of life that will be affected or improved by the conscious direction of the energy implied by the aspect.

JUPITER–NEPTUNE SQUARE. The square aspect always indicates a frustration, for the energies or qualities symbolized by the planets involved work against each other. Jupiter indicates "I relate," and shows us how we reach out to other people, how we reach out to absorb new ideas and how we see ourselves in perspective to the universe around us. Neptune symbolizes our creative dream, what we wish we were, and brings the quality of illusion or delusion to anything it touches. In other words, Neptune veils and clouds issues that may need to be handled from a more conscious point. When Neptune is involved in a square, you can be fairly sure that the energy will be that of delusion because the hard aspects imply the more unhealthy usage of the planet's qualities. Only through conscious behavior can the energy be turned around and reapplied from a healthy point.

When Neptune clouds the relating issue, the individual doesn't consciously recognize or take responsibility for what he puts into a relationship. The problems he may have will probably come from the signs involved in the square. He may look for relationships that are formed because of some "ethereal" connection he feels for the other person, those qualities having no foundation in real life. He may misjudge the kind of energy he puts into his relationships, totally missing the fact that his partner is not the only person with relating problems!

Perspective is the key issue here, for if he wants to become conscious, or self-responsible, he must gain some perspective about what a relationship is and what true spirituality is. Then his insights can be applied to something that counts. His insights (coming from Neptune) may increase his relationship possibilities as well as help him to reach out to new experience from a more knowing or accepting point of view.

JUPITER–NEPTUNE TRINE. Here the addiction comes up again.

This person will be in pursuit of the perfect spiritual relationship and may be drawn up sharply when he discovers that other people don't relate the way he does, or that other people don't want the kind of relationship he wants. He wants some lovely pie-in-the-sky kind of relationship that just happens. The reality of having to compromise with another person, the reality of having to face the necessities of survival—like working and paying the rent, etc.—may bother him. This personality may not want to take self-responsibility in the real world. When this happens, he attaches himself to other people without looking to see what the other party wants from him. He may not recognize what the possibilities of the relationship are.

On the constructive side, this aspect indicates a person who is naturally interested in religious philosophy and the pursuit of metaphysics, and even orthodox religion may give solace. However, it's important that he really learn how to relate, for he will feel better about himself if he does. When Neptune clouds relationships, it really indicates that he doesn't fill half of the relating requirement—he doesn't take the time to determine what the other person wants from a relationship, what the other person needs, or even if the other person is available. Unrequited love relationships are not the answer. He must learn to listen to the other person. As he develops perspective, he will find himself in more fulfilling situations.

JUPITER–NEPTUNE OPPOSITION. Jupiter indicates "I relate," and Neptune symbolizes the creative dream. When the opposition takes place, the individual's dreams or spiritual concepts interfere with the process of relating to others. This person may reach out for new experience without any conscious realization of what he is doing, or who he is doing it with. He may not wish to look at the various relationship dilemmas he gets himself into for the reality of the relationship may be unpleasant. When he doesn't like seeing what he has created, he may withdraw into the sugar, alcohol or drug refuge, so that he can continue to live in a world that he has created.

The Neptune energy implies a need for conscious spiritual development, and it doesn't matter whether he pursues the more orthodox forms of religious observances or if he explores the world of metaphysics, philosophy or other occult avenues. The important thing for him is that he gains a perspective on universal energy, that he gains a perspective on what a relationship is all about. This way he won't be as hurt as he can be when he pursues situation after situation that brings no peace. When he takes responsibility for the situations he creates, he will be able to transform the Neptunian illusion into an inspirational kind of energy, lending the qualities of inspiration or a different spiritual consciousness to what he does.

JUPITER–NEPTUNE QUINCUNX. The quincunx is not a very

difficult aspect between Jupiter and Neptune. There are probably more important squares, oppositions and conjunctions in the chart that will indicate more serious personality dilemmas.

The relating principle (Jupiter) is affected by the illusions and delusions of Neptune. Some vague disturbance can be working on an internal level because this individual dreams of having an inspiring and special kind of relationship that may not occur. Probably all relationships are somewhat disappointing because he reaches out according to the sign that Jupiter is in and dreams of handling his life differently.

For example, Neptune in Virgo dreams of being critical, analytical, and pursues the details of a critical intellect. Jupiter in Aquarius, on the other hand, wants to relate to the world from an unconventional or unorthodox point. Probably criticism is delivered and not accepted in return. Perhaps the unconventional relationship causes this person the anxiety that is brought about by wondering if he should have chosen someone who was less apt to be criticized by others.

JUPITER–PLUTO ASPECTS

When the relating principle symbolized by Jupiter is tied to the unconscious motivation symbolized by Pluto, many different kinds of energy manifest. On the one hand, the individual may feel a strong need to be in control of any relationship he forms, or he may be interested in transforming people he has relationships with. If Jupiter symbolizes a need to develop a perspective between macrocosm and microcosm, and Pluto indicates the content of the collective unconscious, a combination of energy between the two planets can indicate a person who may be tremendously creative about manifesting the relating principle.

These aspects may indicate one who can relate to the needs of the masses, for Pluto also symbolizes the masses of people, the common folk. The aspects may also indicate the type of person who needs to control all attempts at relating with the masses, or with people in general.

JUPITER–PLUTO CONJUNCTION. Because Pluto is one of the slow-moving outer planets, many people born in any given year when Jupiter is transiting the same sign as Pluto will have this aspect. It creates a mini-generation of people who will have choices to make as to how they pursue relationships. If the conjunction is unafflicted by other planets it can be diagnosed by the sign and house placement.

It indicates that relationships will be affected by the unconscious motivation caused by the conjunction to Pluto. It can indicate a person who may need to control all his relationships, a person who needs to stay on top, needs to manage those around him. He may reach out for new experience with great care and caution because he doesn't want to feel out of control. This person may be extremely sensitive about relationships in general, for a chance word overheard can send his subconscious self on a trip that will analyze and re-analyze anything that bothers him because of certain kinds of early childhood experience.

For example, Pluto conjunct Jupiter in Leo creates the kind of individual who is overly sensitive in the approval and respect departments. Any relationship will be colored by this sensitivity, and the overly sensitive reactions to respect and approval will be motivated by some unconscious desire for approval that ties into early childhood experience. This oversensitivity can be worked out by examining childhood experience that relates to the formation of such sensitivities.

JUPITER–PLUTO SEXTILE. This aspect is common to a fairly large group of people born in the same year. It indicates the potential for relating to large groups of people; it indicates a person who may work well with groups or for the furthering of group interests. Relationships formed will be similar to those of the contemporary generation, and relationship ideals will vary with the generation's standards. The mass interests will interest this individual, so the problems of the generation will affect his personal life.

Because Pluto can indicate the collective unconscious and all the mythic images contained therein, this individual may be either creative in the kinds of relationships he forms, or affected by those images in some way. Any problems that can be related to universal or mythic images may be solved by pursuing the studies of that subject and relating the information into the personal life.

JUPITER–PLUTO SQUARE. The relating principle is squared by the images from the collective unconscious. Relationships may be colored with the qualities of the sign of the Pluto square. A strong need to control relationships will emerge, as well as the unconscious motivation caused by early childhood memories. Too much sensitivity may be brought into the picture when relationships occur, for some confusion may exist in regard to what relating is. This individual may confuse relating and sharing with being in control or staying on top of any situation.

Pluto can indicate a need to stay in control that can get so out of hand that it causes certain obsessions. This individual may need to "win" so bad that he obsesses over any relationship that doesn't go his way. Getting locked into obsession games obviously defeats the purpose of relating, for relating indicates a voluntary sharing of time and experience. As soon as the obsession begins, the other party is not allowed to volunteer but is required to share. This defeats the purpose.

Since Jupiter has something to do with keeping a perspective between self and universe, the Pluto square does not help the perspective to develop. The control urges and the continuing fear of being controlled by others can cause the relating principle to become stagnant. When this occurs, relationships become control games, or role-playing rituals that don't allow this individual to receive the pleasure of sharing time with another person.

Volunteer sharing is one of the most exciting pleasures a person can have, for it is exhilarating to know that another person really likes being with one. When the Plutonic energy is used for control, although one may spend time with another, it's not time spent because it just happens. Therefore, the security that can be engendered by sharing self with another cannot take place.

JUPITER–PLUTO TRINE. Jupiter indicates the relating principle, and Pluto symbolizes the unconscious motivation within an individual. When these two planets are in a trine aspect, it indicates a person who enjoys relating to the masses, who enjoys the generation into which he is born, who enjoys reaching out to others in a cooperative venture. When the trine is in effect, the more unhealthy qualities of Pluto (like control or manipulation) don't manifest.

These individuals are more apt to become involved in traditional relationships and tend to marry, raise a family, and participate in the more accepted cycles of adult behavior. They may be victims of the "fad" of their day, subscribing to the faddy kinds of behavior that are popular from moment to moment. They may overrelate to the value system of their generation. For example, when it became fashionable to have a swimming pool and a color television set, these people could relate to those values, and may not understand that there is more to a relationship than having what the Joneses have.

Because the symbolism of Jupiter involves a changing perspective, and because Pluto symbolizes the needs of the collective unconscious, these individuals may need to analyze their relationships more thoroughly than they want to when they are younger. Age and maturity help their drives for they have the capability of combining archetypal images and patterns into their relationships, if they so desire.

JUPITER–PLUTO OPPOSITION. Jupiter indicates how the relating principle will manifest; it tells how we reach out and open up to another person, to new life experience. Pluto indicates our unconscious motivation, those sensitive qualities caused by unhappy memories that come from early childhood.

When the opposition occurs, every relating experience will be influenced by the unconscious motivation caused by a need to control outgoing and incoming experience. These individuals will want to stay on top of all relationships, so they may be controlling or manipulating; but the need to do this comes from a subconscious point. In order to develop a free and easy relating ability, they must become conscious of their personal motivations in the matter. Once this occurs, they can then use some of the creative energy that can be theirs, because the opposition is a strong aspect. They can proceed to care more about people and constructively use the mythic images alive in their psyche instead of fearing them.

For example, Pluto in Leo opposing Jupiter in Aquarius will manifest the following pattern: Jupiter in Aquarius indicates an individual who is interested in unusual kinds of relationships, or relationships with an unorthodox kind of person. Relationships will be handled in a more humanitarian or new-age manner. This individual may extend himself in an unconventional manner when he pursues a new perspective on life, or a new relationship. But Pluto in Leo wants to be properly respected and indicates an inordinate need for approval. If the planet in Leo was something other than Pluto, the problem caused by the opposition might be easier to absorb consciously. But Pluto indicates the unconscious motivation—which means that a chance word overheard in a random conversation can influence this person's attitudes. If he hears a word that makes him feel he is not being properly respected, or if he thinks he is not approved of by those people with whom he is relating, he can go into all the control games that are played by people who need to be in total control of circumstances around them. This controlling or manipulative type of behavior is not necessarily conscious, and in the process of curing these kinds of attitudes a lot of conscious effort must be put into the cure.

A relationship, whether with a friend, a lover or a family member, is a process that involves sharing. You listen to them and respond and care, and they listen to you and do the same. The relating process is a special sharing process whereby one personality is integrated with another for a moment in time. This process engenders a feeling of closeness and caring that surpasses the idyllic love fantasies that are projected on another, for there is genuine feeling going on in the relating process. When Pluto opposes the Jupiter principle, the issues become cloudy because of the inner motivation to be in control. When this control need is recognized and let go, the individual may flounder for a time, much like a ship without a rudder. But eventually this same individual will begin to recognize how much fun this relating process can be. The biggest single factor discussed by clients who have worked on this aspect is that of the inner security that can be realized when a friend or lover likes them—not because of excess giving and other little manipulation games, but just because "you're you."

JUPITER–PLUTO QUINCUNX. The issues here are less obvious, as all issues are when involved in a quincunx aspect. A strain takes place between the relating needs symbolized by Jupiter and the unconscious motivation factors indicated by Pluto's sign and house placement.

Relationships are influenced by a vague feeling that one must be in control of something, but what the "something" is may be difficult to self-diagnose. Jupiter in Pisces and Pluto in Leo in a quincunx aspect indicates a person who relates as a Pisces, with great sensitivity, perhaps a touch of martyrdom, one who has the ability to relate to the sufferings and misfortunes of others. This may be a person who recognizes the needs of the underdog, a person who can give much warmth and sensitivity to friends, lovers and family. Pluto will worry about approval—is this underdog properly respecting my help? Are my friends approving of my relationships? And of course, the pain comes in when a love relationship is formed with an emotional underdog (a person who can't relate, or a person who hurts what he loves), and here comes the Pluto approval attitude. When one loves someone who doesn't love himself, how can you get respect?

The strain caused by the quincunx can be handled on an intellectual level, and both facets of personality as well as the personal qualities symbolized by the sign of the quincunx can be incorporated into the personal life. Then the strain will disappear.

SATURN REPRESENTS THAT PART OF US THAT NEEDS TO mature. The ancients considered Saturn as Father Time, for after three rounds of Saturn a lifetime was usually ended. Saturn has been called the Grim Reaper, the energy that cuts us down. It can be, but primarily Saturn is the tester, the teacher who tests our maturity in the school of life. If we grow, mature, pass the tests of the various life cycles, if we understand universal law, we find Saturn a friend. If we wish to cling to our childhood ideas and illusions, if we wish to remain ignorant of natural law, if we think the universe owes us a living, Saturn seems to generate fear and apprehension. The fear is not caused by Saturn but by our own inner apprehensions, for Saturn seems to relate to each individual's conscience. Somewhere within we inherently know when we have not cooperated with cosmic law.

Early in life, Saturn indicates the individual's weak point, the point of insecurity that can manifest on a physical level (indicating frail health) or on an intellectual level (indicating an apprehension regarding intellectual ability) or it can influence one's feeling of self-worth. Children who don't feel worthy feel guilty about taking up space in the universe, for they are seldom recognized by anyone they consider to be an important authority figure early in the life.

According to the symbols of the unconscious, the first authority figure we meet is that of our father. If Saturn is poorly aspected, it usually indicates that the father has an unhealthy or unconstructive impact on the developing child's psyche. The aspects Saturn makes to the personal planets in the horoscope begin to tell what affect the father has on which facet of the child's personality. That affect influences children's attitudes when they begin to pursue adult responsibilities; the influence can touch any part of the personality ranging from expressing sexuality to career aspirations. Often the more psychologically based Saturn afflictions are best worked out in analysis for they may be time-consuming to uncover.

One of my clients who had undergone years of therapy mentioned having sexual difficulties as an adult. The aspects in her chart indicated some unhealthy influence from her father early in life. She was amazed, for under hypnosis she discovered a memory of sexual abuse that had been committed by her father. Because the memory was so painful, she was unable to consciously remember that period in her life even when shown pictures of herself. Another client blocked so many memories she couldn't recognize pets she held in her arms in family snapshots because the surrounding detail of the childhood was too painful for her conscious mind to accept. The blocked memory doesn't always indicate a sexual dysfunction, it can indicate parental behavior that offended the child. The offensive behavior can be diagnosed through the signs that the planets appear in, and problems with the father will be attached to Saturn aspects. It's important that the astrologer doesn't put words in a client's mouth—people will remember what they need to when the time is right.

Saturn represents the mundane area in life that we regard with caution or what we approach with fear. The sign and house placement of Saturn is important. When Saturn is in the first house, for example, it indicates a self-imposed restriction placed on the beginnings of activities. The individual may be apprehensive during childhood about facing authority figures or new school situations; as an adult the apprehension may involve any new beginning ranging from a relationship to a new job.

When Saturn sits in the fifth house the apprehension does not involve new beginnings but, rather, those matters indicated by the fifth house: there may be apprehension regarding taking risks, a fear of gambling, a fear of love relationships, apprehension about entertaining, about having babies, about the children one has given birth to. Since the fifth house represents the children of our minds as well as those of our bodies, the Saturn caution may also include apprehension about the creative ability. We spend so much time being cautious about Saturn, about our fears, that eventually they become our strong points and the Saturn location becomes an area of strength and maturity. As we learn to face our fears and apprehensions, Saturn turns into a friend.

We can often cure our fears when we observe how our father reacted in similar situations. For example, when Saturn is in the first house, not only was the father apprehensive about beginning new situations but he was unsure of himself when dealing with those in authority, and he passed those fears onto the child. He may have enforced the child's feelings of insecurity as well by belittling everything that the child did, or by disapproving of the child's attempts at self-expression. With Saturn in the natal fourth house, the environment of the early childhood was harsh, cold, extremely formal. The effect of the father on the child's psyche will manifest as some apprehenison about making a home of one's own. The early environment is so dreary that people with this configuration may subconsciously fear they may recreate the environment if they attempt to establish the parental experience.

Considering Saturn from a spiritual level, it has been mentioned that Jupiter and Saturn were the cross-over planets according to the ancients. If we understand the concepts symbolized by these planets we can lift the consciousness to more evolved levels. Saturn, as tester, symbolizes that energy must be expressed in a responsible way; we cannot merely satisfy our personal drives in a willful fashion. They must be channeled to meet universal needs. In the natural zodiac, the Moon rules the fourth house and the Sun the fifth, symbolizing that we are a combination of our environment (fourth) and our creative endeavor (fifth). In the ancient wheel Saturn opposes both the Sun and Moon for it rules the signs Capricorn and Aquarius. The universal forces do not inhibit self-expression, but they do not indulge selfish expression either. As we learn to express the self maturely, the energy becomes productive rather than restrictive.

Recently a number of articles have appeared disclosing the amount of industrial waste that lies buried indiscriminately near suburban housing and water supplies. The industrial waste is poisonous to the land, kills wildlife, infects water and causes certain kinds of disease to develop in people raised in these areas. Someone irresponsibly solved an immediate problem and got rid of waste material without considering what would happen to surrounding land and the ongoing generations of people. "The sins of the fathers are visited on the sons for seven generations." The philosophical approach to Saturn as reflected in the Bible conforms with the Saturn cycles of seven lean years and seven good ones; irresponsible fathers infect their own children. Saturn monitors the destructive behavior in the universe. The universal flow requires that we be responsible for ourselves; if we aren't the irresponsibility will have to be "ironed" out.

From a symbolic point, the natural opposition between Saturn and the Moon indicates that emotional responses cannot be totally selfish; Saturn opposing the Sun indicates that creative expression must be tempered with conscience. The opposition forces maturity, and it gives us the wisdom of the ages.

Saturn aspects to the personal planets indicate the part of the personality that must mature in this life. Some people have to consciously make an effort to express or develop facets of the personality; the difficulties will be shown by the Saturn ties. These ties don't keep us from being, but emphasize the importance of that area of life. The more Saturn aspects people have, the more intense the need to break the ties with inherited experience and become self-responsible. When people can break from the past, when they can free themselves to explore all the mythic images describing the process of maturity, the soul can assimilate the responsibility of higher consciousness.

SATURN–SUN ASPECTS

See Chapter 1 in this section.

SATURN–MOON ASPECTS

See Chapter 2 in this section.

SATURN–MERCURY ASPECTS

See Chapter 3 in this section.

SATURN–VENUS ASPECTS

See Chapter 4 in this section.

SATURN–MARS ASPECTS

See Chapter 5 in this section.

SATURN–JUPITER ASPECTS

See Chapter 6 in this section.

SATURN–URANUS ASPECTS

When the restrictive principle, or the maturation principle as some call Saturn, combines with Uranus (the behavior of a generation) the behavioral attitudes of an entire generation come to grips with the concept of maturation. Each time Uranus changes signs new ideas about human behavior spring up that can be directly related to the sign through which Uranus is transiting. When Saturn affects these new ideas, it tests them, tries them, and sorts out the constructive from the vain.

In a personal sense, the psychological influence of the father will have some affect on the individual's behavior. In order for the process of individuation to take place, people with these aspects will have to confront the beliefs and fears of the father. Symbolically, this may indicate the biological father, or the effect of his family's beliefs and traditions. In either sense the traditions will change.

SATURN–URANUS CONJUNCTION. If Saturn represents the affect of the father on the individual's developing psyche and Uranus indicates the behavior of a generation, the father will have some unusual or unconventional affect on the child. In the personal chart, Saturn represents the part of ourselves we are "cautious" about, that part of personality we view with apprehension. The conjunction to Uranus can also indicate certain kinds of erratic or self-willed behavior that directly relates to a father influence. The conjunction indicates a person who may be unruly or recalcitrant about his fears. He may hang onto beliefs long after they have been proven invalid.

Since Saturn represents authority the conjunction indicates that the individual has little respect for it, that his life may be bound up in learning about his concept of authority. The Uranus influence can indicate that he has the energy (in his generation) to lift the consciousness of tradition to another dimension. If the conjunction is involved with hard aspects to other planets, it can indicate an individual who may be an erratic and eccentric hard-nosed kind of person who wants to win at all costs.

A young person with this conjunction will be involved with group values, or the establishing of a personality in the face of what he considers a stringent world. After the age of thirty, the personality will be somewhat settled and other aspects of maturity become visible.

The conjunction indicates the ability to rise above the father, to remedy the father's influence, to change and uplift the traditional. This individual may be able to bring into being a new approach to tradition because of his work and his attitude toward life. Because Uranus can represent willfulness, it's important to consider it in this conjunction—this may be the mark of a self-centered individual, one who is interested in living a personally erratic or eccentric life at the expense of those around him. When this occurs, check the other aspects in the chart that may also indicate a fear of approaching life—i.e., if the Moon afflicts this conjunction, the individual may be emotionally apprehensive, and because of that apprehension he may be excessively harsh with others.

SATURN–URANUS SEXTILE. The sextile is more easily turned into constructive action than the conjunction. Saturn indicates the influence of the father on the individual's psyche; its sign indicates what the father causes this person to regard with caution. Uranus indicates the behavior of a generation as well as the possibilities of transformation or enlightenment in a personal sense.

When these two energies coincide harmoniously, there is potential for positive growth and awareness. As the talent is discovered and consciously applied, the individual becomes capable of working with large groups in order to make slow-moving, constructive changes in the environment.

SATURN–URANUS SQUARE. The square indicates the potential to be a world changer. Saturn indicates how the influence of the father affects the individual's psyche. This marks the caution point in the youthful personality. The sign Uranus occupies symbolizes the behavior of a generation, its regard for morality and consciousness.

The square indicates that these individuals are born in a time when people rebel against old traditions, old concepts of authority, old or established concepts of behavior, because they want to create something else. These people grow to question authority, for the nation was questioning authority when they were born. This square was in effect when "Watergate" occurred: young people were questioning the military system; the masses were saying "no" to the previously accepted behavior of authority figures. Citizens started looking at political figures, questioning graft; the media began reporting the sexual indiscretions of certain public figures; students rebelled in the classroom. Any time this square takes place the general public begins to examine established behavior patterns. Each time the question occurs, those who have this aspect have choices to make, for this energy can be used to make productive changes in society or it can be used to service rebellious causes.

Because the hard aspects between Saturn and Uranus indicate a break with past traditions, this aspect becomes important when it ties into the personal planets. When this occurs, people will be confronted with a need to pull away from the father, in the personal sense, as well as removing themselves from family traditions. Here consciousness and the individual need for it is hampered by the *familiar*, by the family experience. These individuals can mature in several directions, depending on how strong the family ties are. When the need for family relationships is too strong, resentment and a resentful personality may occur. A strong family tie may not be a constructive one, it can indicate powerful family traditions or a powerful sense of family failure. A child born under a welfare program, for example, may see no alternative to his life style, and resentment regarding society will occur. When encouraged to become responsible for his own consciousness, remarkable changes can take place in his attitude.

SATURN–URANUS TRINE. The trine indicates children born into a generation that wishes to cooperate with established forms of authority. The father's affect on the individual's psyche can be used constructively because Dad was cooperative with his peers. Dad's values may be expressed differently, but this person is exposed to the concept of a changing consciousness.

If the trine ties into the personal planets, or if the trine ties to the chart of the nation, this individual may be drawn to work in the political arena, for he relates to contemporary events. In the personal sense, his need to develop a "personality" works cooperatively with his drive for maturity.

SATURN–URANUS OPPOSITION. Saturn represents the effect of the father on the psyche of the individual; Uranus represents the behavior pattern of a generation, as well as the personal point of eccentricity. The opposition aspect sometimes indicates that during childhood this person may be the bane of his father's existence. He will rebel against the authority of the father as well as against authority figures in general. If the father was eccentric, erratic or self-willed, this can indicate an individual with an eccentric personality. It can indicate a person who flaunts his actions in the face of authorities.

A person who isn't using this energy constructively may not listen to anyone, and his relationships become limited. A boss cannot give him instructions, his girlfriend has no rights nor do his friends. If the opposition includes ties to the Sun, Moon or Ascendant, it gains in strength and will become an important part of this individual's development, for maturation and eccentricity will be a part of the expression of the other planets involved.

This aspect doesn't occur often, so the generation which has it will mean something as far as making history is concerned. It was a part of the atmosphere in World War I (World War II manifested a conjunction between Uranus and Saturn). Children born during war time are exposed to the idea of fighting for a cause. Loyalties are changed, people take a stand, the child absorbs that energy and it becomes a part of the personality. Traditional attitudes are thrown off because the world is in a state of chaos and traditional "niceties" are no longer affordable. When the war is over, the nation wants to resume "business as usual," but the child influenced by this energy in his birth chart cannot return to a family tradition with which he isn't familiar.

SATURN–URANUS QUINCUNX. Saturn represents the personal apprehensions of the individual as well as the influence of the father on the developing psyche. Uranus indicates the behavior pattern of a generation and the point of consciousness in the individual sense.

The quincunx indicates a strain between the influence of the father and the process of individuation. This person may not feel comfortable with the maturation process. It brings a vague feeling of discontent when the attempt is made to free the self from the traditions of the father. In order for the energy to function easily, both signs involved in the quincunx need to be expressed. As the individual becomes conscious of the difference between the Saturn and Uranus function, the discontent can be handled.

SATURN–NEPTUNE ASPECTS

When Saturn combines with Neptune, tradition and father influence are tied to the concept of creativity and spiritual love. The father influence becomes cloudy because Neptune brings the veil of Maya (illusion) to whatever it touches. This may manifest in the personality as either some delusion or inspiration about one's roots. It can indicate one who has skeletons in the family closet or one who worships the family. It can indicate one who wants to explore the creative consciousness or one who is afraid of it. Sometimes Neptune adds additional apprehensions or phobias to the exploration of the Saturnian fears; then the exploration of consciousness becomes more difficult.

In order to take our place in the universe, Saturn requires that we become conscious of the affect of our father; we must mythologically explore the concept of Father, and that exploration ranges from understanding the physical man who is the personal father to the mythic symbolism of heredity as it forms the basis for tradition. Neptune represents our capacity for spiritual love and the universal creative urges. When the aspects between these two universal symbols are easy, the generation is not inhibited unless a third aspect is introduced. When Saturn–Neptune aspects are hard, the ability to free one's self from the bonds of tradition becomes more arduous...but the labor is well worth it. The hard aspects can bring more energy, more stimulation to the process of individuation.

SATURN–NEPTUNE CONJUNCTION. Saturn indicates the psychological influence of the father on the psyche of the individual. It indicates that part of the personality that one is most apprehensive about, the facet of self that one regards with caution. Neptune brings a sense of creativity or illusion-delusion regarding insight concerning the father.

People with this aspect may not really understand the kind of affect their father had on them. This influence may be determined from other aspects to Saturn or the Sun. There have been cases where mother-dominated children have been deluded about the father, especially if he was missing. There have been instances when a child is unpleasantly surprised about paternity itself, for not every legal father is a child's physical father. These situations are difficult to diagnose and more difficult to discuss; they must be handled with tact.

When a father-dominated person has a Saturn–Neptune conjunction, there may be some idealization of the father. When a mother-dominated person has the conjunction, the mother may misrepresent the father in some way: the kind of man he is, some delusion about the family or inherited family responsibilities may be engendered. The delusion about the father influence may merely be that the person doesn't know about the family influence or interests. These people will be influenced by certain delusions or illusions regarding authority figures; they may be hurt by the reality of the traditional approach, for they want to support illusions.

SATURN–NEPTUNE SEXTILE. This aspect brings a talent; the individual's psyche has been affected by the father and his search for spirituality. Dad may not have chosen the same road his child will choose. If so, this individual may not feel comfortable making choices in the realm of spiritual or creative discovery; but the energy will eventually manifest according to the signs and house placements involved.

The search for spirituality may come about when the individual becomes as old as the father was at the time of the individual's birth. In terms of personal growth, this person will have a good feeling about the effect of family and tradition upon himself; he may be a person who is proud of his heritage.

SATURN–NEPTUNE SQUARE. Saturn represents the effect of the father on the developing psyche of the individual. Neptune can indicate the "grand delusion," so this person may be born into a family that has illusions or delusions regarding the father, heredity or family influence.

The father will affect the individual's concept of creativity, perhaps impeding the development of some form of creative expression. Because of the square aspect, the influence of the father will work against the individual's dreams or goals, or even the development of spiritual goals. The aspect may indicate the person who has to pull away from the family experience in order to find himself. He may not see authority figures for what they are; he may be supportive of people who disappoint him.

It's interesting to note the house placement of the square for the misunderstandings will involve the departments of life ruled by the houses. Inner conflict may be present, for the influence of the father is subconscious, keeping the individual from using the creative energy of the Neptune placement until he learns to recognize the Saturn influence.

SATURN–NEPTUNE TRINE. The trine indicates that the father's influence will not inhibit the dreams and goals of the individual, although the effect of the environment may not show up until the person becomes thirty.

The individual absorbs Dad's influence and wants to use those interests as a foundation for spiritual goals. However, if there are other aspects indicating a rift between father and child, the individual may not pursue spiritual or creative goals as freely.

People with this aspect want to uphold and uplift tradition, to maintain the family "roots," to maintain pride in a family heritage. The need for creative development is pursued through traditional means; these are people who often support the established church.

SATURN–NEPTUNE OPPOSITION. If Saturn symbolizes what one regards with caution and Neptune indicates what one deludes oneself about, the opposition may be considered to indicate an individual who may delude himself about his fears. He may delude himself about what he regards with caution, or even what tradition is. The affect of the father may keep him from expressing his dreams, his goals, his creativity, for he may not value his creative ideas. In order to develop creative potential with this aspect, the mundane effects of the opposition must be understood. The father affects the psyche so that exploring the realms of the incredible fantasy world of the inner self is restrained in some way.

Saturn can represent the tradition of the day. Neptune can represent the uplifting of consciousness, the development of universal love. Neptune, as the higher octave of Venus, involves impersonal or universal love. The opposition indicates that after the father image and the delusions or illusions about him are understood, this person can combine tradition with a new dimension of caring for people.

SATURN–NEPTUNE QUINCUNX. The strain of the quincunx aspect indicates the discontent that occurs when Saturn (as a symbol of the influence of the father on the psyche) ties to Neptune (the symbol for ideals, illusion and dreams of being creative). The energy is not overwhelming; it may merely cause apathy in the individual, for some nagging ideal in the mind keeps one from handling responsibilities.

Creativity may not have been respected by the father, and the individual may not have been openly criticized for what he did, but he knew he was not appreciated. As he entered adult life, he may have assumed that authority figures didn't like what he was doing either. Once the energy is understood, both sides of the quincunx can be expressed somewhere in the life, and the signs involved can be worked into the life style.

SATURN–PLUTO ASPECTS

Saturn represents Father Nature, or Father Time. Saturn also represents the affect of the father on the developing psyche of the individual; the father's fears indicate what the individual will approach with caution in life. Saturn is teacher and tester, indicating what boundaries are placed on the soul's expression. Pluto represents a part of the collective unconscious, those archetypal figures (discussed by Jung) that run the depths of the psyche and force us to change. On a mundane level Pluto indicates how we manipulate and attempt to control conscious expression, no matter how those concepts disagree with universal law. Many people born in a given time period will have the same Pluto aspect and it will only become important when it ties into the personal planets.

The hard aspects of Saturn to Pluto may be difficult to diagnose because the manipulation games played by the father of the individual may not be those of power or aggression but, rather, those of the tyranny of the weak. In any event, in order to let go of one's fears and apprehensions, in order to rescind the ties of inherited behavior patterns, the individual must learn to comprehend the game (or the riddle) and enter into the Hero venture alone.

Because the effect of Saturn is unconscious and Pluto represents unconscious motivation, it may take a few years before the father's fears and attitudes can be accurately diagnosed. If they are not, the individual will behave much like his father but won't really know why. Many of the personal fears will repeat the pattern that the father established, causing the family pattern to be re-created over and over.

SATURN–PLUTO CONJUNCTION. Saturn represents the influence of the father on the individual's psyche, the caution point in the consciousness, the teacher or tester; Pluto represents unconscious motivation. The conjunction indicates a person born into a generation when people unconsciously take the law into their own hands. Rationally, they may say that the "law" is wonderful, but personally one hears them talking about how one "must" do something. Free will may be discussed intellectually, but in actuality they subconsciously feel that they should be the law-makers.

The father's influence on these individuals was most probably manipulative; it may be difficult for them to see just how they are influenced by the father. The aspect indicates people who may think their urges toward traditional concepts are conscious, but who may be motivated to react to life experience on an unconscious level.

Consider Saturn conjunct Pluto in Leo: This indicates people who consider respect and approval seriously, who may feel they are not being respected enough. They unconsciously react with hurt feelings and sensitivity when they are not treated in an approvable manner. They may not realize that the hurt feelings have something to do with the fact that their father didn't treat them well when they were little, and here is this life experience doing it to them again! These people will be motivated to consider the "law" and all its ramifications whenever they are offended. They may not explore *why* they are offended, but merely that they are.

Saturn conjunct Pluto in Virgo will express differently. These people are apprehensive of criticism, and they may be suspicious of their own intellectual ability. As they get older, because of Saturn in Virgo they are apt to develop the intellect. Subconsciously they are more apt to respond to criticism or innuendoes because Pluto is there, and it unconsciously reminds them of the criticism they felt from Dad when they were small. They may find themselves being uncommonly critical of others, as is their entire generation. This aspect becomes really important when tied into the personal planets.

SATURN–PLUTO SEXTILE. The father's influence on the individual's psyche, plus the concept of caution or fear in the personality caused by his influence, will be handled constructively.

These people can work well with groups for the father taught them how to cooperate. There are no strong urges to control coming from this aspect. As these individuals mature the energy can be used to effectively handle the problems of career, community and personal relationships.

SATURN–PLUTO SQUARE. The father's influence on the individual's psyche may remain subconscious. There may be attempts to rationalize fears or to avoid facing them. When personal security patterns are threatened, the subconscious drive to control life events may become apparent.

If there are no ties to personal planets, this aspect indicates people who were raised in a manipulative atmosphere, but they didn't feel it personally. When personal planets are involved these people may unconsciously attack traditional authority figures, starting with the father. There may be little respect for the family traditions or for those within the community, or little respect for accepted standards.

Saturn in Cancer square Pluto in Libra indicates the following pattern: Saturn says "I regard emotions with caution, I take emotional situations seriously, I fear that I lack emotion or emotional response in my life." Pluto in Libra is unconsciously motivated to be a part of an elite group. The elite group (or special group) will be chosen by each of these individuals and formed by the personal environment. The father may have encouraged them to forego emotional contacts in favor of public acceptance. As adults, the aspect indicates a need to handle the conflict between personal emotional needs and the attitudes of peers. If they were born in an environment of "free love" they will curb their emotional fears and try not to be possessive, but underneath they really will be. If the world moves into a spiritual phase and emphasizes the depersonalization of emotional values, these people will have another conflict to work out—for they need love and emotional security in the personal sense.

The father was manipulative in some way; the secret of understanding the kind of manipulation or control involved will be shown by the other aspects to the Sun and Saturn, as well as by the houses involved. If one is to free oneself from the power of the father image, the aspect needs to be understood. Often these people will imitate the father's pattern in adult life, attempting to control those around them in a similar manner.

SATURN–PLUTO TRINE. The father influenced this person's psyche in a constructive manner, teaching him how to cooperate with peers. The fears and cautions in life can be faced and handled; they will be similar to the father's and described by the sign and house placement. The father's role can be reviewed with little problem.

The aspect indicates a natural concern for the needs of the times, the needs of the masses, the need for communication as it affects groups. It indicates individuals who fit in comfortably with the status quo.

SATURN–PLUTO OPPOSITION. The father's influence on the psyche of the individual during early life will be difficult to comprehend on a conscious level. In order to overcome weak points, fears, feelings of failure (caused by Saturn's placement), these feelings must be acknowledged consciously.

The Plutonic energy from the unconscious may confuse the image of the father with the unconscious or mythic image. This aspect may indicate individuals who have an obsession about the father, who don't know how to begin the journey toward self-discovery. If the aspect also includes personal planets, these people may attempt to revolutionize society because they go against the father, authority and tradition.

This energy can be used in a positive manner for these folks are world changers. Before the aspect can be used constructively, however, personal understanding of the influence of the father must be achieved. If not, these individuals can be manipulators of situations whenever they become afraid. They can take the law into their own hands; they can be vigilante types.

SATURN–PLUTO QUINCUNX. Here the archetypal images of the unconscious may affect the relationship with the father but it will be a vague influence. The aspect indicates a strain, for self-responsibility (Saturn) is vaguely affected by unconscious motivation. The father image may not be clearly defined. The unconscious motivation may be hampered by family and traditional values.

The resentments toward family may be vague or disconcerting, for hurt feelings and the inner motivation for action may not be clearly thought out. Both energies must operate. Understanding the signs and houses involved will help this individual learn to work with both energies.

URANUS WAS DISCOVERED IN THE 20TH CENTURY AND has replaced the masculine side of Saturn as the ruler of the sign Aquarius. As astrologers traced the type of energy that seemed to emanate from Uranus, they found it tied in with the concepts symbolized by Aquarius, that it indicated an opportunity to expand consciousness, to advance human development in the humanitarian sense. Some people don't have lives that are personally affected by this planet except at a cursory level—they simply live in a generation born with Uranus in a particular sign and are therefore a part of that generation's particular behavior pattern. However, when Uranus aspects personal planets, these people become involved in matters that are important to their generation, they become a part of a team of world changers.

Uranus seems to indicate certain behavior patterns. It can indicate a certain attitude that may conflict with planets which represent other facets of personality. The Sun symbolizes the "I am" part of the personality; the Moon represents "I feel"; Venus stands for "I want", Mercury stands for "I talk", Mars for "I act", Jupiter for "I relate"; Saturn for "I fear"; and Uranus comes along with "I behave."

One may question the difference between "I am" and "I act" and "I behave," but there are subtle differences. The "I am" part of the self may never manifest; it cannot as long as the person doesn't resolve how he is different from humanity, and how his needs differ from those people he may imitate. Mars, as representative of "I act," indicates how he will take physical action to express himself. Uranus will, however, indicate *behavior* which can be very different from action. For example, consider the bully who rants and raves and threatens everyone in sight, but when confronted in turn, his actions don't match his words or his behavioral attitudes. He may behave as though he were pugnacious, and in reality act like a coward.

In terms of behavior, one can consider the Uranus placement the point of eccentricity in the chart, for whatever the planet touches by aspect can be diagnosed as a part of the personality that will be handled in an unorthodox, unconventional or eccentric manner. Uranus also represents a point of increased consciousness, and its location indicates the growth point in every individual's life. If we understand the placement of Uranus and consider how we can use this planet (or facet of personality) in the process of "finding" ourselves, Uranus can be a friend indeed. The Uranus point may be called the rebirth potential, perhaps it indicates the bursting of the cocoon for some. Transits of Uranus seem to bring a chance for us to raise our consciousness, to break old patterns; the cycles of Uranus force us to re-evaluate our position in life.

URANUS–SUN ASPECTS

See Chapter 1 in this section.

URANUS–MOON ASPECTS

See Chapter 2 in this section.

URANUS–MERCURY ASPECTS

See Chapter 3 in this section.

URANUS–VENUS ASPECTS

See Chapter 4 in this section.

URANUS–MARS ASPECTS

See Chapter 5 in this section.

URANUS–JUPITER ASPECTS

See Chapter 6 in this section.

URANUS–SATURN ASPECTS

See Chapter 7 in this section.

URANUS–NEPTUNE ASPECTS

Uranus indicates the capacity to accept the possibilities for expansion of consciousness, and Neptune indicates the potential for creative ideas, our inspiration or delusion. The contacts between these planets are both personal and impersonal at the same time.

In the impersonal sense, they interact and cause a particular type of generation to emerge, one that combines inspiration and eccentricity, one that combines inspiration and heightened consciousness. When an aspect between these two planets also involves a personal planet, this individual may be very creative. The aspect should be read in terms of the effect on the personal planet involved.

URANUS–NEPTUNE CONJUNCTION. This aspect has not taken place since the early 1800s and won't happen again until the 1990s. It seems that the conjunction of these planets would make for some interesting life experiences—the concept of individuality or humanity is brought together with that of creative expression. These are the times when important changes in attitude and/or consciousness take place.

In the 1800s the world got Mary Baker Eddy, Dostoevski, Clara Barton, Louis Pasteur and Johann Strauss to name but a few. If this conjunction also involves a personal configuration, a personal kind of creativity emerges—for example, Clara Barton had this conjunction also conjunct her natal Sun.

URANUS–NEPTUNE SEXTILE. This group can learn to combine creative expression with the process of individuation. The potential for consciousness will have to be developed or the sextile may remain latent.

The aspect produces a generation of people who may have highly individualistic dreams or goals. Some of them will be unproductive, some will use this energy to present advanced concepts in the field of scientific endeavor or spiritual development.

URANUS–NEPTUNE SQUARE. The square aspect indicates a tendency to use the energies against each other. The dream or ideal of the generation (Neptune) may not be reflected in the behavior pattern of that generation (Uranus). When this aspect ties into the personal planets, the square becomes important in the personal sense, for these individuals will need to work out the frustration in order to realize the full potential of growth possible.

For example, consider the Sun conjunct Neptune square Uranus. The creative energy of Neptune will influence the Sun. The aspect indicates some delusion regarding the father; either he was misrepresented or the individual doesn't know who the father was, or the person has some delusion in regard to his heredity or inherited responsibilities.

The Uranus square will make him willful, eccentric—and he will behave in a manner that might not enhance the expression of his Sun sign energy. In order to use the aspect constructively, he will need to consider his Sun sign needs and how highly individualistic behavior would best support those interests.

URANUS–NEPTUNE TRINE. Compassion, understanding, creative expression or inspiration (Neptune) blend with the expression of new-age ideas (Uranus), so that theory and feeling meld together to express a form of universal love and understanding. This trine has occurred in recent years; people born around 1940 have it.

These are the people who have taken courses in meditation, inner awareness, spiritual development, etc. They are searching for the inner self. This generation may produce new philosophies that will emerge at the turn of the next century.

The trine can also foster the great dreamer—the energy from the Uranus–Neptune combination can produce highly individualistic ideas that may not be put into practice unless there is an aspect in the chart that indicates the potential to take action.

URANUS–NEPTUNE OPPOSITION. Uranus represents the potential for the individuation process and Neptune indicates the dream or goals of a generation. Spiritual love and compassion may be at odds with individualistic expression in the generation when this opposition occurs. The process of discovering the self may be veiled by the Neptunian dream. Human behavior may take on new dimensions. During the last opposition, the Hollywood movie came into being and people were presented with a Neptunian concept of personal and family life. The filmmakers wove a web of illusion that influenced the behavior of generations of men and women. The human psyche is still trying to recover from the effect of the "movie miracle"; people saw one kind of behavior on the screen and felt something else in their personal lives.

When people have this aspect involving personal planets as well, the influence of dreams and creative fantasies may either inspire or de-energize the search for self. For example, the Sun conjunct Uranus opposing Neptune provides the following circumstances: the individual will have an unusual father who is spiritually deluded in some way, or a father who is shrouded in mystery. Depending on the Sun archetype, the individual will have a confused image of self caused by the Sun–Neptune opposition, and he will have the potential to be an outstanding "ahead-of-his-time" sign type because of the conjunction between the Sun and Uranus. Will he be able to express his unusual ideas (Sun–Uranus) with the Neptune opposition there? Will he delude himself? Will he use his natural energies well, or will he be so unsure of himself that he never develops any follow-through? The creative energy is there but may not be expressed constructively until he searches out the riddle or the mystery attached to the father image.

URANUS–NEPTUNE QUINCUNX. The quincunx aspect implies a strain that will involve the process of individuation, the eccentricity or behavior of a generation (Uranus), and the dream of compassion and universal love (Neptune). The generation's behavior pattern will not agree with the creative dream.

For example, consider the generation born with Neptune in Virgo and Uranus in Aquarius. These people are somewhat eccentric, somewhat unorthodox, often wanting to establish unusual kinds of life styles, yet they are highly self-critical. The era of the photographer, painter, and writer as social critic, comes from this energy. But they don't go anywhere with the criticism—they paint a word picture that makes no conclusions.

The strain can be read in terms of the signs involved in the quincunx. This is not an important aspect unless the personal planets are also tied in.

URANUS–PLUTO ASPECTS

Uranus represents the process of individuation as it may take place within the personality or within the generation. Pluto represents either the mass unconscious of a given generation or, in the personal sense, the unconscious motivation of the individual. When these planets are in aspect the generation will be moved by the urge to change what has been. In terms of personal growth, the aspects are only important when they also involve a personal planet.

Although the energy indicates the possibility for personal growth, it also indicates that parental influence affects the process. In order to determine the effect on personality, it will be necessary to look at the aspect as it ties into the configuration with the personal planet.

URANUS–PLUTO CONJUNCTION. The keyword for Uranus is "I behave" and the keyword for Pluto is "I am unconsciously motivated." The combination doesn't occur too often; it last happened in the 1960s. Here the process of individuation can be either confused or overwhelmed by some unconscious force or energy. The behavior may be controlling or strangely eccentric.

Pluto rules the underworld in mythology; it has something to do with the archetypal energies of the unconscious depths. In the 1960s people became interested in hallucinogenic drugs. Some of them experienced an inner exploration of the self induced by chemicals. Literature has been written comparing the drug experience to that of the mystical path of Oriental philosophies. People also became involved in supporting "people" rights and the peace marches began—the march on Washington occurred as well as marches supporting young people's rights to refuse to fight in the Vietnamese war.

Children born during those years will be highly individualistic and unorthodox. Whether this energy will express creatively or destructively will be apparent in the coming years.

URANUS–PLUTO SEXTILE. The behavior of a generation, or the generation's attitude, can learn to cooperate or be supportive of the needs of the people.

In a personal sense, the process of individuation will take place while integrating the ideas of the collective unconscious; these people will explore the archetypal images with ease and interest. This energy may remain latent unless tied into the personal planets.

URANUS–PLUTO SQUARE. The concept of personal individuation is at odds with the needs of the masses. There may be an unconscious attempt to control behavior and relationships. If Mercury is involved with the square it can indicate an attempt at controlling the mind as well as the behavior.

Behavioral attitudes may be unconsciously motivated and the individual may find himself living out the archetypes or having them lived out on him. People with this aspect will be interested in moving away from the family environment into some new approach to life. If the aspect concerns personal planets as well, it becomes more powerful.

URANUS–PLUTO TRINE. The person born with this aspect will find it important to "know thyself." The needs of the people correspond to the needs of the individual, and the developing behavioral attitudes will reflect the needs of the community as a whole.

It seems that people born in this time reference will be interested in raising consciousness, changing the status quo, but in a constructive sense.

URANUS–PLUTO OPPOSITION. This aspect indicates a generation that may use coercion to establish accepted behavior patterns. Pluto can represent control needs; Uranus expresses a point of consciousness, and on an undeveloped level, can represent self-will. If we force our will on others, or if we are born in a generation that forces itself or its ideas on others, we are not developing our consciousness. These individuals can be influenced by peer group members, or can be influential in a peer group situation.

The archetypal influence from the collective unconscious or the inner self can influence the developing behavior patterns; these people may react to life experience based on urges from the unconscious. This can indicate a powerfully fertile and creative mind. Since Pluto has something to do with obsession, this aspect can be indicative of obsessive behavior.

URANUS–PLUTO QUINCUNX. Here the behavioral attitudes are strained, for vague obsessions may impede the search for freedom or place a strain on any attempt made to pursue the process of individuation.

NEPTUNE IS A SLOW-MOVING PLANET THAT WAS NOT A part of the ancient horoscope. It was given rulership over the sign of Pisces and replaced the feminine side of Jupiter in the ancient wheel. Neptune, or Poseidon, is the god of the sea; and in myth as in psychology the sea symbolizes a part of the unconscious. In astrology, Neptune represents spiritual or universal love; that love which includes compassion and understanding, that love which is more universal than personal, so it is often associated with spiritual love in the universal sense. Neptune represents the dreams, the fantasies, the daydreams, the vagaries, the illusions, the inspirations and the delusions in the personality. If a person is born without strong Neptune aspects to the personal planets, the dreams of the generation he is born into will be a part of his reality but he won't be strongly involved in the energy of the planet. If his personal planets are involved in powerful aspects to Neptune, he will be a part of the creativity of the generation; he will need to explore his spiritual needs; he will be sorting out concepts of reality and fantasy.

In a personal sense, close ties to Neptune indicate a natural bent toward the creative fantasy; the poetry and prose of creative endeavor lie close to the surface. Seldom do clients come to an astrologer to learn about deeply hidden talents, for most people know when they are able to think and dream the dream of the creative. Most often, a person with strong Neptune ties in the chart needs help sorting out the difference between illusion and fantasy, and those kinds of confusions are most often caused by the hard aspects. Neptune's aspects can tell where one will most often be deluded, where one tends to see fantasy or illusion rather than insightful complements to intellectual concepts.

The house placement of Neptune tells us how we can be deluded by self or others. For example, Neptune in the sixth house clouds the issues of fellow employees as well as those of service and health. The placement can be easily diagnosed—this individual will serve in an atmosphere he doesn't understand, so he may be the victim of political maneuvers on the job; a medical diagnosis may not accurately reflect his health condition and he may therefore be wise to explore the concept of medicine by familiarizing himself with the basic body functions; he also may want to explore the alternative or self-help healing approaches available such as herbology, homeopathy and the concept of preventive medicine.

If Neptune is natally in the eleventh house, the cloud will reflect bewilderment regarding the motives of friends, advisors may not understand our needs, we can be confounded or misled by those we consider to be friends. We are not "stuck" with the natal placement's worst potential. Knowing that we may not choose good advisors, knowing that we may be confused by friends or associates, we can examine the information brought to us by those people and determine our own answers rather than counting blindly on the ties of friendship. Had Richard Nixon understood basic astrology, he may not have so readily accepted the counsel given him. The combination of a Capricorn Sun and Neptune in the eleventh house in his natal chart didn't help him to wisely select his advisors; the Watergate situation clearly indicates those close to him were not helping him see things rationally.

The aspects to Neptune indicate the creative energy or the blind spots we develop based on early environmental exposure. After considering the power parent—that is, the parent most influential in the development of our personal philosophy—look to Neptune to discern if this planet influences our concept of that parent. Neptune aspects involving planets symbolizing the mother or father can give insight into the possibility of a distortion of that parent's role. Our distortions of reality, those distortions that encompass unreasonable fears or unreasonable concepts, will be indicated by Neptune aspects. For example, the Neptune–Venus hard aspects will indicate a distortion which involves the ability to appreciate love. The individual with this natal aspect will have some difficulty establishing a relationship with another person for he may not be understood by his mate. His concept of love may be so ethereal that it confounds the other person; it may be so spiritual that he is perplexed as to how to combine the fantasy of love with the living experience of it. The aspect only hurts when it interferes with the possibility of developing close relationships.

Because Neptune involves fantasy, its aspects to Mercury can be disconcerting, for it develops the psychic power and combines it with the thinking or mind processes and confuses one as to what mental stability is. Again, the creative portion of any Neptune aspect won't be an issue, but the distortions and fantasies caused by Neptune will. Any Neptune aspect can be used creatively, for it symbolizes a creative source, a fountain of ideas within the personality. The hard aspects compel us to work for the bonus; the easy aspects bestow the natural talent, and because we don't work for it we sometimes don't appreciate or use it.

The Neptune aspects have been discussed individually in the preceding chapters. To search them out, look in the chapter describing the other planet involved with the Neptune aspect.

NEPTUNE–PLUTO ASPECTS

Neptune is a generation planet as is Pluto. When there are aspects between these energies they are common to a great number of people within that generation. Pluto represents the mass unconscious, the unconscious motivation of a generation. Neptune symbolizes the universal dream. The merging of the energies symbolizes the possibility of integrating the mass unconscious and its creative dream.

In the Hindu creation myth the "god" (or creative essense) is immersed in a dream of a world. In this dream state nothing happens; ideas float around but nothing materializes, nothing is realized. In order to actualize consciousness, the "god" realizes that some manifestation must take place. So he splits himself up into millions of pieces and becomes the universe—the planets, the sky, the earth and its waters, the vegetation, the animals, the grass, the rock. The universe teeming with life, all struggling to survive, is the conscious realization of that dream.

When aspects take place between these two representative forces, great changes take place in our world. When we are born with these aspects, great changes take place within us. The dream becomes intermingled with the unconscious motivation; the dreams bring the contents of the collective unconscious into realization. Unless the aspect between these two planets also ties into a personal planet, the effect will take place in our generation; when they are tied to the personal planets in our chart we have a chance for profound personal transformations.

IT SEEMS THAT THE NEWLY DISCOVERED PLANETS—
Uranus, Neptune and Pluto—symbolize our potential to become conscious. Uranus replaces the masculine side of Saturn in its rulership of
Aquarius; Neptune replaces the feminine side of Jupiter and its rulership of
Pisces; Pluto replaces the feminine side of Mars in its rulership of Scorpio.
Because the planets are symbols themselves, in order to understand them
we need to explore the philosophical and religious symbols of many
cultures in order to discover the subtle meanings relating to them. Because
they are symbols, the understanding has to be felt, it has to be synthesized
into the familiar astrological terminology so that this symbolism can be
related to energy manifesting in the chart of a person.

On one level, Pluto has been called the key to the mass unconscious of
any given generation. It stays in one sign for about twenty years so it influences a large group of people in each sign. It gives a symbolic message
about the strivings and struggles of a generation; it can be used to indicate
how a particular group of people will be motivated, how they will pursue
consciousness. Everyone will feel the effect of Pluto for everyone is a part
of a generation. It seems that whenever Pluto changes sign a new group of
people makes an attempt to free themselves from bondage, to shed the protective or restrictive bonds of strong governmental policies, to become a
self-responsible and citizen directed group. The planet's motion can be
observed as history is being made and we can watch it indicate the struggle
for power, for transformation, for freedom on our own planet.

Pluto becomes personal when it attaches itself to one of our personal
planets by aspect. This means that the values of our generation or the consciousness of our era are important to us in a very personal way. We
become more involved in our generation's struggle for consciousness,
although each of us will use the energy differently. In the family experience, the aspects between Pluto and the personal planets indicate that

we are raised in a family that uses the energies of Pluto as a part of the family experience. If the aspects are easy, we are taught cooperation in the home. The easy aspects also can indicate a person who may be a victim of the goals of a generation (following blindly along with the generation of the moment), or one who can offer his energies to the furthering of the needs of the masses because he is trained to do so. For example, Pluto trine the Sun indicates several options—it may indicate someone who works with labor unions, for the community, for the media, or who works easily with groups; or someone who follows the group and becomes a ''pot-smoking'' teen-ager who smokes because all his friends do. Obviously as we become more mature we are better able to make decisions about how we want to use this energy.

The hard aspects to Pluto usually indicate that rather than cooperation, the energy of coercion is used in the childhood. Which parent is involved in manipulating the family energy can be seen by observing the aspects: do they come from the father, the mother, or both? When Pluto aspects a planet symbolizing the father (Sun or Saturn) the pursuit of consciousness is important, for one's very existence and the quality of one's existence will be self-established. The energy manifests on either a low or high level and the choices range from being obsessive and controlling to being at the height of conscious development—the choice is ours. The decisions to use this energy will involve becoming aware of the power in the universe, how to use and understand universal law, and how that understanding can further consciousness.

When Pluto aspects planets that symbolize a coercive mother image (Moon or Venus) one needs to free oneself from the confusion caused by a controlling mother and her affect on the image of the feminine in one's psyche. Until the confusion is understood, it may be difficult to develop the feeling side of the self.

Several astrologers feel that Pluto is the Great Mother, the chthonic mother, that mother figure who is devouring. Pluto, as ruler of Scorpio, does have a tie to motherhood. The feminine side of Mars (the ancient ruler of Scorpio) has to do with reproduction and sex for reproductive purposes. Sex in this sense is not the romantic kind that we think about when we fall in love, but rather the kind used in the mating process, the type which draws any species to mate because of the instinctive and biological urges.

In Hindu symbolism the figure Maya/Kali has been used to symbolize Mother Nature, the constant teeming of life that devours itself on an unconscious level. The figure is both a beautiful woman (Maya) who symbolizes illusion and what we hanker after unconsciously, and Kali, the devouring mother who gives birth at one end and eats her children at the other. She is often pictured wearing a belt of shrunken heads; she is awesome and horrible, but she is real. Mother Nature is involved in a round of death and rebirth, and the sign of Scorpio symbolizes that for us.

Shiva is another symbol of life and death in Hindu symbolism. He is an androgynous figure, both male and female; he has many arms and is called The Lord of Death and Destruction—and Regeneration. Most Westerners forget the regeneration part and see Shiva as only a terrifying figure. But, he dances the dance of life and death. When we know Pluto well, we know about the round of life and death, we understand the teeming life force present in our environment, and what remains is to free consciousness from its familiar surroundings and allow it to expand to include the whole.

The hardest image to free ourselves from is that of the Mother. The Mother figure represents so much to the psyche, it becomes so complicated that unless the image is pursued on a conscious basis, most of the time it will lie in some confused state within us. When Pluto ties to the Moon, we must break the tie with Mother; we must understand who our individual and physical mother is and free her from the image we have of universal Mother in the psyche. When Pluto aspects the Moon, the job may be difficult, but also important if we wish to gain a sense of self. Our mother is the person who feeds us, cares for us, nurtures us, gives us a pattern to follow in terms of our emotional responses. She appears in our psyche as well in the impersonal form of Maya/Kali, the Great Mother in the universe in mythology. We can easily confuse all of these images and make them one. They aren't.

In order to become free, the myths tell us that we kill the father and overpower the mother. Obviously we don't do either in the physical sense, but the psyche must become free of the personal parents in order for consciousness to take place. Jung, in his *Symbols of Transformation*, says: "The empirical truth never frees a man from his bondage to the senses; it only shows him that he was always so and cannot be otherwise. The symbolical truth, on the other hand, which puts water in place of the mother and spirit or fire in place of the father, frees the libido from the channel of the incest tendency, offers it a new gradient, and canalizes it into a spiritual form. Thus, as a spiritual being, becomes a child again and is born into a circle of brothers and sisters; but his mother has become the 'communion of saints,' the Church, and his brothers and sisters are humanity, with whom he is united anew in the common heritage or symbolical truth."*

The symbols free us from the confusion of physical images, for we may not understand the quest if the symbols are those physically close to us. It is harder to break the tie with our mother than with our father. The symbolism is rampant here, for the mythic sperm is never seen, yet the birth is visible. The imagery of the material universe is seen in terms of "Mother

---

The Collected Works of C.G. Jung, trans. R.F.C. Hull, Bollingen Series XX. Vol. 5: *Symbols of Transformation*, copyright © 1956 by Princeton University Press. From the Harper Torchbooks edition, New York, 1962, p. 226.

Earth'' and the Father is some personalized god in the sky who sees everything we do. For the personality to free itself, it must become conscious of the symbolism around it and become a part of it. When we have strong Pluto aspects it becomes more difficult to do this, for the Plutonic energies seem to convince us that we each must "wrest" a universe away from that which is teeming outside ourselves.

People who are locked into the Plutonic vibration attempt to control love, to control children, to control the environment, to control the rain, and some of them even try to control their transits! The battle is a long and arduous one, and no matter how hard they fight they never seem to win. There is another side to the Plutonic energy, however, and it bestows fantastic creative energy and insight on those who are brave enough to use it.

Religion has its sources in symbolism, and those people who have wholeheartedly become involved in some religious transformation have "given themselves *up* to God" for they have stopped trying to control the universe and have decided to "trust in the Lord." People who are not religious converts may be interested in "giving themselves up to the creative energy within" for the Plutonic energy is vastly creative. In order to use this energy one must let go of the power and control trip; for the urge to power, the urge to control, is always blinding to the owner.

For example, consider the person with Pluto conjunct the Ascendant who is determined to obsess and control the loved one. He doesn't ever feel sure of the loved one, for he never gives the person a chance to love him. When manipulating people, when giving in order to control, he can never be sure if the loved one is there because she is being manipulated, or because she wants to be. A sense of personal security cannot be established, for nothing "just happens," it is always arranged. If you throw a pebble in the middle of a pond the ripples spread all over the surface—and if you throw power and control into your relationships the ripples spread all over your relationships. When can you relax? If you relax, will you lose control? Consider the tension that is caused merely because of the need to know where you stand. Is it worth it? Why not sit back and let people show you that they care—for then you'll really know! When the edges and boundaries are taken away, new ideas burst forth and the beauty of consciousness can take place. Symbols always have a low form and a high one—we are free to choose.

Because Pluto is the slowest moving planet, the aspects have been discussed under other headings. To consider Pluto's aspects go to the chapter that covers the other planet included in the aspect.

SOME ASTROLOGERS FEEL THAT THE ASCENDANT IS MORE important than the Sun or the Moon, and some feel that it is not important at all. Jung described the conscious development of personality as the "persona," that part of ourselves which we use to confront the world. It seems that persona is a good word to use to identify what the Ascendant does for us. When we are born, the Ascendant (or rising sign) marks the horizon. It sometimes describes the physical characteristics we have, and when people play "guess your Sun sign" they often guess the Ascendant rather than the Sun.

The Ascendant indicates what we are trying to be rather than what we are. The Sun is the "I am" principle; the Moon indicates how we respond to life; the Ascendant gives the key to what we are trying to *be*. It doesn't reflect what we *are*, but how we attempt to be someone else—we attempt to be other than ourselves. In diagnosing the early childhood experience, the Ascendant can be used as an indicator (along with the fourth house) of the environment to which the individual was exposed. It seems that when the parents won't accept the individual's Sun sign characteristics, or the early school system won't accept them, they *will* accept the qualities of the Ascendant. These are the qualities that we use when we are "putting our best foot forward." The Ascendant characteristics are donned like our "Sunday best" and we exhibit behavioral traits that may be somewhat out of character.

We put our best foot forward when we begin something new—so the qualities of the Ascendant are used for every new beginning that we make—a new job, a new neighborhood, a new beau, even the first trip out on the dance floor at a party! When we fall in love, we usually fall in love with the other person's Ascendant and he or she with ours. However, after the relationship has gone on for a while, one finds out that the other has a Sun and a Moon; the masquerade of the Ascendant seldom covers the qualities and drives of the Sun/Moon for long. It does for a while, though; the Ascendant covers us, it hides the self, it protects the self, it develops a persona. The persona is necessary for survival: it keeps us from being as vulnerable as we might be, it serves as the third party in the inner trinity of personality. The trinity of personality is represented by the Sun, Moon and the Ascendant, and if we can express all the qualities of the triad, we have a chance at knowing ourselves.

The Ascendant masks the self, and when we are younger it can cause great confusion. We go around trying to be something or someone that we aren't. When we do this, we sometimes marry the wrong person, or avoid the development of the real personality within. We tend to behave as expected—and other people expect us to behave like the Ascendant. However, the Sun must manifest at some time or other, and if it doesn't we begin to feel lonely and rejected. As we mature, as we pass the age of thirty, the Sun characteristics express more easily. However, a person in the twenties period may have difficulty diagnosing the source of personal problems, for he may be trying to be who others think he should be.

The Ascendant can be used to discover the kind of career we may wish to pursue, and it can be used to see just how we will work after we get the job. It represents the qualities of the sign we are trying to be; it can be put to good use on a job, for the Ascendant marks the point where we strive the most valiantly. We cannot *be* the Ascendant, for we already *are* something else. The pursuit of career goals will put this energy to good use for we have the physical energy of the Ascendant sign available to us. This energy can mask who we are while we work at a profession; the qualities of the sign rising can be added to those of the Sun.

For example, consider an Aries with Cancer rising. The Aries qualities will have to manifest sooner or later. The personal life will reflect the qualities of the childhood of the Aries archetype (see Chapter 5, Section I) and the Cancer energy at the Ascendant level will cast a caring and nurturing element to the Aries intellect. This individual will be idealistic and intellectual, but will appear to be caring, emotional and nurturing. The combination of the energies will tend to soften the Aries qualities, and this individual will do well in some teaching profession. Remember that teaching doesn't mean just teaching in the local elementary school—all kinds of things can be taught, and teaching can be done in extremely unconventional circumstances.

It has been said that the Ascendant exhibits the worst qualities of the sign type characteristics! The more obnoxious qualities of the signs are apt to show through the Ascendant energy because that is what we are trying to be. So Aries rising will appear to be more aggressive than the Aries Sun, for the Aries Sun is already an Aries and probably has a different sign rising. The Ascendant is a cover.

It should be mentioned that it is possible to have the Sun, Moon and the Ascendant appearing in the same sign. If the Ascendant represents the persona, or our "cover," then how can we have all three points of personal character in one sign? It is possible! When the Sun and the Ascendant are in the same sign, the person is born to experience life; that is, rather than going out to look for experience, it seems to come to him. He has less cover, less persona, than the other signs. He is more honest, more direct, and the personality is less complicated. Don't confuse less complicated with easier—for each combination of signs presents its own special problems.

The Ascendant can be treated much like a planet. It represents how we start things, how we manifest ourselves in our career. The aspects are discussed in general, but with a special emphasis on the conjunctions.

ASCENDANT–SUN ASPECTS

Generally speaking, if the Sun and the Ascendant are well aspected, it indicates individuals who are easily able to execute a career. These individuals are capable of manifesting the qualities of the Sun in daily activities.

When the Sun squares or opposes the Ascendant, there is more difficulty in expressing these qualities. A square generally comes from the fourth or tenth house, so goals reached for (tenth) or the early childhood environment (fourth) might stand in the way of Ascendant expression. Constructive action may not be easily taken until these individuals become conscious of the sign dilemma. For example, Sun in Cancer square Ascendant in Aries: a Cancer person will take indirect action to express the Sun qualities, for Cancerians are intuitive people who usually consider a crisis on a personal level, who will consider what part they may play in this crisis, and act accordingly. But Aries rising acts aggressively in any new situation. How can the Sun express itself? These people will seem to be far more aggressive than they really are, less sensitive than they really are: people may be drawn to their Aries energy rather than to the Cancerian sensitivity. If one is aware of the two kinds of energy available, one can use all of it, but at appropriate times and in appropriate places.

When the Sun opposes the Ascendant, the opposition often takes place from the seventh house. Because the first house indicates how we begin things, and the seventh indicates how we cope with our partners, the opposition would indicate some kind of compromise between self-initiation and relationships. This may indicate individuals who feel they must give up a great deal of freedom and personal decision-making in order to marry and have a partnership. If the opposition is between Aries and Libra, the Aries Ascendant will appear to be aggressive, perhaps direct, overly bold and blunt. The Sun in Libra will be more genteel, seeking to balance the life experience, seeking a gentler, more democratic expression than the Aries "me first" attitude. Again, when the energy is understood, it can be used in the appropriate places.

ASCENDANT-SUN CONJUNCTION. This aspect is a special one, for it indicates people who are born in an atmosphere that is most encouraging of their sign type. The inner self, the qualities of intimate personality, will be manifested any time these individuals begin a new endeavor, a new stage in life.

The qualities of the Sun are bound up in the life style, the personality is entwined with any new endeavor: the best foot forward is a part of the inner personality. Any new start, any new beginning is extremely important to these individuals, for the concept of self-worth is wrapped up in all new activities. This can indicate people who need a great deal of personal attention, or it can indicate individuals who overreact to each new life experience, for the "I am" principle is manifested in career, every new start, every new beginning.

If the Sun is well aspected, this energy can be highly productive. If the Sun is afflicted, the energy involved in the difficult aspect will be used better when it is understood and perhaps rechanneled.

ASCENDANT-MOON ASPECTS

If the Ascendant represents how we begin things and the Moon represents how we respond emotionally, the combination of the two energies generates a higher than average emotional response to any new endeavor. The emotional response can indicate a caring, feeling, intuitive response to all new projects; it can indicate individuals who are emotionally involved in the work they do, who care about what they do in a highly personal sense. It also can indicate individuals who overreact emotionally to every new project, who may be afraid to start something new for fear of becoming emotionally vulnerable. It's important to consider the other aspects to the Ascendant and the Moon to fully understand how these individuals will react to their own energy.

If the aspects are easy, these are·people who have been taught to respond to life in an emotionally constructive manner during childhood. If the aspects are difficult, they see life as a difficult emotional experience. If the aspects include a square or an opposition between the Moon and the Ascendant, each new beginning in childhood may have been an emotional trauma—they were afraid to start school, they had difficulty moving to another school during the early years, or perhaps they resisted the various phases of growing up.

If the Moon squares the Ascendant, it indicates that the emotional needs of these individuals are not easily expressed by the "persona." The career drive may suppress the emotional nature, or the masquerade that is presented to the public may in fact mask a tender emotional structure. This causes inner tension, for the emotional needs have to find expression.

For example, Moon in Scorpio square a Leo Ascendant: The Scorpio Moon feels emotionally unwanted, it needs more warmth and security than other signs. The Leo Ascendant needs attention (which can support the Scorpio factor) but there is an additional need for respect and approval. Hurt feelings are covered by Leo energy, for one doesn't show such a personal reaction in public. The need for approval may require these individuals to participate in activities that the Scorpio Moon resents, and tension begins to be created. It isn't tension from the environment as much as from the inner self attempting to proceed in two different directions at the same time! In a crisis situation, these types may put up a "proper front" rather than asking for what they need.

In the case of the opposition, consider a Leo Ascendant opposing the Moon in Aquarius. What kind of emotional distress might that combination present? The Aquarian Moon will probably be in the seventh house, which indicates a sensitivity concerning partners, perhaps an overly emotional response to any action taken by the partner. How will that affect the emotional self? Would it cause a compromise in some way? The Moon symbolizes the physical effect of the mother when the individual is very young. In some way the mother (Moon) compromised the child's actions—every time the Ascendant reached out to do something, mother stood in the way. The individual will respond to life much like the mother did as far as the emotions are concerned, so the same apprehensions that Mom projected when the person is a child will be projected by the person as an adult. Each new job will bring inordinate trauma, each new beginning will contain trauma.

When adding the qualities of the signs to the opposition, the compromise will involve the dichotomy between Leo and Aquarius: Leo rising indicates a "proper" front, an idealistic approach to new things, a need to be respected when putting one's best foot forward. The Aquarius Moon indicates an unorthodox approach to life, a less personal approach, so these individuals may be involved in some humanitarian endeavor but feel repelled when they aren't approved of by their peers or by the group they sell their Aquarian idea to. How can they approach their career with new ideas, with the Aquarian intuitive approach, with an Ascendant that needs approval, an Ascendant that doesn't like being laughed at?

In romantic situations, this dichotomy becomes the "proper front" that covers the expression of the emotional needs. When hurt feelings are hidden, how does the partner know that feelings have been hurt? Would these individuals begin something new from a conventional point of view because they need approval from the partner or the public and sacrifice the emotional joy of experiencing something out of the ordinary?

ASCENDANT–MOON CONJUNCTION. This aspect is not an easy one. The Ascendant symbolizes the body according to the house system. The Moon represents the physical body in the language of the planets. When the two are combined it indicates an inordinate sensitivity to any new experience. Obviously a Cancer Moon conjunct the Ascendant will be more sensitive than the conjunction in Aries; but this person is oversensitized to the surroundings no matter what the sign is. The Moon also symbolizes the physical mother and how she carried herself when the individual was forming a personality. The emotional reactions felt by the mother are absorbed by the child, and in this case, the emotional reactions will be directly tied to the pursuit of any new stage of life, new people, new situations, new jobs.

These individuals will acutely feel any sensitive feeling experience, and it's hard to make it past third grade with your peers with this kind of sensitivity! So these children develop a veneer to cover the emotional reactions—and the aspect is often tougher on boys for they are supposed to be rough-tough people in our culture.

The mother of these individuals reacted emotionally and they reacted to her—emotional difficulties can be traced back to their response to her. The body is abnormally tense, for it is constantly prepared to cover or hide any emotional shock it may experience in the environment. These individuals are apt to interpret conversations in a most personal way, not understanding the editorial "you" and assuming that all conversations are directed their way in a personal fashion, and that any criticism is directed at them in a personal sense. This can indicate people who are overly defensive or overly sensitive.

The conjunction also gives an unusually strong intuitive ability which when properly channeled can be most helpful in the decision-making processes. But, it also can hinder the personality if the cultural or ethnic background frowns on intuitive reactions. For example, a boy raised in a "macho" family may feel insecure about his masculinity if he feels too much, if he is too sensitive. If this is the case, he may become defensive and therefore hard to communicate with.

Each of the signs must be read individually, for the Aries Ascendant will respond very differently than the Cancer Ascendant, and so on around the zodiac. The conjunction intensifies the activities governed by both the Ascendant and the Moon. Any additional aspects to this conjunction should be considered when discussing this aspect, for hard aspects can alter an interpretation considerably.

ASCENDANT-MERCURY ASPECTS

If the Ascendant represents how we begin things and Mercury indicates how we communicate, these two energies combine so that the persona may represent itself differently than the conversation indicates it should. The Ascendant represents how we present ourselves, the kind of energy we put out when we attempt something new; Mercury can be used to understand how we communicate, how we talk, how we think. We may say one thing and do another. The dichotomy can be understood when we consider Mercury in relationship to either Mars or the Ascendant, for either placement can symbolize the action we take.

If Mercury sextiles or trines the Ascendant, the individual was taught constructive communication in childhood, and he or she can use that knowledge creatively. If the square or opposition occurs, the personality will become conscious of the faux pas it creates in the middle of the most delicate maneuvers. For example, Aries rising square Mercury in Capricorn: Mercury will talk management, tradition; communication will sound as though this individual has strong feelings toward traditional approaches to career situations. Aries rising indicates an aggressive front, perhaps thoughtless action. Because Aries is an intellectual sign and prides itself on rational thinking, the mature person with this combination of energy can learn to use the energies constructively, but the process will be acquired.

If there is an opposition between the Ascendant and Mercury, there will be some compromise involving the thinking/communicating function and every new beginning. When Aries is rising and Mercury is in Libra, these types communicate in a democratic manner, often smoothing the troubled waters of others' relationships (Libra), only to turn around and take aggressive action (Aries) that the Mercury placement doesn't warrant. Again, this aspect can be channeled, the energy can be used at the appropriate times and places.

ASCENDANT-MERCURY CONJUNCTION. This conjunction indicates that the Sun is in close proximity. The Mercury placement may be outweighed by the Sun energies.

People born with this conjunction are able to put their thoughts into action for Mercury rules the mind, the ability to communicate. The Ascendant indicates how we start things, and how we function best in career. These may be talkative people, but the energy can be channeled to help them to get their point across.

ASCENDANT-VENUS ASPECTS

If the Ascendant represents the masquerade, the persona, how we start something new, and Venus symbolizes what we want from life, what we desire, how we appreciate love, this combination will indicate how we manifest our desire nature in our personal life. In romantic situations these aspects shape the life for they indicate the degree of comfort or discomfort that will be experienced as we accomplish our goals, or cope with our frustrated romantic aspirations.

People with a trine or sextile from Venus to the Ascendant easily attain their affectional needs, for their persona manifests traits similar to that which they appreciate in general. People with a square or opposition may find their "wants," their ability to receive love, thwarted or frustrated in some way.

Consider a Gemini Ascendant square Venus in Virgo: the Gemini Ascendant appears to be controversial, a bit contrary, one who can talk about anything, listen to anything, who can be approached with any new idea in any of its experimental stages. Venus in Virgo is symbolic of highly critical energy; affectional ties will be formed because of a worthy reason; it enjoys pursuing the world of the intellect, sharing an intellectual idea with another person. Venus in Virgo also indicates a pristine view regarding the concept of love; love should be special, and feelings are easily hurt when approached with ideas and concepts regarding the love bond that are not traditional. Both qualities, the attributes of both Gemini and Virgo, are present in the personality; both attributes will manifest in attitudes presented to others. This combination will have to learn how to allow both energies to flow. However, the square is most often an indication that its owner will live one end and suppress the other, finding it difficult to attain the compromise necessary so that both energies can function at the same time. If the "best foot forward" battles with the concept of love, all relationships will encompass a strain, and permanent relationships will be difficult to build.

When the opposition takes place between Venus and the Ascendant some kind of compromise must take place between the "persona" and the desires. The career drive may be confused or the personal relationships may be difficult.

Consider the Gemini Ascendant opposing Venus in Sagittarius: the Ascendant in Gemini indicates one who puts a controversial foot forward when beginning new relationships. The energy manifested at each new beginning seems to be airy and intellectual, controversial, perhaps contrary, extremely open. Venus in Sagittarius wants to be free, but one can't be free if one needs an audience. Controversial behavior needs an audience. Venus in Sagittarius will enjoy personal independence, yet Gemini rising prefers living with someone, having people around. These individuals will appear to be looking for a different kind of relationship than their Venus in Sagittarius wants. Until the compromise is understood, relationships may change frequently.

ASCENDANT–VENUS CONJUNCTION. When the Ascendant conjuncts Venus the energy expresses according to the sign involved in the conjunction. The Ascendant represents the persona, the masquerade, the "best foot forward." Venus indicates how we appreciate love, how we wish to be treated, our concept of the feminine principle and, therefore, how we regard femininity and womanhood.

This conjunction often indicates a warm and social personality. It can indicate individuals who are capable of being generous and responsive to what pleases them. However, the generosity reflected will be influenced by the images coming from the mother's sphere early in the life, and the aspects to the conjunction will indicate if the energy operates freely or not.

The conjunction in Gemini will be more intellectual than the conjunction in Taurus. It can be a blessing or an indication of a neurotic type, depending on the other aspects involved in the conjunction. If Venus indicates the personal concept of femininity, the regard for femininity in this developing personality, it's possible that a woman with this conjunction might be defensive of herself whenever she is confronted with a new beginning, a new situation. If she has been taught that the feminine side of life has no real importance, she may approach each new beginning with a feeling of second-class citizenship. She may be too defensive of herself, she may even subconsciously assume that her female friends or co-workers have no validity. This response to life will occur if the hard aspects to Venus remain unresolved.

ASCENDANT–MARS ASPECTS

This combination is important for the Ascendant is the house symbol of the action taken, how one starts things; and Mars is the planetary indicator of the action taken. Mars generally indicates how the Sun sign qualities are put into action. When Mars sextiles or trines the Ascendant, the individual was taught constructive action as a child, and action taken as an adult will complement the persona. If Mars squares or opposes the Ascendant, it is not easy to energize the creative potential in the personality in an appropriate manner. When the square appears, the action taken doesn't complement the persona.

For example, consider a Taurus Ascendant square Mars in Aquarius: the Mars will take unorthodox or unconventional action to express the Sun qualities, and the Taurus Ascendant indicates one who appears to be practical, rational, scientific. These individuals will appear to be reasonable employees but may end up taking action in an unconventional manner. The action taken may not express the career interests for career moves may not be perceived appropriately. Goals may be confused. Since Mars also rules sexuality, the sexual expression may not make sense either, for the career may be affected by the choice of sexual partners, or the career life style may not connect in with the love life.

When the opposition occurs a compromise is indicated, for the persona, the public attitudes claimed while we put "our best foot forward," may not agree with the action taken in life, or with the sexual needs. Consider an opposition between Taurus rising and Mars in Scorpio: although the Taurus Ascendant indicates a practical approach to life, when the feelings are hurt Mars in Scorpio thinks about being vindictive. Career goals might be confused with personal partnerships, so that the marriage partner might provide a problem when trying to get ahead in the business world—or people with this aspect may perceive the marriage partner as an obstruction. The Taurus Ascendant understands the practical side of competition and the Mars in Scorpio considers retribution. Some compromise will have to take place in order to get these two energies working together. Practical transformations, scientific research may be one way to use the energy. When these people understand the various possibilities regarding manifestation of this energy, they can make conscious decisions regarding how they wish to use it.

ASCENDANT-MARS CONJUNCTION. This is a powerful aspect for it indicates a high energy potential. These individuals will make quick, perhaps rash, decisions. The early childhood environment will be very active, it may even be somewhat violent. These individuals will be familiar with anger, and the kind of anger they were exposed to as children will be indicated by the sign in which the conjunction occurs.

For example, the conjunction in Aries indicates a household with a short fuse but easily forgotten flare-ups of temper. The conjunction in Pisces indicates a more maudlin type of anger—one that is projected with guilt attached to it, perhaps anger that is caused by overly sensitive reactions to life.

The emotional reaction to life will have to be handled constructively or this person might spend too much time overreacting to ordinary life situations. Career decisions will need to be thought out carefully to overcome the natural inclination to jump into new situations thoughtlessly.

ASCENDANT-JUPITER ASPECTS

The Ascendant is the masquerade, the indicator of how we project our persona; it reflects how we handle our new beginnings. Jupiter indicates how we relate ourselves to others, and how we relate to our personal needs. We either relate (or understand) what we start, or we don't. If we relate easily, we tend to do well professionaly; if not, we have to be really brilliant in order to get ahead. People born with the sextile or trine relate to others by using a similar energy to that of the Ascendant. They tend to open up (Jupiter) in a manner complementary to the persona they have put forth.

When Jupiter squares the Ascendant the relationship needs argue with the persona. Consider Jupiter in Aquarius square Scorpio rising: the persona is protective and cautious about new beginnings, yet the Jupiter position indicates an unconventional or unorthodox response to life. The Jupiter position indicates an open personality, yet the Scorpio Ascendant reflects a person who is apprehensive. New experience will begin with difficulty for the square indicates a frustration of energy. These individuals may not be conscious of the fact that their response to new relating experience will be perceived differently by those viewing the Ascendant reactions.

When Jupiter opposes the Ascendant, a compromise between new beginnings, the persona and the ability to relate to what is being projected, becomes an issue in the life. Usually the opposition is active between the first and seventh houses (the personal projection versus the needs of a part-ner). When the opposition takes place between Cancer and Capricorn the following conflict may take place: Cancer rising indicates a person who wants to nurture, to care, to protect and may project a little boy/girl or big momma/daddy image. When Jupiter is in Capricorn, it indicates a need to relate in a traditional manner. How does a traditional approach to relating affect the little boy/girl projection? It becomes confusing. These people may object to being treated as a child but may not recognize the projection of those qualities. The energy can be handled constructively when the signs are understood.

ASCENDANT–JUPITER CONJUNCTION. People born with this aspect were born into fairly comfortable circumstances. They tend to be overexpansive, or they tend to overrelate to the situations they become personally involved in.

The Ascendant indicates "our best foot forward," and Jupiter there in-dicates a tendency to throw all the energies in each new beginning. Life is not approached with caution unless the Ascendant sign is a cautious one. It brings the quality of "too much" into the life style. In order to use the energy constructively, the concept of "too much" will have to be thought about and determined where it occurs in the life. "Too much" can be determined by the reactions of others to whatever we are relating to in an overly exuberant manner.

ASCENDANT–SATURN ASPECTS

If Saturn indicates what we regard with caution and the Ascendant represents the persona, or how we begin something new, the aspects be-tween Saturn and the Ascendant will indicate caution or circumspection. The sextile or trine indicate people who were raised in an atmosphere of careful decision making. Work done and values considered are those that cooperate with authority and tradition. Action taken will probably be mature because the childhood environment encouraged it.

When Saturn squares the Ascendant the approach to any new beginning is clouded with conflict, for early in the life the father was not encourag-ing. These individuals will commence new activities with caution or ap-prehension. Some of the conflict will be caused by an inner lack of self-confidence, for early problems with the father image usually manifest as problems with authority figures later on.

The square indicates a self-worth predicament that can be coupled with the sign quality dilemma indicated by the square aspect. Consider a Cancer Ascendant square Saturn in Libra. The self-worth predicament is obvious for the father influenced this person in some way. The signs will tell the story. Cancer rising indicates a soft approach, a need for love, a possessive approach to life, perhaps an ability to nurture others that can be used in a profession. Saturn in Libra indicates that the father's values (at the time the individual was born) had to do with belonging to a special or an elite group on a social level. Every time this person reaches out to begin something new, there will be an inner concern or apprehension in regard to being accepted by the peer group or by an authority figure. The Cancer Ascendant indicates a natural inclination for the intuitive approach, yet the Saturn in Libra may not respect the intuitive hunch. Both needs of the signs will have to be incorporated into the personality.

With the opposition of Saturn to the Ascendant there will also be an early childhood conflict with the father, there will be a need for authority approval, or a feeling of caution attached to any new beginning. A feeling of compromise occurs because the needs of the partner (or the partner's opinions) will influence the new steps forward in life. Cancer rising indicates an emotional approach to life, and Saturn in Capricorn indicates a need for tradition; yet the traditional approach is not often emotional or intuitive. The urge to nurture, foster or care for others may not fit in with the understanding of life as it is, for Capricorn seldom nurses the underdog; but the Cancer Ascendant will want to do that. There will be an image in the psyche that comes from the father, indicating a feeling of insecurity regarding new ventures, for seldom did Dad approve of this person's "best foot forward."

ASCENDANT-SATURN CONJUNCTION. Saturn represents what we approach with caution, our feelings of insecurity. The Ascendant indicates how we start new ventures, as well as the persona we project. Saturn conjuncting the Ascendant indicates individuals who are often insecure about their abilities when they are young, for a self-worth facet in the personality needs development. In early childhood there was a rejection by the father in some way; these people didn't feel accepted or encouraged by him. As young adults they feel apprehensive about being approved of by those in authority; they may deem it necessary to work too hard in order to attain whatever life experience they seek.

The self-worth dilemma will be indicated by the sign in which the conjunction occurs. As these people mature and earn a concept of worthiness, a personal strength will emerge, for Saturn in the first house can indicate the ability to persevere.

ASCENDANT-URANUS ASPECTS

The Ascendant indicates how the persona will manifest, how new projects will be approached, while Uranus indicates the ability to develop consciousness or the capacity for eccentric behavior. When a sextile or trine between the Ascendant and Uranus occurs, these individuals are exposed to new ideas and new attitudes because the parents were encouraging of new concepts.

The square or opposition brings in conflict, for the behavioral attitudes of these individuals were probably not accepted as a part of their persona. When putting their best foot forward, they may not be comfortable. Consider Aquarius rising square Uranus in Taurus: the Ascendant indicates a person who appears to be unconventional, unorthodox, open to new-age ideas, yet the Taurus placement for Uranus indicates a person who behaves in a practical manner or who is stubborn in some way. Because Uranus indicates a behavior pattern and Taurus indicates the possibility of establishing ruts, the behavior may be too eccentrically stubborn to conform with the Aquarian attitudes of human compassion and understanding.

When the opposition takes place, the behavioral attitudes are compromised with every new beginning: the approach to life may not reflect the behavioral attitudes. Consider Aquarius rising opposing Uranus in Leo. Although these people appear to be open and unorthodox, when their feelings are hurt their behavior pattern will reflect the qualities of Leo—perhaps reacting in an overly sensitive manner, being too involved in a need for respect or approval from others. If the Aquarius Ascendant wants to become involved in new-age ideas, how can those visions be enacted when one also needs immediate approval from peers? A compromise must be made. In a personal sense, the opposition between Aquarius and Leo indicates people who want to project an unconventional persona, yet they want to have an approvable partner, since this opposition usually reflects the first and seventh house positions.

ASCENDANT–URANUS CONJUNCTION. The Ascendant indicates the persona, how we present ourselves to others, the person we are trying to be. When Uranus conjuncts the Ascendant the self-expression becomes unique. The qualities of the rising sign will be enhanced, the approach to life will be unorthodox or unconventional, and this personality will have a chance to manifest a more highly conscious reflection of the rising sign qualities than those without this conjunction. A Taurus Ascendant will be a highly unusual Taurus, and the personality may be eccentric or even willful.

Because the Ascendant reflects the approach to new life experience, this conjunction indicates a tendency toward an unusual approach, an unpredictable approach to new situations. This conjunction can be exciting, sparking off an unusual life experience, or it can cause much inner conflict depending on how Uranus is aspected to other planets. The unorthodox approach will only bring contentment when used to further develop the facets of personality that must have expression. In order to diagnose the personality needs, look to the personal planets.

ASCENDANT–NEPTUNE ASPECTS

The Ascendant represents how we meet people, how we start something new, the persona projection. Neptune symbolizes our dreams, our fantasies, our illusions, delusions and capacity for inspiration. When Neptune ties to the Ascendant, a need for spiritual development is indicated as well as the potential for creative endeavor. The creative energy may not be expressed until the veil of illusion is lifted so that we can get a better insight into what we are manifesting.

Trines or sextiles between Neptune and the Ascendant indicate individuals who were raised in a somewhat spiritually evolved atmosphere; their dreams and fantasies were encouraged by their parents rather than discouraged. When a square or opposition aspect is formed, it indicates a difficulty assimilating the world of fantasy into the persona or in the beginnings of new life experiences. In plain English, the hard aspect can signify people who don't know what they are doing for they can't see themselves or the impression that they make on others.

Consider a Virgo Ascendant square Neptune in Sagittarius: the Virgo Ascendant will approach work and any new endeavor with a great deal of self-criticism. These individuals are raised in a critical environment which causes the development of analytical skills. Neptune in Sagittarius dreams of freedom, responds to grand ideas pertaining to political freedom or independence. Virgo looks for the analytical job; in close personal relationships the persona manifests an attunement to detail, yet the dream urges and goals reflect a desire to be free as a bird, following the pursuit of the ideal. Learning how to do a little of both will present a difficulty, for when the square aspect occurs the tendency is to pursue one end of the square for a while and then give it up to pursue the other. In order to accomplish anything worthwhile both ends of the square have to function comfortably at the same time.

The opposition between the Ascendant and Neptune will involve a compromise. If Neptune is in Virgo, the individual will dream of being a person who is critically analytical, able to separate the wheat from the chaff, one who is aware of all the details. Pisces rising indicates sensitivity and compassion, perhaps an apprehension regarding the pursuit of the critical approach for it might hurt the other person. The Pisces Ascendant will approach love from a spiritual, sensitive standpoint, perhaps becoming a martyr in love situations or being involved with an unrequited love. Neptune in Virgo will enjoy criticizing the partner, and if its placement falls in the seventh house it might force the owner of the chart to learn the difference between blind compassion (Pisces) and learning how to pick a partner from a conscious point (Neptune in the seventh). The Neptunian dream might not bring pleasure, and people with this aspect may have to learn that any misery they encounter in relationships may be caused by the fact that they have not understood what they are doing, that they are pursuing a dream or fantasy that doesn't provide satisfaction for their needs.

ASCENDANT-NEPTUNE CONJUNCTION. The Ascendant represents the persona, how each new venture in life is started, the qualities that we project as observed by those around us; Neptune indicates our dreams, inspirations, illusions. The conjunction indicates the ability to use this energy creatively or illusively, depending on the personal awareness of its existence.

New beginnings may be inspired on the one hand and delusory on the other, for Neptune conveys the characteristic of vague or ambiguous activity. People born with Neptune conjunct the Ascendant may not seem to know what they are doing! They may appear to be preoccupied or absent-minded. An Aries type of energy on the Ascendant indicates a tendency to rush headlong into any new venture; but Neptune there indicates people who drift into new circumstances—or who look as though they dreamily get started in some new venture. This can be a most advantageous placement for Neptune, because the rest of the world can't see what the plans are!

The childhood circumstances were Neptunian. The conjunction can indicate that these people were not related to, or they did not really relate to childhood activities as other children do. There is a strong drive toward the spiritual and some form of spiritual philosophy will be developed in life.

ASCENDANT–PLUTO ASPECTS

The Ascendant indicates how we will approach the career, how we approach new situations or people, how we put our "best foot forward." When Pluto attaches to the Ascendant, an unconscious motivation is added to the drive for new beginnings. These individuals have been exposed to some kind of manipulation or control in their early environment, and the story will be told when the other aspects to Pluto are taken into consideration. This energy can be either productive or not, depending on the needs of the generation signified by Pluto's sign.

The sextile or trine between Pluto and the Ascendant reflects a childhood environment that was encouraging of group participation and cooperation. It sometimes indicates an individual who may be totally involved in the needs of the generation, an individual who strives for the peer group goals without questioning why the goals are important.

When Pluto squares or opposes the Ascendant the life takes on a different meaning, for the hard aspect indicates individuals who were raised in a strongly manipulative atmosphere. How the manipulation works and who was doing it will be revealed by the other aspects involved with Pluto.

When the square occurs there seems to be an excessive need to be in control of the environment, of the circumstances of the life; new starts will be hampered by some unconscious motivation that is reflective of the early childhood experience. For example, consider Pluto in Leo square Scorpio Ascendant: Pluto's sign indicates an unconscious need for respect and approval while the Scorpio Ascendant reflects an emotionally bleak childhood which adds a feeling of apprehension to each new beginning. These individuals will question whether any new venture will be wanted or appreciated by another. The Pluto position will heighten the apprehension; each new beginning will be colored with a need for approval. The need may not even be a conscious one, but some vague inner feeling of anxiety. This can even manifest as an attack—for every new beginning is controlled by presenting an offensive. The less productive end of the square might even mean that these individuals want to control and manipulate others before new ventures can be started. When the energy is turned into a productive phase, the need to control the environment has been let go and the inner motivation becomes joined with approvable action; they cease to view life as something that must be planned and the energy can flow.

When Pluto opposes the Ascendant another dilemma begins to show itself. It may look as though these individuals have chosen a controlling partner, but more likely some kind of internal battle is going on that concerns a desire to control both new activities and partnerships. Giving may be a response to love that ends up being "smother love," for the early childhood environment was strongly colored with controls.

Before one can eliminate unconscious needs to control, an understanding of the need to manipulate must take place. We are a species of imitators; if our parents play manipulation and control games, we will too, because we only have one childhood experience upon which to draw our concepts of normal behavior. In order to let go of old patterns we must first recognize that they exist. Then each individual can consciously examine the need to continue. Unconscious patterns are the most difficult to break for the patterns were formed many years ago and are not easy to recall.

In order to get the most out of the Ascendant qualities, the Pluto opposition needs to be understood for it will cause a compromise to take place that ends up compromising every new endeavor. Once consciousness is applied to this aspect, it becomes a strong one indeed and can be used in the transformation process.

ASCENDANT–PLUTO CONJUNCTION. When Pluto conjuncts the Ascendant the qualities of unconscious motivation are added to every new beginning. Either the energy of the archetypal or mythic images can be added to each new endeavor or the need to control each new event in life will take place.

When Leo is rising and Pluto is in Leo conjunct the Ascendant, an emphasis of Leo qualities will be present. Leo needs respect and approval; it symbolizes idealism, and high ideals can foster many sensitive repsonses to life. Because Pluto functions on an unconscious level, these individuals may have to cope with both the conscious need for approval signified by the

Leo Ascendant, as well as the hurt feelings engendered by Pluto. The Pluto in Leo sensitivity relates back to something learned in the early childhood regarding a need for approval or the feeling of its absence. Many new ventures will be motivated by some unconscious need for expression, and the energy can manifest on many levels. The controlled personality, the person who approaches life very carefully, can be indicated by this conjunction, as well as the person who has great healing abilities, or one who has wonderful ideas that can benefit society.

III: EXAMPLES

GENERALLY SPEAKING, EACH PLANET IN A BIRTH CHART symbolizes a certain aspect of personality. The planets each represent a number of attitudes toward life, and the dispersion of energy by house placement and aspect gives insight into how the energy will affect or confuse the personality. Astrology students often say "It's such-and-such planet doing it to me." But it isn't. The planet is merely a symbol that gives us a "handle" on how we may be reacting or overreacting to our life experience. Planets are code words or keywords symbolizing human behavior in astrological language, nothing more. They can be used to help us understand ourselves. The basic keywords of the planetary symbols appear at the end of this chapter; a more complete description of each planet can be found in Chapters 1-11 in Section II.

When we begin interpreting charts the symbols in the wheel can appear confusing to diagnose, for it is difficult to know where to start—which aspect to read first? Or the student may become interested in attempting to "call the shots" with a client and wind up playing the fortune-teller role.

Each personality will reflect the Sun, and the planets in the chart add or detract from the Sun, or life energy. The Sun is the core of personality and the planets, signs and houses become the branches on the tree of life. An astrologer discussing another individual's life is free to discuss potential and possibility only, since the client has the right to choose the manner in which the energy will express. Each aspect will work differently, for everyone is born in a slightly different environment. In *Astrology the Space Age Science** the author discusses the lives of a prince and a pauper born on the same day. Obviously the environment will be different between these two people, but there will also be similarities because both individuals will

---

*Joseph Goodavage, *Astrology the Space Age Science,* Parker Pub., 1966, p. 27.

share common interests and common dilemmas of personality.

The astrologer doesn't have to guess events in the client's past, but can be really helpful to a client in helping him to discover the riddle of the life path. An astrological chart can be a valuable diagnostic tool for an individual who is searching for identity, for meaning in life, for cause factors, for clues as to why certain aspects of life are painful and others not. The astrologer can help a client to discover uncomfortable personality blocks as well as emphasizing natural talents and proclivities. The client is free to use the information any way he wishes.

This chapter is intended to help those who wish to begin reading charts. In the astrologer-client relationship it must be remembered that a relationship is taking place since we can only read another's birth chart in terms of our own consciousness. Each time we do a reading we have a chance to grow, too, for we have been exposed to the details of another person's life experience. As we look at the details of another's life in some kind of order, we have a chance to review our own lives in that kind of order; we have a chance to extend our consciousness to understand another's way of being. It can be an exciting experience.

We begin with the Sun sign to see how the planets reflect the energy of the Sun, how the elements and modes indicate different interests and attitudes.

THE SUN

The Sun is the starting point in the life. It animates us when we are born and it's that part of us that leaves the body when we die. We enter the zodiac, or universe (in our galaxy), at the particular point in the circle where the Sun is posited. It is hoped that we will learn to express the creative essence symbolized by the Sun in our lifetime.

In traditional astrology the Sun represents whether or not we are well-born. It can be used as an indicator of our success with authority figures; it indicates how we can be successful in a career, etc. However, when looking at a chart in terms of *potential*, in determining the environment an individual was raised in, and in looking to see how an individual can free himself of any unhealthy life energies, the relation of the Sun to the other planets becomes very important in the diagnosis.

The Sun indicates the basic archetype. An evaluation of each archetypal image is presented in Chapter 5, Section I. Once we have determined the basic life pattern, interest pattern and social reaction pattern, these patterns are modified and made even more special and individual by the aspects made to the Sun from other planets.

THE MOON

The Moon indicates the feeling function. It symbolizes how we respond to our life experience, what our emotional needs are, how we react to others, how we feel about motherhood, femininity, etc. The Sun and Moon placement by sign and house help to diagnose the personality archetype and how the individual will respond emotionally to that archetype. Spiritual needs are more important when the Sun and Moon are at odds; and the personality will include inner tensions.

The Sun represents the physical father and the Moon the physical mother. The combination of the two gives the foundation upon which to build a sense of human interrelationships.

MERCURY

The planet Mercury moves so quickly in the zodiac that it never gets too far away from the Sun. It can be used to diagnose how we will express ourselves in relation to our Sun sign.

The diagnosis is simple: if Mercury is in the same sign as the Sun, we tend to talk, hear, see, feel, taste in a manner agreeable with the qualities expressed by the Sun. If Mercury is in the sign before or after the Sun, we may say things that don't express the needs of the Sun sign; we communicate differently than we are. This is both easy and difficult, for it enables us to "cover" ourselves in the world, yet it also helps us to present ourselves in a misleading manner so we don't get what we want because we haven't asked for it!

The other planets aspecting Mercury will show how the senses are affected by other influences. This gives even more understanding of how we use our senses individually.

VENUS

Venus never gets too far from the Sun either, so the only aspects of Venus to the Sun will be the conjunction (or one of the minor aspects which aren't discussed in this volume).

The Venus placement helps to diagnose what we want from life versus what we are (Sun). It can help to determine if our "wants" really satisfy our soul urges. Venus indicates what we appreciate around us, how we appreciate love, our home, our friends, how we think of ourselves in a love situation, what kind of love or romance we want, how we receive the love we say we're looking for.

Venus also represents the psychological influence of our mother, what she may have projected when our personality was forming that will affect our concepts of adult relationships. Other planets aspecting Venus tell more about the mother's influence and how our concept of love becomes altered by her attitudes.

MARS

When Mars relates to the Sun by aspect, or merely by its presence in the chart, it shows how a person will act out the Sun sign characteristics. No matter where Mars is in the chart, no matter what sign it's in, it can only act out or enforce the characteristics of the Sun sign. (See Mars, Chapter 5, Section II.)

Mars determines our kind of energy level, our ability to act, to do: it indicates how we experience our own sexuality. The action we take must in some way reflect the energy of the Sun. When diagnosing a chart the relationship between Mars and the Sun (even if there is no aspect) should be considered by sign. Some people have unrealized creative potential because creativity can't easily express itself when the Sun and Mars are not working together.

In Chapter 5, Section I, the archetypal images which come from the Sun sign are discussed. Mars should be considered by sign in respect to how that sign will work with the energy of the Sun. Confusion can occur in the individual if it doesn't. For example, consider an Aquarian Sun with Mars in Libra with no aspect between them. Mars in Libra acts in a socially acceptable manner, soothes the troubled waters, acts in a manner that will keep the status quo. How do the unorthodox or unconventional creative needs of the Sun manifest when the action taken is diplomatic, or, at worst, ingratiating?

The understanding of the Sun's needs and consideration of the Mars energy in relation to those needs can free individuals so they can consciously determine when and where they wish to use the energy. All the energy in a horoscope must be expressed, but we can choose how we wish to do it.

JUPITER

Jupiter added to the Sun indicates how an individual will relate to others. The Sun indicates the solar archetype, the parental atmosphere, etc., and Jupiter shows how people in the early environment related to the individual, as well as how he will naturally tend to reach out to relate to others as an adult.

The sign Jupiter is in is important here, for it tells the manner in which relating will be expressed. Jupiter indicates how we are willing to open up to others, how we will expand our consciousness. I once had a student with Jupiter in Virgo. He came to my classes and criticized nine of them before he could admit that astrology had something to offer in his quest for self-understanding! A person with Jupiter in Pisces will not be critical: he will relate to the qualities of the Sun sign in a martyred way, relating how he has suffered. He may open up to people he feels sorry for rather than to those he considers his peers. In some way he must feel superior to those he can be open with.

When Jupiter is afflicted it can be diagnosed as a block, for it stops the Sun sign from expressing its characteristics in a constructive manner. The personal dilemmas may be too personal, there may be some lack of perspective regarding how one fits into the world. Since Jupiter is considered representative of the energy of personal individuation, until the energy represented by the planet is understood it keeps us from raising our consciousness, from developing an understanding of ourselves as well as others, and keeps us from understanding the environment of which we are a part.

SATURN

When the Sun interacts with Saturn by sign or aspect, it helps to diagnose what the fears and cautions of this individual may be. The Sun represents the essential spirit, the physical father, and the aspects to the Sun indicate how freely this soul may express itself. Saturn indicates the psychological affect of the father on the psyche of the individual in childhood; it eventually forms the basis of our concept of restriction, our self-imposed limitations, areas of the life that are regarded with caution or apprehension.

When there is no aspect between the Sun and Saturn, a perusal of the sign difference can give insight into the energy. For example, if the Sun is in Cancer the archetypal energies of the Cancerian early childhood environment will affect the individual's behavior. If Saturn should be in Virgo and not in any aspect to the Sun, we may say that the Cancerian archetype prevails. But this person will also regard the intellect with even more caution than the average Cancer, for Saturn in Virgo feels apprehensive about the intellect. When the personality was forming, the father was critical of the individual's first attempts at exploring the universe or making decisions. The Cancer Sun will feel apprehensive about exposing the mind, may feel an even stronger need for a university degree. This type of Cancer may fear criticism from authority figures, and because he is born in the sign of Cancer, authority figures for him may be women.

When Saturn opposes, squares or conjuncts the Sun, it indicates an individual who must learn to become responsible for himself, no matter how much it hurts. The father image is not healthy for the father was highly critical of himself. He affected his child in such a way that this individual feels he must defend himself, that he must constantly prove himself to authority figures (Saturn). This type of person may have an inner resentment regarding work, for he may feel that the world should support him. Yet, in order to achieve the process of individuation, he must become self-responsible. There's an old song, "Something for nothin' is nothin'" and it's true. Without responsibility there is no freedom, for how can we be free when someone else is responsible for us?

URANUS

Uranus added to the Sun shows how individualistic we are. Uranus represents individuality, erraticism, self-will, our general behavior pattern. The generation we're born into has an overall behavior pattern that we will imitate.

How does our behavior relate to the constructive expression of the qualities of the Sun archetype? If Uranus doesn't aspect the Sun (or the other personal planets) it merely indicates something about the behavior of the generation. But when aspects between Uranus and the personal planets take place, it indicates that we are unusual in some way—we are honorary Aquarians, so to speak.

This energy lifts us out of the sign type, and during the lifetime we may be forced to grow. When diagnosing a chart, the Uranus aspects indicate *how* the individual is different, and it also can be determined whether or not the person is comfortable being different.

NEPTUNE

Neptune is another generation planet. It symbolizes what the generation is dreaming, how inspired they are, how deluded they may be, and the sign will tell the inspiration/delusion qualities. As this planet interacts with the Sun, it helps in diagnosing the spiritual or creative needs of the individual.

Was this person exposed to creative development in his childhood environment? How can the creative needs best express in relation to the Sun? Children from educated homes are seldom taught about the glory of physical labor; children from laborer's households are seldom taught about the glories of classical piano. In our present society we are more free to express ourselves according to our needs than to the expectancies of a rigid social structure; so modern children are really free to choose how they wish to use creative energy.

PLUTO

If there are no aspects to the Sun or other personal planets, Pluto will merely represent a generation of people—it will indicate the social consciousness of the day, perhaps the morals of the day, perhaps the power needs of the masses, perhaps the unconscious needs of the "people."

When it affects the personal planets by aspect, it can be used to diagnose the urges toward power and control, our attempts at manipulation, our need for creative expression, our need to understand the mythic images of universal communication.

ORDER

When reading a chart, the interest is in determining the motivation of an individual, and it's important to look at the chart in some kind of order. We start with the Sun, for it's the foundation our "house" is built on.

Then comes the Moon, for it describes the vehicle that the soul is encased in and how the vehicle will respond to external stimuli. Then we look at the Ascendant, for that indicates how we will present ourselves. Notice how many masculine and feminine signs are present in the trinity of personality (Sun, Moon, Ascendant), for that will tell whether this is a thinking-intellectual type or a feeling-intuitive type. Notice whether the individual is comfortable with the natural energy of the self. Women born in a masculine polarity and men born in a feminine polarity are seldom really comfortable being themselves in this society. Perhaps they can be put at ease. (See Chapter 3, Section I).

What do the elements say? What does the individual have an abundance of and where are the lacks? (We will seek what we don't have and are self-conscious about what we have a lot of.) How is the energy level? The Cardinal, Fixed and Mutable signs (the modes) will tell how the person activates himself, how he pursues his goals. Is this energy constructive or is it poorly balanced? If it is poorly balanced, perhaps he can be helped to understand how he goes about the business of self-expression, where the pitfalls are, and how to use the energy constructively.

How does he communicate? What is Mercury doing in the chart? The aspects to Mercury will tell you how he is used to expressing himself. Does Mercury agree with the Sun or not? What house is it in? This will be the area of Mercury stress or interest.

What does the individual want? How does Venus tie in with the Sun? Are the desires in life, the need for love and appreciation cooperating with the Sun sign needs? Will he chase a stranger when he needs the tried and true? The astrologer can't make anyone change but can only apprise a person of his needs. Whether or not the appraisal helps will be determined by the age and the individual's ability for introspection.

How does the individual act? What is Mars doing? Does he act out the needs of the Sun in a constructive manner? Will he "cut his nose off to spite his face?" What are the sexual needs—do they conform with the family background and experience that come from the Sun archetype? If not, will the sexual needs cause the person to become involved in unhealthy relationships? Can that be discussed so he can be helped? It's helpful to compare Venus and Mars, for Mars tells about the sexual act and Venus tells about the intellectual concept of what love is. Do the two go together or is there confusion?

Can this person relate to others? What is Jupiter doing by sign and aspect? If Jupiter afflicts the Sun or Moon, this individual may not recognize or relate to the needs of the spiritual or emotional self. Can he be helped to get a handle on it?

What does he feel limited by? How is Saturn aspected in the chart? What house does it affect, and what will he be cautious about? How has the father affected the psyche—what possible restrictions does the person take with him because of that influence? Can a compromise be worked out? How does Saturn influence the Sun's ability to express itself?

Looking at Uranus—how is the individual different? Is he willful or eccentric? Does that eccentricity get him anything? (In diagnosing the needs of another person, be careful that the needs of the chart are considered and not the personal needs of the reader!) Unconstructive behavior may mean that the Sun sign doesn't get a chance to express itself. The end result is personal discomfort and loneliness.

How is Neptune aspected? Will this person be lost in dreams or can the dream be manifested into some kind of reality? How does the Neptunian dream affect the love life, the career, the concept of the family?

Does Pluto aspect the personal planets? It has something to do with attempting to control the life exprience when it does. Is this person blocking emotionally, does he need to control certain parts of himself? If so, there will be afflictions to the personal planets. Does the energy come from the mother or the father? (Father is indicated by Sun and Saturn ties; mother is Moon and Venus ties.) A constricting family environment in general is indicated by Pluto to the Ascendant or to the fourth house in some way.

Where is the balance of energy? If most of the planets are above the horizon (seventh through the twelfth houses) this individual may be more extraverted than introverted. When talking to a person about the diagnosis, it may be wise to speak tactfully and carefully, looking to see how your words are being heard. If most of the planets are in the bottom of the chart (first through sixth houses) this individual is more an introvert and will better be able to hear what you have to say, for the chances are that he's already thought about it.

If most of the planets are in the eastern half of the chart, (the tenth house through the third) the individual is a self-starter. If the astrologer opens the door an inch, this individual will move a mile on the information. He will take what he hears and run with it, make use of it, use it to guide himself. If most of the planets are in the western half (the fourth house through the ninth) this individual will most often be recommended by others; he is unable to be a self-starter for he needs to work cooperatively with groups. He wants to be free and independent. The self-starter type wants to be helped and gets tired of going it alone; the helped type wants to be independent and doesn't want to be obligated to others. Each must learn to use his energy the way it is presented however, and it's easier to use when he cooperates with the natural tendencies.

When reading a chart, you don't have to guess what the client's previous life has been. You can talk about the possibility of behavior and let the client draw his own conclusions. Each aspect suggests certain kinds of behavior. Even though an aspect can predict that one will react in a certain manner, the individual can either use the aspect or be used by it. Those who don't understand what an aspect means in terms of personality development may feel as though they are victims. Once they understand the childhood circumstances that enhanced the development of a particular conceptualization of life within them, they are free to change their reactions.

Someone who is very young (under the age of twenty-five) really hasn't felt himself yet. He is still experimenting with the idea of being a grownup and will continue to do so until he has passed through the first Saturn cycle (age twenty-eight or twenty-nine). When reading for young people, it's wise to do so gently. As people mature they learn how they react to certain life experiences, and when you tell them about their aspects they will know what you are talking about because they have already felt them. You may help them gain insight into themselves, you may even help them to change their future, for they can already relate what you are saying to their past life experience.

This kind of astrology cannot be used to predict upcoming events, but it can be used to help someone understand what has motivated him to become involved with life from his particular perspective. Once we know why we do what we do we can alter our circumstances.

I recently did a reading for a woman in her late sixties. I was not enchanted at the prospect for she is older than I am, and I had heard that she was not particularly open about astrology. However, a personal crisis had prompted her to accept help from an astrologer. How do you talk to a grandmother about the motivation in her life? Most of it has already happened. How can you help her change what's coming up? And what are your personal views on aging? As a reader, do you think her life is over? Well, it isn't.

This woman is a Sagittarian with a positive sign trinity (Moon in Aquarius and Gemini rising). She has a t-square with the Moon at the point—Saturn in Taurus squares the Moon and opposes Jupiter; Jupiter, as well as Mars, squares the Moon from Scorpio. I began by telling her about the archetypal images of Sagittarius, the power parent, the personal needs. I talked to her about her trinity, the masculine energy, the need to develop her mind. I mentioned career being more important to her than her need to be a housewife, remembering that because she was born in 1910 she may have some guilt about not enjoying housework!

She regarded me with great suspicion. We began to discuss the Saturn–Moon square, how she was distrustful of men, how she wouldn't share her emotional self with her husband (see Saturn–Moon aspects, Chapter 2, Section II). At this point she opened up like a flower and the session began to really progress, because her husband had told her the same thing! She has one child (two others were stillborn) and had been feeling guilty about not having more children. Her chart didn't call for them, it called for a career.

She worked with her husband (they had a business together) and since his death a few years ago she has been handling it alone. We discussed her idealism and how it affects her business relationships. She communicated her problems to me. We talked about whether or not she should keep her business since that was a problem—should she keep her business and was she too old to get married again? She was past retirement age but still going strong, and the business life was good for her. The guilts were removed about the children, for deep inside she knew that she had not wanted to have them; she felt the birthing problems were somehow caused by her, for all good women of her generation and background should want lots of children and she didn't. Her chart didn't need them.

We discussed her right to have a relationship at her age. She began to think she could work out some of the Saturn–Moon square in the next relationship. She said, "Poor..., I wish I could apologize to him for not having been more open."

She later told her daughter that our talk was very good for her, that she really benefited from it. You may not know how you're doing until after the session is over. You don't really help anybody, they help themselves. You merely read the symbols, put them in context with the person's age, and let them draw the conclusions. No matter how old someone is they can still grow, they can still attain consciousness. Between the ages of fifty and seventy, the psyche is most ready to receive spiritual instruction. When we try to become initiates at age twenty-five, the idea is nice but we are giving up a part of our growing experience. After the children are gone, after the major career heights have been attained, that's when we explore philosophy best, for we bring experience and maturity to it.

Each reading you do will be an individual experience. After you've read for fifty people or so, you'll begin to see how astrology works. You'll see the difference between the obvious outer manifestations of personality and the more subtle inner workings of the mind. You'll see that each person is striving for something—that we all have a lot in common. We all seek inner peace, we seek an emotional relationship that brings us comfort. We do the same things from many different perspectives.

People who become involved in astrology are usually looking for answers to their own problems and inner conflicts. They find the subject so interesting they sometimes become professionals. The professional astrologer is usually a person who needs to feel needed, who wants to do something to help people, who enjoys helping people find that which is difficult to attain.

As students and as counselors we have responsibilities. When we do a reading we are involving another person's life in our own. It's important to remember that each person has his or her own individuality, his or her own life path, a different drummer perhaps. We have our life path, too, and although we are talking to someone about their life path, we don't have the right to inflict ours on them. Our political, racial, ethnic, religious and sexual values should be carefully considered, for if we disapprove of a client we will show it. On the other hand, we are going to read the symbols in a chart in terms of how we see life. Most of the time a client will be drawn to us because we have a similar vision.

When you start to do readings, look at your own chart. As you continue to do readings, keep looking at your chart. What have you learned? Are you facing the responsibilities in your own chart that you've discussed in someone else's? Are you using your chart as a cop-out? Have you forgotten those aspects that need to grow? How much theosophy, philosophy, sociology have you studied over the years? Have you studied any psychology? Do you know about metaphysics? Or the humanistic philosophies? Do you still have basic ethnic prejudices? Is one religion better than another? If so, keep reading—you're not there yet. The astrologer is a wise man, a wise woman. Are you?

Keywords for the Planets

Sun I am.

Moon I feel, I respond to the world.

Mercury I communicate, I talk, I learn, I hear.

Venus I want, I want to be, I want to love.

Mars I act, I want sexually.

Jupiter I relate, I open up to, I expand.

Saturn I take seriously, I regard with caution, I'm afraid of.

Uranus I behave, my behavior versus my action, my ability to open up my consciousness, I'm eccentric about.

Neptune I dream of being, I inspire, I aspire, I delude.

Pluto I'm unconsciously motivated, my generation is unconsciously motivated, I'm obsessed by, I want to be in control of.

Keywords for the Signs

Aries intellectual, aggressive, idealistic.

Taurus practical, scientific, building, dictatorial.

Gemini curious, contrary, controversial, ever changing.

Cancer possessive, sensitive, fluctuating, emotional, little boyish or girlish, big Momma, big Daddy.

Leo proud, sensitive, with proper respect, the "should/ought's".

Virgo critical, self-demeaning, detail oriented.

Libra competitive, fawning, placating, democratic.

Scorpio searching, feeling unwanted, strong needs for love, researching.

Sagittarius freedom, independence, hoof-in-mouth disease.

Capricorn proper, traditional, powerful, corporate.

Aquarius unconventional, unorthodox, tenacious.

Pisces martyred, sensitive, long-suffering, spiritual.

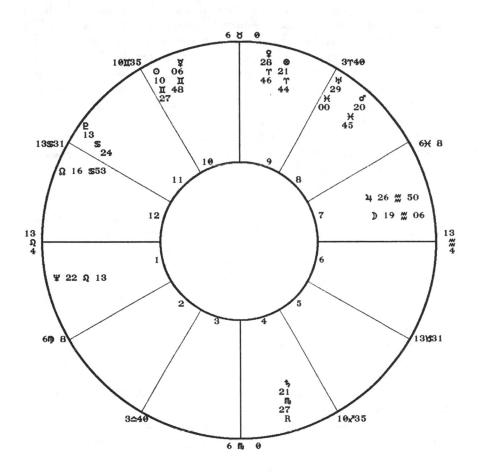

LET US NOW SEE HOW WHAT WE'VE DISCUSSED WORKS when interpreting a chart. In order to determine the motivation of personality by working with a horoscope, we must begin to look for underlying causes for certain kinds of behavior. We cannot determine the career or the life interest of any individual from a really specific point, for each individual experiences a different childhood environment, a different financial and educational background. Bearing that in mind, we will begin our interpretation using this particular system.

This lady has a Gemini Sun, Aquarius Moon and Leo rising. She has 6 planets in masculine signs and 4 planets in feminine signs. If we consider only the Sun in Gemini, we know that she was born into a father-dominated household, that she was a child who imitated her father, or formed her life philosophy because of her father's philosophy. The Sun archetype indicates that her parents communicated with each other in a manner she didn't understand; she would eventually feel deserted by her dad, for he would find other interests; she would grow up to be somewhat suspicious of men. The Gemini sign type, because of the father influence, seeks intellectual development, seeks to understand the words, seeks consciousness by developing the mind.

The Gemini female will be uncertain of her own sexuality. In relationships with men, she prefers some kind of intellectual companionship, and as much as she may need confirmation of her femaleness (because of the six masculine signs and a masculine trinity), she will seek companionship. She will be difficult to understand, for the Gemini type needs new circumstances, new situations; she loves to socialize and to relate to new people. She may be accused of being flirtatious, for her partner feels left out while she explores the new and the different. (When you understand that the Gemini type loves to socialize, you begin to realize that she is not searching for new partners but that she learns from socializing. She may have to learn to share this information with her partner.)

Because she has a preponderance of masculine planets, and because all the planets in her trinity (the Sun, the Moon and Ascendant) are masculine as well, she tends to feel insecure about being a woman, and the insecurity may not even be conscious. This kind of woman needs a lot of reassurance that she is really feminine; and she sometimes confuses men, for they don't understand her needs. She will probably take good care of her appearance: she will wear make-up and pretty clothes, keep her nails done, her hair beautiful. The outsider will see her as a very feminine type. But in the case of the positive sign trinity, the excessive manifestation of femininity is often a cover-up for an inner insecurity about the feminine nature. This leads to insecurity in man-woman relationships, for she will need a lot of reassurance about her beauty, charm and feminine appeal.

Her mind works in what is considered a masculine fashion—she is more a thinker than an intuitive, feeling type; she rationalizes, she will handle each new crisis by thinking it through. Most men have been taught that women feel, that most women make intuitive decisions. They will be confused by this particular woman, for they see her thinking through her decisions, almost sounding like a man's concept of another man. If she is criticized by him for making rational decisions, she may become even more confused or insecure.

So far we've only looked at the Sun, the trinity and the masculine-feminine count. Let's take a look at what her father was doing when she was born, for she is a father-dominated child. We can establish her physical father's state of mind by looking at the aspects to the Sun.

She has the Sun square Mars, which indicates that Dad was in some kind of a self-destructive phase in his life when she was born. He may have been unemployed, or at least extremely unhappy; he wasn't doing anything positive or constructive when she was young. The Sun trines the Moon, so it looks as though the parents were happy about the condition of life they were experiencing. It looks as though they expected to suffer. Because Mars squares the Sun, the child was born into an environment where she was not welcome; the whole family wasn't welcome. This may mean that she was ethnically different, or socially unapprovable in the neighborhood. In this case, was she an illegitimate child? Were her parents disapproved of because they were not married? Or were they married and not working? We don't know.

Mars square the Sun helped her to develop a lack of personal security because the neighborhood vibrated disapproval or contempt, and she began to think those vibrations were normal. She would grow up to have little sense of impending danger; she can walk into situations without considering her safety, she may not consider how unfriendly situations may affect her future. Mars square the Sun indicates that she acts (Mars) against (square) her own best interests (Sun). This means that she can be what is sometimes called self-destructive. We don't know how this will manifest in her life. It may come up for discussion during the session with her.

What did the father do to this child on a psychological level? How did he affect her psyche, what inhibitions and insecurities does she carry that come from him?

Saturn is in Scorpio in the fourth house and it's retrograde. Retrograde action often indicates that one uses the energy of the planet against the self, or that one matures slowly in that particular facet of life. Saturn in the fourth house indicates a severe, unhappy or cold childhood environment. Saturn in any sign in the fourth put a damper on the childhood environment, but the sign Scorpio also indicates that the child was not particularly wanted, or welcomed in the family. The child grows up subscribing to some subconscious feeling of being unwanted. This feeling will combine in this case with the insecurity about femininity that comes from the masculine trinity.

This chart can indicate a female who needs a lot of emotional security. But we're not through yet. Saturn squares Neptune and also squares the Moon. It trines Mars, Uranus and Pluto. Looking at the trine, we see that her father was not uncommon to his generation; many men were disillusioned at the time of this woman's birth. Because we are dealing with a Water sign grand trine, she is creative and can express her creativity in work she chooses in adult life. In a personal sense, there is potential for a lot of emotional suffering and self-imposed martyrdom. Saturn in Scorpio feels unwanted; Pluto in Cancer feels emotionally orphaned on an unconscious level; Mars in Pisces acts like a martyr. So in a personal sense, this can indicate an oversensitivity where sex and love are concerned. In the work department, it indicates a creative energy and an ability to work cooperatively with men, as long as there is no personal involvement.

Because Mars rules the sex life and Pluto rules the unconscious and Saturn symbolizes the feelings of restriction and limitation that we impose on ourselves as a result of the father's influence, the chances are this person confuses sex and suffering. Look at the square to the Moon. As we discussed before in the chapters on aspects, the Moon square Saturn indicates that the father (Saturn) was not understanding of the mother's emotional needs. In the case under discussion, the father also seemed to put a damper on this woman's emotional responses to life during her childhood, so the feeling function is restricted or repressed. Usually this aspect serves to inhibit the emotional life and love relationships more than it affects the career. The aspect tends to produce a person who has the ancient disease called melancholia—modern depression.

A woman with the Moon square Saturn will be apt to have much difficulty expressing her emotional needs to her lover. She can maintain open relationships with men who are friends, but once the relationship includes sex, some kind of withdrawal is likely to take place. Unintentionally, she begins to expect that this man won't want to listen to her, won't respond to her needs, because Dad didn't respond to Mother's and he seldom responded to hers as a child. She has been programmed to think that men don't really care about the things that she cares about. She will be more eager to share her deep feelings and her innermost dreams and ideas with friends, keeping that part of herself from her lover. If she picks a man who is basically an unfeeling or an inconsiderate person, it will not be abnormal; for deep within the psyche is an image of men being that way. Should a really nice man fall in love with her, the chances are she would not appreciate his love because a warm and truly loving man doesn't fit in with her ''normal'' image of man in her subconscious. Her personal concept of what love is doesn't include caring, for Dad didn't care for Mom that much, he didn't support her mother's enthusiasms, so why should any normal man support hers? Or, would she ultimately fall in love with a man who treats her like her father treated her mother?

Looking at Saturn further, we see that it squares Neptune, and Neptune opposes the Moon as well as the Ascendant. This indicates some delusion as to who her father was, what kind of a man he was. The mother may have projected some grand delusion or illusion regarding the father and who he was. When this woman was a child, her mother may have told her that Daddy left because he was irresponsible, unknowingly fostering the image in the child's psyche that men are not to be trusted. Perhaps the mother told her daughter that women are always left by the men they love. Or the father may have disappeared because he could no longer cope with the mother's behavior. We don't know what the real story is here, we just know there's some delusion about her father at play.

Some illusion also was probably attached to the image of what a woman is, what a woman should be, or what kind of woman the mother was, due to the Moon–Neptune aspect. This woman will be apt to imitate her mother's concept of what a woman is, and she may create for herself similar problems to those which her mother faced. The circumstances can be better understood (or explained) by the client herself than by the astrologer, for we don't have to guess the action that has taken place. The additional aspects to the Moon and Saturn indicate some falsehood connected to the parental history; this person may have been raised by parents whose life style was unclear or unfocused during the formative years, engendering a sense of insecurity in this lady.

An astrologer can help a client sort out the parental effect. The client may be interested in doing this if her emotional life is painful enough or difficult enough to cause her to search for her inner motivation of personality. Because the father didn't relate well to the mother, this woman is apt to assume that men don't relate well to women. Her mother and father were both a part of a lie or delusion that was foisted upon her in order to protect the parents' personal secrets. The Neptune creativity can be released once the childhood distortions are made conscious and relinquished.

Saturn squares Jupiter as well. These two planets must work together if we are to be free from the bondage to the parents, if we are to be free to go on in life and achieve freedom and consciousness. Because they are square in this chart, the trip will be difficult. If Jupiter represents how she expands, how she opens up to new situations, and how she relates, the square to Saturn indicates that if she wants to expand, to mature, or to have good relationships, she will have to "kick the father habit." The subconscious effect of her father will inhibit her ability to relate. When the transiting aspects permit the Jupiter facet of personality to open up, they will at the same time activate the Saturn fears of abandonment, of being unwanted, of feeling restricted. So we have here a person who is both open and restricted or inhibited simultaneously.

Because Jupiter conjuncts the Moon and is opposed by Neptune, it seems that this woman will be predisposed to open up through her emotional involvements. The chances are she will be more open to people she meets because of her work or career achievements. The Moon–Neptune opposition suggests that she may open up or relate to people for the wrong reasons, because the opposition indicates a chance for deluding oneself about one's emotional or intuitive responses. As she opens up, or begins to relate emotionally, she will eventually become sexually involved thereby activating the Moon–Saturn square discussed previously.

Venus symbolizes the mother's psychological affect on the individual during the formative years. Venus is in Aries, and some astrologers say that Venus there is a lusty Venus. In modern terms, let's say that this lady has a "lusty" eye for romance, that she may contemplate men in terms of their romantic appeal to her. Venus is tempered by Neptune, suggesting that she will search for a love relationship that encompasses both a chemical reaction on a sexual level (Venus in Aries) as well as a highly spiritual bond (Neptune in Leo). She wants a strong spiritual bond and a meaningful relationship—for that is what will transform sex into something special rather than it being merely "animalistic." (Note: Because of the emphasis on her femininity on a superficial level, this type of mate may be hard for her to find since most men will only see her sexual female projection.)

However, Neptune clouds the issue and the trine to Venus suggests that her mother may have some unusual attitudes about love. If this woman follows in her mother's footsteps, she will not pick her lovers clearly but will pick them because of some fantasy she has. We all imitate our parents, but imitation doesn't mean that we do exactly the same things in exactly the same way the parents did; we are not nearly so obvious. We tend to do a similar thing; but while we are doing it, it looks very different to us. So this lady may delude herself about the men she picks. She may not pick the same type that Mom did, but she may end up being deluded in a similar fashion, just like Mom was.

Before going any further, let's look at the elements. She has 2 Fire, 0 Earth, 4 Air, and 4 Water planets. This will tell us something about her needs as a person. We seek what we lack and we avoid what we have a lot of. Two Fire planets indicate a need for attention. This isn't serious until that need is combined with the Leo Ascendant—which means that she needs both attention and approval. The 0 Earth planets indicate that she is searching for both material and emotional security. This poses a bit of a problem: material security can be attained, but will she ever be emotionally secure? There is a t-square between Saturn, the Moon and Neptune, as well as a grand trine between Saturn, Mars and Pluto. A t-square and a grand trine usually make material success easy to attain, for there is creative energy to fall back on and discordant energy to motivate her to keep going. So the material success will be fairly well assured, if she is old enough to have earned it. But in the emotional department, she needs lots of reassurance because of the 0 Earth.

There are other factors in the chart that will impede her attaining security. First, she is a Gemini—one who wanders and explores the creative mind. She wants to communicate with others, and when she does, her social behavior may be misconstrued as flirtation. Flirtation doesn't bind a relationship because the partner often gets jealous and tends to stop the compliments that the 0 Earth needs. The Moon square Saturn doesn't expect emotional fulfillment, but the 0 Earth needs it. With the Saturn–Moon square, the chances are that she will choose a man who can't fulfill her emotional needs anyway, because she never tells him what they are. Because she has no Earth planets, it's important that she become emotionally secure. How can she work through that kind of dilemma if she doesn't understand what it is? It is only when we become *aware* of our needs that we can begin to make sure they will be fulfilled.

She has 4 Air planets, and this usually indicates a person who is not fond of university degrees. If circumstances permit, she will get a degree; environmental conditions might make it mandatory for her social status. However, if the social position doesn't warrant education, the chances are she will prefer to learn from the "school of life." A degree gives one freedom, but learning from people and from life experience is more fun when one has four Air planets. However, with four or more Air planets, she doesn't know what she wants, and often resents others for giving her the necessary guidance. (This attitude is reinforced by the contrary attitudes which Geminis can sometimes foster as well.) She may need to work in a constantly changing surrounding, for she may be easily bored by routine. A career in the media—radio, television or film will probably satisfy her needs because of the 0 Earth and the 4 Air planets plus the Leo Ascendant and the first house Neptune.

Four planets in Water indicate another facet of personality because they signify a sensitive nature, but one that is afraid to give. Considering relationship potential, lots of Water poses a problem. She will be liable to give more physically than emotionally—she may make love with her body but not with her soul. A great deal of Water in the chart suggests a person who is afraid that she will be destroyed if she is rejected by a loved one—she can become too involved. In order to protect her vulnerability, it's easier to project a certain "hardness" that others interpret as noncaring. Usually, just the opposite is true, for she cares a great deal. In order to derive satisfaction from an emotional relationship, however, it is necessary to relate. The other party needs to feel needed and wanted as well. If she can't open up, if she can't respond emotionally, eventually the other person will withdraw. The high Water count person has to consciously learn how to give emotional support and feedback to her loved ones for she is unfamiliar with the idea.

How will she make changes in her life? The balance of action is determined by counting the modes: the Cardinal, Fixed and Mutable planets. She has 2 Cardinals, 4 Fixed and 4 Mutables. She doesn't have a great deal of energy because she only has 2 Cardinals. She may have less stamina than she thinks she has. Endurance comes from the Fixed planets, as does her stubbornness and rigidity. She doesn't want to change, she will stubbornly endure even when she doesn't have the stamina to keep up with her commitments. The 4 Mutable planets indicate that she is open to change—on occasion. The 4 Fixed and 4 Mutable give her a "sit-and-stew" personality. She will change her mind a lot, for she listens to other people a lot. Then she goes home and worries about it! This kind of energy needs to be channeled; it can waste a lot of time if it isn't. The 4 Fixed planets give a fixity of purpose, the mutability indicates that she will worry about decisions she makes.

Her way of doing things, her way of taking action, will be influenced by the Leo Ascendant as well, for planets in Leo indicate a person who wants approval from others. If her need for approval comes from outside herself, she may tend to put herself into "victim" situations. She wants approval from others; they sense her need and withdraw their approval—she may find herself doing things that she inherently doesn't approve of in order to remain on the other person's good side.

In order for this personality to become emotionally secure, she will have to take responsibility for herself, to understand that she is responsible for the situations she creates. If she understands her needs, she can understand the kinds of partnerships she creates; she can then begin to develop ones that are healthy.

There are many other things that can be said about this chart, but this is the beginning of a session. After talking this much—if the client has let you go on that long—it's time to let her talk, to let her share some of her experience with you.

The personality we have been discussing in terms of her childhood is Marilyn Monroe.* There is a great deal of biographical information available about this woman, and I recommend that interested students check it out. Some of the information will be distorted because she is a famous person, and such information is usually colored with exaggeration. But if a stranger came to you with this chart, would you have made some accurate and helpful statements?

**Born June 1, 1926, 9:30 AM, Los Angeles, California. The data was taken from the Circle Book of Charts, compiled by S. Erlewine.

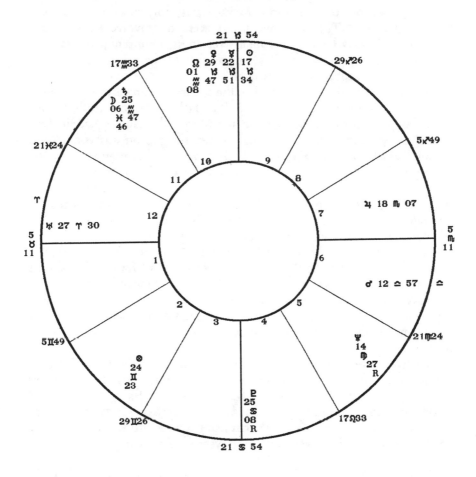

THIS IS THE CHART OF A MALE WITH SUN IN CAPRICORN, Moon in Pisces and Taurus rising. The trinity (Sun, Moon and Ascendant) is in feminine signs as well, so we know immediately that he will be an intuitive, sensitive type. His environment will affect how he uses this sensitivity. For example, someone from a less educated background may develop a strong sense of "macho" to cover it. A child from a more educated background may be encouraged to develop creative skills such as painting or classical music. If this person gets self-liberated enough to listen to his intuition, the chart can be most creative.

Seven planets out of ten are in feminine signs; only three planets appear in masculine signs. The masculine sign placements involve Mars, Saturn and Uranus. It may be that this man's maleness, or macho, will emerge only in sexual situations—for it seems as though he might separate sex from love, but we'll go into this later.

His Sun is in Capricorn, so he has the Capricorn archetype: he comes from a mother-dominated background. The father was powerfully passive in this case, for Pluto opposes the Sun and Mars and Uranus square it. Dad was vainly contending for some power when this person was young, and the child would have felt the struggle that went on between the parents. He would have interpreted it as a struggle between Mommies and Daddies, or all men and all women in later years. If he felt this struggle as a child, he would endeavor to avoid being in his father's position when he becomes an adult. He may only become involved in relationships where he either holds all the power, or he gets out.

The Capricorn male learns his behavior patterns from his mother. He wants to be strong like he thought his father was, but for some reason he feels that his father was unattainable. And, in order to gain his freedom, he will have to approach the men that he meets with attitudes similar to those of his mother. His mother "handled" men, and he will handle them in a fashion similar to hers. She was a bit contemptuous of men, and he will be too.

Let's look at how his father affected him. The chart shows a wide conjunction from Saturn to the Moon, if the birth time is right. I'm always suspicious of the time factor, expecially in charts of well-known people, for misinformation is rampant, and even carefully kept records can be wrong. In diagnosing a chart, I have found that using a wide orb works, but many astrologers work with a very different system. You'll have to pick your own.

When Saturn conjuncts the Moon, it indicates that the father adversely affected the mother, that she was unable to receive the emotional caring that she needed from him. In the case of a male child, it can indicate several possibilities—either the child doesn't care for the mother or he over-compensates for his father and cares for his mother too much. When Saturn conjuncts the Moon, the feeling function is restricted in some way. This man may relate to immature women, women who tend to be sick all the time, or women who can't cope with the responsibilities of maturity—such as the sexual or domestic responsibilities engendered by a marriage. He may choose an immature woman because his own feeling function is immature or limited, and in this case, this man will want to feel in control, or superior to the woman with whom he relates.

The Saturn–Moon conjunction also indicates that the father restricted any spontaneous feeling responses that the child had, so the child tends to avoid sharing his dreams and druthers with anyone. He may develop melancholia; moodiness or depressions may occur with no apparent reason. He will tend to be apprehensive of emotional commitments, as if some small voice in the subconscious is saying, "Be careful, you'll get hurt if you reach out to feel this feeling."

The mother seems to be a far more powerful figure than the father, although her affect on this person is somewhat strange. The Moon is in Pisces, which is a sensitive and wistful sign. It suggests that the mother played the role of martyr during this man's formative years—that she suffered and endured great pain, and that she was sure to let him know how she suffered. Some astrologers say that a Pisces Moon indicates a very old soul—or at least one that can feel compassion for other people.

With the Moon opposing Neptune, one begins to wonder about the kinds of misinformation the mother taught this child about women. This opposition is the setup that can keep boys tied to their mothers for life. "Good girls don't have sex, sex is wrong," or "You have to be careful about how you pick a woman to be your wife—be sure she hasn't been messing around," says the mother. She may tell him delusions or fantasies about her past as well, confusing early feeling memories he has of her with the stories she's told. This type of child puts mother on a pedestal and finds it difficult later on to find another woman as good as his mother is. It isn't an incestuous situation as much as it is a bond formed because of early childhood programming. Some illusion/delusion about what the mother is, or about what women are has taken place. The Moon in Pisces indicates inordinate sensitivity, and because it's so sensitive, there may be some feeling for art and music. Because of the closeness to the mother, the feeling for the intuitive-creative side of life may be intensified.

Looking to see how the mother affected this man from a psychological point, Venus is in Capricorn squared by Uranus and opposed by Pluto. The mother was a controlling lady, says the Pluto opposition. When Uranus squares Venus, it indicates that the mother probably made her decisions without consulting the family or her husband. Since the ability to appreciate love, as well as give it, comes from Venus we may conclude that the Uranus square here indicates a person who suddenly jumps into a love affair and as suddenly jumps out, leaving a trail of broken hearts behind him. Because his mother did it when he was forming his behavior patterns, he thinks this is normal behavior.

These aspects create a certain amount of inner tension. If he is a sensitive soul caught in the middle of some early family progamming, it can be explained astrologically and perhaps the tension can be somewhat relieved. Pluto opposing Venus doesn't bode well for the mother influence either, for it suggests she was a controlling and perhaps obsessive individual.

Taurus rising (as well as Taurus planets in a male trinity) indicates that the child may have been used as a pawn between the parents. He may have been used to separate them, to assist in the avoidance of the sexual role that is usually associated with marriage. This Ascendant can indicate a child who slept with his mother, who was allowed in the parents bedroom too often, who conveniently kept the parents from having private time with each other.

This man has Taurus rising and Cancer ruling the fourth house cusp; Pluto is in the fourth, indicating strong power games in the early environment. Pluto in the fourth signifies that the childhood environment was highly controlled. It appears that he arrived in a family that was cold, uncaring, and fraught with personal difficulties between the parents; power games, control games were going on—and the child was used as a "football" between two warring adults. It may well be that the father lost the game, for Saturn is not strongly aspected according to my system, and Mars squares the Sun which further indicates that Dad was in a self-destructive phase when the child was born.

The Sun–Mars square causes the individual to be as careless about himself as his father was. He may be unaware of danger, he may not care about his future when he takes action. With Uranus squaring the Sun from the other direction, he would grow up to be an erratic, eccentric and perhaps self-willed individual who will do what he wishes with himself and those he associates with.

When Uranus and Mars both square the Sun, the individual gets caught in the middle of a lot of destructive energy. Mars square the Sun says "I act against my self," and Uranus square the Sun says "I behave against myself." "My behavior and my willfulness, or my eccentricity, is probably self-destructive and so are my actions." Unless he is careful or conscious, much time can be wasted pursuing unhealthy or foolish goals.

Because he is a mother-dominated male, with a feminine trinity, he may have severe self-worth problems, but we won't know until we talk with him. The father (symbolized by the Sun and Saturn) was self-destructive when this person's personality was forming. Although this man is mother-dominated, he will eventually realize that both he and his father are males, and he may fear that he may grow up to be like his father. He may have apprehension about a lack of "manhood"; he feels the intuitive, sensitive energy and he may think that his response to life is too sensitive, that he doesn't have a "normal male" response. He may also feel that men are "losers" since his father lost to his mother. The combination of energies indicates self-worth problems, self-destructive tendencies and a fear of failing as a man. This type of situation needs tactful, diplomatic and sensitive counseling.

He has three t-squares in his chart, which makes him highly motivated as far as work is concerned. (A t-square is an opposition fenced in by two squares, and it creates tension as well as stimulates action.) He might not consider his problems before he sets out to accomplish his goals. There are no grand trines in his chart, so the work he does will be arduous, and when he gets to where he's going he will still have to work. Easy success needs a grand trine to fall back on.

Because of the hard aspects (the Sun, Moon, Mercury, Venus and the Ascendant are all afflicted), he has a great deal of energy to bring to any career, and a lot to prove. He may not be able to relate to anyone, he may not have a comfortable personal life, and he may sublimate those problems through his work. He may have a great talent to offer. However, the Mars–Mercury square indicates that he doesn't listen to anyone, probably takes advice poorly, and he may not get his rudiments together. He may have trouble in school; either he was not scholarly or he was a snob. How will that affect career?

Let's look at what he needs from life. He has 1 Fire planet, 4 Earth, 2 Air and 3 Water. We seek what we lack; he lacks Fire, so he is essentially seeking attention and intellectual interests. The 1 Fire planet indicates a need for a great deal of attention. He wants to be known, he wants to be seen, he wants to be recognized. People with few Fire planets should get some public recognition for the work they do—for they can get some of their need for attention satisfied on the job, thereby allowing an emotional relationship to solve other needs. When people have 0 to 1 Fire planet, there is a tendency to be extremely demanding. This person may attempt to be "center-stage" all his life, constantly demanding reverence and homage from his peers. It can be difficult to love this person, for he may need to totally control everyone around him. The behavior can manifest as someone who stands and waves his arms in the air when everyone else in the room is sitting; or a person who interrupts any conversation not started by him; it may be a person who hits the booze or drugs for spite when he doesn't get enough attention. Adding this to the Mars–Mercury square indicates a possibility that he may really sulk if he doesn't get his own way.

He has 4 Earth planets which suggest that he is sturdy and in many ways self-secure and stubborn; he wants what he wants when he wants it. So he can be considered selfish. He will not sell his soul for love or money; he has too many Earth planets for that. He will probably enjoy his pleasures and comforts but not at the expense of his freedom. The Earth count suggests that he will be difficult to change, for he doesn't care about emotional or material security. The low Fire count indicates he needs attention, but he can get that from anyone. If a lover says, "You must change or I'll leave," he will let her leave. If an employer says, "You must cooperate or you'll be fired," the chances are he will quit. He doesn't really care about your opinion of him. If he can learn to give in a little, learn to cooperate a little, he will feel better, and perhaps he will have better friendships. The Earth count does make him quite secure; it helps him to stop some of the self-doubt.

The 2 Air planets indicate that he has a curious mind, and will seek to educate himself during his lifetime. Although he may never earn a college degree, he will be curious—which means he'll read, study and pursue subjects that interest him. He may adore theory and systems, so he'll want to learn a few. He may not be particularly social; he may prefer reading to partying.

The 3 Water planets indicate that he is moderately sensitive and will hold back a bit to avoid being hurt in love relationships. But, if he ever decides to trust someone, he will be able to love. There are other factors in his chart that make loving difficult, however, and he will need to work them out before he is able to give a relationship a fair shake.

How will he expend his energy? He has 6 Cardinal, 2 Fixed and 2 Mutable planets. This guy is a dynamo! Do now, think later! He will involve himself in activities quickly—take the town by storm, so to speak! He will need to learn how to think things through if he is interested in becoming more responsible for his actions. He may solve all his problems by taking immediate action. And because Mars squares his Sun, his actions may not be well planned. Because of the 6 Cardinals and the 4 Earth, he may jump from one conclusion to another without thinking about anything, except that he didn't get his own way. His reactions to someone else's attitudes will be to take some form of action. If he has a relationship problem to work through, he will probably leave the relationship rather than work it out. If his wife or girlfriend disagrees with him forcefully, or even if a powerful man disagrees with him, he may hit the bottle. He might walk away from a troublesome situation rather than cope with it. He may have a reputation for being eccentric or erratic, and that behavior may have something to do with his own self-undoing.

He has 2 Fixed planets, indicating that he has some inner security, but he doesn't have a lot of stamina. He gets some help from the 4 Earth planets as far as stability is concerned, for they help him keep his feet on the ground. His stamina may be more braggadocio than real, more stubbornness than a true belief in what he's doing.

The 2 Mutable planets indicate that he is somewhat open to listening to others—but not much. He prefers to do things his way; he may not be considerate of others needs. If he is self-employed, these characteristics don't matter much, but if he works for a large organization, he will have to learn how to curb his independent tendencies and share his decisions with others.

When considering his emotional needs, this balance of planets matters, for the 6 Cardinal planets might influence his jumping into spur-of-the-moment relationships, as would his Venus–Uranus square.

This chart indicates major problems with emotional relationships. The Taurus Ascendant indicates a person who may concentrate on his sensual appetites. If he can't satisfy them, Uranus conjunct the Ascendant and Jupiter opposing it indicate some lack of cooperation with others. He feels he must always compromise, for the Jupiter–Ascendant opposition suggests that he doesn't relate to the way others see him (the Ascendant masquerade). He may appear to be a little dictator, an authoritarian type, who appears to have little regard for others. He also has little concept of what he looks like to others. The opposition activates marriage problems, for if he relates to his wife's needs (Jupiter in the seventh) he feels he'll have to compromise his life style (the Ascendant) and vice versa. It looks as though he might resent her needs, feeling that they will take from his career, or his self-image.

He has spiritual problems; he needs to develop spiritually, and he may feel guilty about his sex drive because of that. He also may feel that he's a homosexual. If he isn't, he may form relationships with women he can totally control for he will be afraid to have a woman around him who is as strong as his mother was. He may be too close to his mother. This may further accent his fear of homosexuality. There may be a strong love/hate polarity between him and his mother that he may have difficulty breaking. This feeling will be caused by the mother-dominated Sun, the feminine trinity, the Moon–Neptune opposition, as well as the Venus–Pluto opposition. The Mars square the Sun doesn't help. If he can understand the tie to his mother, if he can break away from her, not to hate her, but to put his relationship with her into some healthy perspective, he will be able to separate her from the archetypal Mother image in his psyche. Then he will have more productive relationships. Otherwise, he may be stuck in some form of self-destructive behavior.

This type of information would have to be discussed very carefully. It's important not to remove all the self-protective barriers that he may have set up. He would probably not come to an astrologer for business advice. He might permit a consultation if he is in enough personal pain. People don't come to see astrologers when they feel good—they come when life is uncomfortable or unhappy; they want to hear some alternatives to the pain. This man needs to hear how and why he functions the way he does.

When diagnosing a chart intellectually, you don't necessarily have to discuss all your information with the client—you don't have to prove what you know. But you can use that knowledge to help you discuss his problems, his discomfort, his alternatives. This personality may not be ready to hear all you know. If you are perceptive, you can feed him a little information at a time and watch how he digests it. You may want to suggest some form of therapy, for self-worth problems are not easy to cure. If he's had therapy already, your insights may help him proceed further. He may need someone to talk with, so he can safely share his feelings about himself. The session may be helpful to him if he has a chance to communicate.

Because he is a "famous" person, we may think he's happy because he has more money than we have. When reading a chart for a well-known or prominent personality, it may be wise to keep in mind that he doesn't need his progressions or transits read backwards. He needs the same kind of consultation that you would give an unknown.

The person we have been discussing is Elvis Presley. Perhaps he might still be around if he had talked to a knowledgeable astrologer or an interested therapist. His chart is highly questionable, however. Some new data from the Journal of the American Federation of Astrologers suggests a different birth time. This data is from the *Circle Book of Charts*, compiled by S. Erlewine. He was born January 8, 1935 at 12:20 P.M. CST, in Tupelo, Mississippi. The data was taken from *Elvis, A Biography* by J. Hopkins. The biographical information available can be of help in determining the diagnosis. The data can give a clue as to what motivated the action taken by this personality.

BIBLIOGRAPHY

The following material may have been influential in the writing of this book. People interested in pursuing fields that relate to astrology may find these sources helpful.

Aesop's Fables, New York, 1947.

Arroyo, Stephen, *Astrology, Psychology and the Four Elements,*Davis, California, 1975.

Barker, Raymond C., *You Are Invisible,* New York, 1973.

Bhagavad-gita, New York, 1952.

Brunhubner, Fritz, *Pluto,* American Federation of Astrologers, n.d.

Campbell, Joseph, *Creative Mythology,* New York, 1968.

——,*The Hero with a Thousand Faces,* New York, 1949.

——,*Myths to Live By,* New York, 1972.

——,*Occidental Mythology,* New York, 1964.

Carter, C.E.O., *The Zodiac and the Soul,* London, 1968.

Castaneda, Carlos, *The Teachings of Don Juan,* New York, 1968.

Churchward, Albert, *Signs and Symbols of Primordial Man,* London, 1913.

The Complete Grimm's Fairy Tales, commentary by J. Campbell, New York, 1944.

Coomaraswamy, Ananda, *Buddha and the Gospel of Buddhism,* New York, 1964.

——,*The Dance of Shiva,* New York, 1957.

——,*Hinduism and Buddhism,* New York, n.d.

Dunbar, Flanders, *Mind and Body,* New York, 1972.

Frazer, Sir James G., *The Golden Bough,* New York, 1951.

Freud, Sigmund, *Moses and Monotheism,* New York, 1939.

Goodavage, Joseph, *Astrology, The Space Age Science,* New York, 1966.

Hand, Robert, *Planets in Transit,* Rockport, Mass., 1976.

——,*Planets in Youth,* Rockport, Mass., 1977.

Harding, M. Esther, *Psychic Energy,* New York, 1963.

——,*The Way of All Women,* New York, 1933.

——,*Women's Mysteries,* New York, 1935.

Hesse, Hermann, *Narcissus and Goldmund,* New York, 1968.

Hickey, Isabel, *Astrology, a Cosmic Science,* Bridgeport, Conn., 1970.

Higgins, Godfrey, *Anacalypsis,* New York, 1965.

Hinkle, Beatrice, *The Re-creating of the Individual,* New York, 1923.

Jung, Carl G., *Collected Works, Aion,* New York, 1959, Part II.

——,*Collected Works, Psychology and Religion, East and West,* New York, 1958, Vol. XI.

——,*Collected Works, The Archetypes and the Collective Unconscious,* New York, 1959, Vol. IX, Part I.

——,*Collected Works, Two Essays on Analytical Psychology,* New York, 1953, Vol. VII.

——,*The Undiscovered Self,* New York, 1957.

——,*Symbols of Transformation,* Vols. 1,2, New York, 1956.

——,*Psyche and Symbol,* New York, 1958.

——,*Memories, Dreams and Reflections,* New York, 1956.

——,*Man and His Symbols,* New York, 1968.

——,*Integration of the Personality,* London, 1963.

Jung, Carl G. and Kerenyi, C., *Essays on a Science of Mythology,* New York, 1949

Jung, Emma, *Animus and Anima,* New York, 1957.

Kuhn, Alvin Boyd, *Sex as Symbol* (The Ancient Light in Modern Psychology), Elizabeth, N.J., 1945.

——,*The Lost Light,* Elizabeth, N.J., 1940.

McClain, Ernest, G., *The Myth of Invariance,* New York, 1976.

——,*The Pythagorean Plato,* New York, 1978.

Massey, Gerald, *The Natural Genesis,* Vols. 1,2, London, 1883.

May, Rollo, *The Courage to Create,* New York, 1975.

——,*Love and Will,* New York, 1969.

Neumann, Erich, *The Origins and History of Consciousness,* New York, 1954.

Palmer, Lynn, *ABC Chart Erection,* New York, 1968.

Pryse, James M., *The Adorers of Dionysos,* London, 1925.

——,*The Restored New Testament,* New York, 1914.

——,*Spiritual Light,* Los Angeles, 1941.

Rudhyar, Dane, *Astrology of Personality,* Netherlands, 1936.

Taylor, Thomas, *The Timaeus and Critias of Plato,* New York, 1952.

Wheelright, Joseph, *The Reality of the Psyche,* New York, 1968.

Wickes, Frances, *The Inner World of Man,* New York, 1948.

Wilhelm, Richard, *The Secret of the Golden Flower,* London, 1957.

Wilhelm/Baynes, *The I Ching,* New York, 1950.

Whitman, Edward W., *Aspects and Their Meanings,* London, 1970.

Zimmer, Heinrich, *The King and the Corpse,* New York, 1957.

——,*Philosophies of India,* New York, 1951.

——,*Myth and Symbols in Indian Art and Civilization,* New York, 1962.